THE SECRETS
OF FRENCH HOME
COOKING

THE SECRETS OF FRENCH HOME COOKING

Marie-Pierre Moine

Photography by Peter Williams

CONRAN OCTOPUS

To Colin MacIvor with love

Acknowledgements

I would like to give a very big thank you to all the team who produced this book:
Lewis Esson who patiently sorted out my diskettes as well as textual muddles, Jane Suthering and Peter Williams who made dishes look so inviting, Paul Welti who designed the book. My thanks also go to Anne Furniss who commissioned me, to Mary Evans, to Louise Simpson and to Helen Trent and Emma Patmore. Thanks go to the many friends, relatives and acquaintances who helped me so generously in France and in London. I would also like to express my gratitude to Catherine Manac'h who guided me in the wine selections and to Sophie Vallejo and Sopexa for all the information they gave me. M-P M.

The Publishers would like to thank Valerie Crowther at
Antiques & Things, 91 Eccles Road, London SW11,
for providing props for photography.

Throughout the book recipes are for four people unless otherwise stated.
Both metric and imperial quantities are given. Use either all metric or all imperial,
as the two are not necessarily interchangeable.

Editor & Project Manager: Lewis Esson
Design: Paul Welti
Photography: Peter Williams
Styling: Helen Trent
Food Styling: Jane Suthering assisted by Emma Patmore
Editorial assistant: Penny David
Production: Mano Mylvaganam

First published in 1994 by
Conran Octopus Limited,
37 Shelton Street,
London WC2H 9HN

Text © 1994 Marie-Pierre Moine
Photography © 1994 Peter Williams
Edited text, design & layout © 1994 Conran Octopus

Cataloguing in Publication Data: a catalogue record for this book
is available from the British Library

ISBN I 85029 644 8

Colour separations by HBM Print Pte Ltd, Singapore
Printed and bound by the Tien Wah Press, Singapore

CONTENTS

INTRODUCTION

I am very bad at keeping secrets, especially happy ones. Good news and information that is likely to be enjoyable or useful are there to be shared. Writing *The Secrets of French Home Cooking* has been the most enjoyable of tasks. It gave me the opportunity to think about, to perfect, to formulate as clearly as I could, and to pass on all the tricks and techniques I have learnt and enjoyed practising over nearly two decades as a French home cook.

If there is any guiding principle behind French home cooking, it is that it tries to make the most of what is available – the ingredients, the kitchen equipment, the time, the cook's level of expertise – to produce dishes that taste as good as possible in the circumstances. To do this, it uses a number of techniques and combinations that have worked for centuries, with a greater or lesser degree of refinement.

I have spent many of my cooking years outside France in kitchens that were often indifferently equipped and I have frequently been in a hurry, but I have always cooked in a French style. Like languages and manual skills, cooking is best learnt through watching and copying: my early repertory relied almost exclusively on the family recipes, the 30 or so dishes with which my sisters, my cousins and I were brought up and felt safe cooking once we were thrown in at the deep end in our own kitchens. As I got more interested and experimental, my repertory of recipes increased and my techniques got more subtle and a little finer. I was lucky to have good mentors at an early age, but it is easily possible to learn about French home cooking from detailed recipes – especially when they are illustrated by photographs. Even in novice hands, the basic recipes of the French kitchen can, and do, produce palatable results. The techniques are not complicated, and the ways of combining ingredients are tried and tested.

Some time ago, when I was finishing work on the recipes for this book, I attended a very interesting food seminar in Biarritz, at which people gathered to discuss Basque gastronomy. One of the participants remarked that the best cooks and chefs of previous generations would cook quite differently if they were alive today. Their recipes would be less complex in some cases, more refined in others, and lighter most of the time. For this reason French home cooking should not be regarded as a holy cow; it is not fossilized and recipes change with the times. I have felt free to update some classics and to make them more appropriate for the tastes and palates of the '90s.

The following introductory remarks examine the ingredients, equipment and the fundamental simple techniques you will need to cook the recipes in this book. If this is a brief chapter it is because there is nothing very complicated or intimidating about any of the topics. It is my hope that the recipes in the book are self-explanatory.

EQUIPMENT

The French home kitchen is not crammed with the latest equipment and gadgets. If you are happy with your own kitchen, you will have all you need to cook the recipes in this book.

I use a standard gas cooker in London and an electric one in France, equally happily. I find the French oven a little hotter, but have not quantified the difference scientifically. Since the recipes were cooked both in London and in France, I suggest that you do not follow the oven temperatures too literally; if you know that your oven is very hot, take that into account. In general, it is usually safer to be one notch cooler.

One piece of equipment I could not do without is a food processor. Another I can live without but enjoy using in France – where I have access to an orchard – is my ice-cream maker. Although I only mention microwave cookers a couple of times, I use mine like a lot of other cooks I know – regularly but not very creatively. The only microwave *truc* I am currently proud to pass on is my quick Mushroom Fumet (see page 10).

On the subject of pots and pans, I have to recommend those two great sturdy cooking vessels – the cast-iron *cocotte* and the heavy sauté pan. The *cocotte* is the best of stewing pots, perfect for nurturing casseroles, while the sauté pan is an ideal medium for a lot of French top-of-the-stove dishes (see Useful Techniques, opposite). A small pan with a heavy base will be useful for sauces – I have a dedicated copper sauce pan, which does the job nicely.

Use the knives you feel most at ease with and sharpen them (or get them sharpened) regularly. I feel more comfortable with smallish cook's knives and have three which I use constantly. Large wide knives are great for slicing a whole row of vegetables at one time and for smashing garlic (use the flat of the blade and peel after crushing rather than before). Scissors are good for snipping fresh herbs, bacon and rolled-up ham and I also sometimes wield my double-handed chopper for shallots, mushrooms and onions.

For baking, in addition to some loose-bottomed flan tins, assorted soufflé dishes and ramekins, no French home cook's kitchen would be complete without a *moule à manqué*, a fairly deep round pan with a slightly curved edge (see Tarte Tatin, page 160).

My most frequently used gadget is my salad spinner, which draws off water from wet salad leaves in seconds without bruising them. I sometimes store salads in the refrigerator, sitting in the inside basket of the spinner.

Favourite small items include graters, zesters, assorted sieves, several pastry brushes and a length of muslin or cheese cloth for lining strainers and bagging up herbs and spices before putting them into stews. I also have to admit to being

My heavy sauté pan in use making Onglet aux Échalotes *(page 122).*

a profligate user of recycled paper towel. Amongst its many uses, it is an ideal mopper-upper of grease and excess moisture, it skims off surface fat and wipes marks from serving dishes.

USEFUL TECHNIQUES

The recipes in *The Secrets of French Home Cooking* are explained in some detail and I hope you will not find them unduly complicated. What follows is a quick résumé of a number of techniques frequently used by French cooks.

Beurre manié is a classic thickening agent made of a small amount (2 teaspoons each) of soft butter and flour mashed together.

Blanchir (to blanch): to plunge ingredients in boiling water for a few minutes. This primes the ingredient and makes it more supple and easier to cook. It also eliminates excess salt. Blanching is used in preparing bacon, white meats (such as veal, with a little lemon juice to keep the flesh whiter), leaf and other vegetables, using salted water to preserve the colour.

Déglacer (to deglaze): is a favourite way of creating a very short sauce from the pan juices. After transferring the cooked meat or fish to a warmed serving dish, you pour in a little wine, stock, cream or water into the pan and stir until simmering, scraping up the tasty sediment. Adjust the seasoning, stir in a snipping of fresh herbs and a knob of butter and trickle over the dish.

Dégorger (to degorge): to sprinkle salt over an ingredient, such as cucumber or aubergines, and leave to stand with a weight on top to force out bitter juices and/or excess moisture. After at least 30 minutes, rinse and pat dry.

Fricassée is the name given to dishes in which ingredients are first browned or seized over a moderate to high heat in a little fat, dusted with flour and seasoned, then cooked in a little liquid, usually wine or stock. A little cream or butter is often added at the end. The sauté pan is a good utensil for such recipes.

Infuser (to infuse): to let flavouring ingredients stand in a (usually) hot liquid before cooking. Useful when preparing milk-based savoury and sweet sauces.

Liaison is a mixture of cream and egg yolk used to thicken sauces. Beat the cream and yolk in a bowl, stir in a few tablespoons of the hot liquid you want to thicken, then whisk the mixture back into the pan.

Mariner (to marinate): soaking ingredients (often meat or fish) in an aromatic flavoursome liquid or paste before cooking to tenderize them and improve their taste and texture.

Réduire (to reduce): turns a cooking liquid into a sauce. Take out the cooked meat, fish or other ingredient to stop it from over-cooking and toughening up

and keep it warm. Turn up the heat and let the liquid boil until it thickens and has the right texture. Adjust the seasoning, whisk in a few dice of chilled butter or a little cream. Chilled butter helps make the sauce smooth and glossy. The technique of vigorously whisking pieces of chilled butter into a sauce is known as *monter une sauce*, to mount or lift a sauce. It takes no time at all and makes a lot of difference.

INGREDIENTS

Most of the ingredients you will need to prepare recipes from *The Secrets of French Home Cooking* should be available from large well-stocked supermarkets. Much as I enjoy multi-stop shopping at specialist suppliers, it tends to be a luxury my normal schedule does not allow. Having said that, like anyone who enjoys cooking, I do of course make regular and enjoyable visits to Oriental stores and trusted delis for goodies that will add that little *je-ne-sais-quoi* to dishes.

I am often asked what I bring back from France. The answer is, fewer and fewer things. I used to come back weighed down with overflowing baskets, but the food shopping scene in Britain – especially London – has improved enormously in the last six years or so. Unless you want to eat it the day after you come back, forget about bringing back a *plateau de fromages*. Cheese does not travel well in family cars or suitcases. A ripe Camembert will be over the top after a few hours on the move and an unripe specimen is unlikely to mature very satisfactorily.

My current list of pet purchases from France includes chocolate with a high cocoa bean percentage (over 70%), the only instant coffee I like (Ricoré, a blend of coffee and chicory), small cans of stock powder (relatively low in salt and fine-flavoured, marketed under the corny name of Astuces Gourmandes – 'gourmet tricks'), coarse-grain mustard, jars of tiny gherkins, aspic powder with a touch of Madeira, vanilla pods and small

sachets of vanilla sugar, canned goose fat and *confit d'oie* or *de canard*, individual cans of tiny petits pois and flageolets. Lentils from Le Puy are also easier to find and *bon marché* in France. I sometimes also bring back charcuterie: a pot of *rillettes* for the Editor of this book, and *andouillettes* or a good *boudin* for immediate consumption.

Vegetables, Fruit and Herbs

Whenever possible, I buy loose vegetables rather than pre-packed ones, in order to get the feel of them and avoid unpleasant surprises later. One exception is potatoes, which come selected these days in appetizing but expensive little punnets. Designer baby vegetables look picture-pretty on the plate, but for stocks and flavour you should use more mature specimens. Unwaxed oranges, lemons and limes are preferable, especially if you are going to use their zest.

A snipping of fresh herbs never fails to bring a dish to life. To my mind, parsley and tarragon are probably the most French of all herbs, closely followed by chives and chervil. Curly parsley is best rinsed and patted dry (I use a mini salad spinner) before being stored like other fresh herbs in a plastic bag in the salad compartment of the refrigerator. This is a more efficient way of keeping them than in a romantic bunch in a jar or jug of water.

Other herbs are wonderful fresh, but not always available. Unless a dish specifically calls for a large quantity of a particular fresh herb, use dried thyme, rosemary, oregano, marjoram, sage, savory and bay leaves. Keep these away from daylight and for no longer than three or four months. Basil and coriander are better fresh or preserved in jars of olive oil.

Salads I rinse, spin-dry and store in zip-lock plastic bags – they keep much longer that way and save you the bother of last-minute rinsing and draining every time you want to prepare a salad.

This will not come as a surprise, but you will regularly need garlic, shallots and onions to cook from this book. They all come in different shapes, sizes and colours and get more assertive and pungent with age, so buy them in reasonably small quantities. Look out for loose garlic bulbs absolutely free of sprouting shoots and still completely enclosed in skins that do not peel off like dried parchment. The cloves inside should feel firm and plump.

Less in vogue than garlic and to my mind underrated by many home cooks, shallots are a versatile and useful ingredient. The small greyish ones have a delicately sharp flavour, the milder and larger pink varieties keep better, in a cool well-ventilated place rather than in the refrigerator.

Unless a dish requires the powerful tang of red onions, Spanish onions are a good all-rounder. Large pale white onions from the Mediterranean have a unique sweet mildness which makes them perfect for tarts (see page 63), but they are only to be seen on market stalls from time to time in mid- to late-summer and very seldom on supermarket shelves.

A personal favourite are spring onions, which I always have in the refrigerator and rely on every day and when all else fails. Finely snipped, the green parts stand in for chives; and the white bulbs – especially, when they are large, taste pleasingly sharp raw and more mellow but still distinctly oniony when cooked.

Poultry

One-third of the chickens bought in France carry a *label rouge*, a quality symbol that means they are free-range and bred according to strict regulations. Free-range birds have a superior taste and texture, they are perfect for roasting and other simple dishes. Like a good wine, they need no bush. Most corn-fed poultry tends to be a little more fatty – I like using it jointed for baking and grilling.

The taste of guinea fowl, *pintade*, has a delicate hint of the game bird which comes off well in fricassees. Poussins, or *coquelets* in French, are too young to have developed much of a flavour but they grill quickly and are nice stuffed and pot-roasted – be generous with the seasoning.

Look out for Barbary duck when cooking *à la française* – it has fine firm flesh and strikes a happy balance between dry and fatty.

Often stored near the poultry cabinets in supermarkets are tubs of fresh chilled stock. They are as good as home-made and I often buy them, particularly veal and lamb stock which I very seldom make. Freeze what you don't intend to use in the next few days.

Lardons

With the renaissance of robust rustic dishes and country cooking, these little cubes of diced bacon have become a fashionable ingredient and much easier to find on supermarket shelves. Experiment with different ones and shop around: lardons should be neat but juicy and substantial, rather than so minuscule as to be tasteless. You can always make your own by chopping up thick slices of smoked bacon, speck or pancetta (*ventrèche*). Blanch your lardons before cooking (see page 64).

Fats & Oils

The regional cooking of France has always been flavoured with the fat of the land: butter and cream in the north and north-west, goose fat in the south-west, olive oil in the south, pork fat everywhere. Unsalted good-quality creamery butter will serve you well when cooking from this book. If butter is the *raison d'être* of a recipe – for instance when it is named in the title of a sauce, you might like to try a fine Normandy or Charentes butter. The grass is always greener: I love a slice of bread buttered with salty English farmhouse butter but keep it for eating 'raw'.

Panaché de salades aux Petits Lardons (*page 126*).

If you work on the basis that every ingredient stored in your kitchen has to work for its space reasonably regularly before its use-by date, you will stock a limited range of oils: groundnut or sunflower seed oil, a good supermarket virgin olive oil, plus a sumptuous designer bottle of extra virgin olive oil with which to anoint dishes at the last minute. Walnut oil, just like walnuts, is glorious when fresh and 'green-tasting', but it deteriorates faster than most oils – I occasionally buy a small bottle and try to remember to make the most of it while in its prime. Throw it away the moment it gets stale – never neutral, it can taste unpleasant enough to spoil a dish.

I never store pork fat (I use bacon and lardons instead) or dripping, but there is usually a little jar or can of goose fat lurking in the refrigerator. It keeps for months and does wonders for poultry, potatoes and beans. A spoonful of crème fraîche is the panacea of French home cooking. If I don't have it in the refrigerator, I use creamy Greek-style yogurt or a fromage frais that is still held together by an honest percentage of fat – the lowest-fat varieties available produce disappointing results in cooking. The same goes for cream cheese – go for lower-, rather than very low-, fat. Single and double creams can replace crème fraîche in most recipes (its texture falls somewhere in the middle) and you can always beat in a few drops of lemon juice for extra acidity.

Condiments

Condiments are one of my many kitchen-management downfalls – I love experimenting with them and keep far too many little jars and tubes. Some – like sea salt, coarse and fine – are easy to justify. Black peppercorns are a must, and mixed peppercorns a nice option. Green peppercorns in brine you will use time and time again when you cook from this book. Keep freshly opened jars of cayenne and paprika – both lose their edge in a matter of months, at least as fast as other spices.

Vinegars can be kept down to red or white wine, sherry, balsamic and raspberry (if only to be used to dress warm leeks). I keep far too many mustards: Dijon, coarse-grain, English powdered (so far, so good) and also green Japanese horseradish wasabi, sweet Swedish, honey, lemon and tarragon mustards.

Capers are an essential, preferably fat ones, as are creamed horseradish, good tomato concentrate, anchovy purée and canned or bottled anchovies, soya sauce, Worcestershire sauce, tomato ketchup (yes, a few drops are an excellent rescue remedy for a dull sauce) and Tabasco. Find a hot pepper paste or sauce you like – my favourite is harissa, a fierce but rounded chilli and spices paste from North Africa.

Cans and Miscellaneous Store-cupboard Items

I have already mentioned flageolets, goose fat, *confits* and petits pois. Also useful are cans of white haricot beans, beef consommé (for emergencies, see Instant Stocks right) and, of course, tomatoes – chopped and whole.

You will need both icing sugar and caster sugar. I store a few vanilla pods (much better than essence) in a jar with sugar. Use the pod as required, rinse, pat dry and replace in the sugar, which will develop a subtle vanilla flavour.

Alongside the usual pasta and rice, I also have on my shelves pre-steamed bulghar (cracked wheat) and couscous.

Breads and Pastries

Like many of my compatriots, I am no home-baker. I buy fresh bread regularly, keep small baguettes in the freezer and usually have a brioche loaf in the refrigerator – it is good slightly stale for making quick *croûtes* or superior breadcrumbs and croûtons. I also often store cans of chilled croissant dough and ready-rolled puff pastry (chilled or frozen).

SOME USEFUL BASIC RECIPES

Beurre Clarifié

Clarified butter is sediment-free, very pure and unlikely to burn. It is best made with unsalted butter. Simply melt at least 55g/2oz (it is not worth the effort for a smaller amount) over a low heat without stirring. Scoop out the surface foam with a teaspoon. Carefully pour the melted butter into a cup, taking care not to disturb the sediment which will remain in the pan and can be discarded.

Croûtons

Use somewhat stale bread. To make large plain toasted croûtons, cut off the crusts (if you like) and bake in a moderate oven for 10 minutes. For garlic croûtons, rub the bread with the cut sides of a garlic clove before baking. A baguette cut on the slant produces a good result.

To make small croûtons for salads and soups, use a sandwich-style tin loaf or a slightly stale brioche loaf. Slice and cut off the crusts, then cut the bread into small squares (say 8-12 pieces per slice). Brush these lightly with olive oil or clarified butter, spread in a heavy sauté or frying pan and place over a moderate heat. Dry-fry for a few minutes, stirring a few times, until the bread is uniformly crisp and golden. Spread the croûtons on absorbent paper to dry them a little. For garlic croûtons, rub the pan as well as the slices of bread with garlic before heating.

Court-bouillon

To make a flavoursome liquid for poaching fish: in a saucepan, bring to a simmer 800ml/1¼pts of water with a few black peppercorns, a bay leaf, a few sprigs of parsley and thyme (or 2 tsp dried thyme), a celery stalk, ¼ Spanish onion, a chunk of carrot and 3 tbsp wine vinegar. Simmer for 20 minutes, leave to cool then drain.

The basic mixture is flexible and can be reduced. After you have poached non-oily fish, you can use a few tablespoons of the court-bouillon in a sauce or as fish stock.

Fish Stock

In a saucepan, put bones and skin from non-oily fish, prawn and crustacean shells (these can be used on their own), a few peppercorns, parsley, thyme, a few strips of lemon zest, and a few tablespoons of lemon juice or white wine. Add at least 800ml/1¼pts of water and bring to a simmer over a moderate heat. Simmer for 15 minutes only, strain well and skim if necessary. Adjust the seasoning before using.

Once strained the stock can be reduced to make a more concentrated liquid or a fish *fumet* – don't hesitate to let the stock bubble away: a proper fumet will be reduced down to a few tablespoons. Don't over-season in the early stages and adjust the seasoning at the end.

Instant Stocks

Use better quality, not too salty, stock cubes. I also often add a few teaspoons of soy sauce to cooking liquids to create a stock effect, or stir a teaspoon into a sauce to intensify its flavour.

A can of beef consommé can be strained into a stew in place of beef stock.

Mushroom Fumet

This adds a delicately dark earthy note to sauces. I make it in minutes in my neglected microwave.

Wipe and thinly slice at least 115g/4oz small brown mushrooms. Place in a suitable dish. If you like, season lightly with salt and pepper. Cover with cling film and microwave on full power for 2-3 minutes, until soft. Drain and use the mushrooms – they will be excellent for sautéing or marinating *à la grecque*. Strain the liquid through a fine sieve and adjust the seasoning.

If you like, you can flavour the fumet by adding to the sliced mushrooms before microwaving a few sprigs of tarragon and a sprinkling of Madeira or a little grated citrus zest.

Quick Chicken Stock

The best of all chicken stocks, a comforting gold bouillon with a fine flavour, is made by slowly simmering a whole bird with aromatic herbs and vegetables (see page 22).

If you are using a jointed bird to make a fricassee, chop of the wings and the least meaty tail end of the carcass. Rub a sauté pan with oil, add the chicken pieces and a chopped shallot and spring onion, and brown over a moderate heat. Now pour in about 575ml/1pt boiling water and a dash of white wine, season with salt and pepper and throw in a few sprigs of parsley and a bay leaf. Bring to a simmer and cook for about 30 minutes – 40 if possible, 20 if you are very pushed for time. Turn up the heat for the last 5 minutes and bubble vigorously to reduce the stock. Strain through a muslin-lined sieve.

Vegetable Stock

For a rich stock with a touch of a caramelized taste: in a large heavy pan, sauté a thinly sliced Spanish onion in a tablespoon of oil over a moderate heat until lightly golden. Add a chopped large carrot, a few chopped celery stalks or pieces of fennel, a small bunch of parsley, a bay leaf, a little thyme and several black peppercorns. Stir for a few minutes, then cover with plenty of water and bring to a simmer. Simmer for at least an hour. Strain and season.

For a lighter stock, do not sauté the vegetables and use a smaller onion and a leek. Vary the herb mixture to suit your purposes with chervil (delicate), coriander and lemon, a little lovage (assertive).

Vinaigrette

No two salads taste the same and everybody prepares vinaigrette differently.

For a small salad (say for 2-3 people) mix the vinaigrette in the bowl – I prefer to use a wide and fairly shallow bowl rather than a deep one. For a bigger salad, mix the dressing in a small jug or cup, pour half into the bowl before you put in the salad, toss lightly, then trickle the rest over the salad and toss again.

Vinaigrette should not be too acidic. For a simple vinaigrette that will dress about 100g/3^1/₂oz of mixed salad leaves (enough for 6 people, to follow a

Croustades aux Champignons *(page 147) served with Champagne.*

main-course or as a side salad): pour into a cup 4 tbsp oil (groundnut, sunflower seed or olive, or a mixture of neutral-tasting oil and olive oil or fresh walnut oil). Season generously with sea salt and lightly with pepper. Mix, then add 2 teaspoons of vinegar, lemon juice or a tablespoon of red wine.

Mustard will thicken the vinaigrette and should be added very sparingly – the idea is to coat the leaves with the lightest of films rather than drench them. An added spoonful of leftover mayonnaise makes a good but thick dressing, and an additional teaspoon or two of single cream is nice when you dress sharp leaves (baby spinach, sorrel, rocket, romaine) without olive oil. Always make sure the leaves are free of water when you dress the salad.

A FEW WORDS ABOUT WINE

Without exception, all the French people I know support their local wines (or the wines of the region from which they or their family originated) with great passion and loyalty. Although *The Secrets of French Home Cooking* makes no claim to be a regional cookbook, a great many French dishes have regional origins and overtones. When suggesting wines to sample with recipes, I have tried whenever possible to make the most of this regional connection. I am not a wine expert, but I enjoy wine with my food and have had great fun matching dishes and wines. I ask wine buffs to forgive my more eccentric suggestions.

In the course of my various experimental *dégustations*, I was very impressed with the vitality, drinking quality and fresh new appeal of a number of *vins de pays*. I was totally unfamiliar with many, others I rediscovered with pleasure – they seemed more consistently palatable and better made than in the past. If perceptive readers notice a bias towards Touraine-Anjou wines and towards rosés, it is only that I too am loyal to the first wines I tasted.

Chapter One

LES SOUPES ET LES POTAGES

Soups and Stocks

À la soupe! It is not by accident that the old colloquial way of summoning people to the table focuses on soup. In one form or another, *la soupe* has always been at the heart of French eating.

The low Latin word *soppa* described the bread dipped in liquid, milk, wine or stock, the sop in the gravy. Soup has remained a favourite way of starting a meal. The nomenclature of *soupes* is rich and varied, a puzzling mixture of local words and technical cooking terms reflecting the long history and importance of the dish.

Technically, the term *soupe* still refers to the more rustic preparations. The *bouillon* is the liquid left at the end of boiling meat, fish or vegetables. *Consommé* is a clarified and reduced stock. In the *potage* there should be a somewhat higher level of refinement, and the ingredients will be puréed or pushed through a sieve. Still higher up the gastronomic ladder, *velouté* tends to describe a soup enriched with a liaison of egg and cream and *bisque* a preparation based on a richly spiced purée of seafood.

LEFT
Potage à la Purée d'Ail (page 14) served with
Petits Croissants aux Anchois (page 62).

POTAGE À LA PURÉE D'AIL
Garlic Soup

Thickening a soup by whisking simmering stock into a little pool of egg yolk is a traditional method. Work the first few spoonfuls of liquid very thoroughly into the yolk before you add the rest and also make sure both the stock and the tureen are really hot at the outset.

Serves 4
Preparation: about 15 minutes
Cooking: about 15 minutes

6-9 large fresh garlic cloves, unpeeled
850ml/1½ pt good-quality chicken or vegetable stock
2 egg yolks
100ml/3½ oz crème fraîche
55g/2oz roasted hazelnuts, almonds or walnut kernels, finely chopped
several sprigs of chervil, finely snipped
sea salt and freshly ground black pepper
TO SERVE:
hot buttered toast or croûtons (see page 10), or Petits Croissants aux Anchois (page 62)

1 In a small saucepan, bring to the boil some lightly salted water. Add the garlic and bring back to the boil. Reduce the heat a little and simmer for 10–15 minutes, until the garlic is very soft (the fresher the garlic, the faster it tends to soften).

2 Meanwhile, heat the stock over a moderate heat in a large saucepan until piping hot.

3 Drain the garlic and refresh in cold water. Working over a warmed tureen, squeeze each clove between your thumb and forefinger until the flesh pops or squirts out.

4 Add the egg yolks to the garlic and mash to mix. Then gradually whisk in the crème fraîche until blended. Now pour in 3 tablespoons of hot stock and whisk well to combine. Season generously.

5 Still whisking vigorously, gradually pour or ladle in the rest of the stock, keeping the pan over a low heat until it is empty. Adjust the seasoning.

6 Stir the chopped nuts into the soup, sprinkle with the finely snipped chervil and serve immediately with pieces of hot buttered toast, croûtons or small croissants.

POTAGE SAINT-GERMAIN
Pea Soup

If you see the words Saint-Germain or Clamart on a French menu, be prepared for a dish involving *petits pois*. Clamart is a suburb of Paris where peas used to be grown before urban development took over. Peas were also grown in Saint-Germain in the Île de France.

The delicate soup below can be served chilled, particularly when it is made with fresh peas, but you can also use frozen peas. Fresh mint is an alternative to the chervil.

To make into a purée which is good with veal and duck, reduce the amount of stock and/or water to a scant 125ml/4fl oz in the recipe below and don't bother about sieving.

Split peas, *pois cassés*, can be cooked in the same fashion. First soak the peas, then boil them for 15 minutes. Rinse and cook as described for peas, allowing an extra 40 minutes and adding a pinch each of dried thyme and sage and more generous seasoning. This purée, which is good with pork and sausages, will need pushing through the sieve and lubricating with plenty of butter.

Serves 4
Preparation: about 20 minutes
Cooking: about 45 minutes

1 tbsp oil
45g/1½ oz butter
leaves of 1 small soft lettuce, chopped or snipped
white parts of 4 large spring onions, chopped
450g/1lb freshly shelled baby garden peas (about 800g/1¾ lb unshelled)
about 1 litre/1¾ pt mixed chicken or vegetable stock and water or plain water
1 medium or large egg yolk
3 tbsp crème fraîche
1-2 tbsp Madeira or port (optional)
few sprigs of chervil
sea salt and freshly ground black pepper

1 Put a sauté pan or large heavy saucepan over a moderate heat. Dribble the oil into the hot pan, tilt the pan around until it is well coated, then add half the butter. When the foaming subsides, add the lettuce and spring onions. Reduce the heat a little and sweat for 5 minutes, stirring frequently.

2 Add the peas. Season lightly and cook for another 5 minutes, stirring occasionally. Meanwhile, heat the stock in a separate pan or bring a kettle of water to the boil.

3 Pour the boiling liquid into the pan of vegetables and bring back to the boil. Then reduce the heat, cover and simmer for about 20 minutes, or until the vegetables are very tender. Leave to cool a little.

4 Pour the contents of the pan into a blender or food processor and whizz until smooth.

5 Push the soup back into the pan through a fine sieve, mashing the vegetables with the back of a wooden spoon to push through as much as possible. Reheat gently over a low heat.

6 In a cup or small bowl, combine the egg yolk and the crème fraîche with 2 or 3 tablespoons of the hot soup. Using a whisk, stir this liaison into the pan a little at a time. Season to taste.

7 Just before serving in a warmed tureen or individual bowls, stir in the Madeira or port, if using. Whisk in the rest of the butter and snip over a little chervil.

SOUPE AU CRESSON
Watercress Soup

This sharp green soup tastes distinctly fuller and more rounded when made with stock rather than water. Follow the same simple method to make spinach or sorrel soup.

To save time – but not necessarily work – use less liquid in the actual cooking. Pour in just enough boiling liquid to cover the vegetables and keep the rest warm. Use it to rinse the emptied bowl of the food processor and add to the soup through the sieve.

Serves 4
Preparation: about 15 minutes
Cooking: about 30 minutes

1 tbsp oil
30g/1oz butter
about 170g/6oz peeled potatoes, cut into roughly 2.5cm/1in dice
about 170g/6oz watercress
about 1 litre/1³/₄ pt chicken or vegetable stock, a mixture of stock and water,
or plain water
2 heaped tbsp crème fraîche, cream or cream cheese, plus 1 extra tbsp to finish (optional)
sea salt and freshly ground black pepper

1 Put a sauté pan or large heavy saucepan over a moderate heat. Dribble the oil into the hot pan, tilt the pan around over the heat until it is well coated, then add half the butter. When the foaming subsides, tip in the potatoes and sauté for 1 minute. Add the watercress and simmer for a few minutes.

2 In a separate saucepan, heat the stock until simmering or bring a kettle of water to the boil. Add the boiling liquid to the potatoes and watercress, season lightly and bring to the boil. Reduce the heat, cover and simmer for 15–20 minutes, until the potatoes are cooked. Leave to cool for several minutes.

3 Pour the soup mixture into a blender or food processor and whizz until well blended.

4 Strain the soup through a sieve into the pan, using the back of a wooden spoon to push as much through as possible.

5 Whisk in the crème fraîche, cream or cream cheese. Reheat over a low heat until piping hot, stirring frequently. Adjust the seasoning, whisk in the rest of the butter and serve very hot in warmed soup bowls. If you like, swirl a little dollop of extra crème fraîche, cream or cream cheese into each bowl.

SOUPE AUX FÈVES ET AU BASILIC

Tomato, Basil and Broad Bean Soup

Omit the pork and use an extra tablespoon of olive oil for a lighter and vegetarian version of this clean-tasting soup. If you are using frozen broad beans, add them halfway through the simmering.

Serves 4
Preparation: about 15 minutes
Cooking: about 55 minutes

1 tbsp olive oil
85g/3oz smoked belly of pork or thick-cut bacon,
blanched (see page 65) and finely diced
1 Spanish onion, finely chopped
2 small carrots, thinly sliced
1 garlic clove, crushed
550g/1¼ lb baby broad beans, shelled
350g/12oz ripe tomatoes, blanched, skinned,
deseeded and chopped
1 tsp sugar
about 18 basil leaves
8 tsp extra virgin olive oil
sea salt and freshly ground black pepper

1 Heat the olive oil in a large heavy-based pan over a moderate heat. Add the diced pork and the chopped onion. Sauté for a few minutes until golden, stirring frequently. Tip in the carrots, garlic, broad beans, tomatoes and sugar. Stir well and season lightly with salt and generously with pepper. Sauté for a few minutes, stirring a few times.

2 Meanwhile bring to the boil about 850ml/1½ pts of water in a kettle. Put two-thirds of the basil in the centre of a muslin square, bring up the edges and tie to make a secure bag.

3 Pour the boiling water over the vegetables, stir well and add the bag of basil. Cover and simmer gently for about 40 minutes, stirring occasionally.

4 Just before serving, remove the basil bag. Adjust the seasoning if necessary. Ladle the soup into warmed individual soup bowls and dribble 2 teaspoons of extra virgin olive oil over each. Tightly roll up the rest of the basil leaves into mini-cigar shapes and snip shreds over the soup. Serve hot.

GRATINÉE AUX CHAMPIGNONS ET AUX ÉCHALOTES

Shallot & Mushroom Soup

This soup is made just like the traditional French onion soup *gratinée à l'oignon*, but the combination of shallot and mushrooms is perhaps at the same time more fragrant and easier on the stomach than the onions.

Serves 4
Preparation: about 15 minutes
Cooking: about 25 minutes

30g/1oz butter
3 shallots, finely chopped
550g/1½ lb small brown or white
mushrooms, finely chopped
250ml/8fl oz dry white wine
600ml/21fl oz chicken or vegetable stock
1 day-old small French baguette, sliced
85g/3oz Gruyère or Farmhouse Cheddar cheese,
grated
sea salt and freshly ground black pepper

1 In a large heavy-based pan, heat the butter over a moderate heat. When the foaming subsides, add the shallots, reduce the heat a little and soften for a few minutes, stirring frequently.

2 Add the mushrooms, season lightly and cook for a few minutes.

3 Pour in the wine and the stock and bring to a simmer over a moderate heat, stirring occasionally.

4 Meanwhile, heat the grill to medium and lightly toast one side of the bread slices. Keep the grill on.

5 Divide the soup between 4 flame-proof bowls. Top with the bread slices, toasted side down. Sprinkle with the grated cheese.

6 Grill for 5 minutes, until the cheese is golden brown. Serve immediately.

(RIGHT) *Rear:* Soupe aux Fèves et au Basilic; *foreground:* Gratinée aux Champignons et aux Échalotes.

LE POT-AU-FEU

Boiled Beef

Serves 6
Preparation: about 20 minutes
Cooking: about 3½ hours

at least 900g/2lb boned shoulder of
beef, bone reserved and coarsely chopped
at least 900g/2lb boned beef
silverside
at least 900g/2lb shin of beef (meat
and bone)
3 large mature carrots
4 turnips
4 medium-to-large potatoes
1 Spanish onion
6 cloves
9 small soft white onions
6 leeks
2 small heads of celery
3 bay leaves
several sprigs each of thyme and parsley
1 large marrow bone, or more
(optional)
sea salt and freshly ground
black pepper
TO SERVE:
2 pieces of toasting bread for the
marrow, if using Dijon mustard
coarse grain mustard
coarse sea salt mixed with finely snipped
parsley (optional)
small gherkins
creamed horseradish

Arguably France's national dish, *pot-au-feu* is a set piece of a soup. It will involve you in a trip to a proper butcher's and half a day in (or in-and-out of) your kitchen. It is a dish for the downright carnivorous. Take a look at the list of ingredients — shoulder of beef, silverside, shin and marrowbone. Well over 2.7kg/6lb of beef for 6 people. If the meat allowance seems to be over-generous, it is because meat reduces by nearly 40% during the boiling process. Nor is the mixture of cuts used extravagant — the combination of lean, fatty and gelatinous pieces gives the *pot-au-feu* its unique richness. Silverside, shoulder and shin work well, as do brisket, oxtail and blade — be guided by your butcher — and do ask for extra bones. It might be an idea to give him advance warning...

One of the joys of *pot-au-feu* for the home cook is that not only is it one of the world's greatest one-pot dishes, but it also provides an ideal opportunity to make *consommé* with the rich golden beef and vegetable *bouillon*. The best *bouillon* is achieved by putting the meat into cold water and gently bringing it to a simmer. This enables the goodness of the beef to seep fully into the stock — which, of course, means that a little eating quality will be lost. If the *bouillon* is not a priority, you wait until the seasoned stock simmers before you add the meat. Having tried both approaches, I tend to put the meat into the cold pot, since it still tastes pretty good at the end and also produces a magnificent *bouillon* that can be enjoyed separately.

1 Select a very large heavy-based saucepan or flameproof casserole and put the bones in it. Now prepare the meat: trim off some of the visible fat, then cut the meat into large pieces (no smaller in size than about 7.5cm/3in) and tie them together with string into 3 or 4 packages of mixed cuts.

TIE THE TRIMMED MEAT INTO PARCELS OF MIXED CUTS.

2 Put the meat parcels on top of the bones. Cover with plenty of cold water, and very slowly bring to a simmer over a low heat. Season lightly with salt and pepper. Wait until a solid layer of thick dirty scum has built up and skim it off with a slotted spoon. Turn up the heat a little. As soon as bubbles appear, add a small glass of cold water and bring back to a simmer. A new layer of greyish scum will gradually come up to the surface. Let it build up a little, then skim again. If the scum is still thick and dirty, repeat the operation one more time.

TIE THE LEEKS, PROTECTED WITHIN A CIRCLE OF CELERY STALKS

3 Meanwhile, prepare the vegetables: peel the carrots, top and tail them, then cut across into 2 or 3 segments. Peel the turnips and halve or quarter

them. Peel and halve the potatoes. Peel the Spanish onion and stud it with the cloves. Neatly peel the smaller onions. Trim the leeks, cut them half open lengthwise, then wash them carefully. Trim and rinse the heads of celery, then cut them into stalks. Tie together the leeks and celery in 3 neat parcels, putting the leeks in the centre.

SKIM THE SIMMERING LIQUID SEVERAL TIMES TO PRODUCE A GOOD CLEAN STOCK

4 Skim the meat again. After it has been simmering for about an hour, add the prepared vegetables with the bay leaves, the onion stuck with cloves and the herbs. Bring back to a very low boil and skim off any new scum. Season lightly.

5 Now reduce the heat so that the surface of the stock just trembles and partly cover. Cook very gently for another 1^1/$_2$ hours or so, until the meat and vegetables are tender (this is not a dish in which you want an *al dente* texture). About half an hour before the end of cooking, wrap the marrow bone or bones, if using, in muslin and add to the pot.

ADD THE PREPARED VEGETABLES AND THE HERBS

6 Leave the pot-au-feu to settle for 5 minutes while you toast the bread for the marrow, if using. Cut the toast into as many pieces as you will need to satisfy those who appreciate beef marrow.

7 Skim off any surface foam from the pot-au-feu. Lift out the meat and vegetables with the slotted spoon, cut off and discard the strings. Arrange the meat and vegetables in an attractive heap on a warmed platter. Halve any pieces of meat or vegetables that seem unmanageably large. Discard the onion stuck with cloves, the bay leaves, parsley and thyme. Keep the serving dish and its contents warm.

8 Remove the muslin from the marrow bones, if using. Scoop out the marrow and spread it over the pieces of toast. Serve these on a small plate.

9 Strain the stock through a muslin-lined sieve into a clean saucepan. Bring to a simmer over a low heat and adjust the seasoning. Ladle a little over the

USE A KNIFE OR POINTED TEASPOON TO EXTRACT THE MARROW AND SERVE ON TOAST.

meat and vegetables. Pour more bouillon into a warmed sauce-boat or serve as a first course in warmed soup bowls while you keep the pot-au-feu warm.

10 Traditional accompaniments to pot-au-feu are Dijon mustard and coarse grain mustard, small gherkins, coarse sea salt (I mix it with a little finely snipped parsley), black pepper and creamed horseradish.

To drink: a Chinon or Pécharmant.

NOTES: any *pot-au-feu* left over will be delicious cold the next day, particularly served with a thick mayonnaise flavoured with a little lemon juice or a spoonful of creamed horseradish. Don't leave the *pot-au-feu* sitting with the vegetables in a pool of *bouillon*, as the vegetables will give a sourish taste to the stock if left overnight. Strain the remaining *bouillon* and store it in coldest part of the refrigerator for up to 3 or 4 days.

LE CONSOMMÉ
Clear Beef Broth

With a little extra but satisfying work, left-over *bouillon* will produce that rare treat — genuine home-made *consommé*.

Serves 4
Preparation: about 10 minutes
Cooking: about 1 hour

1.5 litres / 2½ pt chilled well-skimmed beef bouillon
2 leeks, finely chopped
1 carrot, finely chopped
2 stalks of celery, finely chopped
250g / 8½ oz lean minced steak
crushed shells and whites of 2 eggs
sea salt and freshly ground black pepper
TO SERVE:
few sprigs of chervil or tarragon
Madeira or port (optional)

WHISK THE EGG WHITES AND THE CRUSHED SHELLS TO A THICK FOAM.

fork until well combined. In a bowl, using a fork or whisk, froth up together the egg whites and crushed shells. Tip this mixture into the meat and vegetables. Gradually whisk in the simmering stock, a little at a time. Put the pan over a low heat and bring to the boil, whisking constantly.

3 As soon as the mixture starts to bubble, reduce the heat to very low and stop whisking. Scum will soon start foaming up. Leave it to thicken and simmer for 1 hour, resisting the impulse to stir.

1 When you take it out of the refrigerator, the *bouillon* will have a lid-like layer of fat on top. Lift this off with a slotted spoon and discard. Tip the bouillon into a saucepan and bring it to simmering point over a low heat. The stock is now ready for clarification, the process of getting rid of its hidden fat and impurities.

2 Put the prepared vegetables and the meat in a second saucepan. Mix with a

STRAIN THE STOCK SLOWLY THROUGH A SIEVE LINED WITH DAMPENED MUSLIN.

4 While the stock is simmering, rinse a large piece of muslin in hot water. Wring out excess water and use the dampened muslin to line the inside of a sieve. Grind a generous amount of black pepper over the centre of the muslin and place the sieve over a bowl. Take the stock pan off the heat.

5 Using a slotted spoon, push the scum to one side of the pan. Ladle out the clear stock through the muslin-lined sieve into the bowl. Adjust the seasoning and the consommé is ready. Serve piping hot, with a little snipped chervil, or a dash of Madeira or port and a few tarragon leaves.

NOTES: if you chill the *consommé*, skim off the thin fatty layer that will have formed on top of the wobbly jelly. Use within 3 days or freeze.

BOUILLON DE POULET
Chicken Broth

There are speedier and more economical ways of making chicken stock (see page 11), but the flavourful clear *bouillon* produced by gently simmering a whole bird is by far the best. Use it as base for soups and sauces.

Makes about 1.1 litre / 2pt
Preparation: about 15 minutes
Cooking: about 3 hours

2 carrots, chopped
3 leeks
1 head of celery, chopped
1 onion, coarsely chopped
1 large chicken or boiling fowl, preferably
with its feet
several sprigs each of parsley and thyme
or tarragon
2 bay leaves
few strips of lime or lemon zest
6 green peppercorns
sea salt and freshly ground black pepper

1 Put the prepared vegetables in a large heavy saucepan or flameproof casserole. Put the chicken on top and season lightly. Add the herbs, lime or lemon zest and green peppercorns. Cover with plenty of cold water (about 2.25 litres/4pts) and bring to the boil over a low heat, skimming the surface when necessary.

2 As soon as the surface bubbles, turn down the heat a fraction, partly cover and cook for 1$^{1}/_{2}$ hours, skimming occasionally. After the bird has been simmering for about 50 minutes, lift it out and put it on a dish. Cut out the breasts, serve with Sauce Poulette (page 30) or another accompaniment of your liking. Return the rest of the bird to the pan and continue cooking until the bird is practically falling apart.

3 Lift the bird, vegetables and flavourings from the pot – the meat can be used in another recipe.

4 Turn up the heat. Partly cover the pan and simmer the stock for another hour, until it has reduced by about half. Strain the liquid through a muslin-lined sieve. Adjust the seasoning.

NOTE: to make it into a pale gold *consommé*, clarify this *bouillon* as described for beef Consommé (page 21), replacing the minced steak with minced pie veal.

BOUILLON DE LÉGUMES
Vegetable Broth

This clean-tasting stock will keep for several days in the refrigerator. Use it to give a fine flavour to those soups, sauces and other preparations in which meat or fish are surplus to your requirements.

Makes 1.1 litres / 2pts
Preparation: about 15 minutes
Cooking: about 45 minutes

3 large carrots, chopped
2 turnips, halved
1 Spanish onion stuck with 6 cloves
2 garlic cloves
3 leeks, chopped
1 small head of celery, chopped
3 bay leaves
several sprigs each of thyme and parsley
few strips of lemon or orange zest
1 tsp dried fennel seeds
sea salt and freshly ground black pepper

1 Put all the ingredients in a large heavy saucepan. Cover with about 1.1 litres/2pts of cold water and season lightly.

2 Bring to a simmer over a moderate heat. Partly cover and simmer for 30 minutes.

3 Lift out the vegetables. Chop them up to add to the bouillon to serve as a light soup. Alternatively, drain them well, chop them and use with Sauce Mornay (page 33) or in another recipe.

4 Line a sieve with muslin and place it over a bowl or saucepan. Strain the stock through the sieve. Reheat or chill until needed.

SOUPE DE POISSONS BRETONNE
Fish and Vegetable Chowder

Fish soup is the most flexible of dishes and no two *soupes de poissons* will ever taste quite identical. Even if you follow a given recipe to the letter, the texture and flavour of the fish always differ a little. The method below gives the ingredients plenty of time to marinate and develop their flavours before they are cooked – useful if the fish available is neither particularly exciting nor varied.

The list of ingredients may seem dauntingly long, but the result is a stew that is good and filling enough to serve 6 people as a sociable main course. It can also be largely prepared at your convenience well ahead of the meal.

If the tastes of the Mediterranean appeal to you more than those of Brittany, use olive oil, extra tomatoes, garlic and saffron. Also leave out the leeks and shallots, and add instead an extra bulb of fennel and generous pinches of aromatic herbs from the *maquis* – marjoram, savory and oregano – and a touch of harissa or chilli paste. Feel free to vary the fish and to add prawns and squid (the latter loves macerating in flavoured oil), but remember not to use the trimmings of oily fish in your muslin bag.

Serves 6~8
Preparation: about 30 minutes, plus at least 1 hour marinating
Cooking: about 30 minutes

450g/1lb potatoes, diced
2 large carrots, diced
4 tomatoes, blanched, skinned, deseeded and chopped
1 fennel bulb, chopped into small pieces
white parts of 2 large leeks, finely sliced
1 Spanish onion, finely chopped
3 shallots, finely chopped
2 garlic cloves, crushed (optional)
1 tsp fennel seeds
several sprigs of parsley and chives, plus extra for snipping
pinch of saffron
4 tbsp oil
cayenne pepper
450g/1lb skinned and boned piece of monkfish, cut into 4cm/1 1/2 in pieces, trimmings reserved
450g/1lb skinned whiting fillet, trimmings reserved
450g/1lb skinned smoked haddock or cod fillet, trimmings reserved
300ml/1/2 pt dry white wine
300ml/1/2 pt milk
4 tbsp single cream
sea salt and freshly ground black pepper

1 Put the vegetables, the fennel seeds, most of the herbs and the saffron in a shallow bowl. Dribble in 3 tablespoons of olive oil and toss gently to coat well. Season with a little salt, a good grinding of pepper and a little cayenne. Cover with the prepared fish, reserving the trimmings. Dribble over the rest of the oil. Season with a little black pepper and cayenne. Cover and leave to marinate in a cool place for at least 1 hour and up to 3.

2 Bring a kettle of water to the boil. Rinse the reserved fish trimmings, drain and place in the centre of a piece of double thickness of muslin. Bring up the edges and tie to make a bag.

3 Pour 1.1 litres/2pts of boiling water into a very large heavy saucepan or flameproof casserole. Add the bag of fish trimmings and the wine. Season lightly and bring to the boil. Simmer over a moderate heat for about 20 minutes. Turn off the heat and set aside until about half an hour before you want the soup to be ready to eat.

4 To finish: lift out and discard the bag of trimmings. Pour the stock into a jug.

5 Put the pan over a moderate heat. Lift the fish from the marinade vegetables and put on a plate. Tip the vegetables, herbs and aromatic juices into the hot pan. Cook for a few minutes over a moderate heat, then pour in the milk and stock. Bring to a simmer, reduce the heat a little, then cover and cook for 10 minutes.

6 Add the monkfish to the stew. Cover and cook gently for about 5 minutes. Cut the whiting and smoked cod or haddock into bite-sized chunks and add these to the stew. Cover again and simmer for 5 minutes, or until the fish and vegetables are just tender.

7 Finely snip the rest of the chives and parsley sprigs into a small bowl. Take the lid off the pan, stir the cream into the stew and adjust the seasoning. Sprinkle with the snipped fresh herbs and serve immediately.

To drink: Cassis or a gutsy Languedoc or Provence white wine.

Delicately flavoured Langoustines à la
Soupière *gets a luxurious edge from the firm
sweetness of the langoustines.*

LANGOUSTINES À LA SOUPIÈRE
Seafood Broth

Large prawns are a fair substitute for langoustines (Dublin Bay prawns or scampi): if they are raw, use exactly the same method, reducing the simmering time in the *fumet* by a minute or so; if the prawns are already cooked: top, tail and shell them and use all the trimmings in the fish *fumet*. Add the prawns to the simmering liquid at the end.

Serves 4
Preparation: about 20 minutes
Cooking: about 30 minutes

16-20 small langoustines (Dublin Bay prawns), heads separated
about 225g/8oz trimmings of non-oily fish, rinsed
1/2 Spanish onion, coarsely chopped
1 small head of celery, chopped
cayenne pepper
juice and few strips of zest from 1/2 lemon
300ml/1/2 pt dry white wine
30g/1oz butter
350g/12oz white button mushrooms, very finely chopped
white parts of 2 large leeks, very finely chopped
2 egg yolks
4-5 tbsp crème fraîche or single cream
1 tbsp finely snipped leaves of your choice
(preferably tarragon, basil, sorrel, rocket)
sea salt and freshly ground black pepper

1 Prepare a fish fumet: in a saucepan, combine the heads of the langoustines, fish trimmings, chopped onion and celery, a pinch of cayenne and the strips of lemon zest. Add the wine and 900ml/1 2/3 pts of water. Season and bring to a simmer over a moderate heat. Continue to simmer gently for 15–20 minutes.

2 Meanwhile, melt the butter in a sauté pan over a low heat. Add the mirepoix of finely chopped mushrooms and leeks. Season lightly, sprinkle with the lemon juice and sweat gently for 5 minutes, stirring frequently. Cover and reduce the heat still further. Cook for about 20 minutes, adding a few tablespoons of water if the mirepoix looks too dry or cooks too fast.

3 Strain the fumet through a muslin-lined sieve into a clean jug.

4 Place the langoustine tails on the mirepoix. Pour in the fumet, season and bring back to a modest simmer. Cover and simmer over a low-to-moderate heat for 5 minutes.

5 Lift out the langoustines with a slotted spoon, draining the juices back into the pan. Leave to cool while you thicken the soup. (The recipe can be prepared ahead to this point.)

6 To finish: keep the heat low under the sauté pan. Put the egg yolks in a bowl. Use a small whisk to stir in the crème fraîche or single cream. Pour in 2 or 3 tablespoons of hot liquid, whisk until blended. Pour the mixture into the sauté pan, still whisking, until the soup is smooth and creamy.

7 Shell the langoustines, keeping the shells for use in another fumet. Add the langoustines to the soup and heat through for a minute. Adjust the seasoning, adding a tiny pinch of cayenne.

8 Pour the soup into a warmed tureen or individual bowls. Sprinkle over a few fragrant snipped leaves and serve immediately.

To drink: an Alsace Riesling.

BISQUE DE CRUSTACÉS
Seafood Bisque

The term '*bisque*' generally refers to a *coulis* – a runny purée – of shellfish laced with cream and brandy. It is named after the old seafaring province of Biscay. Crayfish, *écrevisse*, is the classic ingredient, but langoustines and prawns – combined or separately – give an excellent result. Crush the shells well into the mixture for maximum taste. If you happen to have a little fish *fumet* chilled or frozen in your refrigerator, it will be well used in this fine soup instead of some of the water.

Serves 4
Preparation: about 20 minutes
Cooking: about 25 minutes

900g/2lb langoustines
1¹/₂ tbsp oil
225g/8oz raw prawns
¹/₂ Spanish onion, very finely chopped
3 shallots, very finely chopped
1 carrot, very finely chopped
3 tbsp brandy
2 tbsp short-grain pudding rice
2 tomatoes, blanched, deseeded, skinned and chopped
2 scant tbsp tomato paste
1 bouquet garni
150ml/¹/₄ pt dry white wine mixed with
700ml/1¹/₄ pt water
cayenne pepper
3 tbsp crème fraîche, plus extra to serve (optional)
few sprigs of parsley, finely snipped
sea salt and freshly ground black pepper

1 Separate the heads and thin claws of the langoustines from the tails. Heat the oil in a large sauté pan over a moderate to high heat. When the oil is very hot, tip in the langoustines, prawns, onion, shallots and carrot. Sauté for a few minutes, crushing the langoustine heads with a large wooden spoon.

2 Sprinkle with 2 tablespoons of brandy and, using a long match, flame carefully.

3 Add the rice, tomatoes, tomato paste, bouquet garni and wine mixture. Season lightly with salt, black pepper and a touch of cayenne. Bring to a simmer.

4 Lift out and reserve the langoustine tails and the prawns. Leave the other ingredients simmering for about 15 minutes over a moderate heat, stirring from time to time.

5 As soon as the shellfish are cool enough to handle, shell the prawns and the langoustine tails. Reserve the flesh and return all the shells to the pan. Stir well in to the bisque and let cool for several minutes. Cut the cooked langoustines and prawns into small neat pieces.

6 Lift out and discard the bouquet garni, langoustine and prawn heads and the bigger pieces of shell. In a blender or food processor, whizz the rest of the bisque – tiny shells included – until very smooth. Pour or strain back into the pan.

7 Add the rest of the brandy. Reheat over a low heat. Stir in the crème fraîche and the pieces of cooked langoustines and prawns. Adjust the seasoning.

8 Serve at once in a warmed soup tureen or individual bowls with a sprinkling of finely snipped parsley and, if you like, a swirl of extra crème fraîche.

VELOUTÉ GLACÉ À L'AVOCAT
Chilled Avocado Soup

Use only good-quality chicken stock for this recipe. It combines gloriously with the avocado, while the lemon juice keeps the colour fresh and adds a nice touch of acidity.

Serves 4
Preparation: about 15 minutes
Cooking: about 10 minutes, plus at least 1 hour chilling

1 tbsp oil
15g/¹/₂ oz butter
leaves from 1 small soft lettuce, snipped or chopped
white part of 1 large spring onion, finely chopped
1 garlic clove, chopped
¹/₄ tsp harissa or just a few drops of Tabasco
pinch each of paprika and ground cumin
small handful of chives
few sprigs of fresh coriander or tarragon
900ml/1²/₃ pt good-quality chicken stock
2 large or 3 small ripe avocados
juice of ¹/₂ lemon
sea salt and freshly ground black pepper

1 Put a sauté pan over a moderate heat. Dribble the oil into the hot pan, tilt the pan around until it is well coated, then add the butter. When the foaming subsides, add the lettuce, spring onion, garlic, spices and most of the herbs. Reduce the heat a little and sweat for 5 minutes, stirring frequently.

2 Take off the heat. Moisten with a few tablespoons of stock, stir and leave to cool.

3 Put the mixture in a blender or food processor with half the rest of the stock. Season lightly and whizz until puréed. Push through a sieve into a large jug and reserve.

4 Peel, stone and coarsely chop the avocados into the food processor. Add the lemon juice and remaining stock and whizz until smooth. Pour the mixture into the jug and stir until well mixed. Rinse the bowl of the processor with a little water and stir into the jug.

5 Adjust the seasoning if necessary and chill the velouté for an hour or longer, until ready to serve.

6 Serve in individual plates, with a little extra seasoning, an ice cube and the reserved fresh herbs snipped over.

SOUPE AU CANTAL
Cheese Soup

Leftover bread moistened with stock is the traditional base of many French country soups. This recipe uses the same pleasingly elastic cheese as Aligot (see page 142) and also comes from the Auvergne. Do as the natives do – or certainly did – and pour a little wine into your almost-empty bowl. Rinse it around and drink from the bowl.

Serves 4
Preparation: about 15 minutes
Cooking: about 30 minutes

1 tbsp oil
30g/1oz butter
200g/7oz soft white onion, finely chopped
900ml/1²/₃ pt chicken or beef stock mixed with water
1 bay leaf
cayenne pepper
6 thin slices of slightly stale country bread, crusts removed and cut into halves or thirds
125g/4¹/₂oz young Cantal, Tomme d'Aligot or Caerphilly cheese, coarsely grated or slivered if too soft for grating

1 In a sauté pan or large heavy saucepan, heat the oil over a moderate heat. Add the butter and tilt the pan over the heat until melted. Add the onion, reduce the heat a fraction and sauté for about 5 minutes, until golden.

2 Pour in the stock mixture. Add the bay leaf and a touch of cayenne pepper. Season lightly, bring to a simmer and continue cooking for 10 minutes over a low heat, stirring a few times.

3 Meanwhile, preheat the oven to its lowest temperature setting. Place individual bowls in the oven to warm and fill a soup tureen with very hot water. Pour out the water and dry the tureen.

4 Place a layer of bread in the tureen. Cover generously with grated or slivered cheese. Moisten with a couple of ladles of stock and onion. Repeat until you have used up all the bread and cheese.

5 Remove the bay leaf and pour in the rest of the stock and onion. Adjust the seasoning. Cover tightly and leave in the oven for 10-15 minutes.

6 Serve in the warmed bowls.

POTAGE VELOURS AUX LENTILLES ET AU JAMBON CRU
Creamed Lentil and Ham Soup

The term *velours* means 'velvet' and is used of smooth-textured soups and sauces. Likewise, *velouté* means velvety.

Serves 4
Preparation: about 10 minutes
Cooking: about 50 minutes

2 tbsp olive oil
1 Spanish onion, finely chopped
1 garlic clove, crushed
350g/12oz small dark green lentils, rinsed and soaked as per packet instructions
1 large potato, peeled and chopped
1 leek, washed and chopped
1 bouquet garni
3 cloves
1 generous tsp dried thyme or rubbed sage
800ml/28fl oz chicken or vegetable stock or mixed stock and water
3 tbsp port or Madeira
4 small thin slices dry-cured ham
salt and freshly ground black pepper
2 tbsp extra virgin olive oil or 30g/1oz butter, to serve (optional)

1 Put a sauté pan over a moderate heat. Dribble the oil into the hot pan, tilt the pan around until coated, then add the onion and garlic and stir for a few minutes until golden.

2 Mix in the drained lentils, vegetables, bouquet garni, cloves and herbs. Pour in the stock or stock mixture. Bring gently to the boil, then reduce the heat a little. Cover and simmer for about 30 minutes, or until the lentils and vegetables are cooked and tender. Leave to cool slightly.

3 Lift out and discard the cloves and bouquet garni. Pour the soup in a liquidizer or food processor and blend. Strain through a sieve back into the pan, using the back of a spoon to push through as much pulp as possible.

4 Over a low heat, stir in the port or Madeira. Roll up each slice of ham and snip strips of it into the pan.

5 If the soup looks too thick, thin it down by stirring in a few tablespoons of boiling water. Season to taste.

6 If you like, before serving the soup piping hot in a warmed tureen or individual bowls, trickle in a little olive oil or swirl in a knob of butter.

Chapter Two

LES SAUCES

Sauces and Dressings

The great French statesman Talleyrand
once quipped that there were 360 sauces in France
as opposed to England which has 3 sauces
and 360 religions.
In the large professional kitchen,
sauces – just like pastries – warrant the skills of
specialist chefs. On the home front in France, sauces
are less ambitious, but they still play a crucial role.
'Encore un peu de sauce? (A little more sauce?)' is a question frequently asked of table guests. *'Je ne dirais pas non*
(I wouldn't say no)…' is the equally
frequent positive reply.
Sauces are to be savoured in their own
right as they discreetly season and complement
the food. It does no harm at this stage to remind
ourselves that the word sauce is descended from
salsus, the Latin for salt – that most essential
of condiments.
This chapter focuses on some of the sauces
that are important in French home cooking. It
leaves aside a significant category of sauces – *les petites
sauces,* the reductions and the glorious spoonfuls a
cook creates from the pan juices and a few judicious
extra ingredients. As these are an intrinsic part of the
recipes in which they occur – rather than recipes in
their own right – they are dealt with
elsewhere in this book.

RIGHT
Lotte au Four en Papillote (page 88) served with Sauce
Bourguignonne (page 30).

SAUCE BOURGUIGNONNE
Red Wine Sauce

Also known as *sauce au vin rouge*, this sauce is a classic with fried or grilled red meat. It is also the traditional base of Burgundy's stew of fresh water fish, *la matelote*, a recipe that works well with more readily available monkfish (see page 88).

When making the sauce, match the stock to the food it will accompany. If your *bourguignonne* is intended for fish, make it with a *fumet* (see page 10), *court-bouillon* (see page 10) or a light vegetable stock (see page 11). If you prefer, also omit the bacon.

Sauce bourguignonne can be prepared ahead to the end of step 6 and chilled until needed. Its deep dull vinous colour will come to brilliant life when you whisk in the butter. For a more gentle and lighter sauce, use white wine – you will not be disappointed.

Serves 4
Preparation: 10-15 minutes
Cooking: about 45 minutes

55g/2oz thickly sliced smoked bacon, cut into small dice
1 tsp oil
75g/2¹/₂oz chilled unsalted butter, diced
2 sweet white onions, or 1 Spanish onion, finely chopped
115g/4oz white button mushrooms, finely chopped
1 shallot, finely chopped
2 scant tbsp flour
450ml/³/₄pt red wine
250ml/8fl oz beef or veal stock (see above)
1 bouquet garni
sea salt and freshly ground black pepper

1 Bring some water to the boil in a kettle. Put the bacon in a small saucepan, cover with boiling water and blanch for 1 minute over a moderate heat. Drain well, spread between 2 double layers of paper towel and pat dry.

2 Put the oil in a heavy saucepan and use a small wad of paper towel to coat the base of the pan. Heat the pan over a moderate heat. Add about 15g/¹/₂oz butter to the hot pan and tilt the pan around over the heat until the butter has melted. Tip in the bacon and stir for 2 minutes until golden.

3 Reduce the heat a little, add the onion, mushrooms and shallot and sweat for several minutes over a low heat, stirring occasionally.

4 Season lightly, sprinkle with flour and sauté for 2–3 minutes, stirring until the flour has coloured a little.

5 Pour in the wine and stock, then add the bouquet garni. Now turn up the heat and bring to a simmer, stirring occasionally. Keep simmering until the liquid is reduced by just over half. Stir from time to time and do not allow to boil too fast.

6 Push the sauce through a chinois or fine sieve into a small saucepan. Use the back or handle of a wooden spoon to press through as much liquid as possible from the ingredients.

7 To finish the sauce: place the saucepan over a low heat and adjust the seasoning. Turn up the heat, whisk in the remaining butter and serve immediately.

SAUCE POULETTE
Rich White Sauce

This delicate lemony sauce is excellent with poached chicken and plain white meats – veal in particular.

Serves 4
Preparation: about 5 minutes
Cooking: about 25 minutes

30g/1oz butter
30g/1oz flour
finely grated zest and juice of ¹/₂ large juicy lemon or 1 small lemon
400ml/14fl oz good chicken or vegetable stock
2tbsp mushroom fumet (see page 10, optional)
2 small egg yolks
4tbsp single cream
sea salt and freshly ground black pepper

1 Melt the butter in a heavy saucepan over a low heat. Add the flour and stir for a minute to make a pale roux.

2 Sprinkle in the grated lemon zest and season lightly. Gradually whisk the stock into the roux, followed by the mushroom fumet. Bring to a simmer, stirring vigorously and continuously.

3 As soon as bubbles start to appear, reduce the heat a little. Then simmer gently for about 15 minutes, stirring regularly, until the sauce is thick and smooth. Leave over a very low heat.

4 Put the egg yolks in a bowl and beat them lightly. Then stir in 2 or 3 tablespoons of hot sauce, one tablespoon at a time. Now stir in the cream, and whisk lightly until thoroughly combined.

5 Whisk this mixture into the sauce, a little at a time. Stir over a low heat for a few minutes.

6 Adjust the seasoning, stir in the lemon juice and serve immediately.

Variation: to make into a Caper Sauce for fish and boiled lamb, whisk 55g/2oz diced chilled butter, 1 tablespoon of drained capers and 1 tablespoon of white wine vinegar into the sauce instead of the egg and cream liaison in step 4 and omit the lemon juice.

BEURRES COMPOSÉS
Flavoured Butters

Redolent with synthetic garlic and herbs, the *soi-disant* 'flavoured butters' on sale in supermarkets have little to do with genuine *beurres composés*. A combination of butter and other ingredients, these can be whizzed in minutes in the blender or food processor, rolled into a sausage shape and chilled in waxed paper until needed. Neat disc-shaped pats may then be sliced off as required.

Serves 4-6
Preparation: under 10 minutes

115g/4oz butter at room temperature, diced
sea salt and freshly ground pepper
and one of the following flavourings:

FOR BEURRE MAITRE D'HOTEL
(PARSLEY BUTTER)
2 tbsp finely snipped parsley
2 tbsp lemon juice
1 tbsp mushroom fumet (page 10), optional

FOR BEURRE AU ROQUEFORT
(ROQUEFORT BUTTER)
55g/2oz Roquefort cheese, crumbled
2 tsp brandy
1 tsp Dijon mustard

FOR BEURRE DE CREVETTES (PRAWN BUTTER)
55g/2oz peeled cooked prawns, chopped
small pinch of paprika
1 tsp lemon juice
cayenne pepper

FOR BEURRE D'ANCHOIS (ANCHOVY BUTTER)
4 canned anchovy fillets in oil, well drained and chopped
4 capers, drained
2 tsp lemon juice
cayenne pepper

1 To make *Beurre Maître d'Hôtel*: put half the diced butter in a blender or food processor, sprinkle in the parsley and whizz until blended. Then add the rest of the butter, the lemon juice and season. Scrape the butter off the sides of the bowl with a spatula and whizz again until smooth. Serve with grilled meats and with vegetables. To accompany grilled fish, try adding a tablespoon of mushroom fumet at the same time as the lemon juice.

2 To make *Beurre au Roquefort*: put half the diced butter in a blender or food processor, add the crumbled cheese, brandy and mustard. Whizz until blended, then add the rest of the butter and season with pepper. Use a spatula to scrape the butter off the sides of the bowl and whizz again until smooth. Serve with grilled steak.

3 To make *Beurre de Crevettes*: put half the diced butter in a blender or food processor with the prawns. Whizz until blended, then add the rest of the butter, the paprika and lemon juice. Season with cayenne, pepper and a little salt, if liked. Scrape the butter off the sides of the bowl with a spatula and whizz again until smooth. Spread on canapés or use to enrich fish soups and sauces.

4 To make *Beurre d'Anchois*: put half the diced butter in a blender or food processor with the anchovy fillets and the capers and whizz until blended. Then add the rest of the butter and the lemon juice. Season with cayenne and black pepper. Scrape the butter off the sides of the bowl with a spatula and whizz again until smooth. Spread on toast or canapés or serve with grilled fish or steak.

LA SAUCE BÉCHAMEL

Béchamel Sauce

Makes 575ml/1pt
Preparation: about 5 minutes
Cooking: about 20 minutes

55g/2oz unsalted butter
55g/2oz flour
575ml/1pt milk
pinch of ground nutmeg
sea salt and freshly ground
black pepper

When *nouvelle cuisine* temporarily banished flour-based sauces from the kitchen, some late great gastronomes probably turned in their graves. Among them would have been a certain Louis de Béchamel, Marquis de Nointel. A courtier of Louis XIV, he was as clever at making money as he was passionate about spending it on fine food. This great classic of French white sauces is named after him. The good marquis's original sauce was a *velouté* of herbs, butter, spices and flour blended with cream. The herbs and cream have gone but *la sauce Béchamel* lives on.

Much slandered a decade or two ago as heavy and stodgy, Béchamel is in fact a versatile preparation, crucial in the making of savoury soufflés, other sauces and creamy preparations, and relatively uncomplicated to master. All that is required is a little patience.

OVER A LOW HEAT, BRISKLY
STIR FLOUR INTO MELTED BUTTER
UNTIL SMOOTH.

1 Heat a heavy-based saucepan over a moderate heat, then add the butter, reduce the heat a little and tilt the pan around until the butter has melted. Quickly tip in the flour, and stir vigorously, using either a balloon whisk or a wooden spoon (I prefer the latter at this stage). Stir constantly over a low heat for 1–2 minutes until the mixture is smooth, without letting it colour – you now have a blond (pale) roux.

2 Take the pan off the heat and rest it on a heatproof work surface. Moisten the roux with a little milk, whisking it in well (from this stage on I use a balloon whisk). Gradually pour in the rest of the milk, whisking steadily.

ONCE YOU HAVE A BLOND
ROUX, REST IT OFF THE HEAT BEFORE
WHISKING IN THE MILK.

3 Return to the heat. Increase it a fraction and bring slowly to boil, whisking constantly. As soon as it bubbles, reduce the heat and simmer very gently for at least 8 minutes, preferably 12 and ideally 15, whisking frequently and steadily. This seems endless, but be patient – or your sauce will taste floury (undercooked) or sticky (too much heat and irregular whisking).

WHISKING
VIGOROUSLY, GRADUALLY
POUR IN THE MILK.

4 Season to taste with salt, pepper and a tiny pinch of ground nutmeg.

NOTE: use either full-fat or semi-skimmed milk. If concerned about the fat content, make a *Sauce Blanche* instead, using stock or water.

VARIATIONS: the only successful shortcut I know is to use cornflour instead of wheat flour. It will not have quite as much body, but you need to simmer it for only 3–5 minutes. Some cooks whisk in scalded rather than cold milk. With this method, lumps are more of a hazard. It saves simmering time, but you may well end up spending the time saved sieving.

Sauce Mornay poured over boiled cauliflower florets and briefly gratinéed to make Chou-fleur à la Polonaise (see page 135), the French version of cauliflower cheese.

Béchamel's creator used parsley, chives, shallot and nutmeg to flavour his original recipe. Try adding a few sprigs of fresh thyme (or a good pinch of dried thyme), a bay leaf and a pinch of sage or mustard powder to the milk .

Replace half the milk with white wine, stock, fish or mushroom *fumet* (see page 10). This gives a subtle but pervasive depth to the sauce that is good with vegetables.

For *Sauce Aurore*, add a tablespoon of tomato paste to the *Béchamel*. To make *Sauce Mornay* for fish and vegetables, stir in 55g/2oz grated strong hard cheese.

BEURRE FONDU CITRONNÉ
Lemon Butter Sauce

Serve with poached fish and vegetables. Each 30g/1oz solid butter yields 3 scant tablespoons of melted lemon butter.

Serves 4
Preparation and cooking: under 10 minutes

115g/4oz unsalted butter
juice of ½ lemon
sea salt and freshly ground pepper

1 Cut the butter into slivers and put in a small heavy saucepan over a low heat. Tilt the pan around over the heat until the butter has melted. Season lightly

2 Use a small whisk to stir in the lemon juice. Transfer to a warmed sauce-boat or dribble directly over the food.

SAUCE BEURRE BLANC
White Butter Sauce

This sauce is an exquisite blend of the sweet and the sharp and makes a perfect partner for fine-flavoured ingredients such as scallops, asparagus and delicate fish. The only problem is that – like other butter sauces – beurre blanc requires constant attention and is best used immediately.

Prepare the shallot purée (to the end of step 2) in advance, cover and leave until no earlier than 15 minutes before you are ready to serve.

Serves 4
Preparation: about 10 minutes
Cooking: about 15 minutes

4 shallots, very finely chopped
4tbsp dry white wine
2tbsp white wine vinegar
150g/5½oz top-quality unsalted butter, diced and chilled
sea salt and freshly ground pepper

1 Put the finely chopped shallots in a small heavy saucepan together with the white wine and vinegar. Place over a moderate heat and simmer until reduced by over half so that it is soft and syrupy (this will take a good 10 minutes). Stir regularly.

2 Push the shallot purée through a fine sieve. You should have about 2 tablespoons of liquid.

3 Turn down the heat a little. Whisk the butter into the shallot liquid, a few pieces at a time, working briskly without stopping. Take the pan off the heat for a few seconds to keep the temperature under control. The butter will gradually thicken the sauce and give it a smooth, creamy texture.

4 Season lightly with salt and pepper. Serve immediately. The sauce will keep warm for a short while in a bain-marie, but whisk frequently.

Variations: whisk 1 tablespoon of double cream and a few leaves of snipped tarragon into the finished sauce. Add a sprinkling of finely grated zest of lemon or orange. 1 or 2 tablespoons of fish or mushroom *fumet* whisked in at the end gives a fluffy fragrant *beurre blanc*.

(RIGHT) Coquilles Saint-Jacques au Beurre Blanc *(page 74)*.

LA MAYONNAISE

Thick Mayonnaise

Serves 4-6
Preparation: about 10 minutes

2 very fresh egg yolks (size 1 or 2)
1 tsp red or white wine vinegar or lemon
juice, plus a little extra
if necessary
¼ tsp hot mustard
300ml/½ pt groundnut oil, or
200ml/7fl oz groundnut oil and
100ml/3½ fl oz light-flavoured olive
oil (see Notes right)
sea salt and freshly ground
black pepper

Mayonnaise is the sauce of high summer and sunny days ... a marriage made in heaven between two fundamental substances, egg yolk and oil, so essential with cold chicken and poached fish. It requires no cooking, but careful handling and a little basic understanding of its delicate chemistry. It can be made in a blender or food processor, but the best way to approach it is with a bowl and a wooden spoon.

The making of a mayonnaise starts when you break up the egg yolks and thoroughly beat them with the vinegar or lemon juice and the seasonings until all are combined into a sticky little puddle at the bottom of the mixing bowl. Like Hollandaise and Béarnaise (pages 40 and 41), Mayonnaise is an emulsion – a liquid or fat dispersed in another. Emulsions are tricky combinations, a fragile alliance coaxed between never-the-twain-shall-meet ingredients, such as oil and water.

In my experience, mayonnaise is much less likely to be temperamental if all the ingredients and equipment are at room temperature, but there is no scientific proof for this. The celebrated scientist and gastronome Edouard de Pomiane literally and unforgettably puts his mayo under the microscope – '... a fascinating sight. The tiny particles of yolk of egg, under the light, sparkle like stars' – but makes no mention of temperature. More recently the American scientist and food writer Harold McGee, in his magisterial *On Food and Cooking*, focuses on the complex chemistry of the egg rather than on temperature. He advocates using the freshest possible eggs and only mentions *en passant* that extremes of heat should be avoided.

ALLOW THE INGREDIENTS AND UTENSILS TO COME TO THE SAME ROOM TEMPERATURE.

1 Put your fresh egg yolks in a medium-sized mixing bowl, add a little vinegar or lemon juice, a touch of mustard, a tiny pinch of sea salt and a grinding of black pepper. Do not stir, but cover with cling film. Put the oil (or oils), the flavouring ingredients and the wooden spoon (or a fork if you prefer)

TO BEGIN WITH, BEAT THE OIL INTO THE EGG YOLKS VERY SLOWLY, DROP BY DROP.

next to the bowl and leave for at least 15 minutes – longer if it is more convenient.

2 If you like, wedge the bowl in place on a mat of dampened paper towel (a necessary precaution when you use a hand-held electric whisk – not vital here, but you may find it more comfortable). Beat in a few drops of oil, a drop at a time. As soon as the oil has disappeared into the yolk mixture, dribble in a few more drops, still beating rapidly and steadily – not furiously, but at a speed your arm can

keep up for a while without getting the burn like some martyr of aerobics.

3 Continue adding the oil very slowly, a few drops at a time, until the mixture starts to thicken visibly. This gratifying stage tends to happen suddenly after you have beaten in between one-quarter and one-third of the oil.

4 Rest your arm for a few seconds, then continue adding the oil in a very thin trickle, still beating at the same constant speed until you have used up all the oil.

WHEN THE MAYONNAISE AMALGAMATES INTO THICK SHINY COILS, IT IS ALMOST READY.

Which oil to use? It is a matter of taste. Groundnut oil is a reliable orthodox choice. It tends to produce a clean good all-rounder of a mayonnaise. It is a bit on the bland side, however, and needs liberal seasoning. It reacts happily to being flavoured with lemon juice, mustard, tarragon, chives or parsley. I find mayonnaise made exclusively with olive oil somewhat too heavy and prefer a 50/50 or even 75/25 blend of groundnut oil and olive oil. With a touch of garlic, olivey mayonnaise makes a feast of leftover cold *Gigot d'Agneau* (page 118).

ONCE THE MIXTURE BEGINS TO THICKEN, START ADDING THE OIL IN A STEADY TRICKLE.

5 Now admire your bowl of glossy gold mayonnaise. Taste and adjust the seasoning. A few more drops of vinegar or lemon juice will sharpen the flavour and also slightly loosen the texture. Hand-made mayonnaise should be just thick enough to hold its shape. Cover and chill on the least cold shelf of the refrigerator until needed. Use on cold or lukewarm ingredients only, as mayonnaise disintegrates when you confront it with hot food.

Notes: for larger quantities of mayonnaise or if you require a thinner texture, use an electric whisk and the same amount of egg yolks but an extra 150ml/¼ pt oil. Resist the temptation to speed up the beginning of the process. Build up the mayonnaise a few drops of oil at a time at the outset.

TASTE THE FINISHED MAYONNAISE BEFORE ADDING HERBS OR EXTRA FLAVOURINGS.

Mustard Mayonnaise *mixed with shredded celariac to give the classic starter* céleri rémoulade.

If you are using olive oil, start beating it in once you have used up all the groundnut oil. Ordinary good-quality olive oil works best — extra virgin oil has too strong a flavour and will overpower the mayonnaise and the ingredients it is supposed to enhance.

It is a good idea to have 1 more egg at room temperature in case of accidents. If, despite all your efforts, your mayonnaise curdles, blame it on the cat or the weather. Rinse a clean mixing bowl in warm water to help bring it quickly to room temperature and dry it thoroughly. Break in the reserved egg yolk, then beat in a scant tablespoon of curdled sauce until combined. Beat in the rest of the curdled mixture, a few drops at a time to start with, then in a thin trickle later.

VARIATIONS: for Garlic Mayonnaise to serve with cold lamb and fish, crush a large fresh clove (or more) of garlic and add it to the egg yolk with the other ingredients in the bowl before you start.

For a quick Chilli Mayonnaise somewhat less fiery than Rouille (opposite), add a little crushed garlic and a small blob of harissa (no larger than a small hazelnut) to the other ingredients. Whisk in 1 teaspoon of tomato paste once your mayonnaise has emulsified. Season with paprika or cayenne pepper.

To make Mustard Mayonnaise to serve with cold pork, add an extra scant teaspoon of Dijon mustard to the original ingredients. Lightly whisk a tablespoon of coarse grain mustard into the final emulsion. A few finely chopped gherkins, a teaspoon or two of drained capers and a few sprigs of snipped herbs add extra bite.

ROUILLE
Hot Pepper Mayonnaise

Probably the hottest number in the French sauce repertoire, Rouille is the classic accompaniment to Bouillabaisse (page 78). Also serve it with crudités and croûtons.

Serves 4
Preparation: 1 hour soaking the peppers, if necessary, plus 15 minutes chilling

2 small hot red chilli peppers
1 slice of soft bread, crust removed, broken into pieces and moistened with milk
2-3 fresh garlic cloves, crushed
1 large egg yolk
1tsp tomato paste (optional)
150ml/¹/₄pt olive oil
harissa, if liked
sea salt

1 If the chilli peppers are dried, soak them in water for 1 hour. Drain, if necessary. Discard the stems and seeds and finely chop the rest of the peppers.

2 In a bowl, mash together the moistened bread, crushed garlic, egg yolk, chopped peppers and tomato paste, if using. Season lightly with salt.

3 Wedge the bowl in place on a mat of dampened paper towel. Using a hand-held electric whisk, whisk in a few drops of oil, as for Mayonnaise (page 36). Continue trickling in the oil slowly, whisking constantly, until the sauce thickens.

4 Adjust the seasoning, adding a little harissa if you like your sauce really fiery. Stir in a tablespoon of cold water. Cover and chill for 15 minutes until ready to serve.

SAUCE GRIBICHE
Gherkin Mayonnaise

This coarse-textured piquant mayonnaise (the word *gribiche* was once used to describe a shrewish woman) is good with cold meats, and traditional with poached calf's head, *tête de veau*. Readers of Proust may remember from *Swann's Way* that the young hero had a recipe for *sauce gribiche* that was more sought after than he himself for *diners mondains*.

Serves 4
Cooking: about 10 minutes (for the egg)
Preparation: about 15 minutes, plus 15 minutes chilling

1 large hard-boiled egg
1 generous tsp Dijon mustard
300ml/¹/₂pt groundnut oil
2-3tsp red or white wine vinegar
6 or more small gherkins, finely chopped
few sprigs each of all or some of the following fresh herbs, finely snipped: parsley, chervil, tarragon, chives
sea salt and freshly ground black pepper

1 Separate the yolk and the white of the hard-boiled egg. Reserving the white, mash the yolk in a bowl, then add the mustard and season liberally.

2 Wedge the bowl in place on a mat of dampened paper towel. Using a hand-held electric whisk, whisk in a few drops of oil, a drop at a time, as for Mayonnaise (page 36). Continue trickling in the oil very slowly, whisking constantly, until the sauce thickens, then increase the trickle.

3 Once you have whisked in all the oil, stir in the vinegar, then add the finely chopped gherkins and snipped herbs. Adjust the seasoning.

4 Chop the egg white and stir it in the sauce. Cover and chill for 15 minutes, or until needed.

BEURRE DE MONTPELLIER

Herb Butter

An unusual preparation somewhere between a compound butter and a mayonnaise, this gutsy coarse-textured green sauce is good with grilled meats as well as poached fish.

Serves 4-6
Cooking: 10 minutes to hard-boil the egg
Preparation: about 20 minutes, then at least 1 hour chilling

85g/ 3oz green leaves, made up of all or as many as available of the following: young spinach or sorrel leaves, watercress, parsley, chervil, tarragon and chives
4 canned anchovy fillets in oil, drained and chopped
2 small gherkins, chopped
1 tbsp drained capers
1 garlic clove, crushed
100g/ 3 1/2 oz soft unsalted butter, cut into small pieces
1 hard-boiled egg yolk plus 1 raw egg yolk
3 tbsp olive oil
1 tbsp wine vinegar
sea salt and freshly ground black pepper

1 Bring a kettle of water to the boil. Put the leaves and herbs in a sauté pan. Season lightly with salt, cover with boiling water and blanch for 1 minute over a moderate heat.

2 Drain in a colander and refresh in cold running water. Press well to get rid of as much water as possible. Spread between 2 double layers of paper towel and pat dry firmly. Repeat with fresh paper if necessary.

3 Put the drained leaves and herbs in a food processor, together with the anchovies, gherkins, capers, garlic and half the butter. Season with pepper and whizz briefly.

4 Scrape the green purée down the sides of the bowl with a spatula. Add the egg yolks and the rest of the butter. Whizz again quickly until blended. Scrape away the sauce from the sides of the bowl.

5 With the motor running, slowly trickle in the oil. Stop whizzing once all the oil has all been absorbed.

6 Adjust the seasoning and stir in the vinegar. Cover and chill, allowing at least 1 hour for the flavours to develop.

SAUCE HOLLANDAISE

Hollandaise brooks no interruptions: the point of no return is reached the moment you start whisking. Use extra-fresh eggs and on no account overheat, otherwise the yolks will set and the sauce will curdle. This pretty unforgiving emulsion is well worth every stressful minute of the time it takes to prepare. It transforms poached salmon, asparagus and fresh young vegetables, and is heavenly with poached eggs.

For a lighter, fluffier sauce, whisk the whites of 2 eggs until stiff but still creamy soft and whisk into the finished Hollandaise. To make Sauce Mousseline for fish and seafood, whisk in 2 tablespoons of lightly whipped cream. A few drops of orange juice can also be added for flavour.

Serves 4
Preparation: about 5 minutes
Cooking: under 15 minutes

3 very fresh small egg yolks
1 tbsp lemon juice
125g/ 4 1/2 oz chilled unsalted butter, diced
sea salt and freshly ground black pepper

1 Bring a kettle of water to the boil, then leave the water to cool for a few minutes. Pour the hot water into the bottom part of a double boiler, or into a large saucepan over which you can set a metal bowl or smaller heavy saucepan.

2 Put the double boiler or larger pan over a low heat – the water should be just below simmering point. Off the heat, put the egg yolks, half the lemon juice and 2 teaspoons of water in the top pan. Season lightly and beat until combined and liquid.

3 Place over the hot water – its surface should be just trembling – and whisk until the yolk mixture thickens a little.

4 Still whisking over barely simmering water, work in the butter one piece at a time. Each bit should be completely absorbed before you whisk in the next one. Once all the butter has been worked in, you will have a rich creamy emulsion. If the mixture curdles during the process, take the top pan off the heat, dip its base in cold water and whisk vigorously.

5 Adjust the seasoning, whisk in a few more drops of lemon juice and a scant tablespoon of hot water. Serve at once. Sensitive Hollandaise will keep for a few minutes over a bowl of lukewarm water.

SAUCE BÉARNAISE

Less tricky to prepare than Hollandaise, this rich emulsion makes a splendidly robust accompaniment to grilled red meat. Flavour the sauce with snipped fresh mint if you serve it with lamb. To make colourful *Sauce Choron*, whisk in 2 tablespoons of thick tomato paste, push it through a sieve and serve lukewarm.

Serves 4
Preparation: about 10 minutes
Cooking: about 20 minutes

4 shallots, very finely chopped
several tarragon leaves, finely snipped
4tbsp dry white wine
2tbsp white wine vinegar
2 ultra-fresh egg yolks
125g/4½oz top-quality chilled unsalted butter, diced
few sprigs of chervil, finely snipped
1tsp lemon juice
sea salt and freshly ground pepper

1 Put the shallots and half the tarragon leaves in a small heavy saucepan (or in the top pan of a double boiler) together with the white wine and vinegar. Place over a low to moderate heat and simmer until the shallot mixture is well reduced, soft and syrupy (this will take about 10 minutes), stirring regularly.

2 Meanwhile, bring a kettle of water to the boil. Then leave the water to cool for a few minutes. Pour the hot water into a large saucepan over which you can set the pan with the shallot mixture, or the bottom part of the double boiler if using.

3 Push the reduced shallot and tarragon mixture through a small fine sieve into a cup. You should have about 2 tablespoons of liquid. Return this to the pan.

4 Put the pan with the water or the bottom part of the double boiler over a low heat – the water should be barely simmering. Off the heat, add the egg yolks to the shallot syrup in the other pan or top part of the double boiler, followed by 1 scant tablespoon of water. Season lightly and beat until combined.

5 Now put this on top of the pan of barely simmering water and whisk the mixture until frothy. Still whisking, work in the butter bit by bit. Each piece should be completely absorbed and the mixture smooth before you whisk in the next one. Occasionally take the pan off the just simmering water to stop the sauce overheating. If the mixture curdles at any time during the process, take the top pan off the heat, dip its base in cold water and whisk vigorously.

6 Once all the butter has been worked in, your sauce will have the same kind of texture as a mayonnaise. Adjust the seasoning, whisk in the rest of the tarragon and the prepared chervil. Sprinkle over the lemon juice and whisk it briefly.

7 Serve as soon as possible. Béarnaise will keep for a short while over a saucepan or bowl of lukewarm water. It is better to eat it *tiède* (just warm) than to attempt to reheat it.

Chapter Three

LES ŒUFS

Eggs

No self-respecting working family
kitchen in France is complete without, at the very
least, half-a-dozen eggs inside the
refrigerator door. Eggs are the all-purpose players
of the cooking fields – they thicken a sauce, bind a
filling, glaze a pastry, set a custard, mellow an ice-
cream ... Given a starring role in their own right,
in minutes eggs turn into dishes that are among
the most satisfying and the least expensive of
culinary feasts.

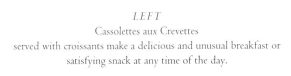

LEFT
Cassolettes aux Crevettes
served with croissants make a delicious and unusual breakfast or
satisfying snack at any time of the day.

CASSOLETTES AUX CREVETTES
Scrambled Eggs with Prawns

Start by preparing the prawns so that you are free to concentrate on stirring the eggs into soft moist perfection over a very low heat. Whisking in small knobs of butter a few at a time helps achieve the desired result by slowing the cooking process and enriching the dish. Another approach is to stir in the last egg (or one extra egg) once the rest is practically ready – a proven rescue remedy if the mixture is at all overcooked.

Wild mushrooms sautéed with a little butter in a pan rubbed with garlic make another delicious centrepiece for a dish of scrambled eggs.

Serves 4
Preparation: about 5 minutes
Cooking: about 20 minutes

12 large prawns, raw or cooked and shelled
55g/2oz butter
small pinch of cayenne
small pinch of paprika
8 extra-fresh eggs at room temperature
1tsp lemon juice
1 generous tbsp crème fraîche
few sprigs of fresh herbs: such as chervil, chives, tarragon, dill
sea salt and freshly ground black pepper
thin slices of light rye bread, to serve

1 If you are using raw prawns, bring a kettle of water to the boil. Put the prawns in a saucepan, cover them with boiling water, season with a little salt and blanch over a moderate heat for 3 minutes. Drain, refresh in cold water, drain again and shell.

2 Put 15g/½ oz butter in a small frying pan and melt over a low heat. Add the prawns and season with cayenne and paprika. Sauté the prawns for a few minutes, turning them over so that they are golden and well coated with butter and spices.

3 Meanwhile, scramble the eggs: first whisk them briefly in a bowl and season very lightly. In a heavy pan, melt half the remaining butter over a low heat. Tilt the pan around over the heat to coat its base and sides with the butter. Cut the rest of the butter into small pieces.

4 Tip the eggs into the pan and cook them slowly, stirring frequently with a wooden spoon. Keep the heat very low. If the eggs set too quickly, take the pan off the heat for a few seconds. Lightly whisk in 2 or 3 pieces of butter.

5 Sprinkle the prawns with the lemon juice, spoon over the crème fraîche and stir to coat.

6 When the eggs begin to look set, distribute the last of the butter over the mixture. Whisk in lightly and take off the heat. Season lightly with salt and more generously with pepper.

7 Spoon the scrambled eggs into 4 warmed individual dishes. Arrange 3 prawns and their cooking juices in the centre of each dish. Snip over the fresh herbs and serve without delay, with thin slices of light rye bread.

To drink: a medium-dry Vouvray.

ŒUFS BROUILLÉS AU BOUDIN
Scrambled Eggs with Black Pudding

The combination of scrambled eggs and *boudin* or good-quality black pudding is an excellent one. Rather than folding it into the egg, pile the slices of *boudin* in the centre or spoon it in a circle around the dish – the very different tastes and textures are much more enjoyable juxtaposed than blended.

Serves 2 as a main course, 3 as a starter
Preparation: 5 minutes
Cooking: about 30 minutes

about 200g/7oz French-style boudin or good-quality black pudding
2tsp oil
55g/2oz butter, or more if preferred
5 extra-fresh large eggs at room temperature
sea salt and freshly ground black pepper
toast or crusty bread, to serve

1 First cook the boudin: if you are using French-style boudin, cut it crosswise into 4 pieces. If using thicker black pudding, cut it into 2.5cm/1in slices.

2 Heat the oil in a frying pan over a moderate heat. Reduce the heat a fraction, add about 15g/½ oz butter and tilt the pan around over the heat until the butter is melted and hot. Add the boudin or black pudding and fry gently. Turn the pieces over after about 5 minutes and continue cooking for another 5 minutes. It does not matter if the boudin falls apart a little during cooking. Remove the pan from the heat. Cover and keep hot while you scramble the eggs.

3 In a bowl, beat the eggs briefly without letting them get fluffy. Season very lightly.

4 In a heavy pan, melt half the butter over a low heat and tilt the pan around over the heat to coat its base and sides with butter. Cut the rest of the butter into small pieces.

5 Tip the eggs into the pan and cook them gently, stirring very frequently with a wooden spoon. Keep the heat very low – and keep an eye on the mixture while you finish preparing the boudin.

6 Take the skin from the boudin or black pudding. Break up the flesh lightly with a fork and season with a little pepper. Cover and keep warm.

7 If the eggs set too quickly, take the pan off the heat for a few seconds. Add 2 or 3 pieces of butter to the pan and whisk in lightly. When the eggs begin to look set, distribute the rest of the butter over the mixture and whisk in lightly. Take off the heat and season lightly with salt and more generously with pepper.

8 Tip the scrambled egg into a warmed serving dish and pile the boudin in the centre. Serve without delay, accompanied by toast or crusty fresh bread.

OMELETTE BRAYAUDE
Flat Country Potato Omelette

Flat omelettes are very much part of France's traditional country cooking. Push the edges of the omelette back towards the centre of the pan the moment they set. This allows the runny egg mixture to brown and crisp cleanly underneath and it helps keep the centre of the omelette meltingly tender.

Serves 4
Preparation: about 10 minutes
Cooking: about 15 minutes

about 85g/3oz waxy potato, peeled and cut into 1.5cm/^{1}/$_2$-^{3}/$_4$in dice
2tsp oil
5 extra-fresh large eggs at room temperature
1tbsp milk or single cream
55g/2oz thick cut ham, diced
1 scant tbsp freshly grated strong medium-hard cheese, such as Farmhouse Cheddar
30g/1oz butter
several sprigs of chives, finely snipped
sea salt and freshly ground black pepper

1 First prepare the potato: bring a kettle of water to the boil, put the diced potato in a small saucepan, pour in the water and season lightly with salt. Bring to a simmer over a moderate heat and cook for 5–8 minutes, until the potato is just tender. Drain.

2 Heat a small frying pan over a moderate heat and add the oil. When the pan is coated with hot oil, spread in the potatoes and sauté for 3 minutes, shaking the pan and stirring.

3 Whisk the eggs briskly with the milk or cream. Season lightly and whisk in the sautéed potato, the diced ham and grated cheese.

4 Cut the butter into 4 equal pieces. Place an 18cm/7in omelette pan over a moderate to hot heat. Swirl 2 pieces of butter into the hot pan. When the butter stops foaming and before it turns brown, tip in the whisked egg mixture.

5 Cook over a moderate heat, shaking the pan and pushing the edges towards the centre as soon as they begin to set, using a heatproof spatula or palette knife. Warm a serving plate (it should be larger than the pan) and have it to hand.

6 When the egg mixture is no longer runny but still moist looking, sprinkle over the herbs, season lightly, then leave to cook for a few seconds. Now put the serving plate over the pan. Carefully turn the omelette out on the plate, browned side up.

7 Swirl a piece of butter into the pan. The moment it melts, slide the omelette back into the pan and cook the underside for about 20 seconds. Slide the omelette back on to the serving plate, lightly trail the butter over the surface and serve at once.

To drink: a vin de pays rosé

Variations: for a finer result, use blanched or sautéed ingredients such as bacon, onion, aubergine, sweet pepper or courgette cut into small dice or pieces no larger than 1.5cm/^{1}/$_2$in. Cheese should be cut into fine slivers, crumbled or grated.

PIPÉRADE
Pepper & Tomato Eggs

The egg dish of France's Basque Country is halfway between a flat omelette and scrambled eggs. The red pepper and tomato purée (cooked to the end of step 3) makes a very good sauce in its own right and mellows still further with slow reheating.

Serves 4
Preparation: about 10 minutes
Cooking: about 35 minutes

1 sweet red pepper
1 sweet green pepper
2tbsp olive oil or goose fat
2 soft white onions, or 1 Spanish onion,
finely chopped
2 garlic cloves, crushed
4 ripe tomatoes
pinch each of dried oregano and rubbed sage
1 tsp sugar
2 slices Bayonne, Serrano or other dry-cured ham
6 extra-fresh large eggs at room temperature
sea salt and freshly ground black pepper

1 Heat the grill to high. Cut the peppers in half lengthwise, then remove the seeds, white core and membrane. Flatten with the palm of your hand and char under the hot grill until the skin blisters and blackens. Leave until cool enough to handle, then peel off the skin and cut the flesh into small strips.

2 Meanwhile, heat the olive oil or goose fat in a large frying pan, then sweat the onion and garlic in it over a low heat for several minutes, stirring a few times. While the onion is cooking, blanch, skin, seed and chop the tomatoes.

3 Add the tomatoes, the oregano, sage, sugar and strips of pepper to the softened onion. Season lightly and cook for at least 20 minutes, stirring occasionally, until you have a coarse thick purée.

4 Roll each slice of ham into a cigar shape and snip into small strips. Add to the purée and stir in well.

5 Break the eggs into a large bowl, season lightly and beat briskly with a fork as for an omelette (page 48).

6 Pour the eggs into the pan and stir lightly to combine with the pepper mixture. Cook for a few minutes over a low to moderate heat, stirring frequently, until just set but still moist.

7 Serve at once, straight from the pan.

To drink: Irouléguy Rosé.

(LEFT) Pipérade *served with* Riz Créole au Basilic *(page 150).*

L'OMELETTE AUX FINES HERBES

Herb Omelette

Serves 2
Preparation: about 5 minutes
Cooking: about 5 minutes

*4 extra-fresh large eggs at room
temperature*
1 tbsp milk or single cream
45g/1¹/₂oz butter
*1 heaped tbsp finely snipped parsley
mixed with 1 or 2 of the following fresh
herbs: tarragon, chives, chervil, plus extra
to finish (optional)*
*sea salt and freshly ground
black pepper*

Baveuse … the French have a word for the perfect omelette … dribbling with moisture, it is a promising golden vision that makes you salivate in anticipation.

The classic French omelette is folded and simple. A true case of less is best, it is often served *nature*. When such an omelette is filled, it is with the lightest of flavourings: a heaped teaspoon of *fines herbes*, a sprinkling of grated Gruyère cheese, a few dice of skinned tomato, thin slices of sautéed mushrooms, blanched asparagus tips, wilted spinach or sorrel, small dice of crispy lardons. Allow 1 tablespoon of filling per person, half that in the case of *fines herbes,* which have to be used with discretion.

A successful omelette starts with the proper frying pan. In an ideal kitchen, the omelette pan should be a dedicated utensil. This may not be possible, so use a smooth heavy-based pan (free of scratches) which is equipped with a steady handle you can grip comfortably. It makes life much easier if the pan is non-stick. What size pan to use? For 2 or 3 eggs and a single serving omelette, use a 15cm/6in pan; for 4 or 5 eggs, use a pan no wider than 20cm/8in; for a 6-egg omelette, use a 24cm/9in pan. Wash your omelette pan with care.

Allow 2 eggs per person – 3 if the eggs aren't very big and your guests are hungry. I find that a 6-egg omelette is the most I can manage in a single pan. Perhaps the optimum size with which to develop your omelette skills is a 4-egg mixture, which gives you just the right amount of mixture to work with and will serve 2 people. Always bring the eggs to room temperature before cooking.

1 Put the eggs in a bowl and season them with sea salt and a few grindings of black pepper. Add a tablespoon of milk or single cream. Take a fork and start beating the mixture briskly, continuing for at least 20 seconds (the idea at this stage is to get in plenty of air). Now set aside the bowl.

2 Add a piece of butter (about 20g/

TRY TO GET AS MUCH AIR INTO THE EGGS AS YOU CAN WHILE BEATING.

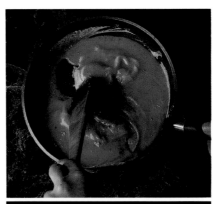

PULL THE EDGES OF THE OMELETTE INTO THE CENTRE AS THEY BEGIN TO SET.

²/₃oz) to the hot omelette pan. Swirl it around to coat the base and sides. Put the pan over a moderate to hot heat. When the foaming stops and before the butter starts to turn brown, it will exude a nutty smell and be just at the right temperature – this is the time to act. Pour the beaten eggs into the centre of the pan and start cooking the omelette.

3 Shake the pan with one hand and use a heatproof spatula (a wooden one does the job well) or a palette knife in

the other hand to push the edges of the egg mixture towards the centre as soon as it begins to set.

4 Cooking a 4-egg omelette only takes 3 minutes or so. Have your warmed serving plate at the ready. Scoop up half the remaining butter with the spatula. The moment your egg mixture is no longer liquid, stop stirring and count up to 5 while you sprinkle the fines herbes (or other light garnish) down the centre.

TILT THE PAN AWAY FROM YOU AND FOLD ONE-THIRD OF OMELETTE BACK

5 Now slide the spatula with the extra lubricant under the omelette and then remove. Tilt the handle-side of the pan down and let the omelette slide down towards the handle and some way up the side of the pan. Fold one-third of the omelette back towards the centre. Tilt the pan the other way and let the omelette slide down the pan and away from the handle. Use the spatula to fold another third back towards the centre. Slide it gently on to the serving plate.

6 Trail the rest of the butter over the surface to make it shine and season it lightly. If you like, sprinkle with extra herbs. Serve immediately.

To drink: a white Côtes de Gascogne or vin de pays.

VARIATION: to make an extra-fluffy omelette, in a separate bowl whisk the white of an extra egg (2 for 6 eggs) until just stiff. Fold this into the beaten egg mixture and make the omelette as described above.

ŒUFS
À L'OSEILLE
Sorrel Eggs

Baked eggs, *œufs en cocotte*, can be prepared in many ways using the method described below. The sharpness of sorrel is traditionally paired with eggs and white fish. Wilted spinach, fresh herbs, freshly grated Gruyère, crumbled Roquefort, diced bacon (blanched and sautéed), a few slivers of dry-cured ham, *Pipérade* purée (see page 47), all combine felicitously with the eggs, butter and cream. Chilling the buttered ramekins first helps prevent sticking during the baking.

Serves 4
Preparation: about 10 minutes
Cooking: about 20 minutes

55g/2oz butter
handful of young sorrel leaves, trimmed and coarsely shredded
freshly ground nutmeg
4 extra-fresh large eggs at room temperature
4tbsp crème fraîche, soured cream or single cream
sea salt and freshly ground black pepper
fingers of hot buttered toast or toasted brioche, to serve

1 Cut the butter into 4 equal pieces and melt 3 of them in a small saucepan over a low heat. Divide this butter between 4 individual ramekins large enough to take an egg, the garnish and cream. Using a pastry brush, coat the inside of each ramekin with the butter. Chill for about 5 minutes.

2 Preheat the oven to 190°C/375°F/gas 5. Meanwhile, put the last piece of butter in a small frying pan and melt it over a low heat. Add the sorrel and stir gently for a minute until wilted. Spread over a double layer of paper towels and pat dry with more paper.

3 Take the ramekins out of the refrigerator and divide the prepared sorrel between them. Season lightly with salt, more generously with pepper and add a touch of nutmeg.

4 Break an egg into a cup, then tip into a ramekin. Repeat with the other eggs. Spoon 1 tablespoon of cream over each egg and then season again.

5 Bring a kettle of water to the boil and line a baking pan with a few layers of newspaper. Put the ramekins in the pan and pour in boiling water to come halfway up the sides of the ramekins.

6 Bake for about 8–10 minutes, until the eggs are set to your liking (the yolks should stay slightly runny).

7 Serve as soon as possible, with fingers of hot buttered toast or toasted brioche.

To drink: Ardèche Chardonnay.

OMELETTE
GARNIE
PÉRIGOURDINE
Cheese and Mushroom Omelette

This delectable omelette scented with goose fat is inspired by the cooking of the Southwest of France. If you happen to be the proud owner of a truffle, here is how to have your cake and eat it: store the truffle with your eggs for a couple of days – their porous shell will allow them to absorb the potent flavour – and you'll then have a magnificent omelette and your truffle will still be intact.

Serves 3
Preparation: about 15 minutes
Cooking: about 10 minutes

1 garlic clove, halved
2 tbsp goose fat
350g/12oz wild mushrooms or a mixture of wild mushrooms and small brown mushrooms, wiped and sliced if large
1 heaped tbsp mixed finely snipped parsley and chives
6 extra-fresh large eggs at room temperature
2tbsp milk or single cream
1 heaped tbsp freshly grated Gruyère or mature Cheddar cheese
45g/1½ oz butter
sea salt and freshly ground black pepper

1 First prepare the mushroom filling: rub a frying pan or sauté pan with the cut sides of the garlic. Place the pan over a moderate heat and when the pan is hot, pour in 1½ tablespoons of goose fat. Tilt the pan around over the heat to coat the base with the fat.

2 Add the mushrooms to the hot pan, season lightly and sauté over a moderate heat for 3–4 minutes, stirring frequently. Tip the mushrooms out on a plate lined with a double layer of paper towel. Cover with more paper towel and pat

gently to draw off the fatty juices. Wipe the pan and return the mushrooms to the pan. Season again lightly and sprinkle in 1 teaspoon of snipped herbs. Keep warm.

3 Whisk the eggs briskly with the milk or cream. Season lightly and whisk in the grated cheese and 1 teaspoon of snipped herbs.

4 Heat the rest of the goose fat in a 24cm/9in omelette pan. Swirl in half the butter and place the pan over a moderate to hot heat. When the butter stops foaming and before it turns brown, tip in the whisked eggs.

5 Cook the egg mixture over a moderate heat, shaking the pan and pushing the edges towards the centre as soon as they begin to set, using a heatproof spatula or palette knife. Put the pan with the mushrooms over a low heat. Warm a serving plate and have it to hand.

6 When the egg mixture is no longer runny but still moist-looking, leave for a few seconds. Now slide the spatula sideways under the omelette, slip in half the remaining butter and remove the spatula. Tilt the handle-side of the pan down and slide the omelette sideways down towards it. Using the spatula, fold one-quarter of the omelette back towards the centre. Tilt the pan the other way and let the omelette slide back down the pan. Fold another quarter towards the centre.

7 Slide the omelette on to the serving plate. Use a knife to slit open the whole length of the omelette and spoon the warm mushroom filling into this gap, allowing it to overspill freely. Trail the remaining butter over the surface of the omelette and sprinkle with the rest of the herbs. Season lightly and serve immediately.

To drink: a Gaillac white wine.

OMELETTE SOUFFLÉE AU HADDOCK
Haddock Souffléed Omelette

Souffléed omelettes are delectable concoctions that take less time to cook than standard soufflés. Use a deep gratin dish.

Serves 4-6
Preparation: about 25 minutes
Cooking: about 20 minutes

300ml/ $^{1}/_{2}$ pt milk
100ml/ 3 $^{1}/_{2}$ fl oz dry white wine
bouquet garni
225g/ 8oz smoked haddock
6 extra-fresh large eggs at room temperature
$^{1}/_{2}$ tsp dried thyme or good mild curry powder
cayenne pepper
3tsp lemon juice
30g/ 1oz butter
sea salt and freshly ground black pepper

1 Combine the milk and white wine in a sauté pan or a saucepan large enough to take the fish comfortably. Add the bouquet garni and an extra 1.5cm/ $^{1}/_{2}$ in depth of water. Bring to a simmer over a moderate heat. Place the fish in the pan, bring back to a simmer and cook gently for about 5 minutes, until you can flake the flesh with a fork. Lift out, drain well and leave to cool for a few minutes.

2 Reserve 3 or 4 tablespoons of the cooking liquid and tip the rest out of the pan. Pour in the cream and place over a low heat until hot.

3 Flake the fish with a fork, discarding the skin and bones. Season with the dried thyme or curry powder, a touch of cayenne and black pepper, then sprinkle over 2 teaspoons of lemon juice. Tip into the pan and combine with the cream.

4 Preheat the oven to 190°C/375°F/gas 5. Generously grease a good-sized gratin dish with the butter. Have ready a large and a medium-sized bowl. Break the eggs, putting the whites in the large bowl and the yolks into the other bowl.

5 Beat the yolks briskly, then tip the haddock and cream mixture into the bowl and beat again. Adjust the seasoning.

6 Add a small pinch of salt and the rest of the lemon juice to the whites and whisk until soft peaks form. Gently fold a quarter of the whisked whites into the haddock mixture, then tip this into the bowl of whisked whites. Fold in lightly, working with swift upward movements.

7 Pour into the prepared dish and bake for about 20 minutes, until risen and golden. Serve immediately.

To drink: Pinot d'Alsace.

ŒUFS À LA LORRAINE
Baked Eggs with Bacon

The cooking of the Lorraine uses lots of eggs and bacon.

Oeufs sur le plat, fried eggs, are perhaps better cooked for a few minutes in a warmed buttered dish in a moderate oven than in the conventional frying pan. The whites will be creamily solid and the yolks will have a shiny translucent film, hence the name of *œufs au miroir*, 'mirror eggs'. The eggs can also be cooked over a low heat, preferably in a covered flameproof dish or pan.

A tasty recipe for *œufs sur le plat* comes from the Bresse area: quickly sauté a finely chopped shallot in the buttered dish; add a few slices of chicken livers and brown them lightly. Then throw in a few thinly sliced mushrooms and cook for 2 minutes. Slip in the egg, cover and cook over a low heat until just set. Serve with a green salad and fresh bread.

Serves 2
Preparation: about 10 minutes
Cooking: about 10 minutes

2 thick slices of rindless streaky smoked bacon
15g/¹/₂ oz butter
2 extra-fresh large eggs at room temperature
2 generous tbsp crème fraîche or thick cream
45g/1¹/₂ oz Gruyère or strong mature Cheddar cheese, finely slivered
cayenne
sea salt and freshly ground black pepper

1 Preheat the oven to 190C°/375°F/ gas 5. Bring a little water to the boil in a saucepan, add the bacon and blanch it over a moderate heat for 1 minute. Drain, then pat dry between 2 double layers of paper towels.

2 Divide the butter between 2 small flameproof gratin dishes (or use a larger dish). Put them in the oven for a minute until melted.

3 Put a slice of bacon in each dish. Place over a low heat and cook the bacon until it is just golden. Turn over after 1 or 2 minutes to cook the other side.

4 Spread 1 teaspoon of crème fraîche over each slice of bacon. Season with a touch of cayenne. Break an egg into a cup and carefully let it slip over one of the slices of bacon. Lightly season the white. Repeat with the second egg. Distribute the slivers of cheese over the eggs. Spoon over the rest of the cream and season lightly.

5 Bake for 3–4 minutes until the cheese bubbles and browns.

To drink: a white Bergerac.

(RIGHT) Œufs à la Lorraine *makes a delicious light lunch served with* Salade de Mâche aux Noix *(page 131)*.

LE SOUFFLÉ AU GRUYÈRE

Cheese Soufflé

Serves 4-5
Preparation: about 25 minutes
Cooking: about 35 minutes

200ml/ 7fl oz milk
½ Spanish onion, coarsely chopped
1 bay leaf
1 tsp dried thyme
freshly grated nutmeg
cayenne
45g/ 1½ oz butter, plus extra for
greasing
45g/ 1½ oz flour
4 extra-fresh large eggs at room
temperature
½ tsp strong mustard
100g/ 3½ oz Gruyère, Comté or any
hard cheese with a strong flavour
sea salt and freshly ground
black pepper

Soufflés are among the big bad wolves of cooking. Many home cooks are so afraid of their temperamental reputation that they have never dared attempt to include them in their repertoire of recipes. They are not the only ones. Food photographers, who make us drool and dream at the ingredients they light up like old-fashioned movie stars, tend to avoid soufflés as if they were wrinkled has-beens. I can't blame them, for soufflés are camera-shy and collapse in a sulky heap if you keep them waiting. Chefs are funny about them too, either ignoring them entirely or turning them into *spécialités de la maison.*

In fact, if you are neither catering for dozens of paying customers sitting a long way from your stove nor dependent on cameras and hot lighting, a soufflé is not difficult to prepare. Two factors are all-important: one is not to take the air out of the whisked egg whites when you combine them with the sauce; the other is the oven temperature.

BRING THE MILK WITH THE FLAVOURINGS JUST TO THE BOIL AND LEAVE TO COOL.

1 First infuse the milk (this is not compulsory, but it helps deepen the flavour of a plain cheese soufflé): bring the milk to the boil with the chopped onion, bay leaf, a pinch of dried thyme and sea salt, a very small pinch each of nutmeg, cayenne and black pepper. Take off the heat and leave to cool until lukewarm, then strain and discard the seasonings.

TIP THE FLOUR INTO THE MELTED BUTTER AND STIR TO MIX.

2 Make a pale roux in a large heavy saucepan: melt the butter over a low heat, add the flour and stir for a minute. Season lightly. Gradually whisk in the milk, a little at a time. Bring to a simmer, stirring vigorously and continuously. As soon as the sauce bubbles, reduce the heat a fraction and simmer gently for about 10 minutes, stirring regularly (the Béchamel for a soufflé should be a thick, smooth sauce).

3 Remove the sauce from the heat and leave to cool for at least 5 minutes,

MIX THE EGG YOLKS INTO THE COOLED SAUCE ONE AT A TIME.

FIRST MIX A LITTLE BEATEN
EGG WHITE INTO THE MIXTURE
TO LOOSEN IT.

stirring frequently. Break the eggs one at a time and separate them into 2 separate bowls: a small one for the yolks and a capacious one for the whites. Tip each yolk into the Béchamel as you deal with each egg and whisk in well.

4 Once you have worked in all the yolks, adjust the seasoning, adding the mustard and a second tiny pinch of nutmeg. Whisk in the grated cheese, a little at a time. The mixture can be set aside for a while at this stage. If it is convenient, cover and chill, but warm it before you finish the soufflé.

5 Preheat the oven to 200°C/400°F/gas6 (if your oven if very fast, use 190°C/375°F/gas5 and if you know it to be slow, 220°C/425°F/gas7). Generously butter a 20cm/8in soufflé dish (or a soufflé dish that can hold at least 1.4 litres/2$\frac{1}{2}$pt). For this amount of eggs, your dish should be no larger than 22cm/8$\frac{1}{2}$in.

6 About 40 minutes before you intend to sit down and eat – this is the point of no return – whisk the egg whites with a pinch of salt, until stiff but not dry. If you prefer a very fluffy airy soufflé to a slightly more creamy one, add the white of an extra egg.

THEN TIP THE LOOSENED
MIXTURE INTO THE REST OF
THE EGG WHITES.

7 Using a spatula or a large metal spoon, gently fold a quarter of the whisked egg white mixture into the sauce to loosen it. Tip this mass into the bowl with the egg whites. It is crucial at this stage not to crush the whites. Plunge the spoon or a spatula in the centre of the whites and gently lift up the mass, while you give the bowl a quarter-turn clockwise. Fold in lightly and quickly carry on until you have completed the turn. Most of the sauce will be folded into the egg whites. Finish folding with a few light swift upward movements to keep in as much air as possible. Do not over-work the mixture.

USE A LARGE METAL
SPOON TO FOLD IN THE
MIX LIGHTLY.

8 Pour into the prepared soufflé dish, level lightly and put immediately into the oven. Bake for about 30–35 minutes (without opening the door during the first 18 minutes), until brown and well risen but still a little creamily soft inside.

9 Have a captive audience around the table, ready to sample your trembling golden creation the moment it leaves the oven.

VARIATIONS: replace the Gruyère cheese with 100g/3½oz mushrooms, 55g/2oz cooked ham, fat removed, and 2 shallots, all finely chopped. First gently sauté the mushrooms and shallots in a little butter for a few minutes, then drain on paper towels. Mix with the ham and a tablespoon of Madeira, then add to the sauce after the yolks.

To make a blue cheese soufflé: whisk 85g/3oz crumbled Roquefort mixed with 1 heaped tablespoon crème fraîche into the thickened Béchamel. Let the cheese melt and blend in before you take the sauce off the heat.

Well-flavoured vegetable purées (cooked asparagus, peas or spinach, whizzed and sautéed over a high heat until drier in texture) make light soufflés. Use the same cooked weight as you would cheese and replace some of the milk in the sauce with stock or a little white wine. If the vegetables are on the bland side, add some freshly grated Parmesan or strong Gruyère cheese.

For 2 people, halve quantities and use a soufflé dish no larger than 15cm/6in which comfortably holds 575ml/1pt. Reduce cooking time by about 10 minutes.

To drink: a white Graves.

ŒUFS EN GELÉE À L'ESTRAGON
Eggs in Tarragon Aspic

Eggs in aspic can also be made with poached eggs (see page 58) but *œufs mollets* (*soft-boiled eggs*) give a prettier and superior-tasting result. This starter is fiddly to prepare but requires no last minute work. Serve with fingers of buttered toast and a scantily dressed little salad of leaves and fresh herbs.

Warm *œufs mollets* make good supper fare with spinach or braised lettuce. For lunch, try them with Salade aux Lardons (page 126).

Serves 6
Preparation and cooking: about 1 1/2 hours, in several 5-10 minute bouts of activity, then at least 1 hour chilling

6 extra-fresh medium or large eggs at room temperature
250ml/8fl oz liquid aspic
4tbsp Madeira (or 100ml/3 1/2 fl oz sweet wine boiled rapidly to reduce it by half)
leaves from several sprigs of fresh tarragon
12 thin strips of top-quality dry-cured or cooked ham
sea salt and freshly ground black pepper

1 First prepare the *œufs mollets*: bring a kettle of water to the boil. Pour about 1.1 litres/2 pts of boiling water into a saucepan wide enough to take a metal egg basket.

2 Immerse the basket of eggs in the boiling water and boil over a moderate heat. After 3 minutes, lift the basket out of the water and turn over the eggs to help centre the yolks. Put the basket of eggs back in the water and continue boiling for 2 or 3 minutes, depending on the size and freshness of the eggs. Lift the basket out and plunge the eggs into a basin of cold water to refresh for a few minutes.

3 Now shell the eggs: take each in your hand and tap gently with the back of a fork to crack the shell. Peel off the shell and membrane, working carefully under a trickle of cold running water. Place on paper towels (or in lightly salted cold water if you aren't using the eggs immediately).

4 In a small saucepan, combine the aspic with the Madeira or reduced wine. Bring to a simmer over a moderate heat, then leave to cool. Adjust the seasoning.

5 As soon as the aspic starts to thicken, pour a thin layer into 6 small individual ramekins large enough to take an egg and the aspic. Tilt each ramekin around until it is well coated with a layer of syrupy aspic. Chill for 15–20 minutes until set. Keep the aspic at a working consistency by putting it over a low heat for a minute whenever it solidifies too much to be workable.

6 Arrange a few tarragon leaves over the aspic at the bottom of each ramekin. Pour a little more aspic on top and chill again until set.

7 Arrange 2 strips of ham in a criss-cross pattern over the aspic. If time allows and you feel patient enough, pour over a little more aspic and chill again. If not, place an egg over the ham and season lightly. Pour in enough aspic to fill the ramekin. Chill for at least 1 hour, or overnight if convenient.

8 To unmould, run a small sharp knife around the inside of each ramekin or plunge the base into hot water for a second. Invert the ramekin on a serving plate, shaking the two gently together until the aspic sits on the plate. Serve as soon as possible.

Variation: follow same method exactly, using a mixture of dill and chives and strips of smoked salmon in place of the tarragon and ham.

To drink: Cabernet d'Anjou.

ŒUFS AU VIN ROUGE
Eggs in Red Wine Sauce

Eggs poached in red wine — also known as *œufs meurette* — are, perhaps not surprisingly, a favourite way of poaching eggs in Burgundy. A less gutsy way of serving *œufs pochés* is on hot toasted brioche, with a few spoonfuls of creamy yogurt flavoured with snipped *fines herbes* and paprika.

Poached eggs taste infinitely better warm than cold — they will keep *tiède* for a while immersed in lightly salted warm (but not too hot) water.

Serves 4
Preparation: about 10 minutes
Cooking: about 40 minutes

½ bottle full-bodied red wine
2 shallots, finely chopped
bouquet garni
few black peppercorns
4 slices of day-old country-style bread
1 garlic clove, halved
4 medium to large extra-fresh eggs at room temperature
55g/2oz soft butter
1 scant tbsp flour
sea salt and freshly ground black pepper

1 Prepare the poaching liquid: in a heavy saucepan, mix about 250ml/8fl oz of water to the red wine, add the shallots, bouquet garni and black peppercorns and bring to the boil over a moderate heat. Cover, reduce the heat and simmer for 15 minutes.

2 Rub the bread with the cut sides of the garlic and grill until lightly toasted. Spread lightly with a little of the butter, put on a warmed serving dish and keep warm.

3 Now poach the eggs, in 2 batches: put each egg in a small ladle and lower it into the barely simmering liquid. Cover and cook over a very low heat for 2–3 minutes. Lift out with a slotted spoon. Drain well and put on a slice of toast. If necessary, give a little trim with some scissors — the eggs should look as neat as possible. Keep warm.

4 Once all the eggs are cooked, turn up the heat and bring the liquid to a fast boil. Partly cover and leave to bubble away vigorously until it is reduced by over one-third.

5 Meanwhile, make a beurre manié by mashing the remaining butter with the flour until combined. Divide this paste into 4 small pieces.

6 Put a fine sieve or chinois over a jug and strain the reduced cooking liquid. Pour back into the pan.

7 Over a moderate to high heat, whisk the beurre manié into the simmering liquid. Allow the sauce to boil for 2 minutes until thickened, whisking all the time. Season to taste and whisk in the rest of the butter. Spoon the sauce over the eggs and serve immediately.

To drink: Beaujolais-Villages.

ŒUFS MIMOSA
Stuffed Eggs

This dish makes a good addition to a summer buffet. Hard-boiled eggs need not be particularly fresh — just under 2 weeks old.

Serves 4
Cooking the eggs: about 10 minutes
Preparation: about 10 minutes

4 large eggs at room temperature
6 canned anchovy fillets in oil, drained
12 small capers, drained
1 tbsp finely snipped parsley
2 generous tbsp well-flavoured Mayonnaise (see page 36)
lemon pepper or freshly ground black pepper
mixed leaf salad or tomato salad, to serve

1 Bring a kettle of water to the boil and pour at least 1.1 litres/2pts of boiling water into a large saucepan. Boil the eggs in it for 10 minutes over a moderate heat. Drain and plunge into cold water or leave under cold running water until cool enough to shell. Tap both ends on a work surface, roll the eggs under the palm of your hand and start shelling from the rounded end.

2 With a sharp knife, carefully cut each shelled egg in half lengthwise. Scoop out

the yolks with a small pointed teaspoon. Reserve the yolk of one egg and put the other yolks in a bowl.

3 Snip 2 of the anchovy fillets and cut the others into 2 strips. Using a fork, mash the yolks with the snipped anchovy and all but 4 of the capers until combined. Sprinkle over half the finely snipped parsley and stir in. Add the mayonnaise and mix well.

4 Using a teaspoon, heap the mayonnaise mixture into the halved egg whites. Cut a little slice off the base of each base if the egg half seems unsteady.

5 Place the strips of anchovy over each egg in a criss-cross pattern. Put a caper in the centre and season with a little lemon pepper or black pepper.

6 Arrange on the serving dish, with a mixed leaf or tomato salad. Push the reserved yolks through a fine small sieve over the eggs. Sprinkle over the rest of the parsley and chill until ready to serve.

ŒUFS VERTS
Eggs with Green Sauce

As long as their yolks are still a little mellow, it does not matter if your œufs mollets have come somewhat close to being hard-boiled, Coat the eggs at the last minute. If you want to prepare ahead, keep the peeled eggs in a bowl of cold water.

Serves 6
Preparation: making the Mayonnaise
Cooking : 10 minutes, plus cooling

6 extra-fresh medium or large eggs at
room temperature
large bunch or sachet of watercress, stalks removed
3–4tbsp crème fraîche or single cream mixed
with 2tsp lemon juice
about 125ml/4fl oz well-flavoured thick
Mayonnaise (page 36)
3tbsp very finely snipped mixed flat-leaf parsley,
chives and chervil
sea salt and freshly ground black pepper

1 Prepare and shell the *œufs mollets* (see Eggs in Tarragon Aspic on page 57, steps 1–3).

2 Bring a saucepan of lightly salted water to the boil. Throw in the trimmed watercress, blanch for 1 minute, then drain well and place on a plate lined with a double layer of paper towel. Pat dry firmly. If you like, reserve 6 pretty leaves to decorate the eggs.

3 Spread the blanched watercress leaves on a board and chop very finely – I like using my small double-handed chopper, but a sharp knife will do the job.

4 Stir the crème fraîche or single cream and lemon juice into the Mayonnaise. Add the prepared herbs and watercress, mix in well – the sauce should be flecked with small green specks – and adjust the seasoning.

5 Put the eggs in a serving dish and spoon over some of the sauce. Pour the rest of the sauce into a jug or bowl and serve at the same time as the eggs. If you like, place a small blanched watercress leaf on top of each egg.

To drink: Bourgogne Aligoté or Alsace Pinot Gris.

Chapter Four

LES QUICHES ET LES PÂTISSERIES SALÉES

Savoury Tarts and Pastries

Savoury tarts and pastries tend to
be put under the general heading of
entrées chaudes — along with a number of egg
dishes from the previous chapter. In the days when
meals were grander and more formally structured,
these were served after the *hors d'œuvre* and before
the *plat principal*. Retrospectively, this seems like an
embarrassment of riches! Savoury tarts are substantial
and distinguished enough in their own right to make a
memorable *plat unique*, probably with a light leaf
salad. Scaled-down and bite-sized, they make
exquisite contributions to a festive
collection of hot canapés.

LEFT
Tourte aux Lardons et aux Pommes de Terre
(page 62) makes a substantial main course served with
Courgettes Poêlées à L'Estragon (page 138).

TOURTE AUX LARDONS ET AUX POMMES DE TERRE
Bacon and Potato Pie

Serves 6
Preparation: about 35 minutes
Cooking: 1–1¼ hours

about 450g/1lb Pâte Brisée (see Quiche
Lorraine, page 64) or ready-made shortcrust
pastry
butter for greasing
flour for dusting
900g/2lb waxy potatoes, peeled and halved if
large
2tsp oil
250g/8½oz smoked belly of pork or thick
streaky smoked bacon, cut into dice, blanched and
well drained
250g/8½oz white parts of large spring onions,
sliced into thin rings
3tbsp finely snipped parsley
2tsp dried ground thyme
1 large egg yolk, for glazing
6 generous tbsp thick cream or crème fraîche
sea salt and freshly ground black pepper

1 Reserve about one-third of the pastry. Roll out the larger piece and use it to line a greased and floured 25cm/10in flameproof moule à manqué pan (page 7). Allow the pastry to overhang a little around the rim. Roll the rest of the pastry into a circle that will fit over the top of the tin. Lightly prick both lots of pastry with a fork and chill while preparing the filling.

2 Prepare the filling: first parboil the potatoes in lightly salted water over a moderate heat for 15 minutes. Drain and refresh, then drain again.

3 While the potatoes are boiling, preheat the oven to 200°C/400°F/gas6. Heat the oil in a frying pan over a moderate heat. Add the pork or bacon and sauté for 2 minutes until golden, then add the sliced spring onions. Reduce the heat and stir for 3 minutes, until the onions are a little softened and coloured. Remove from the heat.

4 Thinly slice the potatoes and add them to the pan. Mix lightly, then stir in a tablespoon of parsley and the thyme. Season very lightly with salt and more generously with pepper.

5 Tip the filling into the prepared pastry case. Use the rolling pin to trim off the pastry overlap. Lightly brush the rim with a little egg yolk mixed with a dash of water. Place the pastry circle on top and pinch the edges lightly together between your index finger and the back of a fork. If you like, draw patterns over the surface with a fork. Lightly brush the pastry with egg glaze. Using a small sharp knife, cut a hole in the centre and insert a funnel.

6 Bake for 20 minutes. Take out of the oven and check the colouring. If the pie is already golden brown, cover loosely with greaseproof paper and continue baking for another 35–40 minutes. At the end of this time, take out of the oven and check that the base is cooked.

7 Using a small sharp knife, carefully work your way around the lid until it is loosened off. Lift gently with a spatula. Spoon the cream over the filling, season lightly and sprinkle with parsley. Replace the lid and return to the oven for 5 minutes. Leave to cool in the turned-off oven for several minutes, then serve hot or warm.

VARIATION: follow the same method to make a splendid pie with leftover *Bœuf Bourguignon* (page 121). Halve the amounts of potato, onion and bacon and prepare as above, then mix with about 450g/1lb cooked bœuf bourguignon. Halve the amount of cream you pour into the tourte towards the end of baking.

To drink: a Bergerac.

PETITS CROISSANTS AUX ANCHOIS
Little Anchovy Pastries

Don't expect these little croissants to come out streamlined and professional – mine usually turn out somewhat uneven and there are sometimes one or two runts in the batch. They do look appetizing, though, and the simple anchovy filling is delicious against the butteriness of the puff pastry. They are excellent with soups and drinks. A sprinkling of grated strong hard cheese makes a good alternative filling and children love playing pastry chef and experimenting with a teaspoon of jam instead.

Makes 16 small croissants
Preparation: about 15 minutes
Cooking: about 20 minutes

8 small canned anchovy fillets in oil, or 4 large
ones, well drained
15g/½oz soft unsalted butter, plus extra for
greasing
225g/8oz cold puff pastry
1 large egg yolk lightly beaten with 2tsp water
and a small pinch of salt
flour for dusting
freshly ground black pepper

1 Prepare the anchovies: snip each fillet across in half, then divide each half again if the fillets are large. Coat with a little butter and season lightly with pepper.

2 Preheat the oven to 220°C/425°F/gas7 (or 200°C/400°F/gas6 if you know your oven to be 'hot'). Lightly butter a large baking sheet. Flour a rolling pin and a cold working surface.

3 Roll out the cold pastry into a 30cm/12in square. Using a very sharp knife or cutting wheel, divide the pastry into 4 equal squares. Cut each square into 2 triangles, then divide each of those into 2 smaller triangles.

4 Place a piece of anchovy along the centre of the wide base of each triangle and loosely roll up each triangle, starting from the wide base and bringing the two ends towards each other to form a crescent shape.

5 Use a little egg glaze to make the central tip of each croissant stick to the layer below. Lightly brush the croissants with the rest of the egg glaze.

6 Bake for 12–15 minutes until the croissants are puffed up and golden brown. Turn off the heat, turn the croissants over and keep warm in the oven until ready to serve or at least for a few minutes.

PISSALADIÈRE
Onion and Anchovy Tart

The onion and anchovy tart of Provence tastes quite different from its Northern relative, *Tarte à l'Oignon* (page 67). Serve in bite-sized squares or rectangles as an appetizer, in larger pieces for a starter or with a salad as a light main course.

Serves 6-8
Preparation: about 1 hour
Cooking: about 25 minutes

FOR THE PASTRY:
350g/12oz plain flour, plus extra for dusting
170g/6oz butter, cut into small pieces
4 tbsp cream cheese or crème fraîche
30-45g/1-1¹/₂oz freshly grated Parmesan cheese
salt and freshly ground black pepper

FOR THE TOPPING:
3tbsp olive oil, plus extra for greasing
900g/2lb sweet white onions, thinly sliced
14 canned anchovy fillets in oil, drained
2tsp sugar
3 garlic cloves, crushed
2tsp dried ground thyme
1¹/₂ tsp oregano
3 tomatoes, blanched, skinned, deseeded and chopped
9 black olives, stoned and chopped
several basil leaves, coarsely snipped
about 1tbsp fruity extra virgin olive oil, for sprinkling

1 First make the pastry: in the food processor fitted with the metal knife blade, whizz together the flour and butter with a pinch of salt until the mixture resembles breadcrumbs. Add the cream cheese or crème fraîche and season with pepper. Whizz again in a few quick bursts until the dough comes together in a rough ball. Wrap in cling film and chill for at least half an hour.

2 Meanwhile, prepare the topping: in a large sauté pan, heat 2 tablespoons of the olive oil. Add the onions and stir over a low heat for a few minutes. Cover, reduce the heat a fraction and sweat gently for about 30 minutes, until the onions are soft and a pale gold colour. Shake the pan occasionally and stir the mixture a few times.

3 Finely chop 8 of the anchovy fillets and snip the rest into long thin strips. Add the remaining tablespoon of oil, the sugar, garlic, herbs and chopped anchovies to the onions. Taste and adjust the seasoning. Cook the mixture for another 10 minutes, keeping the heat low and stirring from time to time.

4 Preheat the oven to 190°C/375°F/gas5 and oil a large baking sheet (the onion mixture will easily cover an area 30cm/12in square).

5 Flour a rolling pin and a cold working surface. Roll out the pastry thinly, then spread it on the prepared baking sheet. Prick with a fork in several places and sprinkle with the Parmesan. Press the cheese in a little. Spoon the onion mixture over the pastry, spreading it evenly up to the edges with a spatula or palette knife.

6 Bake for about 20–25 minutes, then take the baking sheet out of the oven and turn the setting up to 200°C/400°F/gas6. Scatter the pieces of tomato and chopped olive over the sizzling onion mixture. Arrange the strips of anchovy over the top in a loose lattice pattern. Season with a little pepper and bake for another 10 minutes.

7 Leave in the turned-off oven for a few minutes, then take out and allow to cool for several minutes. Scatter the top with snipped basil leaves and drizzle with a little olive oil before serving it warm or at room temperature.

To drink: Bandol rosé.

LA QUICHE LORRAINE

Bacon and Egg Tart

Serves 6
Preparation: 30 minutes, then chilling
Cooking: about 55 minutes

FOR THE PATE BRISÉE:
250g/8oz flour, plus extra for dredging
generous pinch of salt
1 scant tsp sugar
125g/4½ oz cold butter, cut into small
pieces, plus extra for greasing
1 tbsp chilled thick cream or cream cheese
2-3 tbsp iced water

FOR THE FILLING:
250g/8oz piece of smoked belly of pork,
smoked streaky bacon, pancetta or not-
too-fatty speck
1 tsp oil
30g/1oz butter
4 extra-fresh eggs at room
temperature
175ml/6fl oz crème fraîche or thick
cream
grated nutmeg
sea salt and freshly ground
black pepper

The province of Lorraine, tucked away next to Alsace in the north-east corner of the country, has given France the most celebrated of its savoury tarts. *Quiche Lorraine* is a simple cream, egg and bacon custard, usually baked nowadays in a case of shortcrust pastry, *pâte brisée*. In early *recettes* from Nancy, the concoction of *lardons*, egg, and milk or cream was cooked on plain bread dough, like other country pies. The recipe below reflects modern practice and uses a crisp, somewhat crumbly, *pâte brisée* but compromises no further and does not include cheese. Gruyère (which does not, in any case, come from Lorraine) changes the taste of the quiche, making it more salty and detracting from its glorious custardy simplicity. But don't let's get puritanical about this. *À chacun son goût . . .* see the Variations if you prefer a touch of cheese in your *Quiche Lorraine*.

More important still than the presence or absence of cheese for the flavour of the dish is the quality of the pork you use. The French choice is *lardons*, small pieces of belly of pork. These can be fresh, cured in brine or smoked. Alternatives are thick cut streaky bacon, or those great standbys of the deli counter, pancetta or speck. All cuts and cures are improved enormously by first being blanched. This makes them finer, less salty and less likely to toughen or char.

**ADD THE ICED WATER,
A LITTLE AT A TIME, TO THE
CRUMBLY MIXTURE.**

1 First make the pastry: tip the flour into a bowl. Sprinkle over the salt and sugar. Add the diced butter and lightly rub it into the flour, working quickly with your fingertips.

2 While there are still large bits of butter here and there, add the cream. Mix in well (if you prefer not to use cream, use an extra tablespoon or two of iced water or the white of an egg). Add the iced water, a little at a time, mixing the dough until it comes together in a lumpy mass. Dredge this with flour and put it on a cold working surface dusted with flour.

**USE THE HEEL OF
YOUR HAND TO FLATTEN
THE DOUGH.**

3 Flatten the dough 2 or 3 times, chopping it down with the heel of your hands, pushing it away from you, then folding it back. Work fast and do not knead as this will toughen the pastry. Now wrap the pastry in foil, cling film or waxed paper and chill for 30 minutes.

4 Dredge a work surface and rolling pin with flour. Flatten the chilled pastry with the palm of your hand to get it going

LINE THE PASTRY SHELL WITH GREASEPROOF PAPER AND WEIGHT WITH DRIED BEANS.

in the direction you want. Start rolling it out, always rolling away from you with even pressure and rotating the pastry a little each time. Roll out until thin.

5 Grease and flour a 26cm/10½ in loose-bottomed tart tin. Spread the pastry in the prepared tin, using your hands to press it in lightly. Allow it to overhang the edges of the tin a little. Prick the bottom all over with a fork and chill again before using.

6 Preheat the oven to 200°C/400°F/ gas6. Line the pastry shell with foil or greaseproof paper and cover this with a layer of dried beans. Bake blind for 10–15 minutes, checking that the pastry isn't colour-ing too fast: if it is, cover it with foil. Take out of the oven, leave to cool for a few minutes, then remove the beans and lining paper. Cut off any overhanging pastry.

7 About an hour before you intend to serve the quiche, prepare the filling: preheat the oven to 190°C/375°F/ gas5. Bring some water to the boil in a saucepan.

Remove the rind from the smoked belly or bacon, then cut it into slices about 5mm/½ in thick. Blanch these in the boiling water for 1 minute. Drain and pat dry between 2 double layers of paper towel. Snip or cut the slices into 2cm/¾ in pieces.

8 Grease a frying pan with the oil using a small wad of paper towel. Divide the butter into 3 pieces. Cut 2 of the pieces into small blobs. Put the pan over a moderate heat, add the intact piece of butter and allow to melt. Then add the bacon and sauté for 2–3 minutes, stirring and turning so that the pieces colour and crisp

BLANCH THE BACON FOR ONE MINUTE AND DRAIN TO REFINE ITS TASTE AND TEXTURE.

evenly. Leave the bacon to cool for a few minutes, then spread over the pastry base.

9 In a bowl, briskly beat together the eggs and the cream as if you were making an omelette. Season with salt if you like (the bacon is already salty), plenty of black pepper and a pinch of grated nutmeg.

10 Check the pastry: if it feels soft, return the tin to the oven for a few minutes. Another trick is to paint the base with a little egg white before you add the filling. Pour the egg mixture into the pastry case, making sure it does not come right up to the rim as the custard will swell during baking. Dot with the pieces of butter.

11 Put the quiche in the oven for 20 minutes, then check it: if the filling is swelling unevenly, pierce it with a fork; if it is browning too fast, cover it with greaseproof paper. Bake for another 5–10 minutes, then test the custard: it will be done when the tip of a knife comes out clean. Leave the quiche to rest in the turned-off oven with the door open for 5–10 minutes. Serve the quiche either hot or warm.

To drink: an Alsace Pinot Blanc or a white vin de pays from Savoie.

SPREAD THE PIECES OF BACON OVER THE PASTRY SHELL AND POUR IN THE CUSTARD.

VARIATIONS: if you are using Gruyère, grate about 30g/1oz and sprinkle it over the custard tart before scattering the blobs of butter.

Half the crème fraîche can be replaced with cream cheese or curd cheese before beating with the eggs. Try replacing half the lardons with small pieces of cooked or smoked salmon, particularly when using cream cheese.

For vegetarians, omit the lardons and blanch about 300g/10½oz young spinach leaves, drain very well and beat them into the custard. Finish with strong grated Gruyère cheese.

TARTE À L'OIGNON
Onion Tart

This onion tart has a more pronounced onion flavour than most, but the evaporated milk adds a distinct touch of sweetness. About 100g/3½ oz blanched and sautéed *lardons* (see *Quiche Lorraine*, page 64) are an optional extra.

Serves 6
Preparation: making the shortcrust pastry shell, then 1 hour chilling
Cooking: about 20 minutes

26cm/10½ in baked pastry shell (see Quiche Lorraine, page 64)

FOR THE FILLING:
1½ tbsp lard or oil
900g/2lb Spanish onions, thinly sliced
¼ tsp grated nutmeg
1tsp rubbed sage
1tbsp flour
3 extra-fresh eggs at room temperature
150ml/¼ pt evaporated milk
3-4 tbsp single cream
salt and freshly ground black pepper

1 Prepare the filling: in a sauté pan or large frying pan, heat the lard or oil, then add the onion slices. Half cover the pan and sweat the onions for about 40 minutes over a low heat until soft and barely coloured, occasionally lifting the lid to stir the onions.

2 Preheat the oven to 190°C/375°F/ gas 5. Season the cooked onions with a little salt and plenty of black pepper and sprinkle in the grated nutmeg, rubbed sage and flour. Stir, turn up the heat a fraction and cook for 5 minutes.

3 Lightly whisk together the eggs, evaporated milk and cream. Season to taste, then stir this into the onion. Tip the mixture into the pastry shell and distribute the onion evenly with a spoon.

4 Bake for about 20 minutes until browned. Check after 15 minutes and cover with greaseproof paper if the tart is browning too fast. Serve warm or warmish, rather than piping hot.

To drink: a Gamay de Touraine.

FLAMICHE AUX POIREAUX
Leek Tart

Northern French and Flemish in origin, this savoury tart is also traditionally made with pumpkin – asparagus or spinach are other good fillings. Maroilles and Munster cheeses are too soft to grate and may have smells that are a little too pungent for your taste, in which case try the other suggestions.

Serves 6-8
Preparation: 5 minutes, plus making the pastry shell
Cooking: about 1 hour

26cm/10½ in baked pastry shell (see Quiche Lorraine, page 64)

FOR THE FILLING:
45g/1½ oz butter
1kg/2¼ lb leeks, thinly sliced
250ml/8fl oz thick cream
5tbsp milk
3 fresh eggs at room temperature
2 thin slices of cooked or dry-cured ham, trimmed of fat and finely snipped (optional)
at least 30g/1oz Maroilles or Munster cheese, slivered, or young Gruyère cheese, slivered or grated, or Caerphilly, crumbled
pinch of grated nutmeg, if using Gruyère or Caerphilly cheese
sea salt and freshly ground black pepper

1 While the pastry shell is first in the oven, prepare the filling: melt the butter over a low heat in a sauté pan. Add the leeks, stir for a minute, then season lightly and cover. Stew the leeks for about 15–20 minutes, shaking the pan frequently and stirring occasionally until they are soft. Take off the lid and leave to cool for a few minutes, stirring occasionally. Keep the oven at 190°C/ 375°F/gas5.

2 Reserve 2 tablespoons of the cooked leeks and put the rest in the food processor with the cream, milk and eggs. Season lightly and blend to a purée.

3 Push the purée through a fine sieve into a bowl, pressing it through with the back of a wooden spoon. Stir in the reserved leeks and the ham, if using, then adjust the seasoning.

4 Pour the filling into the prepared pastry case, scatter the cheese on top with the nutmeg, if using, and grind a little extra pepper over the top. Bake for about 35–40 minutes, until set and golden.

5 Leave to cool before serving, as this tart tastes much better warm than piping hot.

To drink: a Bourgueil.

FEUILLETÉS AU FROMAGE
Cheese Puffs

Light and flaky pastry makes a great container for cheesy fillings. For these little parcels, try a quick abridged version of traditional puff pastry, or use good-quality chilled ready-rolled or ready-to-roll bought pastry.

Serves
Preparation: about 20 minutes, plus about
1 hour chilling
Cooking: about 25 minutes

FOR THE PROCESSOR PATE DEMI-FEUILLETÉE:
225g/8oz flour, plus extra for dusting
pinch of salt
2 tbsp chilled thick cream or crème fraîche
200g/8oz chilled butter, diced
100ml/3$^{1}/_{2}$ fl oz ice-cold water
1 large egg, for glazing

FOR THE ROQUEFORT FILLING:
150g/5$^{1}/_{2}$ oz Roquefort cheese,
crumbled
2 generous tbsp cream cheese
2tsp crème fraîche
1tsp Madeira
few sprigs of chives
$^{1}/_{4}$ tsp freshly grated nutmeg
freshly ground black pepper
FOR THE CHEVRE FILLING:
150g/5$^{1}/_{2}$ oz ripe chèvre at room
temperature, crust removed
2 generous tbsp cream cheese
4 black olives, pitted and chopped
$^{1}/_{4}$ tsp each dried thyme, oregano and
summer savory, or several leaves of fresh basil,
rolled and finely snipped
cayenne pepper

1 Fit the plastic blade of the food processor. Briefly whizz together the flour, salt, butter, cream and iced water until the dough starts to form a ball and comes off the sides of the bowl.

2 Dust a work surface and rolling pin with flour. Turn the dough out on this prepared surface, then lightly roll it out until it is flattened, roughly rectangular and about 1cm/$^{1}/_{2}$in thick. Fold the top third of the rectangle down towards the centre, then do the same with the bottom third. Press down lightly to seal and refrigerate for 20 minutes. Repeat the rolling, folding and chilling process 2 more times.

3 During the last chilling period, prepare the fillings:

To make the Roquefort filling, put the Roquefort in a bowl and mash well with a fork. Beat in the cream cheese, crème fraîche and Madeira. Snip in the chives, stir, then sprinkle in the nutmeg and season with pepper.

To make the chèvre filling, mash the chèvre in a bowl until softened. Beat in the cream cheese, then stir in the chopped olives and herbs. Season with cayenne.

4 Preheat the oven to 220°C/425°F/gas7 (or 200°C/400°F/gas6 if you know your oven to be 'hot'). Divide the pastry into 2 pieces. Roll the first piece into a rectangle, roughly 20 x 40cm/8 x 16in and no thicker than 5mm/$^{1}/_{4}$in. Divide this into 16 identical rectangles. Divide the Roquefort filling between 8 of these rectangles, keeping it well clear of the edges. In a cup, briefly beat the egg and add a few drops of water. Lightly brush the clear edges of the rectangles with egg. Use a knife to make a criss-cross pattern on the remaining 8 rectangles. Place them on top of the filled rectangles and press gently down to seal, then lightly brush the surface with egg, taking care that the glaze does not dribble down the sides.

5 Roll the rest of the pastry into a circular shape no thicker than 5mm/$^{1}/_{4}$in. Use a small circular pastry cutter to divide this into 16 identical circles rerolling the trimmings, if neccessary. Distribute the chèvre filling between 8 of the circles, keeping it well clear of the edges. Lightly brush the rim of each circle with egg. Use a knife to make a criss-cross pattern on the remaining circles. Place these on top of the filled ones. Press gently down to seal, then lightly brush the surface with egg, taking care that the glaze does not dribble down the sides.

6 Bake the filled feuilletés for about 10 minutes, then open the oven door and continue baking for another 5–8 minutes or until the underside is cooked through. Serve hot.

(RIGHT) Feuilletés au Fromage *make substantial and tasty canapés.*

PETITS CHOUX POUR L'APÉRITIF
Savoury Profiteroles

These make excellent canapés to serve at drinks parties.

Serves 6
Preparation: about 30 minutes
Cooking: about 40 minutes

FOR THE CHOUX PUFFS:
100g/ 3½ oz butter, diced
150g/ 5½ oz flour, sifted
4 or 5 extra-fresh eggs at room temperature, plus
1 extra egg yolk, for glazing
sea salt and freshly ground black pepper

FOR THE PRAWN FILLING:
85g/ 3oz cooked peeled prawns
150ml/ ¼ pt thick Sauce Béchamel (page 32)
3tbsp thick or single cream or crème fraîche
1tsp paprika

FOR THE MUSHROOM FILLING:
30g/ 1oz butter
200g/ 7oz small brown mushrooms, wiped and very thinly sliced
1tsp ground coriander seeds
200ml/ 7fl oz thick Sauce Béchamel
2tsp sherry vinegar
1tbsp thick or single cream, or crème fraîche

FOR THE HAM FILLING:
1 thick slice of top-quality cooked ham, trimmed of fat and snipped into short thin strips
2 thin slices of dry-cured ham, snipped into short thin strips
1tsp dried rubbed sage
1tbsp Madeira
150ml/ ¼ pt thick Sauce Béchamel
3tbsp thick or single cream or crème fraîche

1 First prepare the choux puffs: in a heavy saucepan over a moderate heat, bring to the boil 250ml/8fl oz water with the diced butter and a scant teaspoon of salt. Remove the pan from the heat as soon as the liquid comes to a rolling boil.

2 Tip in all the sifted flour. Using a spatula or large wooden spoon, quickly start mixing the flour and water until the flour is all absorbed. Return the pan to the heat and stir briskly for a minute or two, until the paste is very thick and comes away from the base and sides of the pan in a somewhat sticky mass. Remove the pan from the heat.

3 Add the eggs one by one, mixing each in vigorously and completely before you add the next one. Before you work in the last egg, whisk it lightly in a small bowl – you may need only a fraction of it and you want to end up with a glossy, floppy paste that is at the same time stiff and supple. Continue beating the paste for a minute or two to give it more body and make it shine. Season with a little salt and a generous grinding of black pepper.

4 Preheat the oven to 200°C/400°F/gas 6 and line a baking sheet with non-stick baking paper or grease the sheet if you prefer. Using a wetted tablespoon, spoon the paste into small blobs (the more ball-like the better) on the prepared baking sheet. When you spoon them on the baking sheet, keep the balls of paste at least 2.5cm/1in apart. Mix a little egg yolk with a dash of water and, using a pastry brush, lightly glaze the balls of paste.

5 Bake for about 20–25 minutes, until the little choux buns are puffed out and golden brown. Take out of the oven, pierce each puff with a skewer, then return the baking sheet to the turned-off oven. Leave to dry for a good 5 minutes.

6 Meanwhile, prepare the filling or fillings (each filling should be enough for about 12 small choux puffs – 2 generous teaspoonfuls each):
For the prawn filling, pat the prawns between 2 double layers of paper towel to extract excess moisture. Chop coarsely. In a bowl, combine the Béchamel, chopped prawns, cream and a pinch of paprika. Season.
To make the mushroom filling, melt the butter in a small frying-pan. Add the prepared mushrooms and the ground coriander. Sauté over a moderate heat for a few minutes. Combine in a bowl with the Béchamel, sherry vinegar and cream, then adjust the seasoning.
For the ham filling, combine the cooked and the dry-cured ham in a bowl with the dried sage, Madeira, Béchamel and cream. Season to taste.

7 To assemble: slit open the choux puffs half open with a knife and spoon a little filling into each bun. Replace the 'tops' and pile into attractive cones on a serving dish and keep warm in the turned-off or very low oven. Serve within a couple of hours.

To drink: Champagne or other sparkling white wine.

GOUGÈRE
Cheesy Choux Puffs

The simplest and most classic of savoury choux puffs originated in Burgundy, where *gougères* are served cold to fortify tasters during wine *dégustations*.

This recipe is for a ring of cheesy choux puffs. If you prefer individual puffs, keep the balls of paste at least 2.5cm/1in apart when you spoon them on the baking sheet and reduce baking time by 5–10 minutes.

Serves 6-8
Preparation: about 30 minutes
Cooking: about 40 minutes

100g/ 3½ oz butter, diced
150g/ 5½ oz flour, sifted
4 or 5 extra-fresh eggs at room temperature, plus
1 extra yolk, for glazing
125g/ 4½ oz strongly flavoured Gruyère,
Emmental or mature Farmhouse Cheddar cheese, cut into small slivers
sea salt and freshly ground black pepper

1 In a heavy saucepan over a moderate heat, bring to the boil 250ml/8fl oz water with the diced butter and a scant teaspoon of salt. Remove from the heat as soon as it comes to a rolling boil.

2 Tip in all the flour. Using a spatula or large wooden spoon, quickly start mixing the flour and water until the flour is all absorbed. Return the pan to the heat and stir briskly for a minute or two, until the paste is very thick and comes away from the base and sides of the pan in a somewhat sticky mass. Remove the pan from the heat.

3 Add the eggs one by one, mixing each in vigorously and completely before you add the next one. Before you work in the last egg, whisk it lightly in a small bowl – you may need only a fraction of it and you want to end up with a glossy, floppy paste that is at the same time stiff and supple. Continue beating for a minute or two to give it more body and shine. Stir the cheese into the paste and season generously with pepper.

4 Preheat the oven to 200°C/400°F/gas 6 and line a baking sheet with non-stick baking paper or grease the sheet if you prefer. Using a wetted tablespoon, spoon the paste into small blobs (the more ball-like the better) in a large ring on the prepared baking sheet. To end up with a continuous ring, keep the balls of paste no farther apart than 2cm/³/₄in. If you prefer, use a piping bag fitted with a small round nozzle. Now mix a little of the egg yolk with a dash of water and, using a pastry brush, lightly glaze the balls of paste.

5 Bake for about 30 minutes, or until the choux balls are puffed out and golden brown. Take out of the oven. Pierce each puff with a skewer, then return the baking sheet to the turned-off oven. Leave to dry for a good 5 minutes, then remove and serve hot, warm or cold on the same day.

GNOCCHI À LA PARISIENNE
Baked Gnocchi

Gnocchi can be prepared well ahead and gratinéed at the last minute. A creamy Béchamel is a classic accompaniment, but *gnocchi* are worth trying with a blue cheese sauce (see *Feuilletés au Fromage*, page 68) or with wilted and creamed spinach or *Pipérade* purée (page 47). You can also add them to meaty casseroles towards the end of cooking, or serve instead of potatoes, dotted with butter.

Serves 6
Preparation: about 40 minutes
Cooking: about 25 minutes

250ml/8fl oz milk
120g/4 oz butter, diced, plus extra for greasing
150g/5¹/₂oz flour, sifted
4 or 5 extra-fresh eggs at room temperature
freshly grated nutmeg
30g/1oz freshly grated Parmesan cheese
500ml/16fl oz Sauce Béchamel
(page 32)
2 generous tbsp crème fraîche
55g/2oz mature Gruyère cheese, grated
sea salt and freshly ground black pepper

1 In a heavy saucepan over a moderate heat, bring the milk to the boil with all but 30g/1oz of the diced butter and a teaspoon of salt. Remove the pan from the heat as soon as the liquid comes to a rolling boil.

2 Tip in all the flour. Using a spatula or large wooden spoon, quickly start mixing the flour and milk until it is all absorbed. Return the pan to the heat and stir briskly for a minute or two, until the paste is very thick and comes away from the base and sides of the pan in a somewhat sticky mass. Remove the pan from the heat.

3 Add the eggs one by one, mixing each in vigorously and completely before you add the next one. Before you work in the last egg, whisk it lightly in a small bowl – you may need only a fraction of it and you want to end up with a glossy, floppy paste, which is at the same time stiff and supple. Continue beating the paste for a minute or two to give it more body and make it shine. Sprinkle the paste with a generous pinch of grated nutmeg, stir in the Parmesan and season generously with pepper.

4 Bring a kettle of water to the boil. Pour the water into a saucepan, season lightly with salt and bring back to a rolling boil over a moderate heat. Using a piping bag fitted with a 1cm/¹/₂in plain round nozzle and filled with the choux paste, drop pieces of the paste into the boiling water, cutting each segment with a knife as soon as it is about 2.5cm/1in long.

5 Allow the gnocchi to boil until they come back to the surface. Lift with a slotted spoon and drain well on a clean tea towel or a double layer of paper towel.

6 Preheat the oven to 200°C/400°F/gas 6 and lightly butter a gratin dish. In a bowl, combine the Béchamel with the crème fraîche and half the grated Gruyère. Sprinkle in a little grated nutmeg, stir well and adjust the seasoning.

7 Spread a little Béchamel in the prepared dish. Arrange the drained gnocchi on top, spoon over the rest of the sauce, dot with the reserved butter and sprinkle with the remaining Gruyère. Season with a little extra pepper and nutmeg, if liked. Bake for 20–25 minutes until golden brown.

To drink: Sauvignon de Touraine

Chapter Five

LES POISSONS ET LES FRUITS DE MER

Fish and Seafood

On Fridays the displays of fishmongers are at their shimmering best all over the country. In France Friday is – and has always been – 'Fish Day'. As in other Catholic countries, the regular consumption of fish started in the Middle Ages to comply with the rigorous injunction of the Church of Rome that its faithful should not eat meat on fasting days. This has remained a national habit.

For a food-loving people like the French, a meatless meal never meant an abstemious meal. On lean days, at the courts of kings and on the tables of dignitaries there were veritable extravaganzas of fish and seafood. Take a menu served at the house of the Archbishop of Paris in the sixteenth century: 'Salmon fresh and cured, turbot, lobster, salt cod, mussels, trout, pike, carp, lampreys, crayfish, herrings, mullets and frogs' legs ...' In humbler households, fish courses were more modest, but still varied and appetizing.

Sadly, in France – as elsewhere – fish and seafood have become expensive commodities. A great many fishmongers have closed in the last decade or so, but

RIGHT
Classic Moules Marinières (pages 74 and 76) served with a little of the cooking liquor and a sprinkling of fresh herbs.

fish has somehow kept its place on the regular family menu. You buy what strikes you as the best value for money available on the supermarket counters or on the market stalls. Cod – large *cabillaud* or smaller *colin* – is a universal favourite. Sole, plaice, mullet, trout, sardines, mackerel, herrings and whiting are fairly ubiquitous. Tiny boiled shrimps served with bread and butter are a popular starter. For a family meal you cook fish as plainly as possible, poached in a little *court-bouillon*, prepared in the frying pan with a knob of butter and a squirt of lemon juice, or baked *en papillote*. For special occasions, you choose a finer fish – perhaps shellfish – or you prepare something more elaborate, such as a layered terrine of sole, fish parcels in a creamy sauce or a whole fish cooked in the oven.

MOULES FARCIES
Stuffed Mussels

Buttery stuffed mussels oozing fragrant juices make an irresistible appetizer. Use exactly the same method to stuff large flat mushrooms which have been blanched for a few minutes in simmering water, then drained and painted lightly with melted butter or olive oil.

Serves 4
Preparation: 15 minutes, plus soaking the mussels
Cooking: about 20 minutes

1.1 litres / 2pt (900g / 2lb) large fat fresh mussels, soaked and well scrubbed, discarding any which stay open
1tbsp oil
2 shallots, finely chopped
200ml / 7fl oz dry white wine
few sprigs each of parsley and rosemary
1tsp dried thyme
1 bay leaf
few black peppercorns
30g / 1oz day-old breadcrumbs
sea salt and freshly ground black pepper

FOR THE STUFFING:
2 garlic cloves, crushed
several sprigs of flat leaf parsley, coarsely snipped
few sprigs of chives, coarsely snipped
2tsp finely grated orange or lemon zest
1tsp Dijon mustard
85g / 3oz butter, cut into pieces
2tsp brandy
cayenne

1 Put a large sauté pan over a moderate heat. Add the oil, tilt the pan around over the heat until it is well coated. Tip in the shallots, reduce the heat and stir for 2 minutes.

2 Pour in the wine and throw in the herbs and peppercorns. Turn up the heat and bring to a rolling boil. Tip in the mussels, cover tightly and cook the mussels for 4–8 minutes, shaking the pan frequently, until the shells open.

3 Using a slotted spoon, lift the opened mussels from the cooking liquid. Discard any mussels that haven't opened and leave the others until just cool enough to handle. Strain the cooking liquor into a jug and reserve.

4 Prepare the stuffing while the mussels are cooking and cooling: put the garlic, parsley, chives and zest in the food processor and whizz for a few seconds. Scrape the mixture down the sides of the bowl with a spatula. Add the mustard, butter, brandy and 1 tablespoon of the cooking juices. (The rest of the mussel liquor can be used in another recipe.) Whizz again for several seconds until the green-speckled purée is blended. Season to taste with a little salt, cayenne and black pepper.

5 Preheat the grill to high. Snap off the top shells of the mussels and discard. Using a small teaspoon, heap some butter mixture over each mussel. Flatten this a little with the back of the spoon and sprinkle with breadcrumbs.

6 Place the stuffed mussels in a flame-proof dish, turn down the heat of the grill a little and grill the mussels for a few minutes, until the crumbs are golden.

7 Serve hot, with plenty of bread. If you prefer, serve warm as an appetizer. (Sieve and save any remaining cooking juices for later use as stock.)

To drink: a Coteaux d'Aix-en-Provence red.

VARIATION: to make *Moules Marinières*: follow the recipe to the end of step 3, using a crushed clove of garlic as well as the shallots. Pile the mussels in warmed shallow bowls. If you like, stir a tablespoon of cream into the strained liquor. Pour over the liquor, sprinkle with snipped chives and serve hot.

COQUILLES SAINT-JACQUES AU BEURRE BLANC
Scallops with Butter Sauce

You can make the court-bouillon and reduce the shallots for the *Beurre Blanc* well in advance – after that, however, do not allow any interruptions.

Serves 4
Preparation: 15 minutes
Cooking: 5 minutes plus making the sauce

250ml / 8fl oz dry white wine
1 shallot, finely chopped
2 spring onions, chopped
bouquet garni
2tsp ground dried thyme
few sprigs green or black peppercorns
8-12 fresh scallops, shelled and cleaned
100g / 3½ oz Beurre Blanc (page 34)
2tsp finely grated orange zest
leaves from a few sprigs of tarragon
sea salt and freshly ground black pepper

1 First make a light court-bouillon: bring a kettle of water to the boil. Pour about 6cm/2^1/$_2$ in of boiling water into a sauté pan, then add the wine, shallot, onions, bouquet garni, thyme and peppercorns. Bring back to the boil and season lightly. Simmer for 10 minutes over a moderate heat.

2 Strain the liquid into a jug, discard the flavourings and return the liquid to the pan. Bring to a gently trembling simmer over a low heat.

3 Rinse the scallops under cold running water and separate the orange coral from the white flesh. Depending on the size of the scallops, cut the scallop flesh across into 2 or 3 discs.

4 Make the Beurre Blanc and keep warm.

5 Using a slotted spoon, immerse the white parts of the scallops in the barely simmering liquid, then add the corals. Cook very carefully for 1 or 2 minutes, watching the heat and the timing – the scallops will toughen in seconds if the water gets close to boiling point or if they are at all overcooked.

6 Whisk 2 tablespoons of the cooking liquid and the grated orange zest into the finished Beurre Blanc.

7 Lift out the scallops with a slotted spoon and drain well. If necessary, keep warm for a few minutes on a double layer of paper towel.

8 Arrange the scallops over 4 warmed plates, scrubbed and sterilized concave scallop shells or individual round gratin dishes. Spoon over a little of the Beurre Blanc, scatter a few tarragon leaves over the lot and serve at once. Serve the rest of the sauce in a warmed sauce boat.

To drink: a dry Vouvray.

BRANDADE DE MORUE
Salt Cod Purée

Portugal is said to have as many salt cod recipes as there are days in the year. France has far fewer to contribute, but *Brandade de Morue* is part of the national heritage. Authentic sticky smooth pungent *brandade* includes neither cream nor potato, but these additions may help latent converts acquire a taste for this great palate-challenging dish. Try spreading it on hot *croûtons* as an appetizer.

Brandade is delicious and slightly less pale in colour if allowed to cool and then reheated for 15 minutes in a buttered gratin dish placed in a moderate oven.

Serves 4
Preparation: soaking the fish (at least 12 hours),
then 5 minutes
Cooking: about 40 minutes

675g/1^1/$_2$ lb salt cod
3 or more garlic cloves, crushed
200ml/7fl oz fruity olive oil, plus 2tbsp

TO FINISH
175ml/6fl oz milk
1 large potato, boiled in its skin and peeled
(optional)
3-4 tablespoons single cream (optional)
freshly ground black pepper
Garlic Croûtons, to serve (see page 10)
butter to reheat, if preferred

1 First soak the salt cod thoroughly to remove the excess salt: rinse it well, then place in a large bowl with plenty of cold water; cover and leave in a cool place for about 3 hours, then drain, rinse and place in plenty of fresh cold water. Repeat the process at least 3 more times until the fish has lost most of its salt.

2 Place the fish in a saucepan, cover with fresh cold water and bring to a simmer over a moderate heat. Reduce the heat a little as soon as the water reaches simmering point. Cook the fish gently for 8–10 minutes, until you can flake it easily with a fork.

3 Remove from the pan, rinse and drain well. Leave until cool enough to handle, then discard the skin and as many bones as you can find.

4 Put the fish in a bowl and scatter in the garlic. Shred the fish finely with a fork, mashing and combining it with the crushed garlic. Season with pepper.

5 Rinse out the salt cod saucepan and pour in two-thirds of the olive oil. Place over a very low heat. In a separate pan, gently heat the milk, also over a very low heat.

6 Take the pan with the olive oil off the heat. Tip in the shredded salt cod and garlic. Beat and pound well together, using a large fork, wooden spoon or spatula. Return the pan to a low heat and continue pounding. Gradually trickle in the rest of the olive oil, still beating vigorously.

7 Now work in the warm milk a little at a time – this will take you several minutes after which you should have a thick – somewhat sticky – white purée. If your purée is too runny or if you prefer a more diluted flavour, beat in the cooked potato, a small spoonful at a time. Keep the heat low throughout.

8 To finish: whisk in the extra olive oil and/or cream and season with plenty of freshly ground black pepper. Serve piping hot, with garlic croûtons if you like.

To drink: Corbières or Minervois.

LA MOUCLADE

Aromatic Mussel Stew

Serves 4
*Preparation: about 15 minutes, plus
soaking the mussels
Cooking: about 20 minutes*

*2 litres / 3¹/₂ pt (1.8kg / 4lb) small fresh
mussels, soaked and
well scrubbed,
discarding any which stay open
45g / 1¹/₂ oz butter
4 shallots, chopped
250ml / 8fl oz dry white wine mixed
with 350ml / 12fl oz water
several sprigs of flat leaf parsley
1 bay leaf
cayenne
1 large egg yolk
5 tbsp crème fraîche
2 small or 1 large garlic clove(s),
crushed
¹/₂ tsp paprika
¹/₂ tsp ground saffron
sea salt and freshly ground
black pepper*

TO SERVE:
*few sprigs of chives or chervil
toast or warm bread*

This fragrant mussel stew comes from France's Atlantic coast between Brittany and La Rochelle. A very straightforward dish to prepare, it takes *Moules Marinières* a few steps further up the ladder of excellence and refinement.

1 Put a large sauté pan over a moderate heat. As soon as it is hot, tip in the prepared mussels, one-third of the butter, the shallots and the wine mixture. Add a few sprigs of parsley and the bay leaf and season lightly with salt, black pepper and a touch of cayenne. Turn up the heat and bring to a rolling boil. Now cover tightly and cook the mussels for 4–8 minutes, or until the shells open. Shake the pan vigorously a few times during the process.

DISCARD ANY MUSSELS WHICH HAVE NOT OPENED AND LEAVE THE REST TO COOL SLIGHTLY.

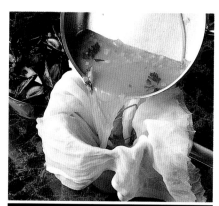

STRAIN THE COOKING LIQUID THROUGH A FINE SIEVE LINED WITH TWO LAYERS OF MUSLIN.

2 Using a slotted spoon, lift the cooked mussels from the simmering liquor. Discard any that haven't opened at this stage and leave the rest for a couple of minutes until they are just cool enough for you to handle. Using a fine sieve lined with muslin or a chinois, strain the cooking liquor to get rid of the flavourings and any grit or sand. Reserve the liquor in a jug. (If you stop at this stage and serve the mussels with a little liquor and a snipping of herbs they will be classic *Moules Marinières* – see pages 72–73.)

3 While the mussels are cooking and cooling, combine the egg yolk with the crème fraîche in a small bowl, whisking lightly until smoothly blended. In a separate bowl and using a fork, mash the rest of the butter with the garlic, paprika and saffron. Season lightly.

4 Now shell all the mussels, except for 12 or so of the prettier specimens. Divide the shelled mussels between 4 warmed serving plates (soup or pudding bowls with a flat rim are ideal). Keep warm in the oven set at its lowest

COMBINE THE EGG YOLKS AND CRÈME FRAÎCHE AND MASH THE GARLIC WITH THE REST OF THE BUTTER.

temperature. If you prefer to cook this dish ahead, moisten the mussels with a little cooking liquor and set aside for a couple of hours before you finish the stew. Then reheat very gently without letting the mussels cook a second time, which would toughen them. A microwave does the job nicely.

5 Rinse out the pan and put it over a low to moderate heat. Tip the flavoured butter into the pan. As soon as it starts sizzling, pour in the liquor and stir for a few seconds. Bring to a simmer, stirring. Ladle out a few tablespoons of the liquor and whisk into the egg mixture. Whisk this liaison back into the pan, stir for a minute or two until piping hot and blended. Adjust the seasoning.

6 Pour the hot soup over the mussels. Decorate with the mussels on the half shell, snip over a few fresh leaves and serve at once, with toast or chunks of warm bread.

To drink: Muscadet.

VARIATIONS: the saffron can be replaced with good curry powder, mixed with I teaspoon of ground coriander and $1/2$ teaspoon of cumin. Snip over a very few fresh coriander leaves at the end.

PETITE BOUILLABAISSE

Fish Stew

Bouillabaisse was originally boiled up by fishermen on the shores of the Mediterranean from the unsold remnants of the day's catch. Like all dishes that are entirely based on locally available ingredients, in its authentic format *bouillabaisse* does not travel at all well. This is a very modest version, but it is neither meek nor genteel. It remains true to the pot-luck nature of the original dish in that it uses plenty of gutsy flavourings and leaves the choice of fish up to you. Salmon is out, but a fresh tuna steak mixes in nicely. Firmish-textured fish is recommended – if you use any soft or very delicate fish, add it to the mixture only at the simmering stage. Prepare the *fumet* from the trimmings of the non-oily fish while the ingredients are marinating (see page 10).

Serves 4–6
Preparation: 20 minutes, plus marinating
Cooking: 20 minutes

5tbsp fruity olive oil
1 Spanish onion, finely chopped
4 tomatoes, blanched, skinned, deseeded and chopped
several sprigs of dried fennel, or ¹/₂ small fennel bulb, trimmed and chopped into small pieces
2tsp fennel seeds
4 garlic cloves, crushed
several sprigs of parsley
several sprigs of fresh or dried thyme
1 bay leaf
3 strips of orange peel
¹/₂ generous tsp powdered saffron
575ml/1pt (450g/1lb) small mussels, soaked and well scrubbed, discarding any which stay open
900g/2lb mixed filleted or skinned fish, preferably including a piece of pre-soaked salt cod and another strongly flavoured fish, left in largish pieces
350g/12oz large raw prawns
300ml/¹/₂pt dry white wine
575ml/1pt light fish fumet (page 10)
sea salt and freshly ground black pepper

TO SERVE:
few sprigs of parsley, coarsely snipped
Garlic Croûtons (page 10)
Rouille (page 39)
boiled potatoes (optional)

1 In a very large heavy saucepan, heat 2 tablespoons of olive oil. Add the chopped onion and tomatoes, season lightly and cook for a few minutes over a moderate heat. Tip in the fennel, garlic, herbs, bay leaf and orange peel, then sprinkle in half the saffron. Stir, reduce the heat and cook for a few minutes, still stirring occasionally.

2 Take off the heat and leave to cool. Tip in the mussels, then place the fish on top. Cover with the prawns. Dribble over the rest of the olive oil and sprinkle with the remaining saffron. Cover and leave to marinate in a cool place for a few hours.

3 About 30 minutes before you intend to eat, pour in the white wine, fish fumet and enough water just to cover the ingredients. Season lightly. Bring to the boil over a moderate heat, then reduce the heat a little and simmer for 8–10 minutes.

4 To serve, pile the fish and shellfish in a warmed shallow bowl and moisten with a little strained cooking liquid. Sprinkle with the roughly snipped parsley and serve immediately. Serve the strained cooking liquid in a warmed jug or tureen. Have a warmed shallow plate or pudding bowl ready for each guest, plenty of garlic croûtons and rouille. Boiled potatoes are a nice extra accompaniment.

To drink: Côtes de Provence rosé.

(RIGHT) Petite Bouillabaisse *served with its traditional accompaniments of* Rouille *(page 39),* Garlic Croûtons *(page 10) and boiled potatoes.*

LA TERRINE DE POISSONS

Fish Terrine

Serves 8-12
Preparation: about 1 hour, plus chilling time
Cooking: about 1 hour, plus cooling and chilling

30g/1oz butter, plus extra for greasing
3 large (but not huge) soles, skinned and filleted
700g/1²/₃ lb skinned and boned salmon fillets
at least 30 large intact spinach or sorrel leaves
sea salt and freshly ground black pepper

FOR THE STUFFING:
250ml/8fl oz milk
45g/1¹/₂ oz fresh white breadcrumbs
500g/1lb 2oz skinned and boned whiting or pike
140g/5oz butter
2 large extra-fresh eggs plus 1 extra yolk
500ml/16fl oz chilled crème fraîche
2tsp each juice and grated zest from ¹/₂ lemon
pinch of cayenne
¹/₄ tsp ground nutmeg

FOR THE SAUCE VERTE, TO SERVE:
1tbsp crème fraîche
1tbsp lemon juice
about 550ml/1pt Mayonnaise (page 36)
few sprigs each of all or some of the following herbs: parsley and chives, chervil, tarragon or dill
small bunch of watercress (optional)

Strictly for *les grandes occasions*, this terrine is a lot of work, but it makes a fine centrepiece for a buffet or a festive first course. Serve with an Alsace Riesling.

Preparations for the terrine can all be carried out the day before the party, or even 2 days ahead if this suits you better. The sauce is best made on the day.

BLANCH THE LEAVES BRIEFLY TO MAKE THEM SUPPLE. REFRESH IN ICED WATER AND DRY WELL.

USE A SHARP KNIFE TO CUT OFF STALKS AND TOUGH RIBS.

1 Start preparing the stuffing: chill a good-sized mixing bowl and bring the milk to the boil in a small saucepan, then tip in the breadcrumbs. Reduce the heat and let the mixture thicken and dry up a little, stirring it occasionally. Leave to get cold.

2 Over a low heat, melt 15g/¹/₂ oz butter in a frying or sauté pan. Dealing with them a few at a time and adding more butter as necessary, place the fillets of sole and salmon in the pan and cook them gently for 2 minutes on each side, turning them over carefully with a fish slice. The fish will stiffen and become just a little opaque. Still taking care not to break up the fillets, lift them out of the pan with the fish slice and put them side by side on a dish. Season lightly.

3 Bring a kettle of water to the boil. Have a bowl of ice-cold water ready. Pour the boiling water into a saucepan, season with a little salt. Bring back to the boil over a moderate heat then blanch the spinach or sorrel leaves for a few seconds. Drain and immediately plunge into cold water to stop the cooking. Spread the leaves on a clean tea towel or a double layer of paper towel. Remove and discard the stalks from the leaves, keeping them as intact as possible.

SAUTÉ THE FISH FILLETS ON BOTH SIDES UNTIL JUST STIFFENED.

PROCESS THE WHITING OR PIKE WITH BUTTER, EGGS AND MILK MIXTURE UNTIL SMOOTH. CHILL.

SET THE BOWL OF STUFFING ON A BED
OF ICE AND WHISK IN THE CHILLED
CRÈME FRAÎCHE A LITTLE AT A TIME.

SPRINKLE OVER THE LEMON
JUICE AND ZEST, SEASON WITH SALT,
CAYENNE AND NUTMEG. MIX WELL.

4 Finish the stuffing: put the whiting or pike in the food processor and whizz until minced, then feed in the butter, eggs and extra yolk, and the milk mixture. Process until smooth. Tip into the chilled bowl and chill again for 20 minutes.

5 Set the bowl in a larger container on a bed of crushed ice and whisk in the chilled crème fraîche, a little at a time. Sprinkle over the lemon juice and zest, then season lightly with salt and a touch of cayenne and nutmeg.

6 Preheat the oven to 200°C/400°F/ gas 6 and butter a 2 litre/3½ pt loaf tin.

7 Assemble the terrine: first line the base and sides of the prepared tin with a layer of leaves, allowing them to overhang. Cover with a layer of sole fillets, if necessary trimming them to fit. Now spoon a generous layer of stuffing over the sole. Knock the tin on the work surface to make sure there are no gaps between layers and smooth with a spatula. Arrange a layer of salmon fillets on top of the stuffing. Now add a second layer of leaves. Reserve the rest for the *Sauce Verte*.

8 Carry on with a second layer of sole fillets, season a little and knock the tin again. Spread more stuffing, then a second layer of stuffing. Bring the leaves over the top of the terrine and add extra leaves to cover any gaps. Knock the tin a couple of times on the work surface to ensure it is well packed.

TRIM THE SOLE FILLETS TO FIT
THE TIN AND USE A FISH SLICE TO
PLACE THEM ON THE LEAVES.

SPREAD A GENEROUS LAYER
OF STUFFING THEN PLACE A LAYER OF
TRIMMED SALMON FILLETS ON TOP.

**PLACE TIN ON NEWSPAPER IN
A BAKING TIN AND POUR IN BOILING
WATER TO HALFWAY UP SIDES.**

**COVER WITH FOIL
AND WEIGHTS BEFORE COOLING
AND CHILLING.**

9 Bring a kettle of water to the boil and line a large baking tin with folded sheets of newspaper. Put the loaf tin in the centre and pour in boiling water to come halfway up its sides. Bake for about 1 hour, until the top of the terrine feels firm.

10 Take out of oven and leave to cool a little, then cover with a double thickness of foil and place weights on top. Leave to get quite cold, then chill for 3–48 hours.

11 Prepare the Sauce Verte: stir the crème fraîche and lemon juice into the mayonnaise. Snip in the rest of the spinach leaves and plenty of fresh herbs and watercress if using. The sauce should be well tinged with green flecks and a little sharp. Adjust the seasoning. Transfer to a large sauce boat or bowl. Cover and chill.

12 To serve: invert the terrine on a plain dish and carefully remove the tin. If you like, surround with tiny sprigs of herbs or watercress. Serve with the sauce.

DARNES DE CABILLAUD À LA MOUTARDE CITRONNÉE

Cod Steaks with Lemon Mustard

Cod steaks can be cooked in many different ways. Choose poaching when watching the calories and, if none of the techniques suggested below appeal to you, try them *en papillote* (see page 88).

Anchovy and lemon give the creamy mustard sauce a nice little kick. Mustard sauce also works well with fresh tuna, sardines, smoked haddock, mackerel and salmon. Add to its intensity by using extra capers and anchovies if you like, but don't overdo the mustard.

Serves 2
Preparation: about 10 minutes, plus
30 minutes marinating
Cooking: under 20 minutes

2 chunky fresh cod steaks, each about
175g/6½ oz and 2.5cm/1in thick
2-3 sprigs of parsley or chervil
2 tbsp olive oil
1 scant tsp dried thyme, or ½ tsp each dried
thyme and marjoram or oregano
2tsp lemon juice
1 bay leaf, halved
sea salt and freshly ground black pepper

FOR THE SAUCE:
25g/¾ oz unsalted butter
2 tsp cornflour
125ml/4fl oz fish fumet (page 10), milk or
water
1 shallot, finely chopped
1 large anchovy fillet, drained and finely snipped,
or 1tsp good anchovy purée
1tsp capers, drained (optional)
1 egg yolk
1tbsp lemon juice, plus extra, if liked
2tbsp single cream
2tsp Dijon mustard

1 First marinate the steaks for 30 minutes before cooking: in a small bowl, combine the olive oil with the herbs and lemon juice. Season lightly. Using a pastry brush, generously brush the cod steaks with the flavoured olive oil and put half a bay leaf on top of each. Cover and leave in a cool place until needed.

2 Start preparing the lemon mustard sauce. In a small heavy saucepan, melt the butter over a low heat. Sprinkle in the cornflour. Cook for 1 minute, stirring briskly, then add the fish fumet, milk or water. Season lightly and whisk for 2–3 minutes until the mixture simmers. Reduce the heat a fraction. Add the prepared shallot, snipped anchovy, capers (if using) and continue to simmer very gently for 5–10 minutes. While the sauce is simmering, in a small bowl combine the egg yolk with the lemon juice and cream. Adjust the seasoning of the sauce, strain into a warmed jug and keep warm.

3 Preheat the grill to high. Start grilling the fish and reduce the heat a little once the fish is cooking. Turn the steaks over carefully after 3–4 minutes, using a fish slice. Reduce the heat still further and cook for 4–5 minutes until cooked right through to the bone.

4 Pour the sauce back into its original pan. Place over a low heat, add the mustard and stir until heated through.

5 Add 2 tablespoons of the hot sauce to the egg liaison and whisk until combined. Then whisk this into the saucepan and adjust the seasoning. If the sauce seems too thick at this stage, thin it down with a few teaspoons of hot water, stirred in one at a time. If you want to sharpen the sauce, stir in a sprinkling of lemon juice.

6 Spoon a little sauce over the cod steaks and serve the rest of the sauce separately, in a small warmed sauce boat or jug. If you like, snip a little parsley or chervil over the fish.

Variations: you can sauté the fish in a frying pan. Follow steps 1–4 of the *Soles Meunière* recipe (see page 89), handling the fish carefully as you turn it over. Do not rinse out the frying pan. To poach the fish, follow step 3 of the *Paupiettes de Poisson* recipe (see page 88). Using a fish slice or wide spatula, carefully transfer the cooked cod steaks to warmed serving plates and keep warm while you finish the sauce.

To drink: a white Côtes-du-Rhône.

RAIE AU BEURRE NOIR
Skate with Black Butter

The classic title of this celebrated dish is a bit of a misnomer because the butter that bathes and complements the skate is in fact brown and closer to *beurre noisette*, hazelnut butter, than to butter which has been allowed to blacken. This dish is quick and easy, but needs constant watching so that you catch both fish and butter at their best. Skate wings are worth taking out your best butter for – the combination of plump smoothness, sharp acidic edge and nutty butteriness can be simply sensational.

Serves 4
Preparation: 10 minutes
Cooking: about 10 minutes

5tbsp red or white wine vinegar, plus 1 more tbsp
to finish
few sprigs of thyme
few sprigs of parsley and 2tbsp finely snipped
parsley
1 spring onion, chopped
4 skate wings, each weighing about 200g/7oz,
rinsed
100g/3½ oz top-quality unsalted
butter
3tbsp capers
sea salt and freshly ground black pepper
1 lemon, quartered, to serve

1 To poach the fish: bring a kettle of water to the boil. In a large sauté pan put the vinegar, sprigs of thyme and parsley and the spring onion. Cover with about 8.5cm/3½in of boiling water and season lightly. Bring back to a simmer over a moderate heat.

2 Place the skate wings in the pan, reduce the heat and simmer for 8-10 minutes, or until the flesh is just tender enough to flake slightly with a fork. Keep the water at a low simmer throughout the cooking.

3 When the fish has been poaching for 5 minutes or so, melt the butter in a small pan over a very low heat.

4 Using a fish slice, remove the skate from the pan. Drain, remove the skin and pat the flesh gently dry with paper towel. Put the fish on a warmed serving dish and keep warm.

5 Turn up the heat under the butter just a little until the moment it turns golden brown and starts exuding a nutty smell. Trickle this over the skate.

6 Add the capers to the pan. Stir over the moderate heat for a minute with the extra tablespoon of vinegar and half the snipped parsley. Scatter this over the skate and sprinkle over the rest of the parsley. Serve immediately, with lemon wedges.

To drink: a white Sancerre

TRUITES À LA GRECQUE
Marinated Trout

Use the smallest trout you can find to make this summer dish. If the fish are larger, double the cooking time and allow 1 fish per person. If the fish are already filleted, bring to a simmer and immediately take off the heat.

Trout are excellent cooked *en papillote* (see page 89, allowing 35 minutes at 190°C/375°F/gas5) for largish specimens, or *meunière* like sole – particularly if you throw a tablespoon of slivered almonds, pine nuts or walnut kernels into the pan for the last few minutes of cooking.

Serves 4
Preparation: 10 minutes
Cooking: 15 minutes, plus cooling and overnight
marinating

8 small trout, cleaned and gutted, or 16 fillets
5tbsp fruity olive oil
5tbsp dry white wine
4 small strips of orange zest
2 garlic cloves, slivered
12 coriander seeds, coarsely crushed
12 green peppercorns, coarsely crushed
2 bay leaves
white parts of 2 large spring onions, cut into thin
rings
1 small lemon, thinly sliced, and 1 extra lemon,
for serving (optional)
2-3 sprigs each of rosemary and thyme
sea salt and freshly ground black pepper

1 Rinse the fish and pat well dry. Put them side by side, head to tail and without overlapping, in a large flameproof gratin dish.

2 In a jug, combine the olive oil, white wine, orange zest, garlic, coriander and peppercorns. Season the fish with salt and pepper and pour the dressing over them. Scatter with the bay leaves, spring onion rings, lemon slices, thyme and rosemary.

3 Place the dish over a low heat. Bring to a simmer, then immediately reduce the heat a fraction and cook for 5 minutes. If necessary, move the dish over the heat from time to time so that the trout can cook evenly.

4 Leave to get cold, then cover and refrigerate overnight. Bring the marinated fish back to room temperature before serving.

5 Serve straight from the dish, but first lift out some (but not all) of the flavourings and adjust the seasoning. If you like, refresh each trout with a squeeze of lemon juice and a grinding of black pepper before eating.

To drink: Sauvignon de Touraine.

(RIGHT) *Lightly cooked* Truites à la Grecque, *using trout fillets, makes splendid picnic fare.*

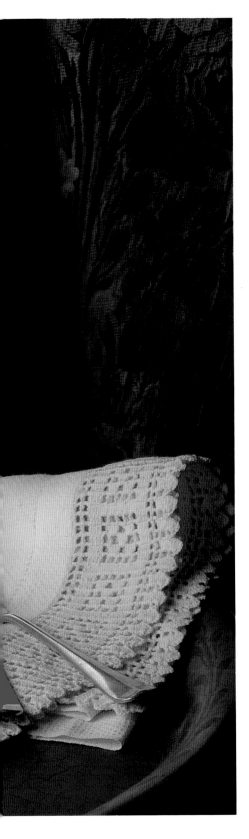

SAUMON RÔTI AUX AROMATES
Roast Salmon with Herbs

Salmon is fast becoming the chicken of fishes. It too is readily available, fair value for money and likely to please – certainly guaranteed not to offend – anyone's palate. Like its counterpart in the poultry world, it also responds magnificently to being roasted at a high temperature on a bed of aromatic herbs. If you are using a whole fish, allow about 225g/8oz per person and ask your fishmonger to bone the fish and cut it into 2 long fillets for you. You may also be able to buy a boned side or filleted tail piece from a larger fish – allow about 170g/6oz per person. Thicker, larger cuts will need an extra few minutes in the oven.

The same simple roasting technique also works deliciously well with whole salmon trout, red mullet and tuna fish steaks. As a safe rule, take any fish out of the oven a few minutes *before* you expect it to be cooked rather than the other way round.

Serves 8
Preparation: 5 minutes, plus about
30 minutes', marinating
Cooking: 15-20 minutes

1 garlic clove, halved
2-3tbsp fruity olive oil
several sprigs each of rosemary and chives, plus
more to garnish (optional)
1 small salmon or salmon trout, weighing about
2kg/ 4¹/₂ lb, head removed, boned and halved
white parts of 3 large spring onions, thinly sliced
¹/₂ scant tsp powdered saffron, or
¹/₂ generous tsp ground ginger
30g/ 1oz butter, diced
juice of 1 small lemon
sea salt and freshly ground black pepper

1 Rub the skin of the salmon with the cut side of one half of the garlic clove. Lightly brush the roasting pan with olive oil, then arrange a few sprigs of rosemary and chives in the centre of pan for the salmon to sit on. Brush these with oil and put the salmon on the herbs, skinned sides up. Paint the skinned sides with olive oil, then scatter over the sliced spring onion, tiny spriglets of rosemary, and snip over a few chive stalks. Season with salt, pepper and a dusting of powdered saffron or ground ginger. Leave in a cool place for 30 minutes or so.

2 Preheat the oven to 220°C/425°F/gas7. Dot half the butter over the salmon, sprinkle with half the lemon juice and season again.

3 Roast the fish for 12–18 minutes, until it is cooked through to your liking.

4 Using a fish slice, wide spatula or palette knife, carefully transfer the salmon to a warmed serving dish and keep warm.

5 Put the roasting pan over a moderate heat or pour the cooking juices into a small saucepan. Add the rest of the butter and lemon juice, stir for a minute, then strain this sauce over the salmon. Snip over a few more chives, if you like and serve soon.

To drink: Mercurey or Montagny.

(LEFT) Saumon Rôti aux Aromates *served with* Pâtes Fraîches à l'Alsacienne *(page 151).*

LOTTE AU FOUR EN PAPILLOTE
Monkfish Baked in Parcels

Fine meaty monkfish is good cooked very simply in foil. To serve it *matelote*-style, mix the cooking juices and sautéed mushrooms with *Sauce Bourguignonne* (page 30). If you find the sauce too deep a purple for the white fish, stir in a teaspoon of tomato paste.

Dressed with a caper *Sauce Poulette* (page 30), still with its mushroom garnish, monkfish makes a delectable *blanquette de la mer*.

Serves 4
Preparation: 10 minutes
Cooking: 25 minutes

1 monkfish tail weighing about
800g/ 1 3/4 lb, skinned, central bone removed, cut into about 16 chunks
cayenne or lemon pepper
white parts of 2 large spring onions, chopped
few sprigs of parsley
6 black peppercorns
2 bay leaves, halved
4-6 strips of lemon zest
45g/ 1 1/2 oz soft butter, cut into small slivers
1 teaspoon each of ground dried thyme and savory
1 tbsp oil
300g/ 10 1/2 oz button mushrooms, wiped and thinly sliced
sea salt and freshly ground black pepper

1 Preheat the oven to 190°C/375°F/ gas 5. Rinse the monkfish and pat dry with a double layer of paper towel. Season lightly with cayenne or lemon pepper and with salt and pepper.

2 Prepare a double layer of foil large enough to wrap the fish very loosely. Scatter the spring onions in the centre of the foil, then add half the parsley, the peppercorns, 2 pieces of bay leaf and half the lemon zest. Put the monkfish on top of this aromatic layer and distribute about 30g/1oz butter slivers on top of the fish. Sprinkle over the dried thyme and savory and top with the rest of the bay leaves and lemon strips. Bring the foil edges together to make a loose but tightly sealed parcel.

3 Bake for 20–25 minutes, until the fish is just bouncy.

4 While the fish is in the oven, prepare the mushrooms: place a frying or sauté pan over a moderate heat, spoon in the oil and swirl it around to coat the base of the pan. Add the remaining butter and, when the foaming subsides, tip in the mushrooms. Season and sauté for 5 minutes, stirring frequently.

5 Take the fish from its foil parcel and put it in a warmed serving dish with the sautéed mushrooms. Strain the cooking juices into a small jug and dribble them over the fish and mushrooms.

Variation: for *Lotte à la Provençale*, replace the butter with 2 tablespoons olive oil and a few drops of lemon juice and add to the *papillote* 1 or 2 cloves of crushed garlic, a sprig of rosemary and 2 chopped ripe tomatoes.

PAUPIETTES DE POISSON À L'ESTRAGON ET À LA CRÈME
Fish Rolls with Tarragon Cream

This is a versatile fish dish which may be made with turbot, sole or whiting, depending on your budget or what your fishmonger recommends. The white wine can be replaced with cider and you can add prawns as an extra — sauté them separately in a little butter.

Serves 4
Preparation: about 15 minutes
Cooking: about 15 minutes

2 tsp oil
30-45g/ 1-1 1/2 oz butter, plus extra for greasing
200g/ 7oz white button mushrooms, thinly sliced
leaves from several sprigs of tarragon
8 skinned fillets of white fish, such as sole (see above), weighing about 550g/ 1 1/4 lb in total
100ml/ 3 1/2 fl oz dry white wine
150ml/ 1/4 pt fish fumet (page 10)
5 generous tbsp crème fraîche or single cream
1 large egg yolk
1 1/2 tbsp lemon juice
sea salt and freshly ground black pepper

1 Heat a sauté pan, add the oil and lightly rub it over the base of the pan with a wad of paper towel. Add the butter and melt it over a moderate heat. Tip in the prepared mushrooms and season. Sauté for a few minutes, stirring occasionally, then stir in half the tarragon leaves and continue cooking for a minute. Using a fish slice, transfer the mushrooms from the pan to a plate lined with paper towel. Do not rinse out the pan.

2 Prepare the fish parcels: wet a large flat knife and press gently along the fillets to flatten them slightly. Season each fillet with a little salt and pepper and spoon a little mushroom and tarragon mixture down the centre – there will be plenty of the mixture left to finish the dish. Starting at the more pointed end, roll each fillet fairly tightly over the filling. Secure with 1 or 2 wooden cocktail sticks or tie with cotton thread.

3 Bring a kettle of water to the boil. Pour the white wine and fish fumet into the sauté pan and place over a moderate heat. Top up with just enough boiling water to cover the parcels when they are put in the pan. Bring to a simmer, then reduce the heat. Using the fish slice, place the fish in the liquid, return to a trembling simmer and reduce the heat again. Poach for 2–3 minutes, or a little longer if the parcels are on the large side.

4 Lift the parcels out of the pan with a fish slice and place them on a warmed serving dish. Carefully remove the cocktail sticks or cotton threads. Scatter the remaining mushroom and tarragon mixture over the parcels and keep warm, covered with lightly buttered greaseproof paper, in a low oven.

5 Turn up the heat and vigorously boil the liquid until well reduced – you should end up with about 175ml/6fl oz. Reduce the heat to low and stir in the crème fraîche or cream. Heat through without bringing to a simmer, still stirring.

6 In a small cup, combine the egg yolk with the lemon juice. Whisk this liaison into the pan and keep whisking for a minute or two, still over a low heat. Adjust the seasoning.

7 Pour this sauce over the fish parcels and mushrooms. Scatter over a few more tarragon leaves and serve at once.

To drink: a white Graves or dry Normandy cider.

SOLES MEUNIÈRE
Fried Sole with Parsley Butter

The sole is a sensitive fish and needs to be approached with a modicum of culinary good manners. *À la meunière* ('in the manner of the miller's wife') is an orthodox technique which agrees with them. It involves dusting the fish in flour (hence the miller bit), sautéing, and finishing with nutty butter and parsley.

Provided you don't cram the soles into too small a pan and let the butter turn acrid, you will have perfect fish on the table within 15 minutes. If you are cooking for 4 people, double the proportions and use 2 separate pans, unless you have a truly enormous pan that conducts heat evenly and efficiently.

Another solution is to undercook the first batch of soles a little and transfer them to a moderate oven while you cook the second lot. Switch off the oven after 1 minute.

Serves 2
Preparation: about 10 minutes
Cooking: under 15 minutes

about 1 tbsp flour
about 200ml/7fl oz milk
2 small Dover soles, cleaned and gutted, dark skin removed
1½ tbsp oil
55g/2oz butter
1½ tbsp lemon juice
1½ tbsp finely snipped parsley
sea salt and freshly ground black pepper

1 Season the flour with a little salt and a more generous amount of pepper. Tip it into a small fine sieve. Pour the milk into a shallow plate and season with a little salt. Dip the prepared soles in the milk, then put them on a clean plate, skinned side up, and dust this side of the fish with the seasoned flour.

2 Heat a large frying pan. When the pan is hot, put in the oil and tilt the pan over the heat to coat its base with oil. Add half the butter over a moderate heat. When the butter starts to sizzle, put the sole in the pan, floured side down. Cook for about 4 minutes, keeping the heat moderate.

3 Dust the top side of the sole with flour. Using a fish slice, carefully turn over the fish. Continue cooking for a further 4–5 minutes, reducing the heat just a little towards the end. The fish should be cooked through to the bone.

4 Using the fish slice, put the fish skinned side up on warmed plates and keep warm. Tip out the fat and wipe the pan with a wad of paper towel.

5 Return the pan to a moderate heat, tip in the rest of the butter and leave to melt. Skim off the white foam, stir in half the snipped parsley and sprinkle with lemon juice. Cook for a few seconds, then dribble the parsley butter over the sole. Sprinkle over the rest of the parsley, adjust the seasoning and serve at once.

To drink: a cool Beaujolais.

Chapter Six

LES VOLAILLES ET LES GIBIERS

Poultry and Game

Henri IV's wish that every family in the land should put a hen in the cooking pot on Sundays, *la poule au pot le dimanche*, is a saying that most French people above the age of seven can quote by heart. Four centuries have passed and poultry is still held in high esteem in France, where it plays an important – almost symbolic – role on the family table.

Alongside the ubiquitous bland offerings of the supermarket shelves, speciality poultry has become a thriving business: chickens, guinea fowls and ducks are ordered days in advance from favourite suppliers for special meals; geese, capons and young turkeys, weeks ahead for Christmas. Quality is rigorously controlled and markets ferociously protected. Cooking methods strongly reflect regional influences: the fat of the land (from the cow, the pig, the goose or the olive) and the local wines are much in evidence.

LEFT
Caneton aux Petits Navets (page 92) served with
Carottes Vichy (page 135).

CANETON AUX PETITS NAVETS
Duckling with Baby Turnips

This is a quick and tasty way to prepare duck. The bed of turnips and onion used during the cooking absorb much of the bird's fattiness. Baby onions can be added to the turnips and glazed in exactly the same way.

Serves 4
Preparation: about 15 minutes
Cooking: about 1 hour

2–2.3kg duck / 4¹/₂–5lb duck, jointed
1¹/₂ tbsp oil
75g/ 2¹/₂ oz butter
about 800g/ 1³/₄ lb unblemished baby turnips
1 Spanish onion, chopped
200ml/ 7fl oz dry white wine or a mixture of white wine and water
1–2 tsp sugar
sea salt and freshly ground black pepper

1 Pat the duck dry with paper towel and season generously. Heat the oil and 15g/¹/₂oz butter in a large flameproof casserole or sauté pan and sauté the duck pieces over a moderate heat until browned on all sides.

2 Remove the duck from the pan and pour out the fat. Select the least attractive third of the turnips and cut them into thick slices. Spread these in the bottom of the pan. Scatter over the chopped onion and put the browned duck pieces on top of the vegetable layer. Moisten with the white wine or wine and water mixture, cover tightly and simmer over a moderate to low heat for about 40 minutes.

3 While the duck is cooking, glaze the rest of the turnips. Bring a kettle of water to the boil. Put the turnips in a single layer in a heavy saucepan, sprinkle with sugar, season and just cover with boiling water. Dot with half the remaining butter and chill the rest.

4 Partly cover the pan with a lid or cover loosely with a layer of foil, then cook over a low to moderate heat until the water has evaporated and the turnips are just tender (the exact timing will depend on the turnips – allow at least 15 minutes).

5 Turn up the heat, take off the cover and allow the turnips to turn golden brown, shaking the pan repeatedly during the process.

6 Add the glazed turnips to the pan with the duck, cover and cook over a low heat for a further 15 minutes. Leave to settle in the covered pan for a few minutes.

7 Lift the duck and glazed turnips from the pan and arrange on a warmed serving dish. Using a slotted spoon, lift out and discard the stewed sliced turnips and onion.

8 Turn up the heat under the pan and reduce the cooking liquid a little, stirring well. Adjust the seasoning. Dice the chilled butter and whisk the dice into the pan until the sauce is smooth and glossy. Strain over the duck and serve immediately.

To drink: a Chinon.

CANARD AUX PÊCHES
Duck with Peaches

Duck and peaches are a happy combination. For the marriage to be truly heavenly, the roasted duck skin has to be very crisp, the meat succulent and the peaches still firm. The sweet flesh of the fruit absorbs and complements the fatty juices of the bird. If fresh peaches are available, poach them in just enough simmering water to cover until the skin peels off easily – this will take 5–15 minutes, depending on the ripeness of the fruit. Use a little of the poaching liquid to deglaze the pan. As the fresh peach season is short, the rest of the time you can use good-quality canned peaches in juice or water (peaches in syrup tend to be too sweet).

Serves 4
Preparation: 10 minutes
Cooking: about 1³/₄ hours

8 canned white peaches in juice, well drained
(reserving 1 tbsp of juice or water) and halved
2tsp runny honey
1 tsp groundnut or sunflower oil
1 tsp green peppercorns, drained and crushed
¹/₂ tsp five-spice powder
1 oven-ready duck, weighing about 1.8kg/ 4lb,
wiped clean and at room temperature
2tbsp crème fraîche
2tbsp brandy
sea salt and black peppercorns

1 Preheat the oven to 220°C/425°F/gas7. In a cup, mix the reserved peach juice or water with the honey. Add the oil, crushed green peppercorns and five-spice powder. Season generously with sea salt and a grinding of black pepper.

2 Season the cavity of the duck with salt and a grinding of pepper. Put in a spoonful each of crème fraîche and brandy. Using a stiff pastry brush, paint the outside of the duck with the juice mixture. Place the bird breast-side down on a rack in a roasting pan.

3 Roast for 30 minutes. Take the bird out of the oven, turn it breast-side up, baste and season again. Roast for 10 minutes, then reduce the oven temperature to 160°C/325°F/gas3. Continue roasting for about 50 minutes, basting several times. Add the peaches to the roasting pan and continue cooking for 10 minutes. At the end of roasting, check that the juices run clear when you pierce the inside of the duck's leg with a skewer.

4 Arrange the peaches on a warmed serving dish. Tip or spoon the creamy juices from the cavity into the roasting pan. Put the duck on the serving dish and leave to settle in a warm place while you make the sauce.

5 Put the roasting pan over a high heat, add 4 or 5 tablespoons of water and leave to bubble for a few minutes, stirring frequently, until reduced and thickened. Stir in the rest of the brandy, reduce the heat and stir for a minute. Then stir in the rest of the crème fraîche, adjust the seasoning and strain the sauce into a small warmed sauce boat. Serve as soon as possible, with the duck.

To drink: an Alsace Pinot Gris.

MAGRETS DE CANARD À L'ORANGE
Duck Breast Fillets with Orange Sauce

The bitter-sweet sauce is also excellent with chicken or pork chops and escalopes. If bitter oranges are available, use the juice of a small orange (or more) instead of a lime.

Serves 4
Preparation: 5 minutes
Cooking: 20 minutes

2 large boned duck breasts, each weighing
300-350g/10½-12 oz
1 generous tsp rubbed thyme
⅓ tsp mixed spice or ground cinnamon
1½ tbsp small thin finely pared strips of orange zest, plus the juice of 2 oranges
juice of ½ lime, or more if preferred
1 tbsp brandy
1 tsp cornflour
3 tbsp Cointreau
15g/½ oz chilled butter
sea salt and freshly ground black pepper

1 Using a small sharp knife, score the skin of the duck breasts a few times in parallel lines deeply enough to cut into the flesh. Season with salt and freshly ground black pepper, then rub in the thyme and mixed spice or cinnamon.

2 Heat a sauté pan until hot. Put the breasts in the hot pan skin-side down over a moderate to high heat. Cook for 10–12 minutes, reducing the heat a little after 8 minutes or so, if the skin chars too much. If the duck breasts are very fatty, tip out some of the fat from the pan as they cook.

3 Meanwhile, in a small saucepan, blanch the strips of orange zest for 2–3 minutes in a little boiling water. Drain well. Pour the orange and lime juice into the pan and heat through gently over a low heat.

4 Sprinkle the duck breasts with brandy. Turn them over (they should be well seized and golden brown), reduce the heat a little and cook the flesh for about 5 minutes or a little longer if you prefer (the timing will depend on how pink or well done you like your duck). Remove the breasts from the pan and keep them warm on a warmed serving dish in a turned-off or very low oven.

5 Pour out most of the fat from the pan and stir in the cornflour. Stir for a minute, then add the hot orange and lime juice, together with the drained blanched zest strips. Stir for a couple of minutes over a moderate heat, until simmering, then add the Cointreau and adjust the seasoning with a little extra pepper. Whisk in the chilled butter, then dribble the sauce over the duck breasts and serve immediately.

To drink: a Bordeaux.

LE COQ AU VIN

Chicken in Red Wine

Serves 4-6
Preparation: about 15 minutes
Cooking: about 1 hour, plus reheating

115g/4oz thick-cut smoked streaky
bacon, cut into small pieces
1½ tbsp oil
45g/1½ oz butter
8 small white onions, peeled, or the white
parts of 8 large spring onions
2 shallots, finely chopped
1 tsp ground dried thyme
½ tsp rubbed sage
1 large free-range chicken, jointed
4 tbsp brandy, plus 2 tsp to finish the
sauce
1 heaped tbsp flour
1 bottle (750ml/27fl oz) full-bodied
red wine
2 garlic cloves, crushed
1 large carrot, peeled, halved lengthwise
and sliced
30g/1oz bitter chocolate (optional, but
recommended)
several sprigs of parsley
1 bay leaf
about 285g/10oz small brown
mushrooms, wiped and sliced
sea salt and freshly ground
black pepper

No French kitchen is complete without at least one of the big black cast-iron cooking pots known as *cocottes*. With their thick heavy bases and sides, rounded edges, high sides and tight-fitting lids, these traditional pans are perfect for one-pot cooking. They can seize ingredients over a fierce heat, then simmer them tenderly for hours, are capacious enough to accommodate soups and conduct heat delicately enough for sauces. A proper *coq au vin* is one of the really great triumphs of *cocotte* cooking.

Coq au vin tastes fuller and more mellow if allowed to cool and then re-heated, and is best made in the morning for the evening or even the day before serving.

1 First blanch the bacon for a minute in simmering water (this too can be done in the cocotte or casserole). Drain well on paper towels.

2 Now put your cocotte, flameproof casserole dish or large sauté pan over a moderate to high heat and tip in the oil. Divide the butter into 4 pieces, put one piece in the pot and chill the rest.

3 As soon as the oil and butter start to sizzle, add the bacon, onions and shallots. Reduce the heat a little and sauté until lightly coloured (golden

SAUTÉ THE BACON, ONIONS AND SHALLOTS OVER A MODERATE HEAT UNTIL JUST GOLDEN.

rather than brown), stirring frequently. Lift out of the pot with a slotted spoon and set aside on a double layer of paper towel.

4 In a bowl, combine the dried thyme and sage and season lightly with salt and pepper. Rub this mixture over the chicken pieces. Put these in the pot and sauté until golden, turning over the pieces after a few minutes so that they colour evenly. Also shake the pan to prevent the chicken from sticking.

LIGHTLY BROWN THE SEASONED CHICKEN PIECES, MAKING SURE THEY DON'T STICK TO THE PAN.

5 Warm the brandy over a low heat in a small pan. As soon as the chicken is tinged with gold, pour over the brandy and carefully set alight with a long match. When the flames subside, use a small sieve to sprinkle the flour over the chicken. Sauté for a minute to cook the flour, stirring well. Return the bacon and onion mixture to the pan.

6 Now pour in the wine. Stir, then add the prepared garlic, carrot, and the chocolate, if using (it will help the dish acquire a deep colour and taste). Stir again, then scatter in a few sprigs of parsley and the bay leaf.

7 Turn up the heat and bring to a fast simmer, stirring and shaking the pot several times. Once you are sure that all the wine has reached the point at which it bubbles, cover and reduce the heat to low. Cook for 40 minutes or until the chicken pieces are just cooked through, stirring a few times and occasionally shaking the pot.

8 While the chicken is cooking, heat a second piece of butter in a frying pan and sauté the sliced mushrooms for a few minutes. Drain them well on paper towel and add to the pot.

DRIBBLE THE WARMED BRANDY OVER THE CHICKEN AND CAREFULLY SET ALIGHT.

9 Adjust the seasoning of the dish and allow to cool completely if not serving immediately. Reheat very gently, adding a little extra wine or water if necessary — but not too much.

ADDING A LITTLE BITTER CHOCOLATE DEEPENS THE FLAVOUR AND ADDS COLOUR.

10 Just before serving, transfer the chicken pieces to a warmed serving dish or keep them warm on a plate and return to the pot when you have finished the sauce. Discard the parsley and bay leaf. Turn up the heat and reduce the sauce by about one-third, stirring and scraping with a wooden spoon. Cut the butter into dice, then whisk these vigorously into the sauce. Sprinkle in the reserved brandy and adjust the seasoning.

11 Return the chicken to the pot or pour the sauce over the chicken, scraping the pot well not to waste any. Snip over a little parsley and serve as soon as possible. Fresh egg noodles (see page 151), plain rice, buttered gnocchi or boiled potatoes are all suitable accompaniments.

VARIATIONS: the dish is best made with a free-range or black-legged bird, both less fatty-skinned than their yellow corn-fed colleagues, and with a robust good-quality red wine — say a red Burgundy, Madiran or Shiraz. In

WHISK IN CHILLED BUTTER TO THICKEN THE SAUCE AND GIVE IT GLOSS.

fact – and this may sound extravagant – to make a generous beautiful *coq au vin,* you may as well be prepared to spend almost as much on the wine as on the chicken. It is the unadulterated red wine that gives the dish its unique colour. If you are using a mixture of wine and water or wine and stock, you will have a perfectly enjoyable chicken casserole but not a genuine *coq au vin.*

Coq au vin blanc is a delicious golden variation, apparently once very popular with the late Georges Simenon: Madame Maigret makes a *coq au vin* to which the Chief Inspector must love to come home. She uses equal amounts of Riesling and light chicken stock, and adds a chopped leek and a pinch of nutmeg to the pot. She thickens the reduced sauce with an egg and cream liaison (see page 7) and finishes off the dish with a spoonful of lemon juice and plum eau-de-vie.

A dry (but not bone-dry) farmhouse cider is a good alternative cooking medium. Flame with calvados if available, then add a few wedges of cabbage, use the cider instead of wine and replace the mushrooms with sautéed apples in step 8.

To drink: a Côte de Beaune, Montagny or the wine used to cook the chicken.

GIBELOTTE DE LAPIN
Pot-roasted Rabbit

Use as many different herbs as you have to hand for this aromatic pot roast. Rabbit is not to everyone's liking, but this recipe is just as flavoursome and pleasingly textured if you use chicken thighs. The cabbage leaves keep the dish moist and can be replaced by a layer of mushroom or tomato slices covered with foil at the end of step 5.

Serves 4
Preparation: 10 minutes, plus marinating
Cooking: about 1 hour

4-6 skinned rabbit pieces, rinsed and wiped dry,
or 8 skinned chicken thighs
4 large cabbage leaves
6 small slices of streaky bacon
5tbsp each dry white wine and chicken stock or
water
15g/ 1/2 oz butter or cream
sea salt and freshly ground black pepper

FOR THE MARINADE:
2 garlic cloves, crushed
2 shallots, finely chopped
1 1/2 tsp grated lemon zest
2tbsp finely snipped parsley
1tbsp finely snipped basil leaves
few leaves of fresh coriander, finely snipped, or
1tsp ground coriander
1/2 tsp each dried thyme and rosemary
4tbsp olive oil

1 Put all the marinade ingredients in a food processor and whizz for a moment until you have a rough paste.

2 Pour the marinade over the rabbit or chicken in a large heatproof dish and toss until well coated. Season generously with pepper and lightly with salt. Cover and leave to marinate in a cool place for a few hours or overnight in the refrigerator.

3 About 1 hour before you intend to eat, preheat the oven to 200°C/400°F/gas6. Bring a kettle of water to the boil. Pour the boiling water into a saucepan and place over a moderate heat.

4 Blanch the cabbage leaves in the boiling water for 2 minutes. Drain well on paper towel. In the still simmering water, blanch the bacon for 30 seconds and drain well on paper towel.

5 Turn the rabbit or chicken pieces over and season again. Cover with the drained cabbage leaves and put in the oven. Cook for 30 minutes, then take out of the oven.

6 Baste well with the cooking juices, then add half the wine mixed with stock. Lay the blanched bacon strips on top of the cabbage and return to the oven. Reduce the heat to 180°C/350°F/gas4 and continue cooking for 20–30 minutes, until cooked through and tender. Leave to settle for a few minutes in the turned-off oven.

7 To serve: arrange the cabbage leaves on a warmed serving dish, and place the rabbit or chicken on top. Snip the cooked bacon and scatter over. Keep warm.

8 Pour the cooking liquid into a small saucepan, add the rest of the wine and stock mixture and simmer over a low heat for 2 minutes. Adjust the seasoning, whisk in the butter or cream and strain (or pour directly) over the rabbit or chicken.

To drink: a Chardonnay or Vin de Pays du Jardin de la France, Normandy cider or Alsace beer.

Variation: replace the white wine in the sauce with dry cider or lager.

LAPIN À LA MOUTARDE
Rabbit in Mustard Sauce

This classic dish accommodates many a variation, but there are two pitfalls it cannot survive: one is a *moutarde* overkill — too much mustard too early will overpower the flavour of the meat; the other danger is an excess of heat which will spoil the final texture and taste of the rabbit. A coarse-grain mustard combines happily with the crème fraîche and is less cloying than the more usual blend of Dijon mustard and butter.

If you want to cook this dish in advance, prepare until the end of step 5, reducing the overall cooking time by 5-10 minutes. Chill or freeze, then reheat gently and finish the dish as below. If you are not a rabbit lover, try the same recipe with pork noisettes or thick chops (the timing will remain the same for the chops and be less for the noisettes).

Serves 4
Preparation: 10 minutes
Cooking: 1 hour

1 scant tbsp rubbed thyme
4-6 skinned rabbit pieces, rinsed and wiped dry
1 tbsp flour
1½ tbsp oil
30g/ 1oz butter
1 soft white onion, finely chopped
2 cloves
2tsp Dijon mustard
100ml/ 3½ fl oz dry white wine
3tbsp brandy
4 generous tbsp crème fraîche or soured cream
1—2 scant tbsp moutarde à l'ancienne or coarse-grain mustard
few sprigs of chervil or parsley, to garnish
sea salt and freshly ground black pepper

1 Sprinkle the dried thyme over the rabbit pieces and press in well. Season the flour lightly with salt and more generously with pepper. Tip into a small sieve or tea strainer and sprinkle over the rabbit pieces.

2 Heat the oil and butter in a large sauté pan over a moderate heat. Sauté the rabbit pieces with the chopped onion and the cloves for a few minutes over a moderate heat, turning the rabbit over regularly. Reduce the heat a little as soon as the rabbit has coloured.

3 Combine the Dijon mustard with the white wine. Add to the pan, stir, cover and cook over a low heat for about 45 minutes until tender and almost ready to flake apart (the exact timing will depend on the rabbit you are using). Shake the pan occasionally and turn over the rabbit pieces once or twice, keeping the heat low throughout.

4 When the rabbit is cooked, warm the brandy and dribble it over the pieces. Set alight with a long match (if it refuses to flame, just heat through for a minute to cook in the brandy).

5 Lift the rabbit pieces and the onion from the pan and keep warm on a warmed serving dish while you make the sauce.

6 In a bowl, combine the crème fraîche with the coarse grain mustard. Tip into the pan and whisk over a low heat for 2–3 minutes, until hot and blended into the pan juices.

7 Dribble the sauce over the rabbit. Snip over a little chervil or parsley and serve immediately.

To drink: Chiroubles.

(RIGHT) Lapin à la Moutarde *served with* Lentilles Tièdes à l'Huile de Noix et au Persil *(page 150).*

Poulet Rôti aux Aromates *served with a portion of* Gratin Dauphinois *(page 132).*

POULET RÔTI AUX AROMATES
Roast Chicken with Herbs

The herb mixture is a flexible one, but I always include fresh parsley and one pungent dried herb. Dried sage and savory work well. A friend from the South-West of France put me on to coating chickens with a little goose fat — it does give the skin extra crispness and somehow makes the most boring bird taste like authentic farmyard-reared poultry.

Lovers of garlic may like to serve this (or plain) roast chicken with an easy *Purée d'Ail*. Put each of 4 heads of fresh garlic in the centre of a large piece of foil, dribble over a teaspoon or two of olive oil, season lightly and bring up the edges of the foil to make a loose but well sealed parcel. Place in the pan and roast with the chicken. Leave to cool a little, then squeeze each garlic clove between your thumb and index finger to extract the garlic purée. Adjust the seasoning, add a dribble of oil or cream and serve with the chicken. This garlic purée is also splendid with *Gigot d'Agneau* (page 118).

Serves 4
Preparation: 15 minutes
Cooking: about 1½ hours, then
10 minutes' resting

1 tsp dried thyme
½ tsp each of dried marjoram or oregano and savory or rosemary
several sprigs each of parsley and chervil, finely snipped, plus extra to finish
1 garlic clove, crushed
1 tsp finely grated lemon zest
55g/2oz soft butter
1 corn-fed or free-range chicken weighing about 1.5kg/3½ lb, wiped clean and at room temperature
1½ tbsp olive oil or goose fat
6 tbsp dry white wine
sea salt and freshly ground black pepper

1 Heat the oven to 230°C/450°F/gas8. In a cup, combine the herbs, garlic and lemon zest with half the butter. Season with sea salt and a generous grinding of pepper.

2 Spoon half of the butter mixture into the cavity of the chicken. Stir the olive oil or goose fat into the rest of the seasoned butter. Using a small spatula, pastry brush or palette knife, smear the mixture all over the outside of the chicken and season again.

3 Place the bird on its side on a rack in a roasting pan. Roast for 10 minutes, then turn the chicken on to its other side and roast for a further 10 minutes. Turn the chicken breast-side up and roast for a further 10 minutes, then reduce the heat to 180°C/350°F/gas4 and continue roasting for about 1¼ hours. Baste with the cooking juices from time to time.

4 Before you turn off the oven, push a skewer into the thickest part of the inside leg of the chicken to check that the cooking juices are running clear. Drain the cavity juices (they too should be golden and clear) into the pan and leave the bird to rest on a warmed serving dish while you make the sauce.

5 Tip some of the fat from the pan, place the pan over a high heat and pour in the wine. Boil until reduced by one-third, then add 2 tablespoons of water. Sprinkle with extra snipped fresh herbs and stir until bubbling. Adjust the seasoning if necessary, stir in the rest of the butter and pour into a small warmed sauce boat. Serve the chicken as soon as possible.

To drink: a Beaujolais or Gamay de Touraine.

LE CHAUD-FROID DE POULET

Aspic-glazed Chicken in White Sauce

Serves 8
Preparation: several hours (off and on)
the day before
Cooking: about 1 hour

8 chicken suprêmes
white parts of 3 leeks, washed and sliced
3 shallots, coarsely chopped
¹/₂ Spanish onion, chopped
few sprigs each of parsley, chervil and
tarragon
several strips of lemon zest and the juice
of ¹/₂ lemon
6 black peppercorns
300ml/¹/₂pt dry white wine
1 sachet (25g/³/₄oz) of good-quality
aspic powder
55g/2oz butter
55g/2oz flour
175ml/6fl oz thick cream
sea salt and freshly ground black pepper

TO DECORATE:
several sprigs of chervil
1 sachet (25g/³/₄oz) good-quality aspic
powder
1 tbsp Madeira, white wine, lemon or
orange juice, to flavour, if required

Chaud means hot, *froid* is cold and a *chaud-froid de poulet* is poached chicken coated in a veritable party frock of gleaming pale sauce. The beauty of *chaud-froid* is that it is a very impressive – but inexpensive – safe buffet centrepiece dish, which can be prepared the day before and is 99% ready to be put on the table and served at the last minute.

1 Early on the day before you intend to serve the chaud-froid, place the suprêmes in a large heavy saucepan, squat fish kettle or cocotte. Add the prepared leeks, shallots and onion to the pot as well as the parsley, a few sprigs of tarragon, strips of lemon zest and peppercorns. Pour in the white wine, then top up with enough cold water to cover the suprêmes. Season lightly with salt and freshly ground black pepper.

2 Bring to a boil over a low heat, skimming off any scummy foam that comes up to the surface. Simmer for about 20 minutes, still over a low heat, then lift out the suprêmes. Check that they are cooked through – if they are still a little pink inside, return them to the pot for a few minutes. Leave them to cool in the cooking liquid. Make plenty of space in your refrigerator.

POACH THE SUPRÊMES
SIDE BY SIDE WITH THE
FLAVOURINGS AND WINE.

3 Once the suprêmes are cool enough to handle, lift them out of the pot and drain well. Leave to get cold, then refrigerate until needed.

4 Meanwhile, carefully strain the stock into a clean saucepan through a sieve lined with muslin and set aside in a cool place. You will use it in the chaud-froid sauce.

5 Ladle off the surface fat from the cooled chicken stock and bring the stock to the boil over a moderate heat. Partly cover and leave to bubble until reduced (you will need about 850ml/1¹/₂ pts – for the sauce and the aspic). When the stock is reduced, prepare about 175ml/6fl oz of liquid aspic jelly, using that quantity of stock and a whole packet of powder (it will be diluted still further with the creamy white sauce) and following the instructions on the packaging.

STRAIN THE STOCK
THROUGH A MUSLIN-
LINED SIEVE.

6 Make the white sauce: melt the butter in a separate heavy saucepan, add the flour and cook for 1 minute over a moderate heat, stirring vigorously until you have a pale roux. Whisk in the remaining hot stock, then bring to a

simmer, still whisking very frequently. Reduce the heat and simmer for about 10 minutes, stirring occasionally. Adjust the seasoning. If at all lumpy, strain through a fine sieve.

7 Remove from the heat and allow to cool a little, stirring occasionally. Whisk in the cream and lemon juice, then the liquid aspic, whisking constantly until combined. Strain through a fine sieve into a bowl and leave to get cold and a little syrupy. The ideal working texture is that of raw egg white.

STIR THE CREAM INTO THE COOLED SAUCE, FOLLOWED BY THE LEMON JUICE AND LIQUID ASPIC.

8 Pat the suprêmes dry with paper towel and trim off any untidy bits. Put over a wire rack on top of a big gratin dish. Using a large metal spoon or a small ladle, carefully coat the chicken with the sauce. You should have some sauce left. Transfer the lot – chicken, rack and dish – to the refrigerator and chill until the first layer is set, then repeat the process.

TRIM THE SUPRÊMES SO THAT THEY LOOK NEAT.

9 Chill the coated chicken for several hours or overnight until the chaud-froid sauce is well set.

10 Decorate the dish before serving: the simplest option is to transfer the chicken to a serving dish and to scatter over tarragon and chervil.

11 For a more festive presentation: at least 2 hours before (or the night before) make some chicken aspic to a syrupy consistency following the instructions on the packet, but flavour with a little Madeira, white wine, lemon or orange juice. Now select pretty sprigs of chervil, dip them in the jelly and arrange them carefully on the chicken. Chill the chicken until needed. Adjust the seasoning of the aspic, pour into a shallow bowl and chill until set.

SPOON THE COATING OVER THE SUPRÊMES, CATCHING SPILLS FOR A SECOND COATING.

12 When ready to serve, using a spatula or fish slice, carefully lift the chicken on to an serving dish. Chop up the jellied aspic and spoon attractively around and between the chicken. Decorate with small sprigs of chervil. Serve as soon as possible, immediately if warm.

13 Serve with hot lightly buttered long-grain rice (flavoured with a handful of pine nuts and a pinch of saffron) and a mixed leaf salad or a medley of warm light-ly cooked spring vegetables, such as asparagus, broad beans and baby green beans.

To drink: a Saint-Véran or Pouilly-Vinzelles.

VARIATIONS: *chaud-froid* sauce using fish fumet or veal stock instead of chicken stock makes an elegant dress for poached salmon, veal chops (gently sauté the meat in butter until cooked but not browned).

PETIT CONFIT DE CUISSES DE POULET
Preserved Chicken Legs

This modest 'mini *confit*' is quick and easy to prepare. You can double the quantities (if you like, top up the goose fat with lard) and store what you don't serve immediately in the refrigerator for future use. Put the cooked chicken in a clean glass jar or earthenware pot, cover with a generous layer of strained goose fat (no meat should surface) and eat within 3 weeks. To re-heat, sauté gently in a little goose fat in a frying pan until hot and browned.

Goose fat is a precious commodity: strain what is left into a clean glass jar, cover and refrigerate until you can use it in other recipes. A tablespoon or two gives a great gutsy flavour to omelettes, vegetables and poultry dishes. It is also worth trying when sautéing or roasting salmon (see page 87).

Serves 4
Preparation: 10 minutes, plus 36 hours'
marinating
Cooking: 50 minutes

1 tbsp sugar
1 tbsp fine sea salt
1 tsp each dried rubbed thyme and sage
¼ tsp each grated nutmeg and five-spice powder
2-3 garlic cloves, crushed
4 fresh chicken leg portions
700g/ 1²/₃ lb goose fat (or a mixture of goose fat and good-quality lard)
freshly ground black pepper

TO SERVE:
450g/ 1lb unpeeled potatoes, parboiled, peeled and sliced, or a sharp green salad

1 In a bowl, mix together the sugar, salt, dried herbs, nutmeg and garlic. With a small sharp knife, make a few deep slits in each chicken leg. Press the mixture well into the chicken pieces, rubbing well so that it goes into the flesh. Season lightly with pepper.

2 Cover the bowl and refrigerate for 36 hours, occasionally turning the pieces over.

3 Wipe the chicken pieces clean with a cloth or paper towel. Heat the goose fat in a heavy saucepan until small bubbles appear. Tip the chicken into this simmering fat and cook over a low heat for 40–45 minutes, or until you can easily pierce a leg with a metal skewer.

4 Carefully lift the chicken pieces out of the hot fat with a slotted spoon. Drain well on paper towels. Keep warm while you fry the parboiled potato slices in the hot goose fat until crisp and golden. You can also sauté the potatoes in 1 or 2 tablespoons of fat. If you prefer, serve the confit cold with a sharp green salad.

To drink: a Bergerac or Côtes-de-Duras.

TERRINE DE FAISAN
Pheasant Terrine

You will find that this lengthy recipe is not as demanding as it may at first seem. It is actually an ideal afternoon's good kitchen fun on a wintry weekend. The unopened terrine will keep for up to a week in the refrigerator and leftovers for 2-3 days. If pheasant is not available or to your liking, use guinea fowl or free-range chicken instead. Serve with toast, unsalted butter, small gherkins and pickled onions or Marmelade d'Oignons (page 148) and a green salad.

Serves 8
Preparation: 1 hour
Cooking: about 3 hours, plus cooling and overnight chilling

breast fillets, coarsely chopped meat and liver, and chopped up bones of 1 plump pheasant hen
about 450g/1lb lean spare rib of pork, boned and trimmed, bones reserved and chopped
1 carrot, peeled and chopped
1 small head of celery, trimmed and chopped
1/2 Spanish onion, chopped
1 1/2 tbsp oil
about 55g/2oz chicken livers, trimmed and chopped
2tsp dried thyme
2tsp rubbed sage
1 scant tbsp finely grated orange zest
2 garlic cloves
3-4tbsp brandy
2 large or 3 small eggs, plus the whites and shells of 3 extra eggs for clarifying the aspic
450ml/3/4pt chicken or veal stock
300ml/3/4pt dry white wine
4tbsp Madeira
few drained green peppercorns
6 slices of rindless smoked streaky bacon
115g/4oz shelled pistachios, chopped
sea salt and freshly ground black pepper

1 Start making the aspic: put all the pheasant and pork bones into a sauté pan and add the carrot, celery and onion. Sprinkle with the oil and brown over a moderate to high heat for about 40 minutes, occasionally shaking the pan.

2 While the bones are browning, mince or quickly process the chopped pheasant meat (reserving the breast fillets) and liver, pork and chicken livers with the thyme, sage, orange zest and garlic.

3 Season the minced meat mixture with a little salt and more generously with freshly ground black pepper. Stir in the brandy, followed by the eggs and work the mixture well, preferably with your hands. Cover and leave to stand for 1 or 2 hours.

4 Using a slotted spoon, remove the bones and vegetable mixture from the pan and put on a double layer of paper towel to get rid of the excess fat. Drain and wipe the pan.

5 Return the bones and vegetables to the pan, add the stock, white wine, Madeira and a few green peppercorns. Cover with 450ml/3/4pt cold water and slowly bring to the boil, skimming off the greasy foam as it surfaces. Partly cover and simmer for 1 hour, skimming occasionally.

6 With a slotted spoon, lift off and discard most of the bones and vegetables. Strain the stock and remaining bits into a clean pan through a sieve lined with muslin.

7 For a clear aspic, quickly clarify the stock: in a bowl, whisk together the whites and crushed shells of 3 eggs and whisk this mixture into the hot liquid. Strain again through a fine sieve lined with clean muslin. Now turn up the heat and reduce this fine stock until you have about 550ml/1pt liquid aspic. Reserve.

8 Meanwhile, preheat the oven to 160°C/325°F/gas3. Stretch the bacon slices with the help of a rolling pin wrapped in cling film or the back of a knife. Line the base of a terrine dish or loaf tin (it should be able to hold a good 1.75 litres/3pt) with 3 bacon slices, then spread in one-third of the meat and egg mixture. Sprinkle with half the prepared pistachios. Cut the breast fillets into long strips. Lay half of these over the meat layer. Cover with a second

layer of meat mixture and lay the rest of the breast strips on top. Sprinkle with the rest of the pistachios and spread the remaining meat mixture on top, then cover with the remaining bacon slices.

9 Cover the dish tightly. Bring a kettle of water to the boil and line the centre of a large roasting pan with a thick layer of old newspapers. Place the terrine dish on top and pour in enough boiling water to come halfway up the sides of the dish. Put the pan in the oven and bake for a good 2 hours, pouring in more boiling water as necessary. Also turn around the dish from time to time so that the terrine cooks evenly.

10 Leave the terrine to relax in the oven for about 20 minutes after you turn off the heat. Remove from the oven, take off the cover and leave for several minutes. Carefully lift the top slices of bacon from the terrine.

(ABOVE) *Served with toast and cornichons,* Terrine de Faisan *makes an excellent starter or snack.*

11 Pierce the terrine deeply in several places with a skewer. If it is too jellied to pour, reheat the aspic and pour into the terrine. Leave to get cold and chill overnight before serving.

To drink: a Rully or Chinon.

FRICASSÉE DE PINTADE AU VINAIGRE DE XÉRÈS ET À L'ESTRAGON

Guinea Fowl with Sherry and Tarragon Cream

The partnership of poultry and tarragon needs little introduction and sherry vinegar is, I believe, purchased by the French in larger volumes than sherry wine. In this recipe, the guinea fowl pieces simmer on top of the stove in tarragon-scented stock and require only a few minutes of actual work. Serve with plain rice and Sautéed Courgettes (page 138). Free-range chicken can be used instead of guinea fowl.

Serves 4
Preparation: 5 minutes
Cooking: about 50 minutes

1 tbsp flour
1 plump guinea fowl or free-range chicken, jointed into 6-8 pieces, or assorted free-range pieces, skinned
1¹⁄₂ tbsp groundnut or sunflower oil
30g/1oz chilled unsalted butter, diced
2tsp finely grated zest and 4tbsp juice from an orange
2tsp brandy
bunch of fresh tarragon sprigs
200ml/7fl oz chicken stock
1tbsp sherry vinegar
2tbsp crème fraîche
sea salt and freshly ground black pepper

1 Season the flour with salt and a good grinding of pepper. Using a small sieve, dust the guinea fowl or chicken pieces with this seasoned flour.

2 Heat the oil in a sauté pan large enough to take the pieces in a single layer. Add one-third of the butter, then stir in the grated orange zest. Tip in the guinea fowl or chicken pieces and sauté over a moderate heat until lightly and evenly coloured, turning them over a few times.

3 Sprinkle in the brandy and stir in well. Snip in the leaves from 5 or 6 tarragon sprigs, then shake the pan and stir the contents.

4 Add the stock, turn over the pieces and stir well. Bring back to a modest simmer, then lower the heat a little. Cover tightly and cook for 30–40 minutes, shaking the pan several times and turning over the pieces halfway through cooking.

5 Lift the cooked guinea fowl or chicken from the pan and keep warm on a warmed serving dish.

6 Turn up the heat, bring the liquid to a low boil and leave to bubble for a few minutes until a little reduced and thickened, stirring from time to time.

7 Reduce the heat, stir in the vinegar and the orange juice. The dish can be cooked ahead to this stage if more convenient.

8 A few minutes before serving, stir in the crème fraîche. Return the guinea fowl or chicken to the pan and stir to coat. Reheat over a low heat if necessary. Adjust the seasoning, snip in several more tarragon leaves and stir.

9 Now, using a slotted spoon, put the guinea fowl or chicken pieces back on the warmed serving dish. Whisk the remaining butter into the pan and dribble the sauce over the chicken. Snip over a few fresh tarragon leaves and serve immediately.

Variation: *poulet au madère* is a recommended variation: replace the sherry vinegar, orange and tarragon with 1 tablespoon of crushed green peppercorns (adding half in step 3, the rest in step 7) and 3 tablespoons of Madeira (also in step 7).

To drink: a medium-dry Vouvray.

OIE À L'ALSACIENNE
Goose with Sauerkraut

Sauerkraut, *choucroute*, makes a good accompaniment to goose. If you prefer, roast the goose – having first seasoned and spiced it liberally. Allow a good 30 minutes per 450g/1lb in a moderate oven, then 20 minutes' relaxing time in the turned-off oven. Degrease the pan juices and baste the bird regularly during roasting to keep it moist. Serve on the bed of *choucroute*.

Serves 8
Preparation: 20 minutes
Cooking: about 2¹/₂ hours

550g/1¹/₄ lb lean mild-cure boiling ham,
pre-soaked
1tbsp goose fat or oil
1 young goose, weighing about 3kg/6¹/₂ lb,
jointed
1 Spanish onion, coarsely chopped
30g/1oz flour
700ml/1¹/₄ pt dry white wine mixed with
chicken stock
2 bay leaves
2tsp mixed spice
1tsp juniper berries
few sprigs of parsley, plus extra for serving
1 scant tbsp rubbed thyme
1kg/2¹/₄ lb canned or bottled sauerkraut
30g/1oz butter
2 shallots, finely chopped
white parts of 3 large spring onions, sliced
8 good-quality Strasbourg or Frankfurter
sausages (optional)
900g/2lb unpeeled potatoes, boiled and peeled
(optional)
salt and freshly ground black pepper

1 First prepare the ham: put it in a saucepan, cover with cold water and bring to a simmer over a low heat. Simmer very gently for about 25 minutes, keeping the heat very low. Drain, leave until cool enough to handle, then cut off the rind and fatty layer. Cut the meat into thick slices and reserve.

2 Using a wad of paper towel, coat a large casserole dish with goose fat or oil. Place over a moderate to high heat. Add the pieces of goose to the hot pan and sauté until browned and well seized, turning the pieces over a few times.

3 Lift out the pieces of goose and reserve. Tip in the chopped onion and cook for a few minutes, stirring frequently, until golden. Return the goose to the pan. Sprinkle with the flour, stir for a minute, then pour in the wine and stock. If necessary, top up with just enough water to cover the goose. Add the bay leaves, mixed spice, juniper berries and herbs. Season lightly. Reduce the heat, cover tightly and simmer very gently for about 1 hour, skimming off surface fatty deposits with a spoon or small ladle from time to time.

4 Add the slices of ham, stir and turn over the goose and cook for another 30 minutes.

5 Lift out the goose, ham and onion and keep warm. Degrease the cooking liquid. Strain into a bowl, stand this over iced water and leave for a moment. With a spoon or small ladle, scoop out and discard the fat which has come up to the surface.

6 Rinse and drain the sauerkraut, then squeeze out any moisture.

7 Put the pan over a moderate heat, add the butter and melt it. Tip in the prepared shallots and spring onions, sauté for a minute, then put in two-thirds of the sauerkraut. Stir and season lightly. Put the goose and ham on top, moisten with a little degreased cooking liquid and top up with the rest of the sauerkraut. Add the sausages and cooked potatoes, if using, and moisten again with a little liquid. Adjust the seasoning, cover and heat through gently until everything is piping hot.

8 To serve, skim and reheat the cooking liquid. Arrange the sauerkraut, goose and ham with the sausages and potatoes, if using, on a warmed serving platter. Moisten with a little more liquid, scatter over a little snipped parsley and serve at once. (Chill any leftover stock and discard the congealed fatty lid before using in another recipe.)

To drink: an Alsace Riesling or Pinot Gris.

Chapter Seven

LES VIANDES

Meat

The French like their meat.
True, they don't consume vast portions of it;
but eat it they do, a little at a time and regularly.
France is a nation of carnivores and, for most people, a main meal without meat is a meal without a
heart. When it comes to preparing meat, there is a
sharp distinction between prime cuts which are
cooked over a high heat for as brief a time as possible, and other cuts which are slowly simmered. As
a result, the frying pan and the stewing pot, *la poêle
et la cocotte*, are favoured utensils. Beef steak, in one
of its many forms — *bifteck, onglet,
rumsteck, tournedos, steak haché* — is almost a symbol
of everyday French meat eating. Seized in the pan
(occasionally on a
griddle) with a little fat, in a technique somewhere
between grilling and frying, it is often plainly
served with its cooking juices. When it is dressed
up (and it often is, for it is ubiquitous — equally at
home in the school canteen and in smart bistros),
le steak is complemented by a quick reduction, a
beurre composé or an elaborate sauce (see the chapter on Sauces, pages 28-41).

LEFT
Cassoulet (page 112) is a magnificent
winter warmer and makes a superb party dish
any time between Hallowe'en and Easter.

CASSOULET
Pork and Bean Stew

The following recipe tastes authentic and is less fatty than most. With one exception, it can be prepared from widely available ingredients – the one ingredient you will have to buy at a specialist shop (or bring back in your suitcase from a French holiday) is the essential can of goose or duck *confit*, with its lovely salt fat and unique flavour. Prepare and assemble your cassoulet one or two days ahead (or freeze) for optimum taste, leaving out the sausages – which can be grilled and dunked into the beans on the day.

Serve as a *plat unique* (one-pot meal), with plenty of bread and a green salad. Drink with Madiran, Cahors or Fitou. A fruit salad or sorbet would be nice to follow.

Serves about 12
Preparation: 15 minutes
Cooking: about 3 hours (in stages)

1kg/ 2¼ lb white haricot beans
1 or 2 meaty pork knuckles, rinsed
1 large bouquet garni
1 Spanish onion stuck with a few cloves
2 large carrots, peeled and halved lengthwise
12 black peppercorns
350g/ 12oz smoked belly of pork
675g/ 1½ lb or more canned goose or duck confit
3 onions, chopped
6 garlic cloves, crushed, plus 2 extra crushed cloves for the crust (optional)
4 tbsp brandy
550ml/ 1pt beef or chicken stock
1tbsp dried ground thyme
1tbsp Dijon mustard (optional)
few drops of Worcestershire sauce (optional)
at least 8 strong herby country sausages, preferably Toulouse
75g/ 2½ oz white breadcrumbs
4tbsp chopped parsley
freshly ground black pepper

1 Rinse the haricot beans and put them in a large pan with plenty of cold water. Bring to the boil and simmer for 10 minutes over a moderate heat. Then drain and rinse.

2 Rinse the large pan and put in the rinsed beans and pork knuckle. Cover with fresh water and add the bouquet garni, onion stuck with cloves, carrots and peppercorns. Bring to a simmer. Reduce the heat a little and simmer gently, half-covered, for about 1½ hours until the beans are cooked but still a little firm. Skim from time to time.

3 Meanwhile, in a separate pan, blanch the smoked belly of pork for 5 minutes in boiling water. Drain, leave to cool for a few minutes, then cut into thick slices.

4 Now put a tablespoon of goose or duck fat from the confit in a sauté pan. Place over a moderate heat, tip the chopped onion into the hot fat and stir for a few minutes until browned. Cut up the goose or duck confit into small pieces, draining off the excess fat (reserve for later use). Any leg or breast bones can go into the bean mixture.

5 Stir the pieces of confit into the browned onion. Add the crushed garlic and the slices of smoked belly, sprinkle with the brandy and cook for a few minutes, stirring occasionally. Then pour in the stock, add the thyme, the mustard and Worcestershire sauce, if using. Season with a little black pepper and cook over a very low heat for 20–30 minutes, stirring from time to time.

6 Preheat the grill to high, then reduce the heat and very slowly grill the sausages until crisp all over and cooked through. Cut into chunks no longer than 4cm/ 1½ in.

7 Now assemble your cassoulet: drain the beans, discard the onion and cloves, any bones, the bouquet garni and the peppercorns. Chop up the carrots and cut up any lean meat off the knuckle bone. Ladle a generous layer of drained beans into your chosen cassoulet cooking pot. Scatter over half the carrot and knuckle meat, half the confit and onion mixture. Cover with more beans, then add the rest of the carrot, meat and confit. Top with a final layer of beans and dunk in the sausages. Set aside in a cool place or refrigerate until about 1½ hours before you are ready to serve.

8 Preheat the oven to 180°C/350°F/ gas4. Bake the cassoulet for 20–30 minutes, pushing any crust down into the mixture. If the cassoulet looks at all dry, moisten with a few tablespoons of hot water.

9 Combine the snipped parsley with the breadcrumbs and the extra crushed garlic, if using. Distribute this over the surface, then dot with some of the left-over goose or duck fat. Bake for a further 20–30 minutes, until the cassoulet has a good thick brown crust and is piping hot. Serve as soon as possible.

To drink: a Madiran, Cahors or Fitou.

PORC FARCI À LA BOULANGÈRE
Stuffed Loin of Pork

Going back to the days when the baker's oven was used by the whole community, *à la boulangère* often describes meat baked on a bed of potato and onion. In order to have as little to do as possible later on, peel and slice the potatoes and immerse them in a bowl of cold water until ready to cook. The onions too can be sliced and tightly covered until required. For a simpler dish you can omit the stuffing and replace the milk with stock.

Serves 6
Preparation: 20 minutes, plus several hours'
marinating
Cooking: about 2 hours

1.35kg/ 3lb loin of pork (ideally taken from the middle), boned, trimmed and tied
350ml/ 12fl oz milk, plus extra if needed
250ml/ 8fl oz dry white wine, plus extra if needed
45g/ 1½ oz butter, plus an extra 30g/ 1oz for finishing the sauce (optional)
675g/ 1½ lb waxy potatoes, peeled and sliced
2 large onions, sliced
¼ tsp each of dried thyme, sage, oregano and fennel seeds
6-8 unpeeled garlic cloves
1 generous tbsp cream, to finish the sauce (optional)
sea salt and freshly ground black pepper

FOR THE STUFFING:
1 garlic clove, crushed
¼ tsp each of dried sage, thyme, oregano and fennel seeds
¼ small fennel bulb, finely chopped
2 tbsp olive oil
85g/ 3oz mild fresh goats' cheese, crumbled

1 First prepare the stuffing: in the bowl of the food processor, combine the garlic, sage, thyme, oregano, fennel seeds and chopped fennel. Whizz for a moment. Scrape down the sides of the bowl with a spatula, season generously and add the olive oil and the goats' cheese. Whizz for several seconds until the mixture is smoothly blended.

2 Using a sharp knife, make several deep cuts into the pork, as if cutting it into medium-thick slices but stopping two-thirds of the way down (work between the pieces of string and be careful not to cut them). Now take a palette knife and insert the stuffing between the half-slices. Insert 2 long metal skewers lengthwise into the pork to keep it all together.

3 Combine the milk and white wine. Put the pork in a freezer bag and add the milk and wine. Tie securely and chill for several hours or overnight, shaking the bag from time to time.

4 Preheat the oven to 170°C/325°F/gas3 and grease a large deep flameproof gratin dish with the butter. Spread the sliced potatoes and onion over the base of the dish, sprinkle with the herbs and season lightly.

5 Take the pork out of the bag, put it on a suitable plate and season with a little salt and more generously with freshly ground black pepper. Drain the marinade juices into a pan. Add the garlic cloves and bring to a simmer over a moderate heat. Pour the simmering liquid and garlic over the potato and onion, dot with butter and cover with foil.

6 Place the dish in a large roasting pan and bake in the oven for about 30 minutes. Remove the dish from the oven. Place the pork over the potatoes and return to the oven without the foil. Bake for about 1¼–1¾ hours, turning the pork over a few times during cooking, until it is cooked through. If the dish looks too dry at any time, heat a little extra milk and wine until simmering and add to the dish. The roasting pan will catch any overspills.

7 Leave the pork to settle for 5–10 minutes in a warm place. To serve: lift the pork out and place on a warmed serving dish. Remove the skewers and strings. Using a slotted spoon, arrange the potatoes and onion around the pork.

8 Finish the sauce: strain the cooking liquor into a saucepan and squeeze the pulp from the garlic cloves into the strained sauce. Heat over a moderate heat, stirring well. Adjust the seasoning. Whisk in the cream or butter, if using, pour into a warmed sauce boat and serve at once with the pork.

To drink: a Beaujolais or Gamay de Touraine.

BŒUF
À LA MODE

Braised Beef

Serves 8
Preparation: about 1 hour
Cooking: about 3¹/₂ hours, plus chilling
if served cold

1 calf's foot, split in half
2 tbsp oil
1.8kg/4lb rolled larded topside of beef
2 marrow bones, chopped
2-3 garlic cloves, crushed
1 Spanish onion, chopped
3 cloves
¹/₂ tsp freshly grated nutmeg
several strips of orange zest
3 large carrots, scraped and cut
in half
1 celery stalk, chopped
several sprigs of parsley
2tsp dried ground thyme
2 bay leaves
bottle (750ml/27fl oz) of dry white
wine, or 400ml/14fl oz white wine
mixed with 350ml/12fl oz water
whites and shells of 3 eggs, to clarify the
stock
1 sachet (25g/³/₄ oz) of good-quality
aspic powder,
if necessary
sea salt and freshly ground
black pepper

TO SERVE:
1.1 litres/2pt light beef stock
8-12 baby turnips, trimmed and peeled
16 baby onions, trimmed and peeled
350g/12oz carrots, trimmed and cut
on the slant
350g/12oz broad beans

This is a recipe for all seasons which should be prepared the day before you plan to serve the meat. A warming *pièce de résistance* of a casserole in winter, this carrot-flavoured beef stew jellies magnificently into a shimmering golden dish that is perfect for summer entertaining. It also keeps well, up to 3 days in the refrigerator.

The vegetables are built in: boiled potatoes and a green salad are suitable accompaniments. White wine is used in the cooking, but break the rules and serve a cool young light red wine, say Bourgueil, Beaujolais Villages in summer, a Bergerac or Côtes du Rhône in winter.

1 Scrub and rinse the calf's foot and blanch for 3 minutes in boiling water.

2 Choose a large heavy pot that has a tight-fitting lid, such as a cast iron cocotte or a flameproof casserole. Place over a moderate heat. Spoon in the oil and tilt around over the heat to coat the base well. Reduce the heat a little, add the beef and carefully brown evenly on all sides, gradually turning it over.

BROWN THE BEEF THOROUGHLY ALL OVER, USING WOODEN SPOONS TO TURN IT GRADUALLY.

3 Add the calf's foot, marrow bones, garlic, onion, cloves, nutmeg, zest, carrots, celery and the herbs. Season and pour in the wine. Bring slowly to a simmer.

4 Once it is gently bubbling, reduce the heat to very low and turn over the beef. Tuck a layer of foil under the lid to seal the casserole and cook very gently for a good 3 hours. Every hour or so, skim off any fatty foam and turn the meat over.

5 If you want to serve the dish hot, preferably leave it overnight in a cool place as the dish tastes much better reheated. Skim off and discard the surface fat and reheat gently the next day over a low heat.

6 Prepare the serving vegetables as described below in step 8 while the beef is reheating. Place them on a warmed serving dish. Remove the beef from the pot, allowing the juices to drip back in. Discard the strings and slice the beef. Arrange the slices overlapping on the serving dish in the centre of the vegetables. Line a sieve with muslin and strain some cooking liquid into a warmed sauce boat. Trail paper towel over the surface to skim off the fat. Dribble some more cooking liquid over the beef and vegetables. Adjust the seasoning and serve immediately.

7 For Bœuf en Gelée, leave the beef to cool for half an hour or so, then remove it from the pot, allowing the juices to drain back in. Leave on a dish until cold. Meanwhile, line a sieve with muslin and strain the cooking liquid into a large saucepan. Discard the flavourings (the calf's foot is worth eating separately).

8 Prepare the vegetables for serving: bring the stock to a low simmer, adjust the seasoning, then add the turnips and onions and bring back to a simmer. Add the carrots, then later the beans and cook until just tender. Drain the vegetables, straining the stock into the pan with the beef cooking liquid. Refresh the vegetables in

cold water and drain again. Spread on a clean tea towel or a double layer of paper towel.

9 While the beef is cooling, clarify and reduce the stock and cooking liquid. Heat it through over a moderate heat. In a bowl, whisk together the whites and crushed shells of the eggs. Whisk this mixture into the simmering liquid. Bring to a boil, then reduce the heat a little. Simmer without stirring for 20 minutes, then strain into a clean pan through a fine sieve lined with dampened muslin. Now bring to a low boil, partly cover and leave to bubble gently until reduced by nearly half.

LEAVE TO COOL
OVERNIGHT AND THEN SKIM
OFF SURFACE FAT.

10 Stand the pan in very cold water and leave the stock to get cold and syrupy. If it fails to jelly, simply bring the liquid back to a simmer and mix with aspic powder as prescribed on the packet. Leave to get cold as before.

11 Cover the cold beef with foil and chill for an hour, then remove the strings and pare off the covering fat. Cut the beef into thin slices and put these on a serving dish, half overlaping neatly. Surround and scatter with the vegetables.

12 Spoon the syrupy aspic generously over the beef and vegetables. Adjust the seasoning, cover with foil or cling film and chill overnight or until just before serving.

ÉMINCÉ DE VEAU À LA CRÈME ET AU CITRON

Veal with Lemon and Cream Sauce

Émincer means to cut into strips or slivers. It is a good way to prepare fine meats for ultra-quick cooking. If you don't like eating veal, substitute strips of pork or beef fillet or poultry breast meat. The lemon juice can be replaced by a teaspoon of tomato paste and the paprika by a tablespoon of port. If you prefer whole escalopes, allow about 4-6 minutes' cooking time for each side. Stewed Baby Peas (page 139) and Glazed Carrots (page 135) make excellent accompaniments.

Serves 4
Preparation: 10 minutes
Cooking: 15 minutes

1 tbsp flour
2tsp finely grated lemon zest and 1tbsp lemon juice
tiny leaves plucked from a few sprigs of thyme or $^{1}/_{2}$ tsp dried thyme
$^{1}/_{4}$ tsp dried savory
scant pinch of paprika
450g/1lb veal escalopes, well flattened and cut into strips about 2.5cm/1in wide and no more than 7.5cm/3in long
1tbsp oil
30g/1oz butter
225g/8oz white button mushrooms, wiped and thinly sliced
white parts of 2 large spring onions, thinly sliced
1 shallot, finely chopped
100ml/3$^{1}/_{2}$ fl oz dry white wine
4tbsp crème fraîche
few sprigs of thyme, chives or parsley, to garnish (optional)
sea salt and freshly ground black pepper

1 In a cup, combine the flour, grated lemon zest, thyme and savory. Season with salt, pepper and paprika. Pat the strips of veal with paper towel, then dredge them lightly with this seasoning mixture.

2 Heat the oil in a large frying pan over a moderate to high heat, tilting the pan over the heat so that it is well coated. Tip in half the butter and, as soon as it is sizzling, place the strips of veal flat in the pan. Cook for a minute until seized and golden, then turn over and seize the other side. Using a slotted spoon, remove the strips from the pan and keep warm on a plate.

3 Tip in the prepared mushrooms, onions and shallot. Cook for 3 minutes, stirring frequently. Season lightly and tip out of the pan on a plate lined with a double layer of paper towel.

4 Wipe the pan with a thick wad of paper towel. Now add the rest of the butter, return the meat and vegetables to the pan and cook for 2–3 minutes, stirring occasionally.

5 Pour in the wine, bring to a simmer and quickly reduce the heat. Simmer gently for 5 minutes. Stir in the crème fraîche and the lemon juice.

6 Adjust the seasoning, adding a touch of extra paprika. If you like, snip over a few tiny leaves plucked from a sprig of thyme, or a few sprigs of chives or parsley, and serve as soon as possible.

To drink: a white Graves or Alsace Pinot Blanc.

CÔTES DE PORC À LA CHARCUTIÈRE

Pork Chops with Gherkins

For a quick *Sauce Moutarde* to accompany pork chops, follow the same method but replace the lemon zest with dried thyme in step 1. In step 5, replace the gherkins with 2 teaspoons of coarse grain mustard and a scant tablespoon of cream.

Serves 2
Preparation: 10 minutes
Cooking: about 30 minutes

30-40g/1-1$^{1}/_{4}$ oz butter
white parts of 2 large spring onions, chopped
2 shallots, finely chopped
1 scant tbsp flour
1tsp finely grated lemon zest
150ml/$^{1}/_{4}$ pt light stock or water
4tbsp dry white wine
1tbsp white wine vinegar
2 large pork chops, trimmed
1tbsp oil
4-5 small gherkins, drained and thinly sliced
1tbsp finely snipped parsley
sea salt and freshly ground black pepper

1 Prepare the sauce: in a heavy saucepan, melt two-thirds of the butter over a moderate heat. Add the onions and shallots and sauté for a few minutes. Season the flour, then sprinkle it over the sautéed mixture together with the lemon zest. Cook for 1 or 2 minutes, still over a moderate heat.

2 Pour in the stock, wine and vinegar. Stir, bring to a simmer, then reduce the heat to low and cook for 15 minutes or until the chops are ready.

3 Cook the chops: slash the fat at regular intervals around the pork and season

lightly with salt and pepper. Heat the oil and half the rest of the butter in a frying or sauté pan. Over a high heat, seize the pork chops all over until browned (start by standing them upright, fat edge down.

4 When the chops are browned, reduce the heat, add a small sliver of butter and partially cover the pan. Cook the chops for 15–20 minutes, depending on thickness, turning them over halfway through cooking. Cover and keep warm while you finish the sauce.

5 Add the sliced gherkins and the parsley to the sauce. Stir in for a few seconds, then take off the heat and adjust the seasoning. Whisk in the rest of the butter.

6 Using a slotted spoon, lift the chops from the pan. Drain quickly and put on warmed plates. Spoon the sauce over the chops and serve as soon as possible.

To drink: a Pinot Noir d'Alsace or Languedoc rosé.

NAVARIN PRINTANIER
Lamb and Spring Vegetables

A light casserole for the spring, *navarin* combines lamb with a basketful of vegetables. White haricot beans or green flageolets also traditionally accompany lamb (or mutton, if you can find it) to make excellent substantial stews. For *Ragoût de Mouton aux Haricots* (or *aux Flageolets*), cook the dried beans as in steps 1 and 2 of the Cassoulet recipe (page 112), using 1 or 2 lamb shanks instead of pork knuckle. Drain well and remove the meat from the shank bone. Start the casserole as described below, omit the vegetable preparation steps and add the beans and shank meat in step 6.

Serves 4
Preparation: 20 minutes
Cooking: 1³/₄ hours

1 tbsp flour
1 tsp each ground dried thyme and rosemary
1 tsp finely grated lemon zest
1¹/₂ tbsp oil
1kg/2¹/₄ lb boned shoulder or chump of lamb, trimmed of excess fat and cut into 5cm/2in pieces
¹/₂ Spanish onion, chopped
2 shallots, finely chopped
1 garlic clove, crushed
300ml/¹/₂ pt vegetable or light meat stock (see page 11)
100ml/3¹/₂ fl oz dry white wine
8 small white onions, peeled, or the white parts of 8 plump round spring onions
8-10 young carrots, scraped
8-10 baby turnips, scraped
2 scant tsp sugar
45g/1¹/₂oz butter
250g/8¹/₂ oz fine green beans, topped and tailed
225g/8oz mange-tout peas
few sprigs of flat leaf parsley, chervil or chives
sea salt and freshly ground black pepper

1 Season the flour: in a bowl, combine it with the dried herbs, lemon zest and season lightly with salt and finely ground black pepper.

2 Heat the oil in a sauté pan over a moderate to high heat. Add the meat and sauté for a few minutes, until lightly browned, stirring and turning the pieces. Remove from the pan and discard the excess fat. Then tip in the prepared Spanish onion, shallots and garlic. Sauté for a few minutes, then return the lamb to the pan and sprinkle with the seasoned flour.

3 Stir and cook for a minute, then pour in the stock and the white wine. Bring the liquid to a good simmer, then cover and reduce the heat to very low. Cook slowly for about 1¹/₂ hours. Skim off the surface fat and foam and stir the meat occasionally.

4 Prepare the vegetables while the lamb is cooking: bring a kettle of water to the boil. Put the onions, carrots and turnips in a heavy saucepan, sprinkle with sugar, season and half cover with boiling water. Dot with half the butter. Partly cover the pan and cook over a moderate heat until the water has evaporated and the vegetables are almost tender (the timing will vary, but allow at least 15 minutes). Shake the pan several times during the process.

5 In a separate saucepan, cook the green beans in lightly salted water for about 5 minutes, tipping in the mange-tout peas after 4 minutes or so. Drain well and reserve.

6 Add the onions, turnips and carrots to the pan for the last 20 minutes or so of cooking. Add the other vegetables 15 minutes later.

7 Once the casserole is cooked, remove the meat and vegetables from the pan with a slotted spoon. Pile in a warmed shallow bowl or serving dish and keep warm.

8 Strain the stock into a jug, return to the pan and turn up the heat. Bring to a fast boil and reduce by one-quarter to one-third. Adjust the seasoning and whisk in the rest of the butter. Spoon over the meat and vegetables. Tuck in a few fresh herbs and serve immediately.

To drink: a Brouilly or Fleurie.

LE GIGOT D'AGNEAU

Roast Leg of Lamb

Serves about 8
Preparation: 15 minutes, plus about 1 hour marinating
Cooking: about 1¼ hours, plus settling

1.8-2kg/4-4½ lb part-boned trimmed leg of lamb
3 or more garlic cloves
2tsp each of dried thyme and rosemary, or finely snipped fresh herbs, plus a few extra sprigs of rosemary and thyme for the roasting pan (optional)
1tsp dried oregano
1tsp finely grated lemon zest
2tbsp olive oil
30g/1oz butter
100ml/3½ fl oz dry white wine, plus extra for the sauce
2tbsp cream
sea salt and freshly ground black pepper

Gigot is the celebration meat of the family table, served with a good Châteauneuf-du-Pape. When the prodigal son (or even daughter) comes home, the French do not kill a fatted calf – they order *un beau gigot* from the butcher. Even uncooked, a part-boned, neatly trimmed leg of young lamb is a handsome piece of meat. In France, unless you specifically ask for the contrary, it will be studded with garlic. The bones will always be there as well, still with enough meat on them to make good stock – or a feast for the dog. Allow at the very least 285g/10oz unboned weight per person, or just over half that if the meat is fully boned.

It is impossible to give a precise cooking time. Most French cooks, butchers and *amateurs de gigot* allow a mere 15 minutes per 450g/1lb at high temperature. This produces very rare meat indeed, especially in the centre. The timing I suggest below is less draconian and will give you rosy meat in the centre and well-cooked end slices. When in doubt, it is always safer to undercook a little: a *gigot* can easily go back to the oven while everyone has another *apéritif*.

If your guests have very partisan views on *bien rosé, à point,* and *bien cuit,* be prepared to return some of the slices to the oven for a few minutes – *gigot* should

MAKE LITTLE SLITS ALL OVER THE LAMB AND USE THE KNIFE BLADE TO INSERT GARLIC SLIVERS.

be a feast for everyone to enjoy and a little flexibility is called for. In general, seizing young lamb at a high temperature, then reducing the temperature to allow it to go on cooking through somewhat more gently, is a good method. If your lamb is more mature, reduce the temperature of the 'gentle' phase of roasting still further (say 150–180°C/325–350°F/gas 3–4) and cook for 15–20 minutes more.

What to serve with *gigot*? It is a dish that brings out the traditionalist in people. Classic accompaniments, Pan-fried Green Beans (page 145) and flageolets (see Cassoulet page 112 for cooking the beans) or canned flageolets (drained and gently reheated with a dash of white wine, a snipping of herbs and a knob of butter), are hard to ignore – and quite rightly so. Herbed baked tomatoes are very good too, as are Glazed Turnips (page 92) and Potatoes stewed in Olive Oil (page 145). Roast or puréed garlic (page 14) makes an excellent extra.

OLIVE OIL AND BUTTER KEEP THE LAMB MOIST DURING COOKING.

❙ First season the lamb and allow it to come to room temperature. Cut the garlic into fine slivers. Using a small sharp knife, make little slits in the lamb and insert the slivers into them. Combine the herbs with the lemon zest and some pepper. Rub the mixture well into the lamb and leave to stand for at least an hour.

HALFWAY THROUGH COOKING, TURN THE LAMB OVER AND BASTE WELL.

2 Preheat the oven to 230°C/450°F/gas8. Rub the fat of the lamb well with salt, dribble over the olive oil and dot with butter. Put the lamb, rounded plump side down, on a rack in a roasting pan (sitting on a layer of rosemary and thyme sprigs, if you like). Roast for 30–35 minutes.

3 Turn the lamb over and baste with the cooking juices and the white wine mixed with the same amount of water. Reduce the oven to 190°C/375°F/gas5 and continue cooking for 30–35 minutes, or a little longer if none of the guests like their meat rosy pink. Baste again and leave in the turned-off oven with the door slightly open for 10 minutes.

4 Get someone to carve the lamb and arrange the slices on a warmed serving dish. Meanwhile, skim the excess fat from the pan and pour the juices into a small saucepan. Add the stock and a splash of white wine. Bring almost to simmering point over a low heat, then stir in the cream. Stir in the carving juices, adjust the seasoning and pour into a warmed sauce boat. Serve with the lamb.

VARIATION: if you like, go easy on the herbs and garlic and add 2 tablespoons of drained capers to the sauce, then whisk in 30g/1oz butter instead of cream.

CARBONNADE AUX PRUNEAUX
Beef and Prune Casserole

From the North and beer country, this sweetish dark casserole has a nice sharp acidic kick. *Carbonnade* owes its unique caramelized depth of flavour to very slow simmering and to the combination of beer, sugar and vinegar. You can do a simpler version by replacing the prunes with a generous tablespoon of brown cane sugar and leaving out the mustard toast. The meat used can vary: braising steak is the traditional choice, but pork and rabbit also work very well. If you decide to put a rabbit in the pot, dust it with flour first and reduce the overall cooking time by 40 minutes.

Serves 6
Preparation: about 20 minutes
Cooking: 2¼ hours

2 tbsp oil
15g / ½ oz butter, plus extra for buttering the toast
1.35kg/ 3lb braising steak, cut into 6cm/ 2½ in chunks, excess fat trimmed off
225g/ 8oz thick cut smoked streaky bacon
3 onions, thinly sliced
2 shallots, finely chopped
1 generous tbsp flour
550ml/ 1pt brown ale
1 heaped tsp ground dried thyme
2 sprigs of parsley
2 bay leaves
200ml/ 7fl oz light stock, if required
140g/ 5oz no-soak stoned prunes
2 tbsp red wine vinegar
6 pieces of toasted bread
1 scant tbsp Dijon mustard
sea salt and freshly ground black pepper

1 Heat the oil in a large sauté pan, cocotte or flameproof casserole pot. Add the butter to the hot oil and tilt the pan around over the heat to coat it well with melted butter. Tip in the meat, season lightly and sauté over a moderate heat until golden, stirring and turning the pieces so that they colour evenly.

2 In a separate small saucepan, blanch the bacon in simmering water for 1 minute. Drain well on paper towel, leave to cool for a moment, then cut into 2.5cm/1in pieces. Add the bacon and the prepared onions and shallots to the sautéed meat. Dredge with the flour, stir well, and cook for 2 minutes until the flour is coloured.

3 Now pour in the beer, sprinkle over the thyme and drop in a few parsley sprigs and the bay leaves. Bring to a low boil and, as soon as the beer bubbles, reduce the heat. Stir well, then cover two-thirds of the pan with a lid (leave a small gap) and cook for about 1½ hours over a very low heat.

4 Add the prunes and vinegar, give the stew a few good stirs and add a ladle or two of stock or water if the mixture looks too dry (it should be a little thickened but not like heavy syrup). Partially cover the pan as before and continue to cook for 20–30 minutes, still over a low heat.

5 Adjust the seasoning and stir well, adding a little stock or water if necessary. Lightly butter both sides of pieces of toast and smear with a little Dijon mustard. Put these over the casserole. Now cover completely and cook for a further 15 minutes before serving piping hot straight from the pan.

To drink: beer or a Côtes-du Rhône.

TRANCHES DE FOIE DE VEAU SAUTÉES
Sautéed Calves' Liver

This delicate classic dish takes minutes to prepare. The light coating of flour protects the meat and prevents any splattering. Keep your eyes on the heat and on the clock – calves' liver does not improve with overcooking.

If you enjoy beef marrow, prepare *Beurre Bercy*: soften 4 shallots in water (*Onglet*, see page 122), then cook these with about 3 tablespoons of beef marrow (see *Pot au Feu*, page 18). Wrap the bone in muslin and poach. Whizz the shallot and the cooked marrow in the food processor with 75g/2½oz soft butter and a generous tablespoon of chopped parsley. Season and chill. Allow this to melt over the sautéed liver for a treat that is well worth the effort. It is also delicious with steak.

Serves 4
Preparation: 5 minutes
Cooking: 10 minutes

4 slices of calves' liver
1 heaped tbsp flour
1 scant tsp dried rubbed sage
2tsp oil
55g/ 2oz butter
1 generous tbsp finely snipped parsley
sea salt and freshly ground black pepper

ONE OF THE FOLLOWING,
TO DEGLAZE THE PAN:
2tbsp good wine vinegar
1tbsp sherry vinegar and 2tbsp Madeira
2tbsp each red wine and light stock

1 Put the liver slices on a double layer of paper towel and gently pat dry on both sides. Season the flour lightly, put it in a small sieve and dust the livers with it. Sprinkle over a little rubbed sage.

2 Using a small wad of paper towel, lightly oil a frying pan large enough to take the 4 slices of liver comfortably side by side. (If you prefer, use 2 pans or cook in 2 batches.) Put the pan(s) over a moderate heat and tip in half the butter. When the foaming subsides, gently place the liver in the pan, dusted side down. Cook for 2–3 minutes over a moderate heat – the idea is to keep the liver rosy pink inside and to seize but not toughen the outside.

3 Dust the top side of the liver with the rest of the seasoned flour and sprinkle over the rest of the sage. Turn over carefully and cook for 2–3 minutes. Reduce the heat a fraction after a minute if the pan juices are browning too much.

4 Lift out on to a warmed serving dish and keep warm while you make the sauce.

5 Add the vinegar or the deglazing mixture of your choice to the pan. Stir for a few seconds, then whisk in the rest of the butter. Adjust the seasoning. Dribble this short sauce over the liver, sprinkle with parsley and serve immediately.

To drink: an Anjou red.

BŒUF BOURGUIGNON
Beef and Red Wine Stew

Bœuf bourguignon improves with age. It keeps for a few days and freezes well. So make twice as much as you need (to the end of step 5) so you have some in store.

Serves 4
Preparation: 10 minutes, plus several hours'
marinating
Cooking: 2¹/₂ hours

1.35kg / 3lb braising steak, cut into 5cm / 2in pieces
2 tbsp oil
3 thick slices of smoked streaky bacon, blanched and chopped
30g / 1oz butter
1 tbsp flour
1 tbsp brandy
3 tbsp red wine
1 generous tbsp snipped parsley
sea salt and freshly ground black pepper

FOR THE MARINADE:
700ml / 1¹/₄ pt full-bodied red wine
1 tbsp olive oil
1 large carrot, peeled and quartered
1 Spanish onion, coarsely chopped
2 shallots, chopped
1 garlic clove, crushed
1 bouquet garni
1 tsp dried ground thyme
6 black peppercorns
few sprigs of fresh parsley

TO SERVE:
450g / 1lb potatoes, boiled and peeled
glazed onions or sautéed mushrooms (optional)

1 First marinate the beef: put it in a large bowl with the marinade ingredients. Toss well to coat, then cover and keep in a cool place for several hours or refrigerate overnight. Stir a few times.

2 To cook the bourguignon: drain the marinade, reserving the wine and separating the rest of the flavouring ingredients from the beef.

3 Heat the oil in a sauté pan, tip in the prepared bacon and sauté over a moderate heat until crisp and seized. Turn up the heat a fraction, add the beef and brown quickly on all sides.

4 Add the marinade flavourings and stir for a minute. Add half the butter, stir until it melts and then sprinkle over the flour. Stir for a minute or two, then pour in the marinade wine. Season and bring to a simmer, stirring occasionally. Chill the rest of the butter until needed.

5 As soon as the mixture is genuinely simmering, stir well, then reduce the heat to very low, cover tightly and cook for about 2 hours. Keep the heat down and give the meat an occasional stir. Add a few tablespoons of hot water if the sauce looks too thick.

6 If you prefer a deeper-tasting casserole, leave the dish to get cold, keep it in a cool place or chill. The next day, spoon off the surface fat, discard the bouquet garni and gently reheat the bourguignon over a low heat.

7 Lift out the meat with a slotted spoon and put it on a warmed serving dish or plate if you prefer to serve straight from the pan. Keep warm.

8 Turn up the heat. If the sauce is too thin, reduce it a little. Stir in the brandy and cook for a few minutes. Pour in the 3 tablespoons of wine, stir and cook for a minute. Adjust the seasoning. Just before serving, dice the chilled butter and whisk it into the sauce. Either return the meat to the pan or spoon the sauce over it in the serving dish.

9 Sprinkle with the parsley and serve at once with boiled potatoes. Glazed onions or sautéed mushrooms are other good accompaniments.

To drink: a Côte de Beaune or Mercurey.

ONGLET AUX ÉCHALOTES

Skirt Steak with Shallot Sauce

Poêler, to grill in the frying pan, is a favourite quick cooking method of the French. The recipe below takes minutes to prepare and combines juicy steak and sharp shallots in a way that will delight lovers of red meat.

Serves 2
Preparation: 5 minutes
Cooking: 10 minutes

30-45g/ 1-1½ oz butter
2 top-quality skirt steaks
4 shallots, finely chopped
2tsp oil
1 scant tbsp finely snipped parsley
sea salt and freshly ground black pepper

1 Prepare the steaks: chill half the butter and divide the rest into 4 pieces. Over a low heat, melt a piece of butter in a frying pan. Tilt the pan over the heat to coat. Take off the heat. Put the steaks in the pan, press gently and then turn over (the idea is to smear both sides lightly with butter). Transfer the steak to a plate, season with pepper and set aside until a few minutes before you want to serve.

2 Put the prepared shallots in a small saucepan and generously cover with cold water. Bring to a simmer. Cook over a moderate heat until the water has evaporated and the shallots are soft (allow 5–8 minutes). Reduce the heat to very low.

3 Meanwhile, cook the steaks: heat the frying pan until very hot over a high heat. Add the oil and the 3 pieces of butter. Season the steaks with salt and add them to the hot pan. Reduce the heat a little and cook until done to your liking, turning the steaks over halfway through cooking.

4 Cut the chilled butter into dice. Turn up the heat under the softened shallot and whisk half the butter dice into this, then tip the buttery mixture over the steaks. Leave in the pan for a few seconds, then transfer to warmed serving plates.

5 Whisk the rest of the chilled butter in the pan, stir in the parsley and dribble this over the steaks. Scrape the pan well in order not to waste any of the mixture and serve immediately.

Variation: an equally appealing and simple variation is *Steak au Poivre Vert*. Using a pestle and mortar, bruise a tablespoon of drained green peppercorns and use one-third to season the steaks before you smear them with butter (step 1). When the steaks are cooked, whisk the rest of the peppercorns into the pan, together with 2 teaspoons of brandy. Cook for a few seconds, then whisk in 2 teaspoons of Madeira and the diced chilled butter. Whisk for a few seconds over a moderate heat and spoon over the steaks.

To drink: a Morgon.

Chapter Eight

LES SALADES ET LES LÉGUMES

Salads and Vegetables

If most of your meals in France — and French meals elsewhere — have been in restaurants, you probably have reason to believe that French vegetable cooking is limited, somewhat chichi and but a minor branch of gastronomy under the general heading of *garniture*, garnish. For it is essentially in the home kitchen that the vegetable riches of the country — so stunning on market stalls, so lacking in ordinary restaurants — are given due respect. Their preparation — judicious but not overly complicated — is perfectly suited to the skills of the home cook (in the large professional kitchen, vegetables are the responsibility of junior chefs). While vociferously not a nation of vegetarians, the French are closet vegetable gourmets. They applaud the first peas or asparagus of the season and sup on a plate of sautéed fine green beans from the garden or a mess of lentils from Le Puy. They swap mushroom recipes, fuss over the proper way to make potato gratin and eat green salad every day. Vegetable cookery is a very important part of French home cooking and one which has been less well explored than most — hence this long chapter.

LEFT
Panaché de Salades aux Petits Lardons with Concombres à la Crème (page 126).

CONCOMBRES À LA CRÈME
Cucumber with Cream Dressing

I am told that salting cucumbers for a long time to extract their bitter juices is no longer necessary with modern varieties. However, old habits die hard and I still like the way this practice transforms the vegetable's texture – it certainly draws out much water. *Concombres à la crème* have a unique cool acidulated taste and a smooth crunchy bite. They are an unpretentious, but genuinely *raffiné* and moreish, light starter.

Serves 4
Preparation: 10 minutes, then about 30 minutes' standing and 30 minutes' chilling

1 large or 2 small firm cucumbers
2tbsp coarse sea salt
several sprigs of fresh tarragon or several mint leaves (optional)
2tbsp lemon juice
100ml/3¹/₂ fl oz sour or single cream
freshly ground black pepper

1 Prepare the cucumber: if you like, first use a cannelle knife or vegetable peeler to strip bands of skin at regular intervals all the way down the cucumber. Then slice the cucumber as thinly as possible, using a mandolin or your sharpest knife (or food processor if yours is fitted with an extra-thin slicing disk).

2 Put the slices in a colander, sprinkle with the coarse sea salt and mix it in well. Place a weighted soup plate on top and leave the cucumber to drain for at least 30 minutes, or up to 1 hour if time allows.

3 Rinse thoroughly with cold running water then drain well, squeezing gently with your hands. Put the slices in a clean tea towel or a double layer of paper towel to get rid of as much moisture as possible and pat dry gently.

4 Put the cucumber slices in a suitable serving dish. If you like, snip over the leaves of a few small sprigs of tarragon, or several rolled up mint leaves. Sprinkle with the lemon juice and mix well.

5 Pour the cream over the cucumber, season with freshly ground black pepper and toss it in lightly but thoroughly. Chill for at least 30 minutes before serving straight from the refrigerator after adjusting the seasoning.

PANACHÉ DE SALADES AUX PETITS LARDONS
Mixed Leaf Salad with Bacon

This classic *salade tiède* is usually made with *frisée*, a spiky chewy salad leaf that has to be in its tender infancy to be palatable. It is much safer to use a mixture of leaves with different textures: romaine, Batavia or oak leaf, a few leaves of soft lettuce, and perhaps a little sorrel, spinach or rocket. Trim, wash and drain them all carefully.

Serves 4-6 as a starter, 2-3 as a snack meal
Preparation: 10 minutes
Cooking: 5 minutes

200g/7oz smoked belly of pork or thick smoky streaky bacon, rindless and cut into small dice
200g/7oz salad leaves
few sprigs of parsley and chives
4tbsp groundnut or mildly flavoured olive oil
sea salt and freshly ground black pepper
1¹/₂ tbsp red wine vinegar

1 Blanch the smoked pork or bacon: bring a little water to the boil in a saucepan, tip in the meat and simmer over a fairly high heat for 1 minute. Drain well and spread to dry on a double layer of paper towel.

2 Put the mixed salad leaves in a shallow bowl. Snip over a little parsley and chives. Sprinkle with about 1¹/₂ tablespoons of oil and season lightly.

3 A few minutes before serving, heat the rest of the oil in a small frying-pan over a moderate heat. When the oil is hot, drop in the bacon and spread it in an even layer. Sauté for 2–3 minutes over a moderate heat, stirring a few times, until the bacon pieces are crisp and coloured.

4 Take the pan off the heat and distribute the bacon over the salad.

5 Return the pan to the heat. Pour in the vinegar and stir well for a few seconds, then sprinkle this hot liquid over the salad. Toss lightly and adjust the seasoning. Snip over a few extra herbs and serve at once – the hotter the dressing, the better the salad will taste.

CHAMPIGNONS EN SALADE
Mushroom Salad

Blanching mushrooms improves their texture and produces a clean salad that is easy to digest. For *Champignons à la Grecque*, boil up the dressing ingredients for *Truites à la Grecque* (page 84) using half the quantities given. Stir into the blanched mushrooms and marinate for several hours or overnight.

Serves 4
Preparation: about 15 minutes

2 tbsp lemon juice
450g/1lb white button mushrooms, thinly sliced
1 tbsp groundnut oil
2tbsp crème fraîche, or 1tbsp single cream and 1tbsp Greek-style yogurt
¼ tsp Dijon mustard
2tsp white wine vinegar
small bunch of chives
sea salt and freshly ground black pepper

1 In a saucepan, bring to the boil some lightly salted water. Add the lemon juice, then throw in the mushrooms. Blanch for 1 minute. Drain well and spread to dry on a clean tea towel or between double layers of paper towel.

2 In a cup, mix the oil, crème fraîche or cream and yogurt mixture, mustard and wine vinegar. Season to taste and snip over some chives.

3 Put the drained mushrooms in a shallow serving dish. Spoon the dressing over the mushrooms and toss in well, then adjust the seasoning. Snip over a few more chives and serve soon.

CÉLERI RÉMOULADE
Celeriac Mayonnaise

The combination of rich mayonnaise and lemony shreds of celeriac is a marriage made in heaven – daily consummated on the deli counters of *charcuteries* all over France. Use home-made mayonnaise, flavour it liberally with mustard and do not drown the celeriac.

Serves 4
Preparation: 15 minutes, plus making the mayonnaise and chilling

450g/1lb celeriac root, peeled and grated
2tbsp lemon juice
sea salt and freshly ground black pepper

FOR THE DRESSING:
about 125-150ml/4 fl oz-¼ pt Mayonnaise (page 36), well seasoned with
1tbsp Dijon mustard, 1tsp white wine vinegar, 2 small chopped gherkins (optional) and 1tbsp finely snipped parsley, plus more to garnish (optional)

1 First blanch the celeriac: in a saucepan, bring some lightly salted water to the boil. Add the lemon juice, tip in the celeriac and blanch for 1–2 minutes. Drain well, squeeze out excess moisture with your hands, then spread the celeriac on a double layer of paper towel and pat dry.

2 Put the mayonnaise in a shallow serving bowl, add the flavourings and stir well in. Adjust the seasoning (the mayonnaise should be quite piquant and peppery). Scoop out 2 tablespoons of flavoured mayonnaise and reserve to finish.

3 Add the celeriac to the dish. Stir well until coated with mayonnaise. If you like the celeriac to be generously coated, stir in the reserved mayonnaise. Chill for 15 minutes, or longer if more convenient.

4 Just before serving, stir again, adjust seasoning and snip over a few extra sprigs of parsley. Preferably eat that day.

POIREAUX VINAIGRETTE
Warm Leek Salad with Egg Mimosa Dressing

This simple starter has to be served within minutes of dressing – while the texture of the leeks is at its best and they are still tiède or tepid. If you like, sprinkle over a small handful of tiny diced *croûtons*, sautéed nuts or even finely chopped anchovy fillets. Asparagus can be dressed the same way.

Serves 4
Preparation: 15 minutes
Cooking: about 25 minutes, plus cooling

12 medium leeks
1tsp coarse-grain mustard
1¼ tbsp raspberry or wine vinegar
3-4tbsp groundnut oil
½ shallot, very finely chopped
2 fresh eggs, hard-boiled and shelled
few sprigs of parsley or chives
sea salt and freshly ground black pepper

1 Season the leeks with a little salt, put in a steaming basket over boiling water and cover tightly. Steam for 15-20 minutes until just tender.

2 Meanwhile, prepare the dressing: put the mustard and vinegar in a cup. Beat in the oil and shallot. Season to taste.

3 Chop up the egg whites, push them through a fine sieve and set aside. Mash the yolks and push through the sieve.

4 Leave the leeks until cool enough to handle, then lightly squeeze them to extract any excess moisture. Pat dry.

5 Arrange 3 leeks on each of 4 salad plates. Whisk up the vinaigrette until it emulsifies and spoon some over each helping of leeks. Sprinkle over a band of the sieved egg whites and one of the yolks, then snip over a band of chives. Finish by snipping over the herbs.

LE CHOU FARCI

Stuffed Cabbage

Serves 6
Preparation: about 20 minutes
Cooking: about 2³/4 hours, in stages

1 extra-large Savoy cabbage
200g/ 7oz fine cooked ham
8 thin slices of smoked streaky bacon,
blanched if preferred
200g/ 7oz good quality sausage-meat
200g/ 7oz minced veal
2tsp oil
45g/ 1¹/2 oz butter
2 red onions, finely chopped
1 large red pepper, cored, deseeded and
finely chopped
4 shallots, finely chopped
1 scant tsp paprika
¹/4 tsp grated nutmeg
1tsp dried ground thyme
¹/2 tsp dried marjoram
1 thick slice of day-old bread, crust
removed
4-5tbsp milk
1 large or 2 small eggs

FOR THE STOCK:
1 Spanish onion, coarsely chopped
1 large carrot, coarsely chopped
1 small head of celery, or 1 small fennel
bulb, trimmed and coarsely chopped
3 cloves
bouquet garni
sea salt and freshly ground black pepper

USE A SMALL SHARP KNIFE TO REMOVE THE CENTRAL CORE FROM THE CABBAGE.

ONCE THE BLANCHED CABBAGE IS COOL ENOUGH, PULL THE BIG OUTER LEAVES AWAY FROM THE CENTRE.

Ponderous green Savoy cabbage, one of winter's bright sights on the market stalls, is the most fillable of vegetables. *Chou Farci* is one of the world's great simple *plats complets*, one-pot meals. It may take an hour to prepare and two hours to cook, but the result is uniquely satisfying.

1 Bring a kettle filled with water to the boil, then pour the water into a large pan. Season with salt. Using a small sharp knife, carefully cut out some of the cabbage core, taking care not to pierce too far in. Put the cabbage in the boiling water, cover and simmer over a moderate heat for 15 minutes. Turn over after 10 minutes.

2 Refresh the blanched cabbage under cold water and drain well. Leave aside in a colander for several minutes until the cabbage is cool enough to handle. Now open up the cabbage by gently pulling the big green leaves away from the centre. With a small sharp knife, cut out the smaller central leaves (between two-thirds and three-quarters of your cabbage should end up being removed), but be careful not to pierce the base. Finely chop half the removed central leaves and reserve the rest for making the stock.

LINE COLANDER OR BOWL WITH MUSLIN OR CLOTH AND CROSS THE BACON SLICES ON THE BOTTOM.

PLACE THE CABBAGE ON TOP AND SPOON THE STUFFING INTO THE CAVITY.

FOLD A FEW INNER LEAVES OVER THE STUFFING, SPOON IN SOME MORE AND ENCLOSE WITH OUTER LEAVES.

3 Prepare the filling: chop together the ham and 4 of the bacon slices. In a bowl, combine these with the sausage-meat and the minced veal. Reserve.

4 Heat a sauté pan over a moderate heat. Grease the hot pan with the oil using a wad of paper towel. Put the butter in the pan. When the foaming subsides, tip in the chopped onion, red pepper and shallots. Sprinkle in the paprika, nutmeg, thyme and marjoram. Season lightly and stir. Sauté for 5 minutes, stirring frequently, then turn up the heat. Tip in the mixed meat, stir to mix and cook for 10 minutes, stirring frequently and vigorously to allow the flavours to blend. Stir in the chopped cabbage leaves after 5 minutes.

5 Take the stuffing off the heat and leave to cool. Soak the bread in the milk for a few minutes. Squeeze well to extract the excess milk. Add this to the stuffing, followed by the egg. Stir well to combine and adjust the seasoning.

6 Now fill the cabbage. Take a self-standing metal colander a bit larger than the cabbage (use a shallow round salad bowl). Line this with a double layer of muslin or a large impeccably clean tea towel. Spread 2 slices of bacon in a cross shape in the centre of the cloth. Sit the cabbage on top. Pull the leaves away from the centre, easing them out so that they rest against the rim of the colander and flop back against the rim. Now spoon the stuffing into the centre of the cabbage. Fold a few inner leaves over the stuffing, spoon in some more stuffing, enclose this with the outer leaves, as it were re-creating the cabbage's original spherical shape.

7 Top the cabbage with the last 2 bacon slices, again stretching them in a cross over the centre. Bring together the edges of the muslin over the top of the cabbage so that it is tightly wrapped. Tie securely with a long length of string, making a generous handle with the ends. Set aside while you prepare the stock.

8 Bring a kettle of water to the boil. In a big pan, put the onion, carrot and celery, the cloves, bouquet garni and leftover cabbage leaves. Season generously. Cover with boiling water and bring to a simmer. Put the colander with the cabbage on top – the base of the cabbage should just be immersed in water. If not using a colander, stand a steaming basket over the stock and place the cabbage in the centre. Bring back to a simmer.

WRAP UP THE CABBAGE TIGHTLY WITH STRING, ALLOWING FOR A GENEROUS HANDLE.

Cover tightly, reduce the heat and steam gently for 2 hours. Regularly open the lid and check the water level, adding extra boiling water as necessary.

9 Lift the colander out of the water. Put over a bowl to drain and leave to cool for a few minutes. Meanwhile, turn up the heat under the stock pot and boil until well reduced. Adjust the seasoning. Strain into a warmed jug and keep warm.

10 Remove the cloth and bacon slices from the cabbage. Add these to the boiling stock. Place the cabbage in a warmed round shallow serving bowl or dish, moisten liberally with strained stock and serve immediately. To serve, cut into wedges with a large wide knife, supporting each wedge with a server fork or spoon as you cut.

To drink: an Alsace Pinot Noir or Côtes du Roussillon.

VARIATIONS: stuffed cabbage is an excellent way of using leftover meat. Replace the ham, sausage-meat and veal with the same weight (550g/1¼ lb) of minced leftover meat. Use all the other ingredients above – and season extra generously.

To make a delicate vegetarian *chou farci*, make a filling from some sautéed onions, garlic, peppers and mushrooms, mixed with cooked rice, pine nuts and chopped olives and bound with egg. Flavour the stuffing with a little cumin, coriander, ginger, paprika, lemon and orange zest and some harissa paste. Reduce the cooking time by 30 minutes.

SALADE DE MÂCHE AUX NOIX

Lamb's Lettuce and Walnut Salad

Serves 4
Preparation: about 15 minutes

about 200g/ 7oz lamb's lettuce
½ garlic clove
1 shallot, finely chopped
several chive stalks
4-6 fresh walnuts, shelled and coarsely crushed
2tsp sherry vinegar
2tbsp walnut oil
1tbsp groundnut oil
sea salt and freshly ground black pepper

1 Wash the lamb's lettuce in cold water. Drain well and separate the bunches if necessary. Then gently pat dry with a clean tea towel or plenty of paper towel – lamb's lettuce is too delicate for the salad spinner.

2 Rub a shallow salad bowl with the cut side of the garlic. Tip the chopped shallot into the bowl and snip in the chives. Then add the walnuts and season generously. Sprinkle with the sherry vinegar and stir to mix. Now beat in the oils, a little at a time. Leave to infuse for a few minutes, or longer if you wish.

3 When you are ready to serve, tip the lamb's lettuce into the bowl. Toss lightly to coat and serve soon.

SALADE DE POMMES DE TERRE

Potato Salad

To make that most enjoyable simple dish, a good potato salad, you have to cook the potatoes over a moderate and steady heat until they are cooked through but still in one piece. Wait a few minutes until you can peel them without burning your fingers, then dress while still warm so that the spuds can absorb the flavours of the dressing.

For *un plat complet*, mix with *Moules Marinières* (see page 76 – shell most of the mussels first, reserving a few on the half shell for garnish), adding a couple of tablespoons of strained mussel liquor to the dressing. Alternatively, stir in crisp *lardons*.

Serves 4
Preparation: 10 minutes
Cooking: about 30 minutes

450g/ 1lb oz not-too-small even-sized salad
potatoes, scrubbed
4tbsp olive or groundnut oil
1 scant tsp Dijon mustard
1 or 2 shallots, very finely chopped
½ garlic clove, crushed (optional)
1tbsp red wine vinegar, or 2tsp
sherry vinegar
1 heaped tbsp single or soured cream
several sprigs of fresh herbs, such as parsley,
chervil and chives
sea salt and freshly ground black pepper

1 Bring to the boil a big saucepan of salted water over a high heat. Add the potatoes and return to the boil. Reduce the heat, partially cover and cook at a steady fast simmer (rather than a rolling boil) for 20-30 minutes, until the potatoes are done but still a little firm (test with a metal skewer – it should go in smoothly and evenly).

2 Prepare the dressing while the potatoes are cooking: in a bowl, mix the oil with the mustard and season generously. Stir in the shallot(s) and garlic, if using, followed by the vinegar and cream. Snip in plenty of fresh herbs. Whisk until the dressing emulsifies and adjust the seasoning

3 Drain the cooked potatoes, refresh under cold water and leave to drain in a colander for a few minutes. As soon as they are cool enough to handle, peel the potatoes and cut them into thick chunky slices.

4 Put the warm potatoes in a shallow serving bowl. Spoon over about two-thirds of the dressing and toss lightly until the potatoes are coated. Cover and leave at room temperature for at least 30 minutes, or until ready to serve.

5 At the last minute, dribble over the rest of the dressing. Toss well, then snip over more fresh herbs.

LE GRATIN DAUPHINOIS

Creamy Potato Gratin

Serves 4-6 as a main course, 6-8 as
a side dish
Preparation: 20 minutes
Cooking: 60-95 minutes, then 10
minutes' cooling

about 1kg/2¼ lb even-sized medium
potatoes (see right)
1 large fresh garlic clove
at least 55g/2oz soft butter, plus extra
to finish
2 medium shallots
generous pinch of dried thyme
generous pinch of ground dried sage
small pinch of freshly grated
nutmeg (optional)
250ml/8fl oz full-fat milk
150ml/¼ pt crème fraîche
sea salt and freshly ground black pepper

With its burnished golden crust and creamy inside, *dauphinois* is the ultimate *gratin* and the most luxurious of potato dishes. It is simple enough fare – sliced potatoes baked in a buttery milk mixture – but no two *gratins* will ever taste quite the same. There is no such thing as the definitive *dauphinois*, but there are, of course, dozens of variations. Before I opened the cookbooks on my shelves to read up the relevant literature, I found I had no fewer than 7 hand-written recipes for *dauphinois* in my 'family and friends' files – some very yellowed indeed. One particularly garlicky *recette* was jotted down in a spidery ink scrawl on the back of an invitation to a wedding near Toulon in June 1912 …

As invariably happens with traditional recipes, cooks argue about the right way to make *dauphinois*. Argument number one focuses on whether or not you soak your potatoes to get rid of some of their starch. The soaking faction will tell you that their *gratin* is lighter, the others that theirs is well-bound thanks to the starch. I compromise by washing my peeled potatoes and patting them dry. The next debate is about the cooking medium – how much milk do you use? Do you scald it first? Do you add cream? What about cheese? How much butter? Having tried several variations, I can report that it is largely a matter of taste and calorie-consciousness. My *gratin* has become lighter and drier over the last few years – I no longer automatically add an egg (whisked into the warm cream and milk mixture) and I use less liquid. I reserve the use of cheese for *Gratin Savoyard* (see page 134). Scalded milk does give the dish its unique *soupçon* of caramel flavour. I find that if the potato slices are on the thick side, they absorb extra cream and butter. Once again, *à chacun son goût* …

What is crucial is seasoning the potatoes generously, then baking them slowly until they are thoroughly cooked. Having done that, the good news is that you cannot mess up a *gratin*. Some may turn out more sumptuously rich than others, but none will disappoint – as long as they have been patiently baked. Never rush a *gratin* and only turn up the heat for the last few minutes.

So, start by buying a good 1kg/2¼lb of top-quality potatoes. I tend to prefer waxy to floury potatoes for my *gratins* (they disintegrate less readily), but I am not too fussed about the type I use and pick the best of the bunch from the medium-sized spuds available. By medium, I mean that 8 or 9 potatoes will make up the required weight. Ideally, the potatoes should be more or less the same size as this will make the slices easier to arrange neatly.

1 Preheat the oven to 160°C/325°F/gas3. Peel the potatoes and drop them into cold water as you go. Drain well and pat dry with a clean tea-towel or plenty of paper towel. Take a trusted sharp knife or fit the slicing disk on the food processor and cut the potatoes into thin slices. Pat dry again.

2 Peel the garlic clove and cut it in half. If you see a little green shoot, extract it with the point of a knife and discard. Press down the garlic with the

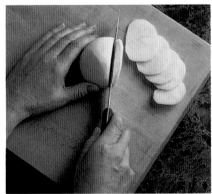

SLICE THE
POTATOES THINLY BUT
NOT WAFER-THIN.

flat side of a knife and rub an attractive medium-sized earthenware gratin dish (I tend to prefer a round one) with the pressed garlic, then discard or use later in another recipe.

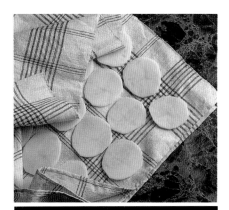

PAT THE POTATO SLICES DRY AGAIN TO ABSORB EXCESS STARCH.

3 Now put a good fat knob of soft butter (about the size of a walnut) in the centre of the dish. Make a small wad of paper towel and use to butter the dish very thoroughly right up to the rim. Scoop up a handful of potato slices and place in the gratin dish against the edge to start the first layer. The potato slices should be at the same time overlapping and well packed together. Continue working inwards a handful at a time until the whole base of the dish is covered with a layer of circular rows of potatoes.

ARRANGE THE POTATO SLICES IN CONCENTRIC CIRCLES, WORKING INWARDS AND SEASONING EACH LAYER.

4 Start seasoning: finely chop the shallots and sprinkle half over the potatoes. Also sprinkle with a pinch of dried thyme and ground sage (or a little nutmeg instead of the sage if you prefer), then season liberally with coarse sea salt and several grindings of black pepper.

5 Heat the milk until almost boiling (I do this not very elegantly in a jug in the microwave for just 2 minutes on full power) and set aside.

6 Dot the potatoes with half of the remaining butter. With a small whisk, stir the crème fraîche into the hot milk. Dribble half of this mixture over the potatoes.

7 Repeat the layering with the rest of the potatoes, again seasoning generously. This time, pour the milk and cream over the potatoes before you dot them with butter. At this stage you can set aside the gratin if it's more convenient for you. Just cover the dish — it will keep quite happily in a cool place for a few hours.

TRICKLE SOME OF THE MILK MIXTURE OVER THE POTATOES BEFORE ADDING THE TOP LAYER.

8 Bake for 55 minutes. Take the dish out of the oven and check tenderness with a skewer – the potatoes will probably need another 5 or 10 minutes, perhaps even longer. Check every 5 minutes from then on until the potatoes start to pierce easily with the skewer. (This is another good time to pause if necessary – take the dish out of the oven and finish it off later).

9 To produce a crusty golden gratin finish, turn up the oven temperature to 220°C/ 425°F/gas7. Dot the potatoes with a little extra butter and season with pepper. Return to the oven for a further 10–15 minutes, until tinged with brown.

10 Leave to cool for at least 5–10 minutes before eating. Enjoy the gratin on its own as a starter or main course, or serve with a roast.

To drink: a white Gaillac or Vin de Savoie

VARIATIONS: make a *Gratin Savoyard* by using 450ml/¾ pt chicken or vegetable stock rather than milk and cream. Flavour with nutmeg and a little cayenne and top with 140g/5oz strong Gruyère cheese, grated.

For *Gratin aux Champignons*, a scattering of thinly sliced wild (or brown) mushrooms sandwiched between the potato layers makes an irresistible addition very much in the spirit of the Savoy region. Use about 140g/5oz wild mushrooms (their flavour will spread through the dish), double the amount if using blander brown mushrooms. Dried ceps work well too.

CAROTTES VICHY
Glazed Carrots

Bicarbonate of soda, aka *Sel de Vichy* in the old days in France, was often used with sugar to prepare carrots. There are still some purists who will tell you that proper *carottes Vichy* have to be cooked in Vichy water … Whichever water you use, this time-honoured recipe is very reliable.

Serves 4
Preparation: 5 minutes
Cooking: about 45 minutes

550g/ 1¼ lb carrots, scraped or peeled and thinly sliced
2tsp sugar
30-45g/ 1-1½ oz butter
few sprigs of parsley
sea salt and freshly ground black pepper

1 Put the carrots in a large sauté pan. Sprinkle in the sugar, add half the butter and just enough water to cover. Season lightly. Cover the pan and bring to a simmer over a moderate heat. Cook for about 20–30 minutes, occasionally shaking the pan, until the carrots are almost done but still a little firm.

2 Remove the lid and turn up the heat. Boil vigorously until all the water has evaporated, still shaking the pan occasionally.

3 Stir in the rest of the butter, snip over the parsley and serve hot.

Variations: for *Carottes à la Crème*, use 2 tablespoons of thick cream instead of the butter in step 3.

For carrot purée, cook to the end of step 1, purée in a mouli or food processor with a little boiled potato for texture (say 100g/3½ oz for the amount of carrots in this recipe), then whisk in cream to taste and season.

CHOU-FLEUR À LA POLONAISE
Cauliflower Cheese

This version differs from the traditional English dish mostly by virtue of the breadcrumbs. The recipe also works well with broccoli or a mixture of broccoli and cauliflower (start cooking the latter 5 minutes before the broccoli). Take care not to overcook the florets.

For a simpler, but still tempting, way to combine cauliflower (or better still cauliflower and broccoli) with unctuous *Sauce Mornay*, add one tablespoon each of cream and water to the sauce. Heat through gently. Arrange the cooked florets (end of step 2) in a saucepan, with the florets facing outwards. Put a plate on top and press down. Replace the plate with the serving dish. Turn the cauliflower over into the dish, rearrange a little, then spoon or dribble the sauce over the mound of cauliflower.

Serves 4
Preparation: 10 minutes
Cooking: about 30 minutes, plus making the Béchamel

30g/ 1oz butter
1 large unblemished cauliflower
30g/ 1oz fresh breadcrumbs
sea salt and freshly ground black pepper
FOR THE SAUCE MORNAY:
1tbsp crème fraîche or cream
45g/ 1½ oz grated strong hard cheese
about 350ml/ 12fl oz Sauce Béchamel
(page 32)

1 Preheat the oven to 200°C/400°F/ gas6. Dot one-third of the butter over a gratin dish and use a wad of paper towel to coat the dish with a thin film of butter.

2 Bring a kettle of water to the boil. Pour the boiling water into a large saucepan, season with salt and bring back to the boil over a moderate heat. Add the cauliflower florets and simmer for 10–15 minutes until almost tender (the stalks should still be a little resilient when pierced with a skewer). Drain the cauliflower florets, refresh under cold running water and drain again.

3 While the cauliflower is cooking, stir the cream and cheese into the Béchamel to make Sauce Mornay. Adjust the seasoning.

4 Tip the cauliflower into the dish, spoon over the Sauce Mornay and toss lightly to combine, taking care not to break up the florets. Season lightly. Sprinkle with the breadcrumbs, dot with the rest of the butter and bake near the top of the oven for 10–15 minutes until golden brown. Serve hot.

RATATOUILLE
Summer Vegetable Medley

A traditional stew of slowly stirred Mediterranean vegetables flavoured with olive oil and garlic, *ratatouille* far too often turns out to be a liquid or greasy mush. In this somewhat unorthodox recipe, I first prepare the vegetables individually in a way that get rids of some excess moisture, then I bake the mixture.

Ratatouille keeps for a few days in the refrigerator and is delicious served cold, sharpened at the last minute with a sprinkling of lemon juice and a touch of fresh garlic.

Serves 6 as a starter, 8 as a side dish
Preparation: about 30 minutes
Cooking: 45 minutes

4 unblemished aubergines, thickly cut on the slant
6 ripe courgettes, thickly cut on the slant
6 ripe tomatoes
2 red sweet peppers
1 yellow sweet pepper
1 green sweet pepper
about 4tbsp fruity olive oil
2 large sweet white onions, thinly sliced
2-3 garlic cloves, crushed
2tsp dried ground thyme
2 bay leaves, crumbled if dried, washed and finely snipped if fresh
2tsp finely grated zest of unwaxed lemon
sea salt and freshly ground black pepper

1 Dégorge the aubergines: sprinkle the slices with salt and leave to stand for 30 minutes. Rinse well, squeezing the slices a little between your fingers. Drain well and pat dry in a clean tea towel or between layers of paper towel.

2 Bring a pan of lightly salted water to the boil, add the courgettes and blanch for 2 minutes. Refresh under cold water, drain well and pat dry like the aubergines.

3 Now bring more water to the boil. Using a sharp knife, cut a small cross on the base of each tomato. Put in a bowl, cover with boiling water and leave for a minute. Drain, refresh and peel off the skins. Cut in half, press out the seeds and cut out excess pale pulp. Cut each half into wedges.

4 Quickly char the peppers, carefully turning them over a flame. Alternatively, put them under a very hot grill for a few minutes until blistered all over, turning them over halfway through — do not allow to cook too long. As soon as the peppers are cool enough to handle, peel off the skin, then remove the core and seeds.

5 Preheat the oven to 200°C/400°F/ gas6.

6 Heat one or two tablespoons of olive oil in a frying pan. Spread the onions in the pan and soften over a low heat for 5 minutes.

7 Season the onion, stir in half the garlic and a little of the thyme and crumbled bay leaf. Cook for a further 5 minutes, still over a low heat, stirring frequently. Spread the mixture over a double layer of paper towel to drain.

8 Oil a large gratin dish and mix the prepared vegetables in the dish. Season, stir in the rest of the thyme and bay leaf. Bake for about 30 minutes.

9 Take out of the oven. Stir in the rest of the garlic and the lemon zest. If you like, dribble over an extra tablespoon of olive oil. Return to the oven for 10–15 minutes. Serve warm or at room temperature.

To drink: a Rosé Vin de Pays du Var.

(RIGHT) *Served warm, tiède or cold,* Ratatouille *makes a filling snack or lunch with good crusty bread.*

SUBRICS D'ÉPINARDS
Twice-cooked Spinach

Subrics (a phonetic rendering of 'sur briques', on bricks) are little cakes, pucks or balls of cooked ingredients often mixed with thick cream or *béchamel* and cooked again – originally on hot bricks. These days they tend to be reheated in clarified butter or baked. Baking is more trouble, but the resulting spinach cakes make a pretty starter, with a well seasoned pepper and tomato *coulis* (see *Pipérade*, page 47) or anchovy butter (page 31) tinged with a little tomato paste. If the *béchamel* (or the cream) is not thick enough, simmer over a moderate heat until thickened, stirring frequently.

Another way to reheat the *subrics* is in clarified butter: make 4 tablespoons (page 10) of the preparation; shape the cakes between 2 spoons; lightly dust with flour and sauté carefully over a moderate heat. They are particularly good with fish and white meats.

Serves 4
Preparation: about 10 minutes, plus making the sauce
Cooking: about 30 minutes

500g/1lb 2oz young leaf spinach, picked and ribbed
55g/2oz butter
pinch of ground nutmeg
1 very fresh large egg, plus 2 extra yolks
100ml/3¹/₂ fl oz very thick well-flavoured Sauce Béchamel (page 32)
1tbsp very thick cream
1¹/₂ tbsp freshly grated strong Gruyère or Parmesan cheese
sea salt and freshly ground black pepper

1 Bring some lightly salted water to the boil in a sauté pan and blanch the spinach for 1 minute. Drain well, refresh under cold water and drain again. Squeeze the spinach gently a handful at a time to extract as much water as possible. Spread on a clean tea towel or double layer of paper towel and pat dry.

2 Melt 15g/¹/₂ oz butter in the sauté pan, add the spinach and nutmeg, season and sauté for 2 minutes, stirring frequently.

3 Preheat the oven to 190°C/375°F/gas5 and generously butter 4 individual 7.5cm/3in ramekins. Bring a kettle of water to the boil.

4 Leave the spinach to cool for a minute, then whizz for a few seconds in the food processor or put through a vegetable mill – the mixture should not be too smooth.

5 In a bowl, lightly whisk the egg and extra yolks as for an omelette. Mix with the thick béchamel, cream and cheese. Season generously. Stir in the puréed spinach and adjust the seasoning. Spoon the mixture into the prepared ramekins. Knock them against the work surface to settle the contents.

6 Bake in a bain-marie: line a baking pan with a few layers of newspaper and put the ramekins in the pan. Pour in boiling water to come halfway up the sides of the ramekins. Bake for about 20–25 minutes until set. Leave to cool for a few minutes in the turned-off oven.

7 Run a sharp knife along the inside of the rim and unmould the *subrics* over warmed serving plates.

To drink: a Muscat d'Alsace.

COURGETTES POÊLÉES À L'ESTRAGON
Sautéed Courgettes with Tarragon

Courgettes are an impressionable vegetable. Their delicate flavour and texture are at their best when the courgettes are past their bland baby stage, just ripe and still firm. Sweating or blanching the courgettes before cooking also helps. There is no need to peel them, but the courgette rounds will look pretty if you use a cannelle or scraping knife to remove a few strips of peel at regular intervals before slicing.

Serves 4
Preparation: 5 minutes plus 1 hour's standing, or 10 minutes
Cooking: about 15 minutes

450g/1lb small to medium-sized firm ripe courgettes, cut into very thin slices
2tsp coarse sea salt (optional)
1 garlic clove, halved
1tbsp oil
2-3tbsp clarified butter (see page 10)
leaves from a few sprigs of tarragon
sea salt and freshly ground black pepper

1 First get rid of some of the courgettes' excess moisture. Put the sliced courgettes in a colander, sprinkle over the coarse salt and mix in. Cover with a weighted plate or bowl and leave to stand for 1 hour. Then rinse under cold water, drain well and pat dry between layers of paper towel or with a clean tea towel. Alternatively, bring a kettle of water to the boil, pour the boiling water into a saucepan and add a teaspoon of salt. Tip in the courgette slices, blanch for 2 minutes, then drain well as above.

2 Rub a frying pan or sauté pan with the cut sides of the garlic. Spoon in the oil. Place over a moderate heat and tilt the pan around over the heat until well coated and hot.

3 Add half the clarified butter and snip in a few tarragon leaves. Add the prepared courgette slices. Season and sauté for 5–7 minutes over a moderate heat, stirring occasionally.

4 Add the rest of the butter and a little more tarragon and continue sautéing for about 5–7 minutes, stirring occasionally.

5 To serve, tip into a warmed dish, season again and snip over a little extra tarragon.

Variation: replace the clarified butter with olive oil and the tarragon with thyme or marjoram and a quarter teaspoon of grated lemon zest.

PETITS POIS À LA FRANÇAISE
Baby Peas with Lettuce and Onion

The simplicity of this favourite French recipe makes it a perfect way to cook freshly picked tender young peas. Variations work well with peas that have been frozen or that are past their infancy – add to the peas and lettuce 3 thin slices of cured ham, rolled and snipped, 2-3 artichoke hearts, slivered; mix into the finished dish a tablespoon of sautéed lardons, 2 tablespoons of meat stock or leftover poultry gravy and 2 tablespoons of crème fraîche.

Serves 4
Preparation: 15 minutes
Cooking: about 30 minutes

55g/2oz butter
leaves from a small soft lettuce, rolled and snipped
white parts of 2 large spring onions, finely chopped
450g/1lb shelled petits pois or tender baby garden peas (about 1.8kg/4lb unshelled peas)
1/4 tsp sugar
2 sprigs of parsley
1tbsp snipped fresh chervil, or 1 1/2 tsp snipped fresh mint leaves
sea salt and freshly ground black pepper

1 In a sauté pan, melt half the butter over a moderate heat. Add the chiffonnade of lettuce and the spring onions to the melted butter. Stir for 2 minutes until softened.

2 Add the petits pois, sugar and parsley. Season lightly and pour in about 150ml/1/2 pt of water. Bring to a simmer, then reduce the heat a little, cover and cook until the peas are just tender (the exact timing depends on the quality and freshness of the peas and should be some 12–20 minutes).

3 Drain, then transfer to a warmed serving dish. Adjust the seasoning and stir in the rest of the butter. Sprinkle over the chervil or mint, stir lightly and serve as soon as possible.

From this end: Steak au Poivre Vert *(page 122)*
with Petits Pois à la Française *(page 139) and*
Artichauts à la Barigoule.

ARTICHAUTS À LA BARIGOULE

Stuffed Artichokes with Mushrooms and Bacon

From Brittany to Provence, artichokes are a controversial vegetable. Eaten by some at every opportunity, they are firmly rejected by others – I yet have to come across a family united in their views about this everyday vegetable. Serious artichoke eaters whose companions do not share their *penchant* may know that the easiest way to prepare your *artichaut* is to wrap it in cling film, pierce the film and microwave on high for 5-8 minutes, depending on size. Leave it to stand for 5 minutes, then enjoy with Vinaigrette (page 11). The recipe below comes from Provence – *barigoule* is a local fungus that is often cooked in the same way and produces a more sociable dish.

Serves 4
Preparation: about 20 minutes
Cooking: about 1 hour

4 fresh globe artichokes
1 tbsp lemon juice
3 garlic cloves
4 tbsp fruity olive oil
115g/4oz button mushrooms, wiped and thinly sliced
1 small onion, finely chopped
85g/3oz finely diced bacon, blanched
1 slice of dry cured ham, cut into small thin strips
1 tbsp snipped parsley
1/2 tsp each dried thyme, oregano and savory
6 tbsp dry white wine
sea salt and freshly ground black pepper

1 Bring a kettle of water to the boil. Trim the artichokes, cutting off the stalk and the top leaves. Pour the water into a saucepan just large enough to hold the artichokes in a single snug layer. Add a pinch of salt and the lemon juice to the water. Drop in the artichokes, bring back to the boil, then reduce the heat a little and boil for 10 minutes. Drain, refresh well and leave upside down in a colander until cool enough to handle.

2 Meanwhile, crush 2 of the garlic cloves and halve the other. Heat a tablespoon of oil in a frying pan over a moderate heat and sauté the mushrooms, the crushed garlic, chopped onion, diced bacon and smoked ham for 2–3 minutes. Season lightly, then snip in the parsley and reserve.

3 With a sharp knife or small spoon, remove the small central leaves and the choke from each artichoke. Spoon in the reserved mixture.

4 Rub the pan with the cut garlic and pour in the rest of the oil. Sprinkle in the dried herbs. Heat through gently over a moderate heat.

5 Return the stuffed artichokes to the pan and season. Pour in the white wine and cover tightly with foil and a lid. Cook over a low heat for about 45–55 minutes.

6 Put the artichokes on a dish. Allow the cooking liquid to reduce just a little over a fairly high heat, then adjust the seasoning. Strain through a sieve over the artichokes. Serve warm or at room temperature.

ENDIVES AU FOUR
Baked Chicory

To turn this side dish into a main course that makes a satisfying winter supper, wrap each head of blanched chicory in a halved slice of cured ham.

Serves 4
Preparation: 15 minutes
Cooking: about 50 minutes

12 small heads of chicory, washed and trimmed
2tsp lemon juice
55g/2oz butter
2tsp sugar
1/2 tsp rubbed dried sage
1/4 tsp freshly grated nutmeg
3tbsp crème fraîche
45g/1 1/2 oz strong Gruyère or mature Cheddar cheese
sea salt and freshly ground black pepper

1 Bring a large saucepan of water to the boil and season with salt. Add the chicory and the lemon juice. Bring back to boiling point and blanch the chicory for 4 minutes, then drain well and leave to steam off until cool enough to handle.

2 Preheat the oven to 190°C/375°F/gas5. Use one-third of the butter to grease a gratin dish just large enough to take the chicory in a single well-packed layer. Gently squeeze the chicory to extract excess moisture.

3 Put the chicory in the dish and season. Then sprinkle over the sugar, sage and nutmeg. Dot with half the remaining butter and cover with foil. Bake in the oven for about 15 minutes.

4 In a bowl, mix the grated cheese with the crème fraîche and season with black pepper.

5 Take the dish out of the oven and remove the foil. Turn up the heat to 200°C/400°F/gas6.

6 Spread the cream and cheese over the chicory. Dot with the rest of the butter and bake without the foil for a further 10–15 minutes, until the gratin is golden and sizzling. Leave to cool a little and serve hot.

ALIGOT
Potato and Cheese Purée

For a classic *purée de pommes de terre*, French creamed potatoes, omit the garlic and stop at the end of step 5. Unlike *Aligot* (which has to be eaten the moment it turns stringy), creamed potatoes will keep nicely warm for up to 20 minutes over a pan of very hot water.

Serves 4
Preparation: 10 minutes
Cooking: about 45 minutes

550g/1 1/4 lb floury potatoes, peeled
55g/2oz butter
2 garlic cloves, crushed
tiny pinch of grated nutmeg
2 or more tbsp single or double cream
4 or more tbsp milk
255g/9oz Tomme d'Aligot or young farmhouse Lancashire or Caerphilly cheese, cut into slivers
sea salt and freshly ground black pepper

1 Bring to the boil plenty of water in a large saucepan. Season with salt, drop in the potatoes and return to the boil over a high heat. Once the water gets to a rolling boil, reduce the heat to a fast simmer. Cook the potatoes for 20–30 minutes, until they are tender but not soft – do not let the potatoes disintegrate and keep the simmering steady.

2 Drain well, refresh under cold water and leave the potatoes in a colander until cool enough to handle.

3 While the potatoes are cooling, melt the butter in the pan and stir in the garlic. Then add the nutmeg, cream and milk. Season and cook for 2–3 minutes over a low heat, stirring frequently, then take the pan off the heat.

4 Peel the potatoes. Mash them using a ricer or a vegetable mill, working as lightly as possible in order not to remove the starch.

5 Put the mashed potatoes in the pan. Using a wooden spoon, stir them well into the cream mixture. Season generously. If the purée looks too stiff, stir in a little extra milk or cream.

6 Return the pan to a low heat and beat in the cheese, a few slivers at a time. Continue stirring vigorously over a low heat for a few minutes, lifting the mass well until the purée is smooth and elastic. Stop beating and serve the moment the cheese starts to make strings.

FÈVES FRAÎCHES AUX PETITS LARDONS
Broad Bean Stew with Bacon and Herbs

Fresh young broad beans are so tender you can nibble them raw. This dish makes the most of them. Use the same method to prepare frozen broad beans or already cooked haricot beans (see Cassoulet, page 112). For older broad beans, increase the cooking time and double the amount of liquid.

Serves 3-4 as a main course, 4-6 as a side dish
Preparation: about 20 minutes, plus pre-cooking the haricot beans, if using
Cooking: about 20 minutes

1 tbsp groundnut or sunflower oil
50g/ 1 1/2 oz butter
white parts of 3 large spring onions, thinly sliced
1 garlic clove, crushed (optional)
4 thick slices of rindless smoky bacon, cut into small pieces, blanched and drained
450g/ 1lb broad beans, podded and preferably skinned, or cooked haricot beans (page 112)
1 tsp dried sweet savory
1/2 tsp dried marjoram
4 tbsp chicken stock
3 tbsp dry white wine
several leaves of lettuce, tightly rolled and snipped into small thin strips
1 1/2 tbsp finely snipped parsley
sea salt and freshly ground black pepper

1 Heat the oil in a sauté pan. Melt half the butter, then add the onions and garlic (if using). Sauté for 2 minutes over a moderate heat. Add the bacon and stir for 2 minutes until crisp.

2 Add the broad beans or haricots, the dried herbs, stock and white wine. Season and bring to a simmer, stirring from time to time.

3 Cover and cook for 10–15 minutes, until the beans are tender. Stir in the rest of the butter, lettuce strips and parsley. Adjust the seasoning and serve hot.

THE SECRETS OF FRENCH HOME COOKING

POMMES DE TERRE À L'HUILE
Potatoes Stewed in Olive Oil

Finely sliced spring onion is a nice addition to this dish – scatter it into the pan at the beginning of step 2. If you are using clarified butter, try snipping in a little fresh tarragon, chervil or chives at the end of cooking.

Serves 4
Preparation: 10 minutes
Cooking: 35 minutes

450g/1lb even-sized new or salad
potatoes, peeled and dried
3¹/₂ tbsp olive oil, goose fat or clarified
butter (see page 10)
sea salt and freshly ground black pepper

1 In a heavy pan large enough to take the potatoes in a single layer, heat the oil, fat or butter over a moderate heat. Add the potatoes, swirl and turn to coat well and season lightly.

2 Reduce the heat, cover the pan and cook the potatoes for 25–35 minutes, until tender. Shake the pan from time to time and keep the heat even and very low throughout the cooking.

3 Season again just before serving.

(LEFT) Pommes de Terre à l'Huile *make a nice snack cold with smoked eel or fish.*

POÊLÉE DE HARICOTS VERTS AUX AMANDES
Pan-fried Green Beans with Almonds

Serves 4
Preparation: about 15 minutes
Cooking: up to 15 minutes

450g/1lb young green beans, topped, tailed
and strings removed
1¹/₂ tbsp olive oil
30g/1oz butter
white parts of 2 large spring onions, very thinly
sliced
1 garlic clove, crushed
2tbsp slivered blanched almonds
2tbsp finely snipped chervil or parsley
sea salt and freshly ground black pepper

1 Bring a large pan of salted water to the boil. Add the beans and bring back to the boil. Keep uncovered at a rolling boil until the beans are very barely tender (small very young beans take 3–4 minutes, larger ones up to 8 minutes).

2 Drain and refresh in cold water. Drain again well, then spread to dry on a clean towel or layers of paper towel.

3 Heat the oil in a frying or sauté pan. Divide the butter into 3 equal pieces and add one piece to the pan. Melt over a moderate heat. Add the spring onion and garlic and stir for a minute.

4 Scatter over the almonds. Cook for 2 minutes, stirring frequently, then tip in the beans and another piece of butter. Turn up the heat a fraction and sauté for 2 minutes, stirring frequently.

5 Sprinkle over the chervil or parsley. Stir in the rest of the butter, adjust the seasoning and serve as soon as possible.

CROUSTADES AUX CHAMPIGNONS
Mushroom Canapés

These creamed mushrooms can also be served as a filling for individual savoury tartlets (see page 64 for the pastry recipe).

Serves 6
Preparation: 15 minutes, plus making the Béchamel, if using
Cooking: 20 minutes

550g/1¹/₄ lb small brown or white mushrooms, wiped and very thinly sliced
2tsp oil
55g/2oz butter
2tbsp finely snipped mixed chives and parsley
4 slices of slightly stale chilled brioche, crusts removed
3tbsp Sauce Béchamel (page 32) or thick cream
1tbsp Madeira
sea salt and freshly ground black pepper

1 Prepare the mushrooms: heat the oil in a sauté pan. Add half the butter, swirl over a moderate heat, then scatter in the mushrooms. Sauté for 5 minutes over a moderate heat, stirring frequently. Reduce the heat a little. Season lightly, sprinkle in a tablespoon of herbs, half the remaining butter and sauté for another 5 minutes – the mushrooms should be very soft and reduced.

2 Meanwhile, preheat the grill to high and prepare the croûtes: cut the brioche into small squares or into small circles, using a round biscuit cutter. Reduce the grill heat a little and grill the croûtes until lightly golden and crisp. Butter them very lightly on one side and reserve.

3 Add the béchamel or cream to the sautéed mushrooms and mix well together over a low heat until hot. Stir in the Madeira and half of the remaining herbs. Adjust the seasoning. (The mushroom preparation can be chilled overnight if required and gently reheated at the last minute.)

4 A few minutes before serving, preheat the grill again and reheat the mushroom mixture. Spread the mushroom mixture over the brioche canapés and grill for a few minutes until piping hot. Sprinkle with the rest of the herbs and serve hot.

Variation: try adding a tablespoon of freshly grated Parmesan, strong Gruyère or mature Cheddar cheese with a few drops of Worcestershire sauce to the mushroom mixture.

To drink: a Champagne or other sparkling wine.

(LEFT) Croustades aux Champignons *make perfect party fare.*

LA MARMELADE D'OIGNONS

Stewed Onions

Serves 4-6
Preparation: 15 minutes
Cooking: about 1¼ hours

55g/2oz butter
900g/2lb sweet white onions (see right), thinly sliced
75g/2½ oz sugar
2tbsp red wine vinegar
2tbsp sherry vinegar
2 shallots, chopped
1 garlic clove, crushed
3tbsp Madeira
sea salt and freshly ground black pepper

Onion *marmelade* is probably the nearest the French get to chutney. This preparation is eaten warm to accompany roast meats. Served cold, it is delicious with pâtés and gamy terrines. It will keep for several weeks refrigerated in a sterilized jar and can be spooned out to enhance sauces and stews.

Sweet white onions melt obligingly in the pan and have the ideal texture and flavour for *marmelade*. Unfortunately, they are less widely available than their golden or red relatives. If you are using Spanish onions or the red onions of Northern Europe, omit the shallots and add a little extra sugar.

TIP THE ONIONS INTO THE PAN AND STIR WELL TO COAT THEM WITH MELTED BUTTER.

KEEP THE HEAT VERY LOW WHILE YOU SOFTEN THE ONIONS.

1 Put a large sauté pan over a low heat. Add the butter and let it melt. Tip in the onions, season lightly with salt, pepper and stir well for a minute or two to make sure the onion mixture is well coated with butter. Now cover the pan and leave the onions to sweat and soften over a very low heat. From time to time, give the pan a good shake or lift the lid and give the mixture a stir. Keep the heat low. If at any time the onions look too dry or start to colour, sprinkle in a tablespoon of water and reduce the heat a fraction.

2 After about 30 minutes, take off the lid and turn up the heat a little. Sprinkle in 2 generous tablespoons of sugar, both vinegars, the chopped shallots and crushed garlic. Season again, stir well, then add 4 tablespoons of water. Continue cooking uncovered for another 30 minutes, keeping the heat fairly low. The mixture will get darker and thicker. If it looks too dry, lower the heat a little and add a tablespoon of water.

3 To finish: sprinkle in the Madeira and the rest of the sugar. Turn up the

STIR IN THE MADEIRA TOWARDS THE END OF COOKING AND TURN UP THE HEAT TO CARAMELIZE THE ONIONS.

heat to high and stir the mixture for a couple of minutes while the sugar caramelizes a little.

VARIATIONS: for a hint of orange in the flavour, add a scant tablespoon of finely grated orange zest halfway through cooking and replace the Madeira with a tablespoon each of Cointreau and orange juice.

If you haven't got sherry vinegar to hand, replace with red wine vinegar, but compensate with a little extra Madeira, oloroso sherry or port for that woody nutty depth of flavour.

A scant tablespoon of dried rubbed sage used instead of the shallots gives a nice herby edge to the *marmelade.*

La Marmelade d'Oignons
served as a relish with Terrine de Faisan
(page 106).

LENTILLES TIÈDES À L'HUILE DE NOIX ET AU PERSIL

Lentils with Walnut Oil and Parsley

To turn this delicate lentil side dish into a salad, add an extra 1½ tablespoons of groundnut oil and a little more lemon juice, wine or sherry vinegar to the dressing.

Serves 4
Preparation: 10 minutes
Cooking: 35 minutes

350g/12oz small blue-green Le Puy lentils, rinsed and drained
1 bouquet garni
1 large spring onion
few sprigs of flat leaf parsley
small pinch of dried rubbed sage
2tbsp walnut oil, or 1tbsp groundnut oil and 1tbsp walnut oil
1 small garlic clove, crushed (optional)
few drops of lemon juice
sea salt and freshly ground black pepper

1 Put the lentils in a heavy saucepan or sauté pan. Pour in water to a depth of 4cm/1½in above the lentils. Add the bouquet garni and the spring onion. Bring to the boil and skim off any surface grey dirt. Season with salt and reduce the heat. Simmer uncovered over a moderate to low heat for 25–35 minutes, until the lentils are just tender.

2 Drain off the excess liquid (it will be a good addition to a soup or stock) and discard the spring onion and bouquet garni.

3 While the lentils are cooking, snip the parsley into a small bowl. Add the rubbed sage, oil, crushed garlic if using, and the lemon juice. Stir well, then season to taste.

4 Tip the lentils into a serving bowl. Dribble over the dressing, toss lightly and serve warm.

RIZ CRÉOLE AU BASILIC

Boiled Rice with Basil

Cooking rice *à la créole* in plenty of boiling salted water then re-heating it in the oven in a gratin dish lightly smeared with butter is a convenient method popular in France. The rice can be prepared well ahead and comes out in clean separate grains. Basil purée makes a tasty contribution. For a plainer dish, simply sprinkle the rice with grated Gruyère cheese before re-heating.

Serves 4
Preparation: 10 minutes
Cooking: 20 minutes, plus 15 minutes re-heating

few drops of lemon juice
about 225g/8oz long-grain white rice
1 large young garlic clove
1½ tbsp extra virgin olive oil
several leaves of basil
1 ripe tomato, blanched, deseeded, skinned and chopped
55g/2oz Gruyère cheese, grated
30g/1oz butter
sea salt and freshly ground black pepper

1 In a large saucepan, bring to the boil at least 1.1 litres/2pts of lightly salted water. Add the lemon juice.

2 Throw the rice into the boiling water and boil uncovered for 12–15 minutes, until done to your liking.

3 While the rice is cooking, using a pestle and mortar crush the garlic with a little salt and the olive oil. Snip in the basil, crush again, then work in the tomato and cheese. Season with pepper.

4 Drain the rice and refresh very briefly under cold running water. Drain again. Reserve until about 15 minutes before you are ready to serve the rice.

5 Preheat the oven to 190°C/350°F/ gas 5 and grease a gratin dish with the butter. Put the rice in the gratin dish and put in the oven until piping hot.

6 Take the rice out of the oven, spread the basil and tomato purée on top, gently stir in and serve immediately. If you like, snip over two or three rolled basil leaves before serving.

PÂTES FRAÎCHES À L'ALSACIENNE
Home-made Flat Egg Noodles

The consumption of pasta is steadily increasing in France, but recipes and techniques are still largely borrowed from Italy. The exception to this rather generalized statement is Alsace, where home pasta-making is very much part of the culinary tradition.

Serves 4
Preparation: 15 minutes, plus resting
Cooking: 15 minutes

300g/10¹/₂ oz plain white flour, plus extra for dusting
1 tsp sea salt
2 eggs
little groundnut or sunflower oil
TO SERVE:
45g/1¹/₂ oz butter (or more to taste)
1 tbsp finely snipped parsley
1 tsp caraway seeds (optional)
sea salt and freshly ground black pepper

1 Season the flour with the salt, tip it on a cold working surface and make a well in the centre. Put the eggs in the well, then start mixing them into the flour, working from the centre outwards.

2 Add a few drops of oil and a little water as you work the mixture into a firm elastic dough. Work it into a ball with the palms of your hands. Knead a few times, then leave to rest at room temperature for 1 hour.

3 Dredge a working surface and rolling pin with flour. Thinly roll out the dough and cut into long ribbons.

4 Use the pasta immediately or leave to dry for 2–3 hours, dusted with a little flour and spread flat on a large rack.

5 Bring a large saucepan of lightly salted water to a fast boil. Add a teaspoon of oil to the pan. Cook the noodles for 3–5 minutes (dried noodles will take a little longer than ones that have been just rolled out). Drain well and serve with butter, snipped herbs and, if you like, a scant sprinkling of caraway seeds.

Chapter Nine

LES DESSERTS

Desserts

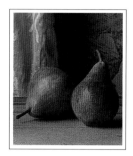

For a truly spectacular dessert, most
French people will rely on the skills of the local
maître pâtissier rather than spend hours attempting
to make their own. The traditional sweets and
cakes of French home cooking are relatively simple
affairs. They require attention to detail rather than
technical skills. Many of the most delicious rely on
the fruit of the season handled with a gentle touch
and absence of fuss – poached in wine or flavoured
with a light syrup, baked in open tarts, preserved
with sugar, or even cooked in a light batter.
Otherwise, the rest of the best French home
desserts make liberal use of everyday ingredients:
sweet butter, dark semi-bitter chocolate, crème
fraîche, eggs and – that great stand-by – caster
sugar, subtly flavoured with a pod of vanilla.
French home cooks may not be passionate bakers
but they all have a solid tried-and-tested repertory
of classic desserts.

RIGHT
Clafoutis (page 154) is given much of its
distinctive flavour by the cherry stones – but do warn
your guests before they break a tooth.

CLAFOUTIS
Cherry Batter Pudding

In some parts of France, *clafoutis* used to be baked on buttered cabbage leaves, a picturesque method which can be abandoned in favour of a more orthodox container. Outside the cherry season, *clafoutis* can be made with plums or apricots (stoned and halved), grapes or apples (cored and quartered).

Serves 6
Preparation: 15 minutes
Cooking: about 45 minutes

4 medium fresh eggs
pinch of salt
55g/2oz caster sugar, preferably vanilla-flavoured (see page 10)
1 heaped tbsp self-raising flour
3tbsp melted butter (not too hot), plus extra for greasing
225ml/7fl oz milk
1tbsp rum or Kirsch (optional)
550g/1¼ lb ripe black cherries, stalks removed
1tbsp icing sugar

1 Preheat the oven to 200°C/400°F/gas6.

2 Lightly beat the eggs as for an omelette. Add a small pinch of salt and the sugar. Mix in well.

3 Sift the flour over the egg mixture and whisk in well, then trickle in the melted butter. Work in until smooth.

4 Dribble in the milk, stirring well to prevent lumps forming. If you like, flavour the mixture with rum or Kirsch.

5 Generously butter an earthenware tart or gratin dish. Arrange the cherries in the dish. Cover with the custard mixture and bake for 40–45 minutes, until set and golden. Check after 25 minutes and reduce the heat a little if the custard is browning too fast.

6 Leave to cool a little before dusting with the icing sugar and serving.

To drink: a medium-sweet Côtes de Bergerac or Côtes de Montravel.

MILLE-FEUILLES
Cream Slices

Not quite the 'thousand leaves' the name of the dessert would lead you to expect, but four fragile layers of puff pastry and rum-flavoured crème pâtissière heaped into a gloriously wobbly sweet concoction. I like adding a touch of raspberry jelly.

You might prefer to halve the quantity of crème pâtissière and replace it with Crème Chantilly (page 164). If you like, glaze the top layer with a little lemon icing (page 172).

Serves 6
Preparation: 15 minutes, plus making the pastry cream
Cooking: 15 minutes

250g/8½ oz ready-to-roll puff pastry
1tbsp granulated sugar
3tbsp raspberry jelly (optional)
thick Crème Pâtissière (see page 156) made with 400ml/14fl oz milk and flavoured with 1tbsp rum
butter, for greasing
icing sugar, for dredging

1 Grease a baking sheet with butter. Roll out the pastry as thinly as you can into a 40cm/16in square and place it on the baking sheet. Prick the pastry with a fork and chill for 10 minutes. Preheat the oven to 220°C/425°F/gas7.

2 Using a brush dipped in water, lightly dampen the pastry, then sprinkle with the granulated sugar. Bake for about 8–10 minutes, until golden and puffed up. Take out of the oven.

3 Using a sharp knife, cut the pastry into 4 equal long strips. Turn each strip over carefully with a palette knife and return to the turned-off oven for 3–5 minutes to crisp up the underside. Close the oven door. Remove from the oven and leave to cool on a rack.

4 If you are using raspberry jelly, warm it gently in a small saucepan until runny. Lightly brush 3 of the pastry strips with jelly, if using. Spread the crème pâtissière over these 3 coated strips.

5 To assemble the pastry, carefully lay the 3 coated strips on top of each other, pressing down gently each time. Place the remaining uncoated strip on top and press down again lightly. Using a small sieve, generously dredge with icing sugar.

6 To serve: using a very sharp fine-bladed knife, cut the large mille-feuille into 6 equal portions.

To drink: an Alsace Gewürztraminer.

SAVARIN AU GRAND MARNIER
Baba Ring with Orange Liqueur

A *savarin* is a ring of yeast pastry (*pâte levée*) generously moistened with an orange-flavoured rum or brandy syrup. Its creators, the Julien brothers – who were *pâtissiers* in Paris during the Second Empire – named it after Brillat-Savarin, philosopher and *gastronome extraordinaire* whose book *La Physiologie du Goût* has remained entrancing reading after more than 170 years.

Roll up your sleeves for these recipes, for they are really messy and sticky as well as being quite hard work (for a few minutes).

Serves 6–8
Preparation: 20 minutes, plus rising
Cooking: about 30 minutes

200g/7oz self-raising flour, plus extra for dredging
7g/¼oz sachet easy-bake dried yeast
pinch of fine sea salt
2tsp caster sugar
3 very fresh eggs
100ml/3½fl oz milk, warmed
75g/2½oz very soft unsalted butter, plus extra for greasing

FOR THE SYRUP:
225g/8oz caster sugar
3tbsp brandy or rum
1tsp each very finely grated orange and lemon zest
2-3tbsp Grand Marnier or other orange liqueur
300ml/½pt Crème Chantilly (page 164)
icing sugar, for dredging

1 Sift the flour and dried yeast into a large bowl. Stir in the salt and sugar. In a smaller bowl, beat the eggs, then stir in 2 tablespoons of hot water. Mix the egg into the flour, a little at a time. Work in the warm milk and the soft butter. Cover with greased cling film and leave to double in size in a warm place (allow about an hour). If you prefer, whizz the dough in the food processor, fitted with the plastic blades, whizzing in short bursts and scraping the mixture down the sides of the bowl until you have a ball of dough.

2 Lightly dredge with flour the bowl or, if you prefer, a work surface. Knead the dough for several minutes until smooth and supple, dredging with a little flour if too sticky. The bulk will shrink back a little as you work.

3 Generously butter a 850ml/1½pt ring mould. Roll the dough into a long sausage shape and put this in the tin, joining up the ends. Cover with greased cling film and leave the dough to rise and fill the tin (allow at least 30 minutes).

4 Preheat the oven to 190°C/375°F/gas5. Bake the dough for 25–30 minutes, until brown and shrinking back a little from the edge of the tin. Check the dough is cooked through with a metal skewer – it should come out clean. If the top is browning too fast, cover loosely with foil for the last 5–10 minutes.

5 Leave the savarin to cool for a few minutes in the tin, then invert on a cooling rack.

6 Make the syrup while the savarin is cooling: in a saucepan over a low heat, dissolve the sugar in about 300ml/½pt water. Boil for 5 minutes, then remove from the heat and stir in the brandy or rum, orange and lemon zest and orange liqueur.

7 Using a metal skewer or a large fork, prick the savarin all over. Put the savarin in a serving dish and pour over the hot syrup. Leave to get cold.

8 Just before serving, spoon Crème Chantilly into the centre of the savarin and dredge with a little icing sugar.

Variation: to make individual babas, use the same yeast dough, but work in 3–4 tablespoons of rum-soaked raisins before you leave the dough to rise. Bake in well greased individual tins for about 15 minutes.

For *Brioche*, use an extra 55g/2oz soft unsalted butter and really knead the dough vigorously, pushing and slapping back, for about 10 minutes. Brush with a little beaten egg yolk glaze before baking at 200°C/400°F/gas6 for about 20 minutes.

To drink: a Cabernet de Saumur or medium-dry Loire rosé.

LA CRÈME PÂTISSIÈRE

Pastry Cream

Makes a generous 300ml/ ¹/₂ pt
Preparation and cooking: 20 minutes,
plus cooling

300ml/ ¹/₂ pt full-fat milk
1 vanilla pod, split
1 level tbsp flour
1 heaped tsp cornflour
3 tbsp caster sugar
2 large or 3 medium very fresh egg yolks
10g/ ¹/₂ oz chilled butter
1 tbsp Kirsch

I always think of *crème pâtissière* as the country cousin of *Crème Anglaise* (page 174). Its taste and texture may be somewhat less delicate, but it is infinitely less tricky to prepare. What it may lose in elegance it makes up for in reliability and versatility. *Crème pâtissière* is a great stand-by of the French home kitchen — the most popular way to fill profiteroles and mille-feuilles, and the smooth lining for many a fruit tart and other desserts.

Crème pâtissière is a custard of flavoured milk, flour and egg yolk. The starch in the flour helps prevent curdling and there is no need to use a double-boiler to prepare it. The two potential pitfalls — lumps and a floury taste — are easy to avoid with a sieve and a little patience.

SLOWLY BRING THE MILK TO THE BOIL, THEN TURN OFF THE HEAT AND LEAVE FOR AT LEAST 15 MINUTES.

1 Put the milk in a medium heavy saucepan, add the split vanilla pod and bring to just below boiling point over a low heat. As soon as small bubbles start popping up here and there, turn off the heat and leave the scalded milk to infuse for at least 15 minutes — the longer you leave it, the more pronounced the vanilla flavour.

2 Meanwhile, sift the flour and cornflour into a large clean bowl, then tip in the sugar. Using a balloon whisk, combine the flour and sugar until well blended — the more you break up the flour the less likely you are to end up with a lumpy custard. Tip in the egg yolks and continue whisking vigorously until the mixture becomes paler and starts to thicken.

3 Remove the vanilla from the milk — it will still be warm at this stage. The split pod can be rinsed, dried and re-used (to flavour sugar, see page 10). Pour the milk into the egg and flour mixture in a thin trickle, a little at a time, whisking well between additions (again the idea is to break up any starch pockets). Carry on whisking until the mixture is smooth. Start pouring it into the pan. If you notice any lumps while you are pouring, tip the custard back into the bowl and strain it through a sieve into another bowl.

4 Bring your lump-free custard to the boil over a low heat, stirring very frequently — this process always seems to be a perfect illustration of the saying that 'watched pots never boil', but the slowness is deceptive: in my experience a neglected custard will always erupt resentfully. Once the cream starts to bubble, keep it boiling gently for about 5 minutes to give the flour time to cook and lose its rather unpleasant starchy taste.

POUR THE INFUSED MILK INTO THE EGG AND FLOUR MIXTURE IN A THIN TRICKLE

5 At this stage the bubbles plop about alarmingly and the custard looks very solid and uneven, but it just means that some parts of the custard have thickened faster than others. Take the sauce off the heat, whisk in the chilled butter and the Kirsch and leave to cool.

REMOVE SAUCE FROM THE HEAT AND WHISK IN THE CHILLED BUTTER AND THE KIRSCH.

6 Again, if you notice any lumps, push the custard through a sieve. You still need to stir several times as the sauce gets cooler, to make sure no surface skin develops. Alternatively, lightly dredge with caster sugar. When quite cold, cover and chill until ready to use.

OTHER FLAVOURINGS: before scalding the milk, add a few strips of orange, lime or lemon zest. Remove before incorporating the egg mixture. Coffee granules (2 teaspoons) or finely grated bitter chocolate (2 tablespoons) can be whisked in while the pastry cream is still hot enough to melt them. Liqueurs are best added very sparingly once the custard has cooled down enough for you to taste what you are doing. Kirsch and rum are the most traditional, but brandy, *marc* and whisky taste fine. Much as I like Cointreau, I find it somewhat cloying in this particular combination.

For a lighter cream, whisk 2 egg whites until stiff and sweeten lightly with caster sugar. Beat this into the pastry cream immediately after taking it off the heat (step 5). If you require a thicker cream, add 1 or 2 teaspoons of flour to the basic amount. For a thin cream, use a little extra milk.

La Crème Pâtissière *used as base for the filling in* Tarte aux Fruits *(see overleaf)*.

TARTE AUX FRUITS
Fruit Tarts

This perennially popular dessert is at its best prepared with the fruit and berries of early and mid-summer. It can also be made all year round with defrosted frozen soft fruit. On occasion, I like using bottled cherries with a little of their syrup – simmered until slightly reduced – as a glaze.

Serves 6
Preparation: 20 minutes, plus 40 minutes'
chilling and making the Crème Pâtissière
Baking: about 30 minutes

FOR THE SWEET SHORTCRUST PASTRY:
225g/8oz plain flour
pinch of salt
140g/5oz unsalted butter, plus more for
greasing
1 egg, plus a little extra yolk mixed with water
for glazing the pastry
45g/1¹/₂ oz caster sugar

FOR THE FILLING:
3tbsp raspberry or other red fruit jelly
about 24-30 very ripe cherries
about 24 medium ripe strawberries
about 300ml/¹/₂ pt Crème Pâtissière
(page 156)
about 24-30 raspberries
1tbsp Cointreau
icing sugar, for dredging (optional)

1 First make the pastry: using the metal blade of the food processor, whizz together the flour, salt and butter. In a small bowl, combine the egg with a tablespoon of cold water, then stir in the sugar. Add to the flour mixture and whizz again in short bursts until the dough comes together into a rough ball. Wrap in cling film and chill for at least half an hour before rolling out. (Make the crème pâtissière while waiting.)

2 Preheat the oven to 190°C/375°F/gas5 and grease a large loose-bottomed tart tin.

3 Roll out the pastry and spread it into the tin, pressing it in gently with your hands without stretching it. Then prick with a fork and chill again for 10 minutes. Line with greaseproof paper or greased foil.

4 Brush the edges of the tart shell with a little egg yolk and water. Fill the lined shell with dried beans and bake for 20–25 minutes, until the pastry is set and the edges are golden. Remove the beans and paper. Leave to cool a little.

5 Meanwhile, warm the jelly for the filling in a small saucepan until runny. Stone the cherries and halve the strawberries.

6 Spread the crème pâtissière into the warm pastry case. Put the fruit on top of the crème pâtissière, strawberries cut side down. The fruit will look equally pretty jumbled up, arranged in overlapping circles or separately, each type of fruit covering a third of the tart.

7 Add the Cointreau to the warm jelly. Brush this lightly over the fruit and leave to get cold.

8 Just before serving, lift the tart and base from the ring. If you like, dust it lightly with icing sugar.

TARTE AUX NOIX
Walnut Tart

Walnuts are a favourite ingredient in the South-west of the country and *Tarte aux Noix* is pretty much France's answer to pecan pie. Fresh walnuts and honey are a worthy match for pecans and syrup, and loyalty to the *spécialité de la région* is just as strong in Quercy and Périgord as it is in New England.

Serves 6
Preparation: making the pastry, plus
20 minutes

Baking: about 25 minutes, plus cooling
Finishing: 10 minutes

225g/8oz sweet shortcrust pastry,
pre-baked in a loose-bottomed tart tin
(see left)
4tbsp runny honey
170g/6oz very fresh walnut kernels
100g/3¹/₂ oz caster sugar, plus a
little extra
3 large eggs
75g/2¹/₂ oz very soft unsalted butter, plus a
little extra for greasing
1 tbsp brandy (optional)
icing sugar, to dust (optional)

1 Preheat the oven to 180°C/350°F/gas4. Brush the inside of the pastry case with honey – if it is not runny enough, warm through gently in a small pan.

2 Reserving a handful of the more attractive walnut kernels to put on top of the tart, whizz the rest of the nuts in the food processor until ground.

3 In a bowl, combine the ground walnuts with the sugar. Stir in the eggs, the soft butter (reserving 1 scant tablespoonful), the brandy and the rest of the honey. Whisk until smooth.

4 Pour the mixture into the prepared pastry case and bake for 20–25 minutes, or until the filling looks firmly set.

5 Meanwhile, dust the reserved walnuts in a little sugar, melt the reserved butter in a small frying pan and sauté for a few minutes. Tip out on paper towels.

6 Remove the tart from the oven and leave until cold. Scatter the walnut kernels on top. Serve cold, with a dusting of icing sugar if you like.

To drink: a medium-dry Vouvray.

LA TARTE TATIN

Upside-down Apple Pie

Serves 6
Preparation: about 40 minutes
Cooking: about 30 minutes

125g/4¹/₂ oz unsalted butter
175g/6¹/₂ oz caster sugar
about 1.35kg/3lb crisp eating apples
such as Cox's

FOR THE PASTRY:
225g/8oz flour
1 tbsp caster sugar
pinch of fine sea salt
125g/4¹/₂ oz chilled unsalted butter,
cut into slivers
2 tbsp crème fraîche

Tarte Tatin is one of the best known of French desserts. Like all such celebrated classic dishes, it comes with an intimidating aura which quite unnecessarily puts many people off baking it at home. It is, in fact, not particularly difficult to make.

Having the right equipment helps a great deal. The best pan, known as a *moule à manqué*, is heavy-based, round and about 5cm/2in deep with a slightly curved rim (you can see mine in the photographs). It made of stainless steel, with an ultra-heavy base that makes it ideal for putting on top of the stove to caramelize the apples (I also use it for cooking flat omelettes) and has been worth every expensive franc it cost me. *Moules à manqué* are available from good cookware or catering equipment stores — invest in a more expensive model with a heavy flameproof base.

Devotees serve Tatin *comme telle*, as it comes, but it can of course be sprinkled with Calvados and/or accompanied by a bowl of crème fraîche or a scoop of fine vanilla ice-cream.

1 First make the pastry: sift the flour into a bowl and sprinkle over the sugar and salt. Stir them in with a large spoon. Now work in the butter with your fingertips. Once all the butter pieces have been absorbed, add the crème fraîche and mix it in. Roll the dough into a bowl and chill it for at least half an hour.

MIX THE SUGAR INTO THE MELTED BUTTER AND TILT THE PAN UNTIL WELL COATED.

2 On top of the stove, melt two-thirds of the butter in your chosen pan over a moderate heat. Sprinkle in two-thirds of the sugar and, wearing a thick oven glove, tilt the pan around over the heat until it is well mixed with the butter. The mixture should coat the whole pan right up to the rim.

3 Now remove the pan from the heat and set aside while you prepare the apples. Peel and quarter them. Cut out and discard the cores and seeds. If your apples are small, simply cut them lengthwise in half — this is the more traditional method. What matters is that you end up with chunky pieces of apple fitting snugly together.

ARRANGE THE APPLES PACKED TIGHTLY IN CONCENTRIC CIRCLES WORKING INWARDS.

4 Arrange the apples in the pan over the butter and sugar, packing them very tightly in concentric circles. I prefer to work my way in from the outside.

5 Sprinkle the rows of apple chunks with the rest of the sugar and dot with the rest of the butter. The apples are now ready for the most important

stage in the making of a Tarte Tatin – they are about to be caramelized.

6 Put the pan over a moderately high heat and cook until the butter and sugar between the apples pops up in small caramelized golden bubbles (this will easily take 20 minutes – I sometimes leave it on top of the stove for 30 minutes). Put your oven glove back on and shake the pan from time to time. Keep watching and reduce the heat after a while to make sure the caramel does not turn too brown and burnt – if you let it go, it will do so in a matter of seconds. This is why a heavy-based pan really pays for itself.

COOK ON TOP OF THE STOVE UNTIL BUBBLES OF CARAMELIZED SUGAR POP UP BETWEEN THE APPLES.

7 Turn off the heat and leave the pan until just cool enough to handle without the oven glove.

8 Preheat the oven to 220°C/425°F/ gas7, or a notch lower if your oven is very 'high' or 'fast'.

9 Take the dough out of the refrigerator, lightly flour a rolling pin and cold working surface and roll out the dough into a thin circle (about 3mm/$\frac{1}{8}$in thick) a little larger than the rim of the Tatin pan, say about 3.5cm/1$\frac{1}{2}$in.

10 Lift the pastry circle and carefully place it over the apples. Using your fingers, ease the edge in between the apples and the side of the pan.

11 Bake in the hot oven for about 30 minutes, until the pastry is cooked and golden. Check after about 20 minutes and reduce the heat a little if the pastry is browning too fast.

PLACE THE PASTRY ON TOP OF THE APPLES AND TUCK IT IN BETWEEN THEM AND THE SIDE OF THE PAN.

12 Remove the tart from the oven and leave to cool for several minutes or longer before serving. Preheat a hot grill.

13 To serve, cover the pan with a serving dish that is slightly larger than it. Holding both the pan (using an oven glove if necessary) and the dish, quickly turn the pan over on to the dish, so that the caramelized apples rest on top of the pastry. Tap the base of the pan a few times, then carefully lift it up. You may find that the apples

require a little rearranging. If necessary, dredge a little icing sugar over the offending area. Give the apples a quick boost under the hot grill for a minute or two just before serving. (This trick also works well if you have had to cut down on the caramelizing time on top of the stove; the other advantage is that it warms up the pie nicely.) Tarte Tatin is best served hot or warm.

To drink: a little Calvados on lots of ice.

VARIATIONS: pears make a delicious *Tatin:* choose them still firm. A more unusual alternative, fresh figs caramelize very well. Beware of peaches, apricots and nectarines, which all shrink back and ooze too much during cooking. If you really want to experiment, try using chicory: trim and halve small heads lengthwise and blanch and drain well before caramelizing.

PETITS SABLÉS
Sweet Biscuits

Makes about 24 round (6cm/2¼ in diameter) biscuits
Preparation: 15 minutes
Cooking: 20 minutes, plus cooling

175g/6½ oz unsalted butter, cut into pieces, plus extra for greasing
85g/3oz caster sugar
8g/¼ oz sachet vanilla sugar (optional)
225g/8oz plain flour, sifted, plus extra for dusting
1–2tsp grated orange zest
1 small egg, plus 1 extra yolk for glazing
TO SERVE (OPTIONAL):
icing sugar
Chocolate Sauce (see right)

1 Fit the metal blade of the food processor. Tip the butter and sugar into the bowl and whizz for about 15 seconds, or until the mixture becomes light and fluffy. Scrape down the sides of the bowl with a spatula.

2 Add the sugar(s), flour, zest and whole egg to the bowl. In short bursts, whizz until the dough comes together in a ball (this takes about 20 seconds).

3 Take the ball of dough out of the food processor and dust it lightly with flour, then wrap in cling film and refrigerate for at least 30 minutes.

4 Heat the oven to 190°C/375°F/gas5 and lightly grease a baking tray with butter. Flour a cold working surface, a 6cm/2¼ in diameter round biscuit cutter and a rolling pin.

5 Take the dough out of the refrigerator and put it in the centre of the work surface, then roll it out until thin (no thicker than 6mm/¼ in). Stamp out discs of dough with the biscuit cutter.

6 Place these on the prepared baking sheet. In a small bowl, combine the egg yolk with 2 or 3 teaspoons of water. Using a brush, very lightly paint the top of the biscuits with this glaze.

7 Bake for about 15 minutes, until lightly coloured. Leave in the turned-off oven to crisp for 5–10 minutes. Take out, slide a palette knife under the biscuits and transfer to a cooling tray to get cold.

8 If you like, dust with icing sugar before serving. Alternatively, dip half of each biscuit in warm chocolate sauce: put a large slightly raised plate on a layer of cling film, carefully prop the biscuits against the rim of the plate, chocolate half down, and leave for 1 hour until set.

SAUCE AU CHOCOLAT
Chocolate Sauce

Use your best-quality high-cocoa-bean-content chocolate to make this sauce and you will not be disappointed by its dark sheen and its intense flavour.

Serves 6
Preparation: 5 minutes
Cooking: 10–15 minutes

125g/4½ oz good-quality dark chocolate
icing sugar or caster sugar, to taste
1 tbsp single cream
30g/1oz unsalted butter, chilled and cut into dice
FLAVOURINGS (OPTIONAL):
1tbsp Cointreau, brandy, rum or whisky or
1tbsp finely grated orange zest or
1tbsp apricot jam, orange marmalade or ginger in syrup, finely chopped

1 Break the chocolate into small pieces. Pour very hot water into the bottom pan of a double-boiler and bring to a simmer. Place the top pan over the simmering water, put in the chocolate pieces and about 6 tablespoons of cold water. Stir from time to time until the chocolate has melted.

2 Once the chocolate has melted, stir in sugar to taste, then the cream and any flavouring(s).

3 Take off the heat. Sweeten to taste with sugar and beat in the butter. Serve or use as a coating while still hot.

CRÈME CHANTILLY
Chilled Whipped Cream

Crème Chantilly keeps in the refrigerator for an hour or two at the very most, but is best prepared at the last minute.

Serves 4-6
Preparation: chilling, plus 10 minutes

400ml/14fl oz double cream or
crème fraîche
icing sugar to taste
1-2 tsp Kirsch, rum or brandy (optional)
1½ tbsp iced water

1 Refrigerate the cream and a mixing bowl until both are well chilled.

2 Put the cream in the bowl, mix in the sugar and flavouring (if using).

3 Using an electric whisk, whip the cream until frothily stiff, starting slowly then increasing the speed. Stop beating before the cream separates into hard butter-like grains.

4 Whisk in the iced water and use as soon as possible.

FRUITS RAFRAÎCHIS
Fruit Chilled with Alcohol

The permanent version of this fruit salad is called *confiture du vieux garçon*, bachelor's jam. It is concocted by pouring a bottle of *eau-de-vie* into a very large sterilized preserving jar or bottle. Add 900g/2 lb caster sugar and shake well. Wash, seed or core the fruit of the season — soft red fruit, berries, peaches, pears, plums, grapes, etc — as they ripen and add them in layers to the bottle. Top with a layer of thinly sliced unwaxed lemon and leave for 2 months or, traditionally, until Christmas.

Serves 4-6
Preparation: 30 minutes, then chilling

well-balanced mixture of some of the
following: fraises des bois, raspberries, pears,
apples, peaches, bananas, oranges, satsumas, kiwi
fruit, physalis fruit, fresh almonds,
redcurrants and white currants, strawberries,
apricots, nectarines, plums, cherries,
seedless white and red grapes
juice of 1 lemon
caster sugar
ground cinnamon
juice of ½ orange
juice of ½ lime
2tbsp eau-de-vie, Calvados or Kirsch
2tbsp Cointreau or Maraschino liqueur

1 Reserve the fraises des bois and raspberries, if using. Peel the pears, apples, peaches, bananas, oranges, satsumas and kiwi fruit (sprinkle lemon juice over the pears, apples and bananas as you work, to stop them discolouring); husk the physalis fruit and skin the almonds; remove any stones or inedible cores from the fruit; remove the stalks from the currants and hull the strawberries. Quarter and thinly slice the apples and pears; slice the peaches, banana, apricots, nectarines and kiwi fruit; halve the plums; thinly slice the oranges and segment the satsumas.

2 Arrange the fruit in a coupe, in well mixed layers. Sprinkle each layer with sugar and a very light dusting of cinnamon.

3 In a small jug, combine 2 tablespoons of lemon juice with the orange and lime juice and the liqueurs of your choice. Dribble this liquid over the top layer of fruit.

4 Put the coupe in a larger bowl packed with ice and refrigerate for 2 hours. After one hour, take out and baste the fruit with the juices.

5 Chill again and serve ice-cold, after scattering the raspberries and fraises des bois over the coupe at the last minute.

(RIGHT) *Serve* Fruits Rafraîchis *with* Petits Sablés *(page 163).*

PROFITEROLES

Caramel Choux Puffs

Serves 6
Preparation: 30 minutes
Cooking: 40 minutes

FOR THE CHOUX PASTE:
100g/ 3¹/₂ oz butter, cut into small pieces
pinch of sea salt
150g/ 5¹/₂ oz flour
4 or 5 extra-fresh eggs, at room temperature

FOR THE CARAMEL:
100g/ 3¹/₂ oz caster sugar
few drops of lemon juice or white
wine vinegar

TO SERVE:
hot Chocolate Sauce (page 163)

TIP THE SIFTED FLOUR INTO THE JUST-OFF-THE-BOIL LIQUID.

BEAT BRISKLY UNTIL THE PASTE COMES AWAY FROM THE SIDES OF THE PAN.

A pile of golden caramel profiteroles is a joyful dessert to behold. It goes by the evocative name of *croquembouche*, 'crunches-in-the-mouth'. Choux paste can be made and chilled in advance (or frozen), but you should serve the cooked profiteroles fairly soon after baking – certainly on the same day.

1 First prepare the choux paste: in a heavy saucepan, mix 250ml/8fl oz cold water with the diced butter and a small pinch of salt. Bring to the boil over a moderate heat, stirring from time to time with a spatula or wooden spoon.

2 Meanwhile, sift the flour into a bowl. Once the liquid has come to the boil, remove the pan from the heat and tip the sifted flour all at once. Using the spatula or wooden spoon, start vigorously and swiftly mixing the flour and water until there are no pools or specks of white left. Keep on stirring briskly, returning the pan to a low heat for a minute or two, until the flour swells the paste (this is where the sifting helps) and it comes away from the base and sides of the pan in a somewhat sticky rough ball.

3 Remove the pan from the heat. Add the eggs one by one, stirring in each completely before you work in the next one. Before you mix in the last egg, whisk it

BEAT IN THE EGGS ONE BY ONE UNTIL THE PASTE IS SUPPLE AND SHINY.

USE TWO DAMP TEASPOONS TO SHAPE THE CHOUX BUNS.

lightly in a small bowl – you may need to use only some of it. What you are trying to get is a supple, firm but floppy paste with a bit of a shine. Continue beating the paste for a minute or two to give it more body and gloss.

4 Preheat the oven to 200°C/400°F/gas6 and butter a baking sheet or line it with non-stick baking paper.

5 Now shape the choux buns: using 2 wetted teaspoons, make walnut-sized balls of the paste and ease them on to the prepared baking sheet. Make sure they are well spaced apart (allow at least 2.5cm/1in between the choux buns).

USE A FORK TO DIP THE COOKED CHOUX BUNS INTO THE CARAMEL.

LEAVE THE CARAMEL-COATED BUNS TO DRY SET ON A DRYING RACK.

6 Bake the choux for about 20 minutes, until they turn into golden puffs. Take them out of the oven. Pierce each with a skewer, then return the baking sheet to the switched-off oven. Leave the puffs to dry for 10 minutes.

7 Now take them out of the oven and leave to get completely cold before dipping in the caramel or filling (see below).

8 For the caramel: use a small heavy stainless steel or copper pan. Put in the sugar and 3 tablespoons of cold water. Melt the sugar over a moderate heat, tilting the pan over the heat this way and that to ensure even cooking. Keep a constant eye on the mixture. Bring to boiling point and leave the syrup to bubble gently until it turns honey-gold – if you like, spread a teaspoon on a white plate to check the colour. Sprinkle in a few drops of lemon juice or vinegar and take off the heat.

9 Dip the choux into the caramel, one at a time but working swiftly, then drain them well on a drying rack placed over a plate. Leave the coated buns to set and harden.

10 Serve with a generous dribbling of hot chocolate sauce.

USE A PIPING BAG FITTED WITH A SMALL NOZZLE TO FILL THE BUNS.

To drink: a Banyuls or Muscat de Rivesaltes.

VARIATIONS: if you like, fill each choux bun with about 2 generous teaspoonfuls of vanilla ice-cream, Crème Chantilly (page 164) or Crème Pâtissière (page 156).

To make a proper *Croquembouche*, pile the choux in a heap shaped roughly like an upside-down cone. If you like, trickle some hot Chocolate Sauce down the mound of profiteroles. Serve immediately, with the rest of the sauce in a heated sauce-boat.

For a simple version of the classic Parisian cake *Saint-Honoré*, roll out and chill a 20cm/8in circle of sweet shortcrust pastry. Pipe a ring of choux paste just within 2cm/¾in of the edge. Bake on a prepared sheet at 200°C/400°F/gas6 for 25–30 minutes. Place caramelized profiteroles over the chou ring and spoon crème chantilly in the centre.

GALETTE
DES ROIS
Almond Puff Pastry Cake

Twelfth-night cake, *la galette des Rois* is still shared on the Sixth of January. The almond puff pastry traditionally conceals a small bean-like china token, *la fève*. Whoever discovers it in their slice of *galette* is crowned king or queen for the evening. Nowadays most people buy their cake from the *pâtisserie* or supermarket, and it always comes with the token and golden cardboard crown.

With its mellow filling, the *galette* below is a simple version of *Pithiviers*, the rich almond cream *spécialité* pastry of the town of the same name near Orléans. If you like, insert a token into the filling before baking.

Serves 6
Preparation: 10 minutes
Cooking: about 35 minutes

about 400g/14oz ready-to-roll
puff pastry
1 tbsp milk, for glazing
icing sugar, (optional)
flour, for dusting
butter, for greasing

FOR THE FILLING:
100g/3¹/₂ oz ground almonds
1 tbsp finely grated orange zest
1-2 tbsp rum
2 egg yolks
85g/3oz caster sugar
100g/3¹/₂ oz soft unsalted butter

1 Preheat the oven to 220°C/425°F gas7.

2 Lightly flour a cold work surface and a rolling pin. Cut the pastry in half and roll out each piece into a circle, about 25cm/10in diameter. Grease a baking sheet and place one circle in the centre.

3 Prepare the filling: put the ground almonds, orange zest, rum, egg yolks (reserve about 1 tbsp for glazing), sugar

and butter in the bowl of the food processor and whizz until smooth.

4 Spread this filling evenly over the circle of pastry, leaving a clear 2.5cm/1in edge all around.

5 In a cup, mix the reserved egg yolk with a tablespoon of milk. Using a pastry brush, moisten the edge of the circle with a little of this glaze.

6 Carefully place the second circle of pastry on top of the filled disc. Press it down lightly with your hands, pressing a little harder around the edge to bring the 2 discs together and seal in the filling.

7 Prick the pastry in several places with a fork. Using the point of a small sharp knife, mark a criss-cross pattern on the surface. Brush the whole surface and edge lightly with the rest of the glaze.

8 Bake for 20–30 minutes until the pastry is golden and puffed up, without opening the oven door for the first 15 minutes. If you like, lightly dredge with icing sugar and return to the oven for 2–3 minutes at the end, for extra glazing. Leave to cool a little and serve warm, preferably, or at room temperature, if more convenient.

To drink: a medium-dry sparkling Saumur.

GLACE À
LA PISTACHE
Pistachio Ice-cream

To make an excellent plain vanilla ice-cream, follow the recipe below but leave out the pistachio mixture.

Serves 6
Preparation: about 30 minutes,
plus freezing in stages

150ml/¹/₄ pt chilled crème fraîche
or double cream
15g/¹/₂ oz unsalted butter
4 heaped tbsp chopped shelled
unsalted pistachios
2 heaped tbsp slivered almonds
2tbsp caster sugar

FOR THE CRÈME ANGLAISE:
350ml/12fl oz full-fat or
semi-skimmed milk
1¹/₂ split vanilla pods or several drops
of vanilla essence
4 large or 5 medium egg yolks
115g/4oz caster sugar

1 Make the Crème Anglaise as described on page 174 in Oeufs à la Neige. Strain the warm custard through a fine sieve and stir it frequently as it cools.

2 Whisk the crème fraîche or double cream until thickened. Carefully fold this into the custard.

3 Pour the mixture into a suitable container and freeze.

4 Prepare the nut mixture while the ice-cream is freezing. In a frying pan, melt the butter over a low heat until the pan is coated. Scatter over the pistachios, almonds and sugar. Turn up the heat a fraction and sauté for 3–4 minutes, stirring and shaking until the mixture is golden and a little caramelized.

5 After 40 minutes, take out the ice-cream container, tip the contents into the bowl of the food processor and whizz for several seconds to break up the crystals. Add the caramelized pistachio mixture and whizz briefly again. Pour back into the container and return to the freezer. Repeat the process after 40 minutes, then again for a third time after the same interval. Leave in the freezer until completely frozen.

6 Remove from the freezer about 10 minutes before serving – so it is a little

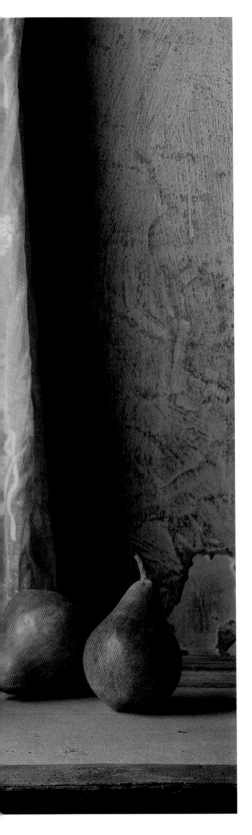

POIRES AU VIN ET AUX PRUNEAUX
Poached Pears with Prunes

The most robust of the fruit and wine combinations, pears in red wine makes a good autumnal dessert. Be careful neither to overcook the fruit nor to reduce the syrup too much. The pears should be *al dente* and the syrup robust but not acrid.

Serves 4
Preparation: 10 minutes
Cooking: 30 minutes, plus cooling

4 just-ripe unblemished Williams pears
575ml/1pt red wine
2-3tbsp sugar
1 vanilla pod, split
8 stoned ready-to-eat prunes
2 tbsp Crème de cassis (optional)

1 Peel the pears, using a very sharp small knife or a vegetable peeler held almost parallel to the fruit so that it does not to cut into the flesh. Keep the stalks on if possible.

2 In a heavy-based saucepan large enough to take the pears comfortably side by side, combine the wine with the sugar and the split vanilla pod. Bring to a simmer over a moderate heat.

3 Stand the pears side by side in the simmering wine, adding a little water if necessary so that the rounded base of the pears is well covered. Bring back to a simmer and poach over a low to moderate heat for about 15 minutes until just tender, basting the top of the pears a few times with a spoonful of the liquid. Add the prunes for the last few minutes.

4 Leave to cool in the liquid for 15 minutes. Then, using a slotted spoon, lift the pears and prunes from the wine. Put on a plate and leave until cold (the pears should be upright if possible).

5 Bring the liquid to the boil over a fairly high heat and keep it bubbling until reduced by almost half, to a light syrup. Remove the vanilla pod, rinse, dry and reserve for future use (see page 10). If you like, stir the Crème de cassis into the wine syrup. Leave to cool, stirring occasionally. Stir in any juices from the pears and prunes.

6 Serve the pears cold – but not chilled – in individual coupes on a modest pool of syrup, with a dribble of extra syrup on top.

(LEFT) *Served en masse* Poires au Vin et aux Pruneaux *make a most spectacular dessert.*

MADELEINES AU CITRON
Lemon Madeleine Biscuits

These little golden cakes are sweetly buttery and memorably good with a cup of fine tea. They are also very easy to prepare. The (unorthodox) icing sugar coating sinks in deliciously and is recommended, particularly if you are baking your madeleines in a plain small bun tin rather than in the prettier traditional scallop-shaped moulds.

Makes about 18
Preparation: 15 minutes, plus standing
Cooking: about 15 minutes, plus cooling

100g/ 3 1/2 oz caster sugar
2 very fresh large eggs
1 generous tbsp finely grated lemon zest
2tsp orange flower water, vanilla essence or grated orange zest
85g/ 3oz flour
100g/ 3 1/2 oz unsalted butter, melted, plus extra for greasing

FOR THE COATING (OPTIONAL):
2tbsp lemon juice
5tbsp orange juice
2tsp very finely grated lemon zest
1tbsp runny honey
3tbsp icing sugar, plus extra for dredging

1 In a bowl, vigorously whisk together the sugar and eggs until pale.

2 Stir in the lemon zest and orange flower water or other flavouring. Sift in the flour, fold in well, then fold in the melted butter. Leave to stand in a cool place for 1 1/2 –2 hours.

3 Grease 2 small-hole bun tins, preferably with scallop-shaped holes, but plain will do. There is enough mixture to make about 18 small buns. Preheat the oven to 220°C/425°F/gas7.

4 Spoon the filling into the holes, leaving a little room at the top for expansion. Put the tins in the oven and reduce the oven setting to 190°C/ 375°F/gas5.

5 Bake for about 10 minutes, until risen and golden. Leave to cool for a few minutes, then tip the madeleines on a cooling rack and leave to get cold.

6 If you like, coat the madeleines. Prepare the coating while they are cooling: in a saucepan over a low heat, heat the lemon and orange juice with the zest, the honey and the icing sugar. Stir until dissolved and syrupy.

7 Using a pastry brush, paint this over the madeleines. Leave until cold before serving, dredged with icing sugar at the last minute.

To drink: chilled Pineau des Charentes on ice or sparkling kir royale.

COMPOTE DE CERISES
Poached Cherries

Time-honoured family sweets, fresh fruit compotes need a gentle touch in order not to disintegrate into a bland pulpy mess. What is nice is the contrast between the texture and acidity of the fruit and the smoothness of the syrup. Cook the fruit carefully until just tender, then drain and reduce the liquor. Compotes keep for a few days in the refrigerator and this particular recipe freezes very well.

Serves 4
Preparation: 15 minutes
Cooking: about 20 minutes

30g/ 1oz unsalted butter
550g/ 1 1/4 lb sweet ripe cherries, stoned
2-3tbsp icing sugar
juice and 1tsp finely grated zest from 1 orange
juice and 1tsp finely grated zest from 1 lemon
1-2tbsp Kirsch
1-2tbsp Crème de cassis or blackcurrant jelly

TO SERVE (OPTIONAL):
madeleines, sweet biscuits, crème fraîche, Greek-style yogurt or vanilla ice-cream

1 In a saucepan, melt the butter over a low heat. Add 6 tablespoons of water, the prepared cherries, the sugar, orange and lemon juice and zests. Simmer for 5–10 minutes, stirring from time to time and keeping the heat low (the cherries should be soft but not mushy).

2 Over a bowl, tip the cherries into a sieve and drain well. Reserve the cherries and pour the juice back into the pan. Bring to a simmer over a moderate heat and leave to bubble gently until reduced by about one-third.

3 Add the Kirsch and the Crème de cassis or blackcurrant jelly. Bring back to a simmer and cook for 2–3 minutes.

4 Scoop the cherries into coupes or glasses. Spoon over the sauce and serve immediately. Alternatively, leave to get cold, then refrigerate and serve chilled with madeleines, sweet biscuits, crème fraîche, Greek-style yogurt or vanilla ice-cream.

GELÉE DE CASSIS

Blackcurrant Preserve

Pectin-rich blackcurrants are easy to turn into a tangy preserve that is dark and heavy with fruit. If you are picking the fruit, preferably do so on a day they have had a bit of sun. If you like, top up with redcurrants.

Makes about 1kg/2¼ lb blackcurrant jelly
Preparation: about 15 minutes
Cooking: about 20 minutes, plus cooling

1.8kg/4lb ripe blackcurrants
about 1kg/2¼ lb caster sugar, or more if needed
(see below)

1 Prepare the blackcurrants: take a large saucepan and, working over it, run the prongs of a fork down each cluster to loosen the currants. Discard the stalks and pick any bits of leaf or dirt from the currants.

2 Add 150ml/¼pt water to the blackcurrants and bring to the boil over a moderate heat, stirring and mashing the currants with the back of a large wooden spoon or slotted spoon.

3 Boil for several minutes, until the blackcurrants have burst and the juice is running. Leave to cool. When the mixture is tepid, strain it through a large fine sieve into a measuring jug. Allow the juices to drip through freely and only press very gently with the back of the spoon.

4 Measure the liquid and the sugar. For each 500ml/16fl oz of strained juice, you need to use 500g/1lb 2oz caster sugar.

5 Rinse out the pan, pour in the juice and the required amount of sugar. Put the pan over a moderate heat and stir until the sugar has dissolved.

6 Bring to the boil, stirring from time to time. Stop stirring the moment the mixture comes to the boil. Continue boiling without stirring for at least 3 minutes or until the jelly begins to set. To check setting, put a teaspoon of preserve in a saucer: leave to cool for 2 minutes, then push the surface with your finger – it should wrinkle a little. If not, boil for another few minutes and test again. Remove from the heat.

7 Rinse out very clean screw-top jars with boiling water, dry well and pour in the hot preserve. Leave to cool a little. Then, if you like, cover the preserve with a disc of waxed paper.

8 Leave to get cold, then seal with the lid and store the preserve in a cool place until required.

VARIATIONS: to make a superlative *Glace au cassis* (blackcurrant ice-cream) for 4–5, take about 900g/2lb blackcurrants and follow the method up to the end of step 3. Whisk in 450ml/¾pt Greek-style yogurt (or a mixture of yogurt and fromage frais). Stir in 5–6 tablespoons double cream or crème fraîche. Sweeten to taste with icing sugar, stirring until absorbed. Churn in an ice-cream maker. Alternatively (this is painstaking work), pour into a suitable container and freeze. After about 40 minutes, whizz in the food processor. Freeze again for 40 minutes, whizz and re-freeze. Repeat the process once or twice until you have prevented crystals forming. Freeze until softly frozen.

Still on the subject of blackcurrants, drinkers of Kir may enjoy preparing their own superior Crème de cassis. Remove the stalks from about 900g/2lb blackcurrants, or enough to three-quarters fill a sterilized screw-top 1 litre/1¾ pt jar. Top up with fruit-flavoured white eau-de-vie. Leave to infuse in a cool place for 4–6 weeks. Push the mixture through a very fine muslin-lined sieve into a clean bowl. Use about 400g/14oz caster sugar and 300ml/½ pt water to make a light sugar syrup, boil it for 5 minutes, leave to cool and stir into the blackcurrant liqueur. Pour into a sterilized bottle and leave to settle for a few days before using (preferably not next to your favourite crystal – I am told there is a slight risk of the mixture bubbling open, but it hasn't ever yet happened to me).

OEUFS À LA NEIGE

Eggs in the Snow

Sweet fluffy egg dumplings flavoured with caramel and washed down with unctuous vanilla custard, *Oeufs à la Neige* has a wonderful old-fashioned quality. Nothing is wasted in the preparation: the milk used for poaching the egg whites is combined with the yolks to make a proper *Crème Anglaise*. This great homely party dessert is best prepared a day or two ahead and left to infuse in the refrigerator.

To make *Île flottante*, floating island, keep the meringuey egg dumpling in one rounded mass and poach carefully. Alternatively, bake in a greased mould in a bain-marie for about 30-40 minutes in a low to medium oven.

Serves 6
Preparation: about 20 minutes
Cooking: about 20 minutes, plus chilling

1 litre/ 1 3/4 pt full-fat milk,
plus extra to top up as needed
175-200g/ 6 1/2-7oz vanilla-
flavoured caster sugar
1 vanilla pod, split
5 large very fresh eggs
1/2 tsp orange flower water
12 sugared almonds (preferably pink), crushed

FOR THE CARAMEL:
100g/ 3 1/2 oz caster sugar

1 Bring the milk to the boil over a low heat in a large saucepan, together with half the sugar and the vanilla pod.

2 While keeping an eye on the milk, separate the eggs. Whisk the whites until they stiffen, then add 2 tablespoons of the remaining sugar and continue whisking until the mixture is very firm. Reserve the yolks.

3 Remove and reserve the vanilla pod. Lower the heat a fraction and keep the milk barely simmering. Scoop up 2 or 3 tablespoons of meringue mixture, slip this into the simmering milk and poach softly for about 1 minute on each side, or a little longer if preferred, turning the dumplings over carefully.

4 Remove the swollen cooked egg dumplings from the milk, drain well in a sieve (letting the milk drip back into the pan). Leave to finish draining on a clean teacloth. Repeat the process until you have poached all the meringue dumplings, making sure the milk stays at a modest simmer throughout.

5 Now make the crème anglaise: strain the milk into a measuring jug and top up with extra milk to make up 1 litre/ 1 3/4 pt (and to have enough custard for 6 servings). Pour into a second pan and add the vanilla pod and orange flower water. Return to simmering point. In the original saucepan, beat the reserved egg yolks with the rest of the sugar until frothy and pale.

6 Place this over a very low heat or, if you prefer, over a pan of boiling water for greater heat control. Remove the vanilla pod from the milk pan (rinse, dry and use to flavour sugar or reserve for another recipe, see page 10).

7 Pour the simmering milk over the egg yolk mixture, a dribble at a time, stirring constantly with a wooden spoon. Cook very slowly, still stirring all the time. Take the pan off the heat occasionally to control the temperature, and continue stirring until the cream is just thick enough to coat the back of your wooden spoon.

8 Remove the custard from the heat and leave to get cold, stirring it occasionally. Then pour it into a serving bowl. Float the meringue dumplings on the surface and scatter over half the sugared almonds.

9 Prepare the caramel: put the sugar and 3 tablespoons of cold water in a small heavy saucepan. Melt the sugar over a moderate heat, tilting the pan over the heat this way and that and stirring a few times. Keeping an eye on the mixture, bring to boiling point, then stop stirring and leave the syrup to bubble gently until it turns golden.

10 Dribble the syrupy caramel over the meringue dumplings and scatter the rest of the crushed sugared almonds over the dish. Refrigerate overnight and serve chilled.

To drink: a Monbazillac.

INDEX

Dad's War

Dad's War

Father, Soldier, Hero

CHRIS TARRANT

2 4 6 8 10 9 7 5 3 1

Published in 2014 by Virgin Books, an imprint of Ebury Publishing
A Random House Group Company

The Random House Group Limited Reg. No. 954009

Addresses for companies within the Random House Group can be found at
www.randomhouse.co.uk

A CIP catalogue record for this book is available from the British Library
The Random House Group Limited supports the Forest Stewardship
Council® (FSC®), the leading international forest-certification organisation.
Our books carrying the FSC label are printed on FSC®-certified paper.
FSC is the only forest-certification scheme supported by the leading
environmental organisations, including Greenpeace.
Our paper procurement policy can be found at:
www.randomhouse.co.uk/environment

Typeset by SX Composing DTP, Rayleigh, Essex
Printed and bound in Great Britain by Clays Ltd, St Ives PLC

ISBN 9780753555101

This book is dedicated to my beautiful kids in memory of the Grandpa you all loved: Helen, Jennifer, Sammy, Toby, Dexter and Fia.

To all the Hackney Gurkhas – no one must ever forget what you did for all of us.

To all young men and women still risking their lives today for us and our freedoms in some godforsaken foreign land.

And, above all, to the memory of a wonderful Mum and the very best Dad.

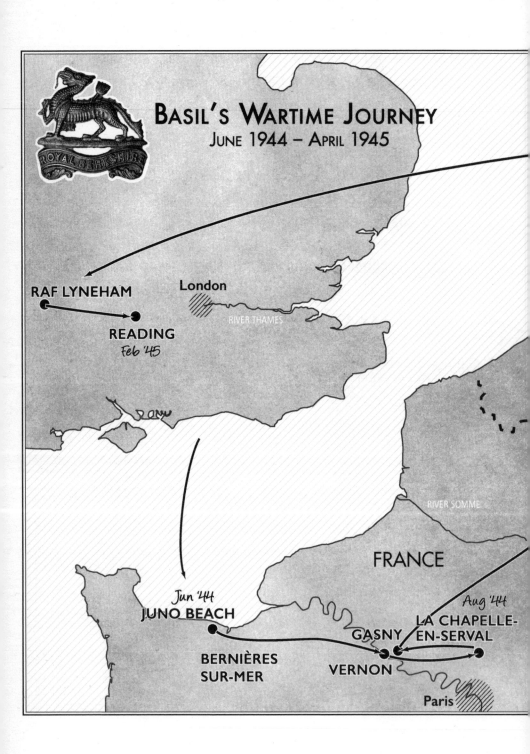

BASIL'S WARTIME JOURNEY
JUNE 1944 – APRIL 1945

ROYAL BERKSHIRE

RAF LYNEHAM

London

RIVER THAMES

READING
Feb '45

RIVER SOMME

FRANCE

Jun '44
JUNO BEACH

Aug '44
LA CHAPELLE-
EN-SERVAL

GASNY

BERNIÈRES
SUR-MER

VERNON

Paris

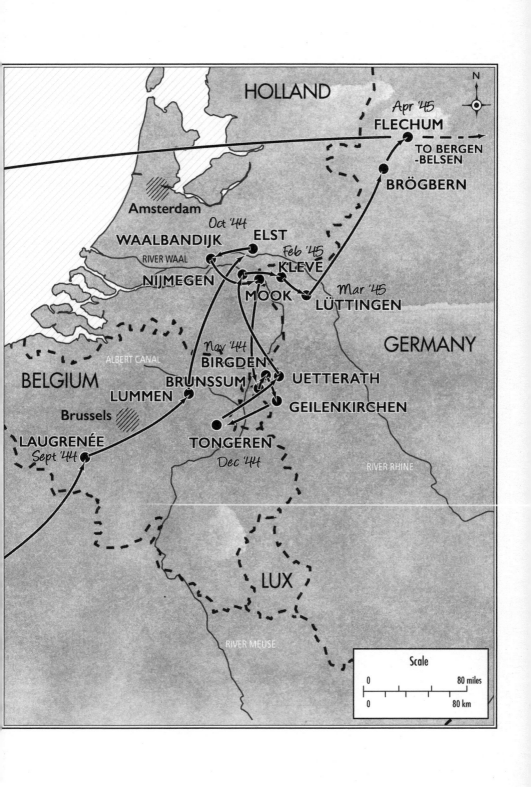

HOLLAND

N

Apr '45
FLECHUM

TO BERGEN
-BELSEN

BRÖGBERN

Amsterdam

Oct '44
WAALBANDIJK   ELST
                                    Feb '45
RIVER WAAL   KLEVE
NIJMEGEN   Mar '45
                    MOOK   LÜTTINGEN

GERMANY

Nov '44
BIRGDEN
ALBERT CANAL
BELGIUM   BRUNSSUM   UETTERATH
          LUMMEN   GEILENKIRCHEN
Brussels
LAUGRENÉE   RIVER RHINE
Sept '44   TONGEREN
                  Dec '44

LUX

RIVER MEUSE

Scale	
0	80 miles
0	80 km

CONTENTS

Introduction

My dad was my closest friend. We had the same strong sense of humour, we played sport together, we watched sport together, I loved him and admired him for nearly sixty years – but, after he died, I realised I hardly knew him at all.

I grew up just after the Second World War and as a little boy our house was always full of former soldiers. Obviously the war was the common bond for all of them, but as I got a little older I realised that the ones who talked about it a lot – the ones who made loud boasts like, 'the Hun were all around us' or 'we gave Hitler the thrashing he deserved' – had never actually so much as crossed the English Channel. The ones who'd been in the thick of the fighting, including my own dear dad, hardly ever said a word about it. It was a generational thing; you buried your memories somewhere deep inside you and just enjoyed still being alive.

Dad became a very successful businessman and showed no obvious signs of trauma from his war years: he didn't wake up screaming in the night or suffer flashbacks. In fact he always seemed very balanced and stable. Yet the things he saw, endured and survived as an infantry officer must have been horrific. As a lieutenant, then a captain, then a major in the Royal Berkshire and Wiltshire Regiments he came back battered but otherwise unscathed from Dunkirk, then went back into France in 1944, landing on Juno Beach on D-Day and fighting the retreating but still bloodthirsty Germans right through France, Holland, Belgium and into the Rhineland.

The mortality rate among infantrymen was high. Among officers it was a virtual wipe-out – yet somehow he survived it all. God only knows what he saw, what friends he lost. It was only when Toby, my son, was old enough to ask, 'Grandad, what did you do in the war?' that he began to release the odd detail. But still so much died with him.

Five years after his death I was approached by Channel 5 about a documentary series they were making, which was called, rather vaguely, *Hero in the Family*. Did I have a hero in my own family who I didn't know much detail about and would I like to try and find out more about him or her? Well yes, my father fitted the bill perfectly, of course, but I was very wary about getting involved. I know rather a lot about television production companies and over the years I've seen some of them being very invasive, inaccurate and callous, so initially I wasn't very keen. As it was not long after his death, anything on the subject of Dad was still too raw, too sensitive, and Mum and all the kids would have been deeply upset by anything that wasn't done with accuracy and respect.

After several phone conversations and a lot of cajoling, however, I did agree to meet up with the production company, but I was very wary and unhelpful. In fact, I was a pain in the arse. I wanted total control of input, scripting, editing – the lot … because it mattered so much to me. It wasn't just another job of work. This was about my dad. It had to be spot on.

Then I met Mike Wadding, the director, and Paul Reed, the

military historian, and I warmed to them both at once. They absolutely understood my reservations and totally reassured me about everything. I was also encouraged to learn that the other names in the series included Ann Widdecombe and Paddy Ashdown, and I knew those two would certainly never accept half measures. Mike promised me every programme would be done with great care and sensitivity, and I trusted him instinctively.

My intuition was correct. As we travelled together through Normandy and on up towards the Rhine, I became very close to Mike and Paul. Although they'd never met my father it was obvious that they respected and rated him for what he and so many others endured. They saw the infantrymen as the bravest of them all. So it was that for the first time I started to piece together just what hell my father must have gone through in the war years.

I saw the beach where he landed on D-Day. I saw where half a regiment was wiped out in minutes trying to cross the River Seine. I saw the place in Holland where they took out two German strongholds in a single mad night. I saw the spot where he crossed the Rhine into Germany. I saw the town of Kleve where he experienced the most savage house-to-house, hand-to-hand, fixed-bayonet fighting. Every morning as we got up to start filming it was for me an extraordinary voyage of discovery.

What seemed particularly extraordinary was that the discoveries about my dear dad's experiences were being made in places that were now lush green meadows smelling of cut grass and wild flowers, with birds singing in the woodlands all around us. It was surreal to think that just sixty years earlier this same peaceful countryside had just been a sea of thick mud and minefields, with the only sounds the rattle and roar of the guns and the only smell the sickly-sweet stench of death.

The final film was beautifully put together and is a real tribute to the man. We had a family viewing where I and all of my own kids – his grandchildren – came together to watch it. It was very teary but we all agreed it had been well made and it had been worth doing. One sadness was that Mum never lived to see it – she had been ill for a long time but had hung on bravely, hoping to at least listen to the film on television because her old eyes could no longer see. I'd been able to tell her so much that I'd learned while I was away filming and I was amazed how little of it Dad had shared, even with his own wife of sixty years. She was thrilled with each new detail I'd bring her back from filming in France and Germany. Mum hung on and hung on, in and out of hospital with an army of carers around her twenty-four hours a day, but in the end she quietly gave in, leaving us on 10 April 2012. *Hero in the Family* aired just ten days later.

By the time the film had gone out I'd already resolved to try to write this book. I had learned so much new information about my father's war from my experiences with Channel 5 but it had only made me hungry for more. It had opened things up just enough but there were so many huge gaps that I wanted to fill in. I went to the Royal Berkshire and Wiltshire Museum at Salisbury and they were wonderfully helpful as I ploughed through mountains of regimental paperwork. I have read every note, every order and every payslip issued during the Second World War that they hold there. I spent hours at the National Archives at Kew and waded through even more mountains of paperwork and computer disks at the Imperial War Museum. In addition, I've read countless war books, including biographies, autobiographies and regimental histories.

But above all, I needed to speak to people who'd been there, in France – people who'd served with Dad – and this was always going to be my biggest problem. I'd known so many as a kid growing up but now they were nearly all gone. To have fought on

D-Day as a young man now you have to be around ninety years old, so clearly there were not going to be many veterans still alive. In nearly two years of research I've found just five, but they are five wonderful survivors from an amazing breed of men and without their help I could never have completed this book. Robert Purver, Doug Botting, Mike Pardoe, Bill Pyke and Donald May's memories are interspersed throughout this book; I am enormously grateful for their assistance.

And then in the sad period after Mum's death, as I prepared for the funeral, a sickening thing happened: Mum's house was burgled. She was so house-proud, so obsessive about tidiness all her life, that it broke my heart to see the windows smashed in and footmarks all over her immaculate worktops. I assume they'd heard on the grapevine that Chris Tarrant's mum had died and seen there were no longer any cars in the drive, so realised they had an opportunity. Fortunately, they took nothing of consequence – cash, a few bottles of booze, a radio, some ornaments, a few medals (though missing all the important ones) – they just caused a lot of damage and left, spilling drink as they went.

When I went into the house and saw what had happened I fell into a blind rage. I felt that everything in my parents' world had been defiled. I went storming out of their old front door, wanting to lay into someone, but perhaps luckily there was just the dark empty street and behind me a house full of memories smashed up forever. I deliberately didn't tell the kids till after the funeral as it would have been just too much for them to bear.

But one positive thing came out of it. The burglars had ripped open Dad's beautiful old desk where he'd sat clunking away on his ancient typewriter for more than forty years. Many of the drawers had stayed locked for as long as I can remember but, as I squatted there sorting out the mess of papers strewn around the floor, something in one of the newly opened drawers caught my eye. It was a diary – an old one, dating back to 1944. It was hard to read and much of it was incomplete. But for the first time I had in my hands my dad's own record of his experiences of the war.

I have included some extracts from Dad's diary in this book, along with quotes from the only in-depth interview about his war experiences that he ever gave before his death, for a project with Martin McIntyre from the Royal Gloucestershire, Berkshire and Wiltshire Regimental Museum at Salisbury, as well as a shorter interview he gave for the *Reading Evening Post*. Both of these were conducted in May 1994, just before the fiftieth anniversary of D-Day.

The book is about Dad and the wonderful times I had with him and what I've learned about him since he left us. The research has been a real labour of love but hard because so many of his contemporaries have died. I have learned a great deal about the extraordinary men and women who fought and gave their lives for us to be free. To have sat and talked to five exceptional men who landed with Dad in Normandy on 6 June 1944 has been an enormous privilege. I have learned so much I am almost ashamed of how little I knew. It is an extraordinary story about an amazing man, written by someone who thought they knew him best.

Boyhood

Part One

CHAPTER ONE

Biscuits and Beer

Basil Avery Tarrant was born in Reading on 22 July 1919 – the firstborn son of Stanley Charles Tarrant and his wife, Edith. My grandad Stan was a wonderful man, my childhood hero, and he was a proud and loving father to Basil when he was growing up. Dad's mum, my granny Edith, was a Scouser born towards the end of the nineteenth century somewhere in Liverpool, although her birth was shrouded in mysterious circumstances that were never really mentioned by the family or resolved. On the headstone on her grave it gives the year of her death, but there is no reference to the year she was born. The family theory is that she was illegitimate in the days when such things were a real stigma, and was given up for adoption.

Stan and Edith fought like cat and dog all their lives, but apparently they were kind enough parents and Basil grew up as a happy little boy. His brother John arrived six years later and, although Dad felt that in later years the younger son seemed to get preferential treatment in many things, including a private education, the two boys remained very close all their lives and shared a terrific sense of humour. I always absolutely loved my Uncle John; he was as daft as my dad and had a wonderful laugh.

As a little boy I remember looking at my grandfather, my father and my Uncle John and thinking, 'I've been born into a madhouse!' And, looking back, I think my early instincts were spot on. Each of them was very loud and very, very silly. I loved it when we all got together at Christmas: the house (usually Grandad's because it was the biggest) would ring with laughter and manic party games, in which cheating seemed to be obligatory.

They were very tall too, these Tarrant men – Stanley and John were both six foot three and Basil almost stunted at five foot eleven and a half inches. Little wonder then that I ended up at six foot two and my son Toby – Igor to us – is six foot five. Now he is twenty-one, I just pray that he has stopped growing, as I'm getting an increasingly stiff neck talking to him.

So Basil Avery came into existence, a sweet little boy with an easy temperament as a baby and the thickest, blackest hair – which does nothing at all to explain my own blond locks, or Toby's, although in many other ways the three of us are horribly similar. Being called Basil was perhaps not the best start in life, though I'm told it was a fashionable-enough name at the time. As for where the middle name Avery came from, nobody ever seems to know. I thought it was a thing that you kept birds in. Anyway, little Basil Avery grew up happily in Reading between the wars, with the smell of biscuits and beer in his nostrils. Large numbers of locals, up to as many as 10,000 men and women at one point, were employed by Huntley and Palmers, one of the biggest biscuit manufacturers in Britain. So the town always smelled of baking, a lovely warm aroma that enveloped the rows of houses like a comforting blanket. One of Basil and John's greatest pleasures was to be in the Kings Road area of Reading, close to the factory, when they were baking ginger nuts. Pure heaven. The sweet smell was unique and unmistakeable.

The other smell that was always in the Reading air came from Simonds Brewery, right in the centre of the town. Years later, Courage's joined them, and beer and biscuits became a major part of the busy town's economy. For two little boys growing up there, though, they were just nice smells. When Simonds were at maximum output, brewing beer in Bridge Street, you could smell the hops ten miles away. Many hundreds were employed in the brewery, either working amongst the barrels or with the horses. In those days, delivery by horse and cart for most things – milk, bread, coal, in fact just about everything – was the norm, and little Basil and John were regularly sent out by Stanley with a bucket and shovel to collect up horse dung for his roses. Piles of manure were a regular sight in the streets and the council were forced to maintain a number of barrows, manually pushed around the town, to clean up after the horses, unless the likes of Stanley and his little helpers had got there first with their shovels. Basil had a strange little ditty that in later years he was to inflict on his son and then all of his grandchildren – all together now: 'Horsey lift your tail up ... and let's see you poo!' This rendition was always followed by squeals of delight from the children and mock horror from Granny, while Basil protested his innocence, saying that it had been handed down to him by his own father. I'm still pretty sure that Dad made it up himself.

Basil was always very bright at school and used to like working hard. He was also a talented all-rounder at sport, good at cricket and running, and regularly appearing as goalkeeper in the school's soccer team. However, in spite of these accomplishments, he was also clearly a bit of a handful. In fact, he must have been a lot of a handful as he was always getting caned, usually four or six of the

best on the backside. It hurt! As I, too, was to learn years later –
God it hurt, especially when the master doing the caning was a
real marksman. If the master had been deadly accurate it meant
that, although he'd received six strokes, on inspection by Dad's
mates afterwards, there would be just the one (often bleeding) line
across little Basil's botty.

It sounds brutal – it probably was – but the boys were never
resentful. Dad just accepted that he'd been out of order and took
the punishment. However much it hurt, it was absolutely
unforgiveable to cry. Some years after he left school, Dad said he
really could not remember his housemaster's face, but could still
describe in detail his shoes and socks and the motif on his carpet.

Most of Dad's problems with authority were for what he
described as 'fooling around'. He was naturally very funny, a great
mimic, and so predictably he was often disruptive in class. He had
similar problems with his Cub master, then his Scout master and
later his poor, exhausted choirmaster.

Even when the young Basil was trying to be good, things had a
habit of going wrong. For example, when he was learning the
rudiments of wood cutting at school, a boy called Eric was foolish
enough to get too close to little Basil, who had an axe in his hand.
Imagine the horror his mum, Edith, must have felt when she
opened the door to find an irate mother standing there with the
headmaster, furiously accusing Basil of cutting Eric's head open. I
think she may have been rather overdramatic but Dad did admit
that Eric was taken to hospital with what seemed like an enormous
amount of blood pouring from his skull. Of course it wasn't
malicious: Basil was looking the other way, as you really should
never do while chopping wood, and Eric just somehow got too
close to the blade. Funnily enough, Eric later became one of my
father's best friends for years. Dad must have been very likeable, or

Eric extraordinarily stupid, because I cannot think of a single one of my childhood friends who I'd have kept in touch with if they'd sliced my skull open with an axe.

In fact, by all accounts, Basil was a popular boy and a natural leader. He loved the Cubs, joining the Reading YMCA Cub pack and enjoying every aspect of it. He adored camping and the great outdoors, although in later life, by early 1945, I suspect that camping was his idea of hell.

At the age of twelve, Dad moved on to the Scouts. He was always very keen and ambitious, and soon became a patrol leader with both arms covered in badges. It was a source of great amusement to the whole family, particularly my mum in later years, when we discovered he'd been awarded a Scout badge of excellence in cooking. None of us ever saw him so much as boil an egg.

Dad was a very strong swimmer and exceptional diver. Mum once showed me the high board that Dad used to dive off into the Thames at Reading Bridge – it seemed miles up in the sky, much, much higher than anything that even the most hardy Olympian would be allowed to dive from now. Health and safety considerations just didn't exist in the 1930s. She told me proudly that Dad and only one other boy had the nerve to dive off the very top.

He also loved to fish, something he'd been taught at an early age by his father. Most of his mates fished a lot, and they would collect birds' eggs and roam around the countryside, cycling everywhere with fishing rods tied on to their crossbars, and tackle and worms in their saddlebags. Dad became the proud owner of a racy Hercules bicycle with a viciously narrow saddle. A Hercules was quite a flash thing to own in the late 1920s, costing him several months' pocket money, but the great (or perhaps not so great) thing about this particular type of bike was that it had a fixed wheel. This made it very fast, but meant you couldn't stop pedalling. Once you got up to a certain speed the wheels just kept on racing round and braking was very hard to do. For a growing teenage boy it was *the* thing to have but, in reality, the saddle was extremely painful and fixed wheels on any bike are a nightmare. Once, when riding fast down a particularly steep hill, into High Wycombe, Dad was rather more than mildly surprised to be overtaken by his own back wheel. Seconds later he crashed into a hedge.

In these days of obsessive health and safety, it's amazing that Dad, or any of his friends, grew up at all – but they did. Perhaps it sowed in them the seeds of what it took for them to survive after 1939. For example, although they could all swim well they loved to push it to the limit. There was a fast back stream of the River Kennet near Burghfield that in the summer months became completely overgrown with stringy weed and water lilies. So that became a challenge. Any fool could swim in clear water but their biggest thrill was to race towards the river at full speed, dive headfirst so that they could go right down beneath the thick underwater growth, then force their way up through the solid weeds and out on to the far bank. The clogging, entangling weeds made the whole thing very dangerous – but of course that was the fun of it.

There was another pool they called the Monk. In the hot, summer evenings, one of the riverkeepers would come along and open the two sluice gates by hand to allow an unrestricted flow of water for a couple of hours or so. That was the signal for Basil and his mates to dive right into the rushing water, push their bodies under the gate and literally race under water through the sluice into the pool on the other side. To us today it sounds terrifying, but when he told his own father about this game much later in life, Stanley just grinned and said it wasn't peculiar to Basil's generation: my grandfather's own gang were doing it before the First World War! It was all part of growing up in those innocent days, with kids making their own enjoyment and fun. Their amusement cost very little and that was essential because in those days they had very little spending money.

One source of a little cash for Basil was the small sum he received each week from joining the church choir. He loved to sing so it suited him, and it had the additional benefit that every summer they had the annual choir trip to the seaside, usually travelling by train. After trying to smoke, which usually degenerated into much gasping and coughing in the train loo, the boys would spend the rest of the journey fighting off an urge to throw up. Strong-stomached Basil never did, which meant he got to eat about eight of the packed lunches around him. Dad always had a voracious appetite and for several years looked on this day out as a chance for a really good feed.

The choirmaster probably only tolerated Basil because he was an excellent young singer. He had a good treble voice until he was at least sixteen. His much more developed schoolmates used to tease him unmercifully, telling him he was going to be a eunuch for the rest of his life. It was apparently good-natured but the squeaky soprano must have been starting to worry. However, as all teenage boys know, these things have a habit of changing dramatically and almost without warning. Suddenly the late-developing Basil could no longer hit the high notes; in fact he became positively deep voiced, rather growly and very hairy. His days as All Saints Church's top chorister were sadly over, but it had been a good run. He'd been paid the handsome sum of two shillings a month (that's slightly less than 10 pence in modern money) and an extra sixpence if he sang solo, which he usually did. In the early 1930s, half a crown a month (that's 12½ pence) was untold wealth for a young boy.

Dad could never seem to sit still – he always had to be doing something. In the summer it was fishing, swimming and camping, with cricket and athletics at weekends. Reading had a strong tradition of producing good athletes and Dad ran for the town's athletics club. A proud fact that, a few years later, he was to bitterly regret telling someone in his regiment! The town also had a good cricket club – they produced Peter May, a great England captain who Dad told me proudly he'd once met ('A very nice man. Very posh!'), and Ken Barrington, another England cricketing legend. Reading Football Club, the town's professional team, known of course as 'The Biscuit Men', played their matches in a small ground near my grandad's house, called Elm Park, and if Dad wasn't actually playing football he was at Elm Park watching it with his father. The town also had a tradition of bull baiting, which was apparently very popular in Reading and Wokingham in the nineteenth century. Mercifully it had been outlawed by the time Basil arrived, otherwise I'm sure he'd have had a go at that as well – he seemed to have been into everything else.

In the winter months it was football, football, football. He formed his own team called Spartan Sports, which were quite successful in the local minor leagues. They were self-financing, mainly achieved through a whip-round every Saturday morning, a few donations from the parents and the automatic selection every week of one boy who wasn't a particularly good footballer but whose dad was a wealthy local bookie. With this income they managed to buy eleven shirts and one ball, pay for a referee and hire a pitch each week. They just about ran to goalposts but couldn't manage the extra for nets, and they couldn't afford the use of a changing room or transport for away games, so they all travelled to matches in a cycle convoy. One of his most vivid memories was all eleven of them pushing their bikes, in the pouring February rain, up the long steep hill into Henley to play Remenham on a pitch where the cows had been grazing and had left steaming cowpats only hours before. They were certainly Spartan. They changed under leafless trees in driving February sleet and changed back again afterwards ready to cycle home with all the mud still intact. No early bath in those days – it was a late one, much, much later, when you'd got back to your mum and dad's house.

Saturday nights were often spent at the Palace, Reading's one and only variety theatre on Cheapside. For teenage boys it wasn't particularly cheap. A seat in the stalls cost about two shillings, but if times were hard, which they usually were, they all trooped up to the gallery for sixpence (that's about 2½ pence). There was a hard wooden bench, nothing more, to sit on and you were a long way from the stage, but you did get two hours of top-class entertainment. Basil was just beginning to appreciate jazz and when a young up-and-coming trumpeter called Louis Armstrong was booked for a week at the Palace, he somehow got the money together and went there every single night. Being so close to London, Reading was on the touring circuit of a lot of stars. Gracie Fields, George Formby, Ted Ray and Billy Cotton and his band all came to the Palace – top entertainment in their day.

But the boys' absolute favourite, and most of the girls too if they were honest, was the comedian Max Miller. By today's standards he wouldn't even qualify as slightly risqué but in the mid-thirties he was forever in trouble with the Establishment. 'Do you want the blue book or the red book?' he would ask his adoring fans. Of course it was the blue book that they all wanted, which was the slightly ruder one, although it was all pretty tame. He would always make local references to the women from Whitley Wood or to staying at the George Hotel in Broad Street, which would go down well with the Reading audience. 'Very strict at the George,' he would say. 'Each night at eleven o'clock the manager checks if you've got a girl in your room. If you haven't, he sends one in.' Or: 'There's an old fellow of eighty from Tilehurst. He is spending his honeymoon at the George. His bride is only twenty-five and very, very pretty. In the bar the other evening my curiosity got the better of me and I went up to him and I asked him discreetly how he fared in bed. How often had he been able to make love to his beautiful young bride? To my utter amazement he told me, "Nearly every night." "Really?" I said. "Yes," he replied. "Nearly on Monday, nearly on Tuesday …"' Needless to say the young Basil had Max Miller's act down to a T.

Of course every Saturday night ended lavishly with fish and chips, liberally covered in salt and vinegar and wrapped in newspaper, from any one of the dozens of corner shops that existed all over town. There you would see the proud banner displayed: 'A super supper every Saturday for sixpence.'

If they had the money, most of Dad's contemporaries used to get into town on the tram. The great majority of people travelled by bus or tram in town and by train out of town, or simply cycled or walked. For years Dad kept an old train ticket, a Reading to Paddington return on what they called the Theatre Special: after 5 p.m. for two shillings and sixpence (that would be 12½ pence in today's money). The steam train from Reading to Paddington usually took thirty minutes, which is pretty much exactly the same time as it takes now, seventy years later.

Basil and his teenage mates were of course beginning to take an interest in girls, although to be honest they tended to get in the way of football and Basil's latest obsession – drumming in a dance band. It was something he'd taken up pretty much as soon as he left the choir and it monopolised a lot of his time. Although he was quite a good-looking, dark-haired, charismatic young man, for most girls of his age he was a hopeless case. One girl called Joan Cox, who'd been with him at Wilson School and who was a year older than him, seemed very taken with the manic young Basil, but in the end it was clear that she found it impossible trying to keep up with his whereabouts. She was a naturally very pretty blonde girl, quite tall, with lovely green eyes, and unsurprisingly never short of boys who would take her out. So, after a few weeks of a pretty hopeless courtship with Basil, she moved on. At the time Basil barely noticed that she'd gone.

In any case it was about time that Basil did a day's work. The depression of the thirties seemed to bypass Reading – there must have been some unemployment but all of Dad's contemporaries found some sort of work on leaving school. Basil left school in 1936, aged just seventeen, and his father Stanley got him a job with a local accountant. He started as a trainee because of course he knew virtually nothing about money movement, book balancing or accountancy and, if the truth be told, he didn't care very much about it either. He was paid the princely sum of ten shillings per week and initially went to the office every day by tram. However, the money he was spending on fares quickly exhausted his funds and he decided instead to walk the 1½ miles to the office, always arriving there punctually just after eight o'clock in the morning, and then walk home again every evening. This meant he could fill up on his mum's breakfast, do a day's work, skip lunch, have his dinner at home and still have enough money to go to the Palace most nights of the week. Unfortunately, though, during the brief period he worked there, this was the only useful bit of accounting that he ever did. To his father's disappointment, Basil was bored stiff with accountancy and wanted out. But what could he do, with so little business experience and no contacts?

His father for a long time had been the buyer at a company called Huntley, Boorne and Stevens, known everywhere as HB&S, a tin-producing firm famous chiefly for making the tins that Huntley and Palmers put their biscuits in. The young Basil heard his father one Saturday talking in hushed tones to Edith about a young administrator from the company who had been summarily dismissed the previous day for sexual indiscretions with a married employee. Dad listened, fascinated, through the door, and then did the most extraordinary thing. That same evening he put on his one and only suit and cycled to Woodley, to the home of the HB&S managing director, knocked on his door and politely asked if he could fill the vacancy. The startled senior executive must have been rather taken with this earnest young man, as he arranged for an interview at the beginning of the next week.

He must have been impressive because the interview for this lowly position was graced by the attendance of the managing director, the company secretary and the chairman. Quite extraordinary for a seventeen-year-old, and his father knew nothing about it until the first day that his son Basil came into work, having flown through the interview and got the job. He started on thirty shillings a week for forty-five hours, including Saturday mornings, plus free parking in the bike shed. He was there, war intervening, for the next forty years and eventually rose to board-room level – the first man from outside the founding families to be made a director.

By now war clouds were looming over Europe and young men began to talk about what might happen and whether they would be called to serve their country. Huntley, Boorne and Stevens, like many companies, were keen to help the military build-up of trained young men just in case war did break out, and encouraged young men like Basil to volunteer for part-time military service. Dad joined the Territorial Army (TA), the Terriers as they were known early in 1937, aged just seventeen, and was thrilled to discover that the annual two-week camp, which of course he absolutely loved, counted as extra to his company holiday allowance. This meant that in all he had six weeks' paid holiday a year and an extra bonus allowance of five pounds for joining up. He attended those camps, in Cosham, near Portsmouth, for the next three consecutive years.

The Terriers was a new experience for him. Basil had joined the Royal Army Ordnance Corps (RAOC) as a clerk (rank: Private), with his role classified as 'Clerk and Mustered', as part of the British 48th (South Midland) Division. This meant that clerical work was his official first duty, but it meant he was to be trained to be mustered for fighting if it became necessary. In general, he enjoyed the TA, although he said the training was pretty pointless. There was a lot of marching up and down and turning left and right, which he hated, and lots of running in full battledress with a heavy pack and weapons, which he also wasn't very keen on.

In addition there was a great deal of bayonet practice, which consisted of screaming at the top of one's voice and then racing, bayonet waving, towards a swinging straw dummy, forcing the blade deep into the dummy's guts and twisting it over and over, still screaming all the while. This was one bit of the training that the young Terriers all rather enjoyed, and they couldn't help thinking it had rather an absurd air about it. It seemed almost impossible to believe that one day soon they might be doing such a horrific thing to any other human, or worse still that it could be their own guts and entrails that were to be ripped out.

Basil stayed with the TA until 25 August 1939, when he was

called up, with war against Germany now seeming imminent. In later years he recalled, 'I loved being in the Terriers. I don't think I learned much about the army, but we had a terrific time … so much fun.' Things for Basil and the rest of his generation had perhaps been too good, too much fun for too long. It was now going to get horribly serious.

CHAPTER TWO

All a Bit of a Shambles

While Basil was busy playing soldiers in the TA and filing paperwork at HB&S, in the wider world events were taking a serious turn. Throughout the 1930s the rise of fascist dictatorships in Europe was starting to threaten the political landscape. In Germany, Adolf Hitler had begun a massive campaign of remilitarisation, flouting the punitive Versailles Treaty that had been agreed in the wake of the First World War. Everyone knew this meant trouble. But with the horrors of the previous 'war to end all wars' still fresh in everyone's minds, British prime minister Neville Chamberlain tried to appease Hitler and agree to his 'reasonable' demands in an effort to avoid giving him an excuse to declare hostilities. The crumbling League of Nations similarly did nothing to prevent German troops marching into Austria in 1938.

However, the policy of appeasement quickly backfired. An emboldened Hitler attempted to reclaim the Sudetenland, an area in Czechoslovakia in which many German speakers lived. The resulting crisis led Chamberlain to meet Hitler three times, culminating in the Munich Conference in September 1938, which was attended by Germany, France, Britain and Italy (Czechoslovakia was not represented). There, Chamberlain decided that the Nazi leader was 'a man who can be relied upon', and along with the French he persuaded the Czechs to agree to hand over the Sudetenland. In return, Hitler promised not to make further territorial demands. Chamberlain returned triumphantly to England waving his famous piece of paper, telling the cheering crowd: 'I believe it is peace for our time.'

In March 1939, however, the flimsiness of the agreement became apparent when German troops marched on the rest of Czechoslovakia. It was clear that Hitler had been lying at Munich. Britain had promised to defend Poland if Germany invaded, and now this seemed imminent. War would surely follow.

Within just a couple of weeks of my father's call-up to the army, the expected declaration came. But still Dad and his mates were more excited about it than frightened or apprehensive. This was, after all, what they had been training for and they still saw it as a bit of a jolly adventure. Little could they know what lay ahead.

Initially Dad had wanted to join the Royal Air Force, although his reasons were pretty spurious: apparently he looked a bit like the bloke in an RAF recruitment poster, his mum said he looked good in a blue uniform and he just fancied flying in a Spitfire. Luckily and very sensibly, on his own initiative, he thought he'd better see first if he suffered from air sickness or nerves. In those days there was an old grass airfield at Woodley, just outside Reading, and there he booked a short flight with a professional instructor. The sun was shining, the air was clear and, flying up over his home town, Basil felt good. Then the instructor put the plane into a steep dive, hurtling down towards the town centre. They could clearly see the terror-stricken faces of the shoppers in Friar Street as they hurtled down towards them before levelling out at about 100 feet. Laughing manically, the instructor said, 'I'll bet half of them down there thought they were going to have an accident.' Dad whimpered back, 'Half of us up here just did have an accident.'

So the RAF was not for Basil and when he was called up it was to become an infantryman. He looked very smart in his new uniform in the three surviving photos I have of him from that period: tall, square-shouldered, slim and fit, with beautiful smiling brown eyes and a head of thick black hair, which he kept glossy with Brylcreem. He was very attractive to girls although he remained as hopeless as ever with the opposite sex.

Nevertheless he had started to meet up again with the pretty blonde girl called Joan during this period. They both used to love going to the dance hall and seeing live bands, but he continued to be erratic and thoroughly exasperating – not unkind, just thoughtless. He always had to be somewhere doing something and he was almost manically fidgety from the minute he woke up – always sickeningly early – to the moment he went to sleep. He also had a terrible habit of disappearing or going fishing when he was supposed to be on a date (many years later, his son was to exhibit very similar patterns of behaviour).

Joan was clearly very fond of the hyperactive Basil, as he was of her in his own selfish way. But it was not really a time to be thinking about a serious relationship even if he could ever be serious. Hostilities had been declared and no one knew what the future would bring, so for any young couple in Britain in September 1939 relationships were always going to be tense. There was a sense of foreboding in the air and a feeling that this was not a time for any sort of commitment to anybody. Although she was very fond of 'Baz', and he of 'Jo', the vivacious Joan Cox was beginning to realise that he was not the young man to pin her hopes on for the future. So, although she wished him well as he went off for his call-up, she did not believe anything would come of their fledgling relationship. As a prospective suitor he was a nightmare and almost certainly mad enough to be one of the first to be killed.

For his part, Basil barely had a thought in his head about the girl he'd left behind, preoccupied as he was with his new life as a young soldier. Dad was just twenty years old when he was called up, no age really, but he was already older than many of the others that went with him. He was now a full-time soldier, still based in Reading with the 48th Division. His rank was now listed as lance corporal, with a further promotion to acting warrant officer – so he was still being paid the same rate as a lance corporal, but he was now acting above his rank due to war being declared. The 48th was a first-line territorial division of the British Army and Dad was poised to be at the heart of the action.

However, although war was declared on 3 September 1939, following Germany's invasion of Poland two days earlier, very little seemed to actually happen until well after Christmas, and those first few months became known as the 'phoney war' as everyone seemed stuck in limbo, waiting for something to happen. All Polish resistance to the German onslaught had been finally crushed by 1 October and although Poland remained occupied until the end of the war, for the next seven months there were no major hostilities in Western Europe, and in fact many people in Britain went from fearing calamity to becoming almost blasé about the German threat during this time. The military high command referred to this period after call-up as 'the tea party'. Memories of the same absurdly euphemistic language they were using in 1914 – what a tea party it turned out to be.

Finally, in January 1940, Basil and his division were sent to

France to join the British Expeditionary Force, the ill-fated BEF, to build defences and prepare for the fighting. Along with most of his mates, this trip to France was the first time that Dad had ever been abroad.

They were stationed on what was called the Gort Line on the border between France and Belgium. This was a long series of concrete bunkers and anti-tank obstacles built by the British Army during the boring months after the declaration of war, when our soldiers had very little else to do. So out of touch were we that, under the British commander-in-chief, General Lord Gort VC, we were preparing for a re-run of the Great War of 1914–18. Static bunkers were thought to be exactly what would be required. Of course, Gort and the High Command had no idea of the sort of highly mobile warfare that Hitler's army would unleash on the rest of Europe in the months ahead.

The first months after the BEF force took up its position in what it believed would be the front line for the coming battle, Dad and his men had neutral Belgium between them and the German border. My father had now been promoted to the position of acting sergeant and, with no sign of any enemy as they went into the early summer, they were all having rather a nice time.

In fact, things were so quiet and pleasant in springtime France that when a spot of leave was on offer at the end of April, Basil wasn't particularly keen to go. He almost begrudgingly went home to Berkshire, but it was good to see his parents, who were of course very proud of him in his uniform and not yet worried for his safety with so little seemingly happening. In spite of the gloomy rantings of a man called Winston Churchill – currently First Lord of the Admiralty – in parliament, the whole war thing seemed to be a bit of a fuss about nothing.

While he was at home in Reading, Dad caught up with a few of his mates and went for some beers along Oxford Road near the barracks. He remembered, years later, being rather naively surprised that several of his acquaintances from pre-war days hadn't been called up and seemed to be working in the very jobs that he and his army mates had been forced to leave behind when they went off to France. Dad was never a particularly bitter man, and it didn't rankle deeply at the time, but six years later it became an understandable source of grievance when some of them were still there, and in more senior positions, after the war.

He also briefly met up with Joan again. He'd known her now on and off for years, since they were both at school, and they were very happy in each other's company, but very little came of these brief few days. They had a few drinks, a couple of dances and a chance to catch up, but this time Basil didn't seem as relaxed as usual with her or anybody else. He was preoccupied with getting back to France, as there were rumours coming across the Channel that it might just now all be about to kick off.

But when he returned to France early in May, it still seemed very much as he'd left it. Behind the scenes, the British Army were continuing to build up their forces and the officers were pushing them steadily through training for whatever lay ahead. But they had no idea what was to come. Events were about to take a massive turn and the war was about to become anything but 'phoney'. What happened just forty-eight hours after Basil's return made it suddenly horribly clear that all the British Army's training and preparations had been totally inadequate.

On 10 May, Hitler's highly trained and mobile troops stormed into Luxembourg, Belgium and the Netherlands as a prelude to the invasion of France. The sheer speed of their troops and tanks caught the world napping. This initially successful German tactic became known as 'Blitzkrieg' or 'lightning war'. As the attack continued, the tanks of the German panzer regiments, with their artillery and air force in full support, raced deep into northern France, bypassing the British Forces. Within a matter of days the ill-prepared and unsuspecting French army was in full retreat. They surrendered or deserted in droves, with only a few pockets of resistance, leaving the British horribly exposed and isolated. My father's regiment, on the French–Belgian border, was suddenly facing the full force of the German attack.

By 22 May the newly installed French commander Maxime Weygand had devised a plan which called for Gort and the British troops to stay and fight with the remains of the French and the already overstretched and exhausted Belgians, to check the German advance and simply push them back over their border. Initially General Weygand got his way, supported by Churchill, who had become Britain's prime minister on 10 May when Chamberlain resigned, his position untenable after the Allied failure to protect Norway from German invasion. Lord Gort reluctantly agreed to send BEF troops, including Dad's 48th Division, to head south and push back the advancing Germans. However, Gort sensed that we would be massacred and thought it wiser to preserve the lives of the BEF for better-planned future battles and the defence of Britain, should there be a German invasion, which of course many believed was Hitler's next goal. There was a stand-off between the two leaders, with Weygand accusing Gort of cowardice and Gort accusing Weygand of recklessness.

Very quickly, from the sheer crushing power of the enemy onslaught, Gort realised he'd been right all along and it was already almost too late. He was sending thousands of men, including Dad, on a hopelessly futile suicide mission. We had been completely wrongfooted. The sheer speed of the German invasion caught everybody by surprise, and Gort, with the backing of Secretary of

State for War Anthony Eden, ordered a massive U-turn. The whole division was to prepare for the evacuation of Europe as best they could, via Calais.

Opinion was divided at the time as to whether Gort was a hero for saving the BEF, or a defeatist for giving in too easily. Churchill initially tended towards the latter train of thought but later was to record Gort's actions in print in his *Second World War* as a 'piece of masterly skill ... ever regarded as a brilliant episode in British military annals'. Some change of heart by Winston but either way the BEF were coming home – if they could. Already they were almost cut off by German forces encroaching on every side and far outnumbered in the air.

Even as the revised new orders were being sent through, Calais was overrun by the Germans. The whole of the old town was set alight and the flames could be seen clearly from Dover. The French government was already talking terms of occupation with Hitler. Holland, Belgium and most of northern France were already in German hands and, with the Americans understandably still refusing Churchill's pleas to join the war, Britain was suddenly terribly alone.

The evacuation, code-named 'Operation Dynamo', was finally rubber-stamped by the War Office on 26 May. Later, in a speech to the House of Commons, Winston Churchill described the events in France 'a colossal military disaster'. He emphasised the seriousness of the situation, reporting gravely that 'the whole root and core and brain of the British Army' had been stranded in France and seemed about to perish or be captured.

Yet in springtime England, events had moved so quickly that most people outside the War Office had no real grasp of the severity of the situation. One young pilot, RAF Fighter Pilot Paul Richey, wounded in France and flying back on a mail plane, was disgusted to look out the window and see Englishmen all in whites playing cricket on the village green. 'With my mind still filled with the blast and flame of a shattered France I was seized with utter disgust at the smug contentedness that England enjoyed behind her sea barrier,' he said. 'I thought that a few bombs might wake up those cricketers and that they wouldn't be long in coming either.'

As a young sergeant, Basil was bewildered by the endless conflicting orders that they were getting. The evacuation of the British troops was switched hastily from Calais to the port of Dunkirk, where the Germans were similarly hell-bent on cutting them all off. Again Lord Gort came in for criticism at the time because some at the War Office felt that all the evacuating troops should head straight for Dunkirk harbour and beach, awaiting transport home. Gort had other ideas, however, and probably saved thousands of lives in the process. He believed, correctly, that the Germans would swoop on Dunkirk as soon as they realised what was happening, and would descend on this massive cluster of exposed troops, wiping them all out – like shooting fish in a barrel. His orders were for some units to form a defensive perimeter around Dunkirk to hold the Germans back, allowing the majority of troops to evacuate, relatively unhindered. Unfortunately for Dad, the 48th Division were one of the units assigned to hold back the rapidly advancing Germans, in order to allow the luckier ones to escape. As for Lord Gort, he was axed from overall command after Dunkirk, but the history books are kinder about his efforts to preserve British lives.

They certainly needed preserving. The British forces were completely outmanoeuvred, pathetically ill-equipped and hopelessly outnumbered by the Germans. They were desperate to get to the Channel, but there seemed to be German units everywhere cutting them off. After his 'jolly nice spot of leave', Dad had sauntered back into hell. The British troops were under constant artillery fire and if they tried to move from their position they were cut down by machine guns. None of the gentle Territorial Army games had prepared them for this.

They were still only young men – Dad was only twenty – but the last two weeks of May 1940 changed their lives forever. Many never got home again. It was the first time that some of Basil's closest friends, young boys that he had grown up with, were killed in action. One young lad from Reading died with a single shot to the head, just falling where he stood, still pointing his rifle. Another died screaming, with his guts in his hands. Such a tragic waste of young life. There were to be many more in the years ahead.

It was also the first time that Acting Sergeant Basil Tarrant and his men were to realise how brutal the German soldiers were prepared to be. His company's brief had been to try to hold the enemy back at the Comines Canal, allowing as many men as possible to be evacuated from the beach. Some groups of soldiers just could not hold the increasing number of Germans off any longer and their divisions were completely overrun. The remaining troops at this point surrendered, but already some of Hitler's finest had scant respect for any of the niceties of the Geneva Convention. Ninety-seven young soldiers of the Royal Norfolks from the hugely depleted British Second Division surrendered, expecting to be taken prisoners of war, but instead were murdered on the spot by the SS in a village called – of all things – Le Paradis.

In the last week of May, at least eighty-six Belgian civilians were taken hostage and murdered near the village of Vinkt – the final victims being ordered to dig their own graves beforehand

– and another eighty soldiers, mainly from the Royal Warwickshire Regiment and in the same division as Dad were rounded up and massacred in a barn at Wormhout, France. A handful survived by lying under the bodies of the dead and mercifully they were later found by a regular German Army unit who had none of the savagery of the SS. They treated their wounds before transferring them to a POW camp, where several of them remained and survived to the end of the war. As stories of these shocking events began to circulate amongst Basil and his comrades, they began to see only too clearly the immense danger they were facing. They knew they had to do everything they could to hold back the German advance while their comrades escaped.

It is infuriatingly typical of my father that, in one of his only ever recorded interviews about Dunkirk, he said, 'We went over to France with the 48th but then on 31 May we retired rather hurriedly and dispiritedly made our way, any way we could, back to England via Dunkirk. It was all a bit of a shambles.'

Talk about understatement. A bit of a shambles? It was an utter disaster. General Alan Brooke, commander of the BEF's II Corps, wrote on 23 May, 'Nothing but a miracle can save the BEF now,' and Lord Gort warned London that the BEF was likely to lose all of its equipment and predicted that only a small proportion of its forces had any chance of getting home. The admiralty estimated that they might only be able to evacuate some 45,000 troops.

Yet, during Operation Dynamo, 338,000 Allied soldiers – 193,000 British and the rest French – were rescued from Dunkirk. The Royal Navy arrived with warships to carry our battered troops across the Channel, backed by a fleet of several hundred small ships. The French army was decimated and the British lost 68,000 men and the bulk of its tanks and artillery, but at least the majority got home, hopefully to fight another day and resist the inevitable invasion of England. As Dad said, 'a bit of a shambles'.

The main reason that so many men got away was that the Germans did not deploy the full might of their army against us at that time. They had trusted too much to the German air force, the Luftwaffe, which the Nazi commander-in-chief Hermann Goering boasted would completely eliminate the British Army. But the German ground troops had moved too far and too fast and the bombers didn't have enough back-up from their fighter planes, who were too far from base to keep refuelling. The RAF were operating from the much closer airfields on the Kent coast and did huge damage to the Germans in the air. Even this, though, was at a high cost – the RAF lost a quarter of its planes over Dunkirk.

Another reason that so many did survive this shambolic evacuation is the famed 'Dunkirk spirit' – the patriotic rallying of British civilians to help get the troops back to Blighty. On hearing about the plight of the BEF, many ordinary non-military seafaring people raced on to the English Channel in a motley armada consisting of almost anything that would float, including fishing boats, trawlers, pleasure boats, yachts, private vessels, lifeboats and tugs, from as far away as Scotland and the Isle of Man. They must have made an incongruous sight, among the huge naval ships, but those civilians and their oddly assorted craft, braving artillery and air attacks to ferry men to and fro, saved hundreds, if not thousands of additional lives.

Meanwhile the terrified, starving, thirsty and exhausted young boys, waiting for the ships to get them back across the Channel, were pounded regularly by the German bombers. Many of them waited for hours, shoulder-deep in the water, causing the Royal Navy sailors who arrived, frequently under fire, to curse them for being so heavy to drag aboard. Many French and Belgian refugee columns were machine gunned and bombed from the air as they tried to crawl away from the carnage that had, perhaps only hours before, been their homes.

All were desperate to get away from this Armageddon. The British civilians who had come to help were greeted, as they approached the Dunkirk coast, by the terrifying sight of wild-eyed men running through the water towards them, some disobeying orders and fighting among themselves simply for survival. Boats capsized in their frantic attempts to climb on board; smaller craft became overloaded by men clamouring for a place and sank. Tragically many men were drowned in this way.

Even when the fleeing troops finally got a place on a boat their problems weren't over. Many craft were torpedoed or bombed and 243 of the 861 ships and boats involved in 'Operation Dynamo' were sunk. A shocking 3,500 young men from the Allied forces were lost on the crossing of the Channel. But it was extraordinary that so many got back from the carnage at all.

My father and the survivors of the 48th Division were among the last British troops to leave French soil. The evacuation took nine days all told, during which time Basil and the rest of his division had to hold back the Germans. The 48th Division's war diary records: 'No sooner were they in position than they were under attack and the battle lasted all day.' This was to be their first battle of many over the next few days.

Dad's men were probably saved by a turn in the weather. Only two days into 'Dynamo', the German panzer divisions mounted a major onslaught on the very part of the town perimeter that they were defending. The 48th Division's position was, according to the war diary, 'precarious in the extreme'. They'd already seen heavy fighting and things looked grim. However, due to heavy overnight rain, the advancing panzer tanks couldn't get a grip on the soggy waterlogged terrain in that area and shifted their focus of attack to a different sector. It had been a close escape for Basil.

It was far from over, though, for the 48th Division, and they had to fight on for several more days. On 31 May, as the mass evacuation reached its climax, all the remaining battered and exhausted defenders braced themselves for a final major onslaught from the enemy, which they knew was inevitable. Fighting to the last, they started getting orders to evacuate themselves, once they were convinced no more BEF troops were stranded and they could get to a suitable embarkation point.

Sadly I have very little knowledge of Dad's actual crossing. Was he picked up by a Navy warship or one of the smaller vessels? How did he feel once he had got aboard a ship and turned his back on the hell that was France? What scenes awaited him as he arrived in England? As Dad chose never to speak to me about it, he took these memories with him to the grave. But what he witnessed at Dunkirk must have stayed with him for life.

This sustained attack on the perimeter of Dunkirk was Dad's first taste of the harsh realities of real warfare, his first experience of hand-to-hand fighting, the first time he had to kill or be killed, and the first time he would have seen friends and comrades falling dead or wounded around him. And of course the first time he witnessed the shocking brutality of the SS. It must have been a horrific wake-up call for the young, happy-go-lucky Reading lad who had joined the Territorial Army as a clerk for a bit of fun and adventure.

After the evacuation was over, Churchill made his famous 'We shall fight on the beaches' speech, hailing the troops' rescue as a 'miracle of deliverance'. It was a typically bulldog-like proclamation, stirring and defiant, yet he and everyone who had been part of Operation Dynamo knew only too well what a close call it had been.

Dunkirk taught everybody a lesson. A lot of young men, including my own father, grew up very quickly. A lot of others in the same action would never have a chance to grow up at all.

CHAPTER THREE

From Sandcastles to Sandhurst

When Dad arrived back from Dunkirk his life had changed. In a few short weeks the young men of the Royal Berkshires had aged considerably, had seen other young men die and experienced for the first time the horrors of war. Hitler's army was now perceived as invincible. It had swept most of Europe before it: Czechoslovakia, Poland, Denmark, Norway, Belgium, the Netherlands, Luxembourg and France were all occupied. It was surely only a matter of time before German troops marched through the streets of London.

Just three weeks after they arrived back on British soil after Dunkirk, with invasion seeming imminent, Basil and the remnants of the 48th South Midland Division were sent to Devon and Cornwall to take over the beach defences. Dad's unit of the TA was part of the RAOC and they were briefed to dig trenches and erect barriers against any forces coming in from the sea and to re-equip the whole division ready for their new role of defence of the UK. It sounds very grand but the men were desperately ill-equipped and there was much despondency amongst the infantry.

It must have been a horrible feeling, waiting for what most

assumed was the inevitable invasion of Britain by German troops and the likelihood of subsequent Nazi occupation. The question wasn't really 'if', it seemed to be more a case of 'when'. And having taken Northern Europe so easily, it was in fact exactly what Hitler had in mind.

A sea and air invasion of the south of England was planned, codenamed 'Operation Sealion'. Only a few weeks after Dunkirk, Hitler deliberately allowed his plans to be known, in the hope that it would encourage Britain to negotiate a surrender to German supremacy in Europe, without the need for a full-scale military invasion. However, he'd underestimated the sheer stubbornness and tenacity of the British people and no such negotiations were forthcoming.

One of Basil and the Royal Berkshire's favourite songs during this time was Flanagan and Allen's popular rendition of 'We're Going to Hang Out the Washing on the Siegfried Line', which cheekily referenced a line of fortifications along Germany's western border (itself named after a section of the First World War defensive Hindenburg line). Apparently Dad and his friends could be regularly heard belting that out into the small hours in the bar in the barracks. It became a national song of courage and defiance but secretly, however loudly Basil sang, after what he'd seen first hand at Dunkirk Dad must not have been at all confident about how we could withstand Hitler's relentless march. After the losses in France, the army was now hopelessly ill-equipped, and Britain was extremely vulnerable to invasion.

Churchill had to act fast. Quickly he committed to a massive programme of rebuilding our armaments and refitting our aircraft. Factories were hastily set up all over the British Isles in places like the Miles Aircraft Ltd aerodrome at Woodley, where Joan Cox and her sister May worked throughout the war (and where Dad had taken his one and only flying lesson). These new factory-line workers, many of them women, raced to properly equip our young servicemen for whatever came next. At Woodley alone, they built over 5,000 planes and repaired over 3,000 between 1940 and 1945. But it seemed impossible to rearm our troops adequately in time. Invasion was surely imminent.

Hitler's next tactic was to prove Germany's might by gaining superiority in the air over the RAF, thus demoralising Britain. The Luftwaffe pounded naval vessels in the Channel and south coast shipping centres like Portsmouth, as well as RAF airfields and aircraft factories. Once again, though, Hitler had underestimated the British and the RAF proved themselves more than a match for the Luftwaffe in what Churchill christened 'the Battle of Britain'. In fact, it was a major turning point of the war: the first time Hitler realised we weren't going to be a pushover. Germany's failure to gain air supremacy over the RAF in the summer and autumn of 1940 led to Hitler quietly shelving 'Operation Sealion'. However, Britain did not of course know that at the time and was still prepared for the worst. And meanwhile, the nightly bombing raids continued.

Since the start of the war, many children had been evacuated out of the big cities into the countryside, bomb shelters had been created in every available space and nightly blackouts were declared so that domestic lights didn't attract attention from German aircraft. Now, in the summer of 1940, the skies all over southern England were lit up every night by searchlights looking desperately for enemy bombers. Sirens howled like ghastly harbingers of doom, and from September to the following May, countless bombs exploded in urban centres over the country, tearing buildings and lives apart, burning homes and leaving many civilians, women and children, among the dead.

The sustained attacks led to a massive uprooting of the populace as families fled from the bombing. At the start of the war, the population of Basil's home town, Reading, was almost exactly 100,000; by the end of 1941 it had swelled to 140,000. This was a huge increase in just eighteen months. Many people had already lost houses and relatives, particularly just forty miles away in London, so moved to Reading to escape the increased danger in the capital. An ever-increasing number of transferred war workers also came into the town to work in munitions factories like the one at Woodley, and many civil servants were moved out of London so they would be safer for the duration of their war work. In addition, Reading was a handy base for defence of the capital and the south coast, so many soldiers were brought in and billeted around the town. Dad later recalled, 'It was packed ... and in fact so overcrowded that by October 1941 the mayor of Reading declared it a "closed town". We were officially chock-a-block; we were legally full up. And without special permission nobody else could move in.'

As well as having to get used to the increased overcrowding, Reading's populace also had to get used to the new wartime regulations. For some reason, Reading at the start of the war had the most appalling record for failing to observe the blackout. In the first year there were nearly 700 prosecutions, but apparently this was massively reduced over the next twelve months by drafting in air-raid wardens who'd been specially briefed to be 'extra vigilant'; the wartime equivalent of today's traffic wardens, perhaps.

During this tense time, British citizens were even urged by the government to put down their family pets in the hope of preventing their future suffering from air raids or starvation – in the twelve months after Dunkirk some 2.5 million pets were humanely destroyed as a result.

As the Blitz continued, Hitler was rattled by our refusal to give in. The Germans were now bombing civilian targets as often as military ones, purely to demoralise Britain and force a surrender. London took the brunt of it, but many British cities suffered terrible losses. The Blitz killed many hundreds of British civilians during these eight months and even after this sustained period of attack Britain continued to be targeted by bombing raids until the end of the war. In fact, one February afternoon in 1943, a string of bombs hit the central shopping centre in Reading and the streets were machine gunned from the air. Dad was very worried for his own parents who loved to shop in that particular part of town but in later years he recalled, 'Miraculously it was a Wednesday – half-day closing – and many of the premises were unoccupied by staff or customers. Even so forty-one died and another 150 or so were badly wounded. It was the first time it really sank in how vulnerable we all were, even in our own town.'

Between June 1940 and March 1943, with invasion remaining a strong possibility, Basil was still stationed with the 48th Division down in Devon and Cornwall, where he had been promoted to corporal. With the war expanding globally, the RAF and the Royal Navy were kept extremely busy, but for army troops waiting to defend the south coast against an invasion – which thankfully never came – life was one long waiting game. Obviously they prepared, trained and kept fit, but it must have started to become very routine. In fact, Dad recalled this period as being rather dull, and boredom was setting in. He quickly became very frustrated. And in spite of the horrors he had already witnessed and the realisation of how lucky he had been to escape with his life from his first taste of action, it seems that even just a few months after Dunkirk he actually wanted to get back into some fighting.

Certainly many other British and Allied servicemen were seeing a great deal of action at this time: elsewhere in the world the war was moving pace rapidly as the conflict became truly global. In the Atlantic a constant battle was raging between the German U-boats and Allied ships defending vital convoys from America, killing some 100,000 sailors on both sides. In June 1941 Hitler ordered the invasion of Russia, beginning a long and grinding war on the Eastern Front. Germany and Italy continued to fight to occupy Europe and North Africa, and Japan was set to dominate the Far East and Australia. Eventually, in December 1941, America was drawn into the war when the Japanese attacked the US naval base at Pearl Harbor, Hawaii, killing 2,500 servicemen and civilians. Meanwhile Britain was still heavily engaged in the Far East, and as Singapore fell in February 1942 some 16,000 British prisoners were taken, along with 14,000 Australians and 32,000 Indian troops, many of whom would die in horrific conditions in Japanese camps in the years to follow.

For Basil, stuck on the south-west coast waiting for an invasion that never happened, it must have felt that the pages of history were being written without him. On a personal level he also suffered another shock around this time. On a spot of leave in Reading he discovered that Joan Cox, the girl he'd always had a huge soft spot for but had treated rather carelessly, had given up waiting for him any longer and gone off to Scotland to marry a young marine called Charlie. She was reported to be blissfully happy, leaving Basil to realise ruefully that he hadn't handled things too cleverly.

Perhaps because of his sense of abandonment, even though it was clearly self-inflicted, and probably also because he was just born to be a soldier, Basil found himself actually missing the comradeship of men at arms. It is possibly no surprise then that by 1943, in spite of his first grim experiences of war, my father decided that he wanted a commission as an officer. It seemed unlikely that he was going to achieve this digging sandcastles on a Devon beach with the Royal Army Ordnance Corps, so he applied to join the officer cadet training unit at Sandhurst with a view to joining a regiment. In fairness I suspect that there was also an admirable patriotism that made him feel he could be doing more for the war effort, and this was a way forward. It was also, for a man like Basil Tarrant, a lot more exciting than accountancy.

So it was that on 5 March 1943, Basil Tarrant – now officially classified as Warrant Officer II – was posted to the 161st Officer Cadet Training Unit (OCTU) based in Aldershot for assessment and training. Non-regular soldiers, called up for the war, were viewed with a certain amount of scepticism by the regular army boys, so they had to prove their worth to be accepted for officer training. This pre-Sandhurst assessment to see if the conscripts were officer material was far tougher than the one that regular soldiers would have had to endure.

Dad once described this period as 'pure guts training'. He and his fellow trainee officers were sent to Luton in Bedfordshire, and then to Wrotham in Kent, an area covered with little tiny streams running into the River Medway. Dad later recalled this four-week period as horrific but probably necessary if you were going to survive as an infantry officer. 'It didn't matter what exercise they gave you and no matter where you were headed for day after day, you were wringing wet all the time. It was still winter so it was bitterly cold, but no matter what the exercise involved you had to get into a stream for cover. There was no fuel in the huts – it was up to you to somehow scrounge your own fuel – but of course with typical army bloody-mindedness that was not allowed. There was a fuel store, but if you got caught stealing coal you were on jankers [put on a charge]. If you didn't get caught then you were a hero because it meant that the stove in your hut was going to be warm that night. If you couldn't do that, then you had to somehow pull down trees and use the green wood. It was up to you. The times I have washed and shaved in ice-cold water down there in Kent are too many to count. It was horrendous and a number of the blokes didn't make it. It really was tough, tough going. You would arrive at four o'clock in the evening in the winter wringing wet, really wringing wet and cold, and you would be expected to be on a bull shine parade the next morning. You had to dry your boots but there was no heat allowed: that's up to you, that sort of thing. So it was dreadful but you soon realised, if you thought about it, that they were trying to sort you out to see if you could take it or not – so I took it.'

Over four gruelling and testing weeks Dad had proved in no uncertain terms that he had 'the right stuff' to train for a commission in the army. The history books would show that he certainly did have what it took to be a successful and respected officer, but before he could attain that rank there were three months of Sandhurst to get through.

Dad hated the 'bull' side of the army, he always did. When he got to Sandhurst he moaned: 'Although there was a war on, and I was going for a commission, I spent the first month of my three months there doing virtually nothing but marching and shining and re-shining my boots ... We seemed to spend almost the whole time doing drill because there was going to be a passing-out parade within four weeks of our arrival. I was part of the junior company and there was no way we were going to be allowed to let down the standard at the parade, so the only way they could get us up to their standard of drill was to continually drill us for a whole month. I just couldn't see the point of it. I never thought it was anything to do with my training, even though I could do the smartest left turn in the British Army. Having said that, the rest of it was excellent. The staff and the direction overall were terrific and when I left I was thoroughly ready to take over a platoon when I was commissioned ... or so I thought!'

Perhaps because of his very smart left turn, Basil Tarrant passed out of Sandhurst at the beginning of July 1943 with flying colours, and because his marks were high enough he was actually given a choice of possible regiments. Dad had no hesitation and joined the 5th Royal Berkshire Regiment. He used to watch soldiers marching in and out of Brock Barracks when he was a little boy, although he had no idea then that those barracks would later become a second home to him and would feature in his life for more than fifty years.

He was genuinely thrilled to be accepted into the Royal Berks and joined the battalion as a subaltern at their base in Kessingland, Suffolk. Rather extraordinarily, their base was a converted holiday camp. His commanding officer was Lieutenant-Colonel Taffs, abbreviated of course by all the men as Taffy, although not to his face. His first platoon sergeant, and a man whom Dad came increasingly to trust and rely on, was called Sergeant Baines. A strong bond was quickly formed between the two men.

Basil thrived on the challenge of meeting his platoon for the first time as a newly arrived officer. He was to have command of the 12th Platoon, B Company. 'I'd been told in officer training that you never forget your first platoon, and that was so true. I will never, ever forget any of them. They were a weird and wonderful bunch of blokes, endlessly chatting, always taking the mickey out of each other and almost certainly me behind my back – funny, stroppy but so brave and so loyal. Great men ... great soldiers ... wonderful.' For a brand-new officer still not quite sure how it was all going to work they were perfect for him. They took no prisoners and he had to learn quickly but he thrived on that. Happily he had found himself in charge of a bunch of blokes that he really liked and could get on with.

The vast majority of the men came from the East End of London, from places like Hackney, Stepney, Bethnal Green and Rotherhithe. They were by and large cockneys and they had a great sense of humour, which suited Dad as he always had a sharp wit. A lot of them had come from really tough and very poor backgrounds, and the legend goes that one senior officer saw this rather undernourished band of Londoners go marching proudly past him in the parade ground and said, 'Good God, they look like a bunch of Hackney Gurkhas!' The name stuck and because of the wonderful fighting record of the original Nepalese Gurkhas the London boys rather liked it, and from then on they were known everywhere as the Hackney Gurkhas Royal Berkshire Regiment, even though many of them had never been out of the East End and only weeks earlier had no idea where Berkshire was, let alone Nepal.

Dad used to recall a great story about what happened to one of these Hackney Gurkhas when he was first called up. This soldier, Tom Gladden, had put down on the form his preference for service on the call-up papers in his chosen order: first, Royal Navy; second, RAF; and third, the army. He eventually got a reply that said he was going to join the 'Royal Berkshire'. He threw a party in his local pub in east London on the Saturday night and it was a real cockney knees-up. My dad recorded how Tom later told the story against himself: 'A bloke came up to me with a pint in his hand and said, "I've never heard of HMS *Royal Berkshire*, Tom, but I'm sure it will be a very good ship if you're going on it. Good luck." It wasn't until the three-ton truck collected me from the station and I was going past the sentry box as you come into Brock Barracks that I suddenly realised: Tom, you're not going into your first choice of the navy at all, you're in choice number three – the army, boy!'

They were quite a bunch, the Hackney Gurkhas, and they accepted Lieutenant Tarrant at face value. Years after the war, Basil said, 'I found that if I could be humorous without letting go of the fact that I was their commander – in other words, there was no way I was going to stand there and exchange dirty jokes with them or anything like that – my humour was such that I could give them a quick answer and I found in a very short time they reacted to this. They thought I was another smart cookie and they liked it, so as long as I didn't do something stupid and become over-friendly, it worked a treat. I'll remember that platoon with so much affection. We all taught each other a lot – we had to. I could still tell you all their names even though so many were lost.'

One of the surviving Hackney Gurkhas who I interviewed for this book, Corporal Robert Purver, remembered his arrival clearly. 'He was a tall bloke and he had a way about him. He was very much in charge but he could relate to the blokes in a very easy way. I didn't like most of the officers – one or two I absolutely hated – but I liked Tarrant. He'd never tell rude jokes or anything like that, but he did have a real way about him and he seemed to like us. He joined in the football and was very good at running with the rest of us, although he claimed not to like it.'

Another former comrade of Basil's, Private Doug Botting, echoed Corporal Purver: 'Lieutenant Tarrant seemed genuine and really understanding. He actually seemed to care about what the blokes were thinking and feeling. He was a bit of a nutter actually – he seemed sort of driven. He played with us at sports, which very few of the officers ever did, and he played it really hard, but he took the knocks, tackles and fouls as well, just like the rest of the lads. He was very much the officer and we were very much the soldiers when we were on duty, but off duty he was one of the blokes.'

Funnily enough, Doug also remembered that Dad loved football but didn't enjoy running. Unfortunately somebody discovered that he was very good at it and had run for Reading Athletic Club before the war. However, his pre-war speciality was the 400-yard dash whereas now he was expected to run over much longer distances. The senior British military commander, Field Marshal Sir Bernard 'Monty' Montgomery, was a great believer in fitness and cross-country running had become an essential part of the training. He had told the men, 'The infantry's biggest task is going to be getting physically tough because there is no doubt at all that living in the open you will have to be physically hard.'

I don't think Dad or any of them at that stage probably understood how much living in the open they were going to have to do. They could have no comprehension of how many cold, frightened nights they would spend sleeping in holes that they themselves would have to dig in the frozen ground through that bitter winter of 1944–45. In 1943 this was all to come and it would be fair to say that Basil Tarrant was less than keen on the endless cross-country runs.

Later he remembered: 'Unfortunately for me, 5th Royal Berks had a damn good cross-country team. Having heard that I was an athlete it was a great thing for the commanding officer to be able to boast that he had an officer in his twenty-man cross-country team even though I loathed it every inch of the way. Even worse, we became so good that we got to the divisional final – seven and three-quarter miles ... and I hated it, hated it, hated it.'

So now, fitter than they'd ever been at any point in their young lives, the Royal Berkshire Regiment trained and waited for the next stage of the war. Meanwhile, back home on leave in Reading,

Dad heard some sad news which he received with mixed feelings. Charles Chapman, the young marine who'd married Joan Cox, had been killed in action soon after their wedding and the widowed young Joan was back in Reading at the home of her parents, Harry and Elsie Cox.

Basil met Joan by chance one evening in Reading and he was able to offer her some genuine sympathy and kindness. She was of course heartbroken by the loss of her young husband, but she and Basil had been close friends since their schooldays and the tragedy drew them together once more. Maybe the flame was starting to flicker again, at least for him, although clearly Joan needed time to grieve. Like many women in wartime Britain she knew only too well the precariousness of life and she would not rush into another relationship immediately. However, it was clear that there was still a strong spark between the two friends, and it was starting to dawn on Basil that perhaps there was a possibility they could rekindle their fledgling romance.

While Basil was coming to terms with the changing nature of his relationship with Joan, the picture was changing on the wider stage too. In Europe, the balance of power was beginning to shift. The Germans had lost millions of men fighting the Russians and, with America now in the war, the threat of Britain being invaded and occupied by the Germans, which had seemed so certain in 1940, was now thought to be much less likely. Indeed it now seemed that the next move for Basil's unit might well be a return to the continent. Those like my father who had survived Dunkirk must, in their quiet moments, have been apprehensive of going through it all again. But for many of the Hackney Gurkhas it was the next great challenge ... and they were positively excited about it.

It was against this background, in amongst all the talk and excitement and nerves surrounding the idea of going back to the continent, that Dad finally realised that Joan, the beautiful girl that he seemed to have known forever, was actually the love of his life. As usual he'd simply been too busy running about like a headless chicken to see it and it was only when she had gone off to marry another man that he had realised what he'd thrown away. It was typically hopeless timing, of course, but despite the tragic circumstances it did seem as if Fate had given him a second chance and this time even Basil wasn't going to mess up. With a return to the front looking increasingly likely, now was the time to act.

Back at home from weeks on manoeuvres at Salisbury Plain, he made his feelings clear, and to his surprise and delight Joan cautiously agreed to give their relationship another chance. He and Joan eventually became a very serious item – whatever that could mean in wartime, with Joan already having been hurt so much. As time passed, though, it was clear they had become absolutely besotted with each other. Basil's parents, however, didn't approve at all. His mum Edith was particularly opposed to young Joan. Her sister May described it as 'sheer jealousy – she hated Joan for her good looks and her smart clothes, always did from day one. She also had a daft idea that Basil was to marry some distant cousin that Edith had decided was to be his wife. But Basil just wasn't interested – he loved Joan to bits.'

There was also the unpleasant underlying notion that Joan was 'soiled goods' because she'd been briefly married before. It seems a very unkind and absurd thought now but attitudes were very different in 1943, even in wartime. Bas and Jo would have none of it. It made them stronger, and in spite of the disapproval of Basil's parents, they began to talk openly of marriage.

Joan and her sister May were still working at Woodley Aerodrome just outside Reading and it became a running joke that Joan's nickname was 'the Iceberg'. Many of the other young girls working with her also had boyfriends serving away in the British Army, but had been seduced by gifts of cigarettes, perfume and particularly nylons that some of the flashy young American soldiers stationed in town were able to offer the lonely girls. Joan and May were unimpressed. May was already married to young Ken Pearce, who was away fighting in the desert, and the Iceberg was determined to wait for Basil to come home. During this period, and for rather longer than anticipated, Basil and Joan communicated almost entirely by letter, each one seeming to have a different postmark as he was constantly being moved.

None of them could have realised how terrifying the next two years were to become and how heavily the odds were stacked against any infantry officer's safe return.

Brotherhood

Part Two

CHAPTER FOUR

A Day at the Beach

By early 1944, Basil and the rest of the 5th Royal Berkshire Regiment were doing endless manoeuvres in Troon in Ayrshire, off the west coast of Scotland, and around the Isle of Arran. Unbeknown to them, many other regiments were doing the same all along the North Sea shoreline. The main reason for choosing the remote Scottish coasts for dozens of similar exercises was that it was as far away as possible from prying German eyes. The Allied High Command didn't want any details of the planned invasion to get out – a breathtakingly ambitious target given the massive scale of the operation. Even more bizarre was that it actually worked. The amazing secrecy in which this colossal invasion of Europe was prepared, down to the most minute detail, without the enemy ever becoming aware of any details, is surely one of the greatest feats of modern military history.

Details were deliberately kept from the common soldier but from the sort of training that Basil and his men were doing, it was clearly going to be a sea landing. The training was harsh. Really brutal. The lads were young, motivated and as fit as butchers' dogs but, despite this, one of the men still had a heart attack during the training, which inevitably spooked his comrades. They were still only at the practice stage and already the Royal Berkshires were a man down.

The training consisted of constantly jumping in and out of little boats and running up cold wet beaches, fully laden with battle gear. Dad spent a lot of time in and out of the freezing North Sea, clambering up beaches – and being sick. Dad was always a lousy sailor, so he was sick a lot. He told me once he even remembered being sick in a boat in Southampton Docks, tied to the harbour wall.

It was a tough time but they all knew that when it came to the day, whenever that would be, it was going to be much, much tougher. After a rough, cold winter of training in the Scottish seas, come the spring of 1944, they moved south again to the altogether gentler channel around Bournemouth and Southampton, near the Isle of Wight. The sea was kinder, the climate was quite a lot warmer and of course they were now closer to occupied Europe.

By this time Basil had become very close to his unit. Corporal Robbie Purver saw a lot of Dad at this time. He remembers: 'He was tall and his uniform was smart, but he always mucked in. Our football games were manic. No goals, one ball, everybody piling on everybody else. None of the other officers ever got involved, the toffee-nosed twits, but Tarrant did. I liked him at once and he seemed to really like the London lads, us Hackney boys, 'cos we were funny and so was he. When it came down to it he was very much the officer in charge, but he'd get down with the boys, take his coat off and have a game of football. He could really give it and take it on the pitch. I remember once he went in for a tackle and came out with his thumb bent right back. It must have been agony, but he just said "my silly bloody fault" and carried on till the final whistle. I liked him, I think most of the blokes did, but he was very much in command of us. He was always in the thick of it. Never minded going in. Later on in battle, the men used to like going on patrol with Basil 'cos he looked out for them; he gave them a good chance of getting back alive. I suppose he was just a good, solid bloke.'

Private Doug Botting also remembered liking Basil, but with reservations: 'He was a good bloke, no question – a very different sort of officer. I fell out with him a few times but you always knew exactly where you stood with him.'

It was a strange time. There was the sense that everybody was anxiously waiting, but nobody actually knew what for. But, for now, young officer Basil and all the Hackney boys just had to keep training and training. Every soldier seemed to know that the Allies were going to invade Northern Europe, but none of them knew when or where. 'It was totally secret,' said Doug, 'but I think a bit of a clue was that we were all given French money!' He added, 'We were all sworn to secrecy, of course. I didn't tell the wife, but I did tell my father-in-law.'

Clearly Doug's father-in-law was a very discreet man, because even if every English Tommy told just one other person it still somehow never got through to Hitler. For his part, Dad never told a soul and in fact almost to the very last night he wasn't really sure exactly what was planned. There was a lot of bluff and double-bluff going on.

In fact, the actual D-Day plan was brilliant, although only Montgomery really believed it would work. The idea was that the Allied forces would invade the Normandy beaches in the early hours of 6 June, in a meticulously planned attack named Operation Neptune. The landings would be conducted in two phases – first there would be an airborne assault landing consisting of 24,000 British, Canadian and American troops, followed by an amphibious landing of Allied infantry and armoured divisions at dawn. Several deception operations had taken place to divert Hitler's attention in the weeks preceding the planned invasion, with the hope that this would give the Allied forces the advantage of surprise.

Many in the British High Command were sceptical of Operation Neptune's success, however, and the Americans were doubters right up to the eve of the invasion. Even Winston Churchill took a lot of convincing. By the end, though, Churchill became so excited by the whole idea they had to beg him to stay away from the south coast, in case prying eyes began to wonder why he was spending so much time down there.

In preparation for the attack – though of course they still hadn't been told when or where it would happen – the Royal Berkshires began a series of long forced marches into Southampton town centre, down to the docks, then running into landing craft and bouncing out to the Needles, off the coast of the Isle of Wight. They would then turn round and come back and do it all again the next day. Cue for Dad to be sick again and again and again …

Each time, the men would go through what Dad called a 'sausage machine' to sort them into smaller groups, so they would start off as a battalion of 1,000 men three or four miles away from Southampton Docks, then they would get sorted through various 'camps' on the way, getting divided into smaller groups each time, so that by the time they were on the road that led directly to the docks, they were down to thirty-six men, the size of unit that they were going to board with eventually. It was a clever system that meant that each platoon would be mixed with others during the landings, so that a whole company of men wouldn't be lost at one time if they got hit. Basil wasn't convinced it would work when they tried it in training but later he admitted he was wrong and it had worked perfectly.

The first few times the Royal Berkshires marched through the streets of Southampton, all the locals thought this was 'it'. Everybody was convinced that Basil and his merry men were going straight to Germany, politely parting the SS to punch Hitler on the nose. So they were cheered through the streets with cries of 'Good luck, lads!' and whenever they came to a halt they were given beer and kisses. However, after they had done the same thing every day for about a week, the locals realised perhaps the Allied invasion wasn't quite so imminent and the beer and kisses dried up. The repeated exercise was a deliberate ploy, though: if there were any spies or enemy aircraft observing their movements, they would have thought the actual landings were just another exercise.

On 3 June they repeated the exercise yet again, with the locals by now not taking a blind bit of notice, only this time it was the real thing. This time there were no morale-boosting goodbyes, no streets lined with well-wishers, not a single beer, kiss or even a peck on the cheek. Silently and apprehensively, the lads were marched into an enormous liner. It was, somewhat incongruously, a P&O luxury cruise ship, the 10,000-ton *Monowai*. On going aboard, Dad noticed that all the lifeboats had been removed and replaced with landing craft. Finally, their time had come.

Once the Royal Berkshires had piled on to the *Monowai*, Dad and his cockney sparrows found they had company: a large Canadian contingent were already on board. Over the terrifying months ahead, they grew to love and admire these men, the Third Canadian Division, as they made their way to the Rhineland. Dad always thought the Canadians were terrific soldiers and their worth was to be proved almost immediately in the battle ahead.

Once fully loaded with 1,800 troops, they set sail and, as the enormity of what was about to take place started to sink in, the men began to get nervous. Dad said there was no panic but some of the more extrovert ones just went very quiet. Many of the lads played cards for money, which was strictly against the rules, but there was a sense of 'given where you're going, why the hell not', and the officers all turned a blind eye. There was a lot of writing home – they had already been encouraged to write their wills before they left. After the years of training, the real thing was suddenly imminent.

But after only a few hours they pulled into Cowes Harbour on the Isle of Wight and there they stayed for another two days, with very little information being passed on to the officers or the men. What they didn't realise was that they were just one tiny part of an enormous fleet being assembled all along the south coast, hopefully without attracting too much enemy interest. And somehow, amazingly, it actually worked.

For forty-eight long hours, the men on the *Monowai* waited and then, after dark on 5 June, the great ship's engines powered up again and they moved out into the open sea. It was then that Dad and the other officers were told that at first light they were going to land in Normandy. They were reassured that their men were all fully trained and as fit as men could possibly be, but that they should expect fierce resistance from the enemy. All the men were shown incredibly detailed models of the beaches where they were due to land, featuring all the landmarks, German-held pillboxes, wire defences, minefields, stations, churches, towers where snipers might operate from, all down to the tiniest detail. 'They were brilliant,' said Dad, 'every detail was spot on.' The officers received a tot of brandy and there was rum for the men. They then slept fitfully until some time before daybreak.

Dad's diary is extraordinarily detailed on the events of the next few hours:

We slept a bit but then, sometime before 4 a.m., we were woken by the ship's crew with toast, great mugs of tea and hard tack biscuits. Within the hour most of the biscuits came straight back up again. It was still dark but the first signs of day were creeping into the sky and we were told we could go up on deck but we had to be completely quiet and we weren't allowed to smoke, presumably because of the lights. I quietly crawled up, not feeling frightened, just intrigued really, and the sight I saw I will never forget to my dying day. It was truly awesome in the fullest meaning of the word.

I have never, ever seen so many ships, nor ever, ever will again. We were several miles off a coast that I assumed must be Normandy and the sea was covered with grey ships of all shapes and sizes. Our British fleet was the closest, maybe six miles off, and the massive American fleet was several miles further out, getting ready to pound the German defences. Years later I learned the exact details of what I saw. Apparently we were off Juno Beach, northern France, and there were 9 battleships, 23 cruisers, 104 destroyers, 71 corvettes and eventually 4,000 landing craft.

As they began to lower the landing craft, the sea looked really choppy. There was a big swell running which would make spotting mines very difficult and a beach landing even tougher. We were all given sea-sickness pills and most of the men were throwing up but surprisingly I wasn't sick at all, nor even frightened I don't think, just apprehensive.

One German soldier, quoted in a British newspaper years after the war, said, 'I looked over the sea and could make out what looked like a black wall across the entire width of the sea, a dark wall in which lights flashed from time to time. That was when I realised, "They're coming. The invasion fleet has arrived!" ... It was so depressing, so hopeless.'

Private Doug Botting sailed along with Dad on the *Monowai*: 'I just remember looking out and seeing one huge armada as far as the eye could see on one side of our great liner. Then I looked the other side and there were even more ships that side. It was very bouncy and very quiet. At first light I got myself some breakfast – eggs, bacon, the lot – but when I went up on deck I found out why it was so quiet: a lot of the blokes were looking really white and scared, but a lot of the others were just white with seasickness. It really was rough. I felt OK but put my eggs and bacon in my top pocket for later ... hoping there would be a later!'

How Dad, the world's worst sailor, wasn't sick on this of all sea trips I don't know. What must he have been thinking in those final hours as the great invasion fleet swept in? Excitement maybe, but also surely anticipation and fear. He was still only twenty-four years old and he was one of the few who'd been through it all once previously at Dunkirk. He had seen men being killed in front of him; did he think this time it would be his turn? In addition, last time he was just a young infantry soldier, but this time he was a lieutenant, an officer, and his decisions in the heat of the now-imminent battle could make the difference between life and death to the young men around him. Getting on with the motley mix of young charges on training exercises, parade grounds and football pitches was all very well, but now he was responsible for their lives. How would he measure up? And how would they react under fire for the first time? All this must have been churning over in his mind that early June morning.

Just on 6 a.m., the great fleet finally announced its arrival and its intent. Almost in unison there was a series of huge bangs as thousands of Royal Navy shells pounded the German defences on the beach. As the long line of guns pumped their rain of death towards the French coast, the noise was ear-shattering. This was followed by a wave of RAF fighter bombers sweeping into Normandy. The vast air and sea armada was the largest amphibious invasion in history. In all there were some 5,300 ships carrying 156,000 men – 83,000 British and Canadian and 73,000 American – backed up by 11,500 aircraft and 1,500 tanks. Some 80 per cent of the planes were British.

The German defences had no idea what was about to hit them. British radio operators on the Norfolk coast intercepting German signals that morning suddenly heard a wave of messages coming through, no longer even bothering to use Morse code: 'Tommy kommt!' ('Tommy is coming!') They were very frightened, clearly in a state of panic.

Dad remembered: 'You could actually hear the trajectory of the shells in preparation for the beach assault. You felt you could touch them going over your heads. Suddenly things were very, very real. I do remember turning to my sergeant with a nervous grin and rather flippantly saying, "I don't think I'm going to enjoy this ..."'

This is the only time in Dad's limited account of that epic morning that he ever uses the word 'nervous'. Of course he must have been, not knowing what he was about to face – and even the top brass had reservations as well. Field Marshal Sir Alan Brooke, Chief of the Imperial General Staff, had written only the evening before, 'I am very uneasy about the whole operation. At the best it will come very far short of the expectations of the bulk of the people, namely all those who know nothing about its difficulties. At its worst, it may well be the most ghastly disaster of the whole war.'

The supreme Allied commander in Europe (and later US president), General Dwight Eisenhower, kept an apology note in his pocket 'just in case things should go badly' and even Churchill sent US President Franklin D. Roosevelt a very untypical 'if we should fail' note. Only Field Marshal Montgomery showed not a hint of doubt – outwardly at least – that Operation Overlord would succeed. In a personal message from the commander-in-chief that was read to all the troops the night before the attack, he wrote: 'The time has come to deal the enemy a terrific blow in Western Europe … On the eve of this great adventure I send my best wishes to every soldier in the Allied team. To us is given the honour of striking a blow for freedom which will live in history; and in the better days that lie ahead, men will speak with pride of our doings … With stout hearts, and with enthusiasm for the contest, let us go forward to victory.'

All very heady patriotic prose, reminiscent of King Henry V on St Crispin's Day at Agincourt, but in truth Dad and the Hackney Gurkhas were at that moment more concerned with keeping the contents of their stomachs down as they awaited what lay ahead.

At this point they were still about five or six miles off the French coast and remained cruising for a long while because the sea was so choppy with a big swell. Eventually the tide was high enough and – with great difficulty in the windy conditions – my father got into one flat-bottomed landing craft while his sergeant got into another, as they had practised back in Southampton, so that if a boat got blown up, the platoon would not be leaderless. Each boat carried thirty-six men in all other ranks, including several Canadians. A large Canadian contingent had already gone ahead, their brief being to take the beach and move fast, not stopping for the wounded or prisoners, and go on to Caen, nine miles inland. The waiting British infantrymen were treated to the incongruous sight of some of the Canadians wading on to the besieged beach carrying bicycles over their heads to speed them on their journey.

The Royal Berkshires' orders were to follow up behind the Canadians, secure the beach and eliminate all German resistance. Having boarded the landing craft, as the overhead pounding by the navy continued, Basil and his B Company had to wait for two long hours until they eventually received the order to land on Juno Beach. This was not easy: there were mines everywhere bouncing up and down in the swell, many of them linked, so if one went up the whole lot would. However, they were very large and visible and one great source of grim amusement to the Hackney boys was the fact that the Germans had put signs up all along the beach saying 'Achtung Minen', basically telling them where the mines were.

As they approached the coastline they were greeted by the chilling and sickening sight of countless Canadian corpses being tossed on to the beach by the waves – the water black with blood – and yet more lifeless bodies littering the beach. 'I kept bumping into bodies as I waded in towards the shore,' said Doug Botting. 'The French Canadians had been hit badly taking the first brunt of it, poor sods, and as you came on to the beach there were bullets whizzing all around us. The noise was horrific and there was a lot of screaming.'

Some of the Royal Berks' landing party were hit by bullets before they were even able to get out of the boats. Tragically the very first was Private Ernest Cloves, who died as he slipped and fell in full battle dress on the ramp coming down from the landing craft and drowned as the others poured past him on to the beach. Cloves was the first in the battalion to die. Another early fatality was the company sergeant major, Joe Snowball. He had ominously told those around him in the landing craft as they raced in towards the beach, 'I don't think I'll be coming back,' and he didn't. He was killed shortly afterwards.

As an officer, Dad was one of the first of the Berkshires ashore. The leading troops were met by the crossfire of machine guns hidden in the sand dunes just at the top of the beach, the shelling of mortars and more distant artillery. As men fell, others stepped up and they kept on running and weaving towards the beachhead. Those that survived, including my father, regrouped at the top of the beach under the sea wall beneath the line of German machine-gun fire, some 100 yards from the sea. 'This was the first time we dared stop running,' said Dad, 'the first chance we got to check what the hell we'd come racing into. There were already many casualties, but the Germans had been badly hit too, and thank God their heavy fire was clearly getting less and less.'

The cockneys regrouped around Dad and the other officers and then moved up over the sea wall. Together they forced their way forward through the entanglement of barbed wire and anti-tank ditches, aiming for the beachhead on the outskirts of the coastal village of Bernières-sur-Mer, the nearest town to Juno Beach.

They had to pass many other casualties but the drill had been hammered into them for months: 'Never, ever stop or look back. Never, ever stand still. Just keep moving from side to side. If anyone falls, never stop for them. You must keep moving. Leave the fallen to the medics. If you stop you're a target and targets get shot.' It was a very basic rule of thumb but it kept many of them alive and many who forgot it, even for a second, didn't see the end of the war.

Another D-Day veteran, Gunner Sydney Riley from the 50th Northumberland Division, remembered years later in a newspaper interview how the landings sharpened the senses: 'Yes, we were being fired at but you expected that. There was shelling too. Anyway, if you hear bullets they've passed you – that's what we used to say. It's the ones you don't hear that cause the trouble.'

By the time the 5th Royal Berkshires streamed on to Juno Beach, in the main the German resistance was starting to lessen, due to the pounding they had received from the navy guns and the full-on assault by the Canadians. There had been machine-gun fire as Dad came up the beach, and certainly many brave men fell around him, but in the main the opposition was nothing like as savage as they'd expected. Bullets seemed to come out of nowhere, but they were sporadic. It seemed that having already been bombarded from the sea and the air, many of the Germans had pulled back to regroup and a full-on panzer reprisal was not expected till later in the day. Many other Germans had already been taken prisoner.

One of Basil's regiment, Captain David Thomas – whose son I met many years later – charged up the beach carrying a Lee Enfield rifle, not the pistol and lanyard that was usually issued to officers. In a written account of that day he recalled, 'Jerry definitely knew that British officers were supposed to carry a pistol and they would use that knowledge to target officers and take them out. It would be like carrying a sign saying, "Yoo hoo, I am an officer! Please shoot me." Also I had won all sorts of medals for shooting a rifle with the Officer Training Corps, but couldn't hit a barn door with a pistol.'

Lieutenant Tarrant didn't like a pistol either. He came running up the beach sweeping the German defences with a Sten gun. As they sheltered under a row of sandbanks beneath the line of sight of German machine guns, several of the infantry with Basil were surprised to find themselves huddled next to Frenchmen and women. The lads weren't too sure what the locals would make of them – they had, after all, been giving their homes a pounding since daybreak. But at this point, they just seemed to be glad to still be alive.

All day there was no time to stop. The Royal Berks had to keep moving forward up the beachhead to secure the area. As they came round the corner of a lonely house, Robbie Purver stumbled on to eight dead Canadian soldiers. It was a horrific sight: one had his head missing, another was dead but still holding a helmet full of blood. They'd clearly all been blown up on a mine. 'It made a lasting impression on me,' he said. 'After the long months of training it was suddenly all horribly real. I was eighteen and they were the first dead bodies I'd ever seen.' Before his nineteenth birthday he saw many, many more.

Another veteran from Basil's regiment, Captain Mike Pardoe, told me, 'The Canadians seemed to have done their stuff well and my group weren't actually fired on until we touched down and started to wade ashore. Small arms fire and some mortars started pounding us from the left, coming from somewhere near St Aubin. I well remember the fury of my CSM when a bullet went clean through the haversack on his back – straight through from one side to the other – just as he reached dry land, thus drilling a neat little hole through everything contained inside. He was furious, not at all fussed about how incredibly lucky he'd just been. It wasn't till we got ashore that the real unpleasantness started. Thereafter it was not funny at all, because the exceptionally high tide soon reduced the serviceable area of the beach to about the size of a couple of tennis courts and the Germans seemed to have an inexhaustible supply of mortar ammunition and some highly trained snipers.'

So many other extraordinary stories emerged from that day. One old French fisherman, whose story was later repeated in a British newspaper, remembered that the Germans had allowed him to put out his lobster pots every morning, some for himself but sometimes for German officers too if they had a sudden liking for lobster. At dawn on the morning of 6 June he went down as usual to inspect his pots and reached the German sentry point on the cliffs just as it was getting light. He could scarcely believe his eyes when he looked out to sea and saw the horizon black with ships of all sorts of shapes and sizes. He nudged the German sentry who was leaning against the concrete side of the pillbox, pointed seawards and said, 'Voilà, la flotte anglaise' ('Look, the English fleet'). The sentry rubbed his eyes, followed the old Frenchman's pointing finger and rubbed his eyes again harder. A look of incredulous amazement came over his face and he was obviously on the verge of panic for a moment. But then his confidence in the invincibility of the Fatherland soon returned and he shook his head contemptuously, spat, and with a patronising air said: 'Non, non, non, pas anglais – allemande' ('No, no, no, not English – they are German').

The old French fisherman continued: 'A few moments later, the first salvoes from the warships came over. It would have done you all good to see the great stupid face of that sentry change as the awful truth dawned on him. He popped back into his little hole like a rabbit, and I just stood there and laughed ... And then I went and cut their telephone wires.'

As my father and B Company continued to make their way inland, with Allied troops still pouring in from the ships behind them, they came upon a pillbox which was resisting with machine-gun fire, raking the men arriving up the beach. 'I started firing my Bren gun from close range into the slits in the pillbox,' says Robbie Purver. 'Suddenly the firing stopped. They were all dead. I think I killed a few but the first one will have been the first person I ever killed. You just got immune to dead bodies. You were an infantryman and you knew your life expectancy was just a matter of weeks, so if and when you got yours you wanted a quick bullet in the head. You wanted one you knew nothing about, you didn't want all your guts hanging out; you just wanted it quick and not even see it coming. Of course you hoped to get through it but the odds for infantrymen were hugely stacked against you.'

Certainly the Allied infantry losses for the D-Day landings were frighteningly high, estimated at upwards of 10,000 men, of which approximately 2,500 to 4,000 were fatalities. There were between 4,000 and 9,000 German casualties on that day too. The losses of the 3rd Canadian Division at Juno Beach alone have been given as 340 killed, 574 wounded and 47 taken prisoner. Anyone who survived that bloody day was extraordinarily lucky to get out alive.

One longstanding friend of Dad's, Captain Bill Pyke, who served with him in the Royal Berks, said that they got used to the dead bodies remarkably quickly once they had landed in Normandy. 'Unless you knew them personally and they were mates you'd seen die, it sounds terrible, but you barely even noticed them.'

Basil, too, was busy dealing with the reality of having death and danger all around him. As they climbed up and over more defences there was still German machine-gun fire raking across the sands, seemingly coming from yet another pillbox at the top. Dad recalled, 'We had to get under the firing line of that pillbox and run, moving from side to side, for perhaps a hundred yards to get under the stream of bullets.' It was actually nothing like as far as a hundred yards but, under fire, it probably felt more like a mile.

A tank put paid to the pillbox with what was actually a lucky hit. Its shell didn't hit the pillbox – its range was way too short – but instead it hit the sandbank in the front of it at its base. This meant the whole pillbox actually fell forward, leaving the gun buried and useless.

The company padre meanwhile busily directed heavy tank fire on to what looked like a very nice French seaside property that clearly held a number of the enemy. The house was reduced to rubble and the padre was heard hoping that his heavenly boss would understand and forgive him.

One more pillbox was silenced by an act of extraordinary heroism by a young officer who became one of Dad's close mates for many years after the war, another Berkshire man called Charlie Spackman. Remnants of a Canadian platoon were scattered across the beach, dead or badly wounded, as Lieutenant Spackman and his group landed. The damage was being done by machine-gun fire from another pillbox at the top of the sand dunes. There was little cover but Spackman and two non-commissioned officers crawled towards the pillbox trying to keep below the line of fire. The Germans then threw grenades, wounding both of the men accompanying Spackman.

Undeterred, but now alone, he moved on up towards the pillbox. Luck seemed to be on his side – one grenade landing near him failed to explode – and somehow he managed to reach his target. However, now he was faced with the challenge of how to take out a pillbox full of German soldiers single-handedly. Realising he was totally vulnerable, the young lieutenant decided to rely on the element of surprise. He charged with just his revolver, shooting and killing the amazed machine gunner before he could fire. The rest of the pillbox were so startled by the manic arrival of this young English officer that they put their hands up and surrendered to him. At gunpoint he got the prisoners to reveal a whole network of German beach defences, taking prisoners as he went. In all he captured no fewer than twenty-six prisoners and was later awarded the Military Cross.

After the war Dad took me, as a young lad, for a beer in the beautiful Thames-side Swan Pub at Pangbourne, where an old mate of his – one Charlie Spackman – was the landlord. He was an amiable, kindly man, a typical friendly Berkshire pub landlord. I think Dad maybe mentioned once vaguely that he'd known him in the war but I feel cheated that I never knew anything of his extraordinary heroism ... and yet in the regimental war diaries the name of Lieutenant Charles Spackman comes up again and again. I just had no idea.

Back in Normandy, after their terrifying charge through the bullets, the remaining Royal Berkshires eventually managed to assemble at the top of the beach outside Bernières-sur-Mer. They had done it. They had overcome the enemy and they were back on French soil.

'After that,' Dad said, 'it all went horribly quiet, much too quiet. I wasn't nervous, not really nervous at all, just exhilarated by everything that had happened since day break, but also very apprehensive.'

At this point, Private Doug Botting remembered the eggs and bacon that were cold but otherwise not even dented in the top pocket of his khaki battle jacket. 'I know it sounds daft,' says Doug, 'but I ate them there and then on the top of the beach and they tasted good. It had been a hell of a morning. I think we all had this silly idea that the invasion, whenever it came, was going to be a great adventure, just like a cowboy film. You were so excited you just wanted to get there ... but once you'd hit that beach you just wanted to get back again as fast as you could. But of course there was no going back.'

Some were already going back of course, but hideously wounded or in body bags. The Hackney Gurkhas that survived that first onslaught came of age on D-Day, and so did Lieutenant Tarrant. For the first time as a brand-new officer he had had the chance to prove himself to his men ... and to himself.

CHAPTER FIVE

A Station Sign and a Rubber Ring

Once Basil and the main body of the Royal Berkshires had secured the beachhead at Juno, and the whole area around Bernières-sur-Mer had been overrun by the Allied forces, the Royal Berkshires' next task was to make sure the coastal area was safe for more incoming troops and supplies and, over the next few weeks, to clear out any remaining Germans from the whole area. They spent most of that first morning lining up prisoners, getting the wounded on to stretchers and inevitably burying the first bodies.

The Canadian regiments that had been first to land were meanwhile pushing on fast towards Caen. They had taken the brunt of the casualties in the first wave of the invasion but their brief was to keep going forward.

The taking of Caen was critical to Montgomery's masterplan. It was the nearest large city to the beach landings and a crucial communication hub, with major routes leading from it, and thus essential to the Allies' advance inland. The enemy had a solid stronghold there, however, and managed to resist the Canadians on D-Day itself. In fact, Caen remained in the hands of the Germans for over a month after the Normandy landings, a fact which somewhat tarnished the glory of Montgomery's D-Day success, the Americans in particular being critical of his failure in this crucial area.

Monty had been opposed to mounting a full-frontal attack as Caen was a beautiful historic city and he was reluctant to decimate it. He was also reluctant to risk the lives of so many Canadian and British troops who were needed for the major liberation task ahead of them. In the end, though, decimation was deemed to be the only answer, and in early July Caen was pounded by a controversial bombing raid that destroyed 70 per cent of this picturesque town and killed 2,000 French civilians. The heavy-handed strategy worked, however, as it also wiped out large numbers of the occupying German troops. This meant that British and Canadian foot soldiers could now enter this 'softened' target and oust any enemy survivors.

Dad always found taking prisoners a thorough nuisance. At this stage, still early in the invasion, he had no dark thoughts of just shooting them, although as the war went on and they witnessed more of the behaviour of the SS, it must have been harder to resist. But on D-Day, once they'd gained the beach, they spent hours taking prisoners and preparing to ship them back to England.

The newly liberated French were in the main delighted to be free from the German occupation. Those locals who were freed by the Canadian forces were puzzled to find the new arrivals speaking to them in French and not English, but made them all the more welcome for that. But Dad's platoon found that some who were rescued by the British were not quite so thrilled. Some of them, of course, still harboured doubts about the dependability of the liberation and were worried about SS reprisals. Others had never really forgiven the British for evacuating at Dunkirk, although with hindsight there was little that the British troops could have done except stay and get slaughtered.

History has shown that the British were right to retreat in 1940. Four years later when my father returned as a veteran officer, it was within a much stronger, better-equipped British army. In addition, the Germans were massively depleted by this time, giving the Allies a much stronger chance of success. By 1944 the German infantry had lost hundreds of thousands of men, particularly on the Russian front, and the Luftwaffe no longer had full control of the skies. It had been the right time to attack, and now Basil and his men, busy rounding up the German prisoners, were the ones in the position of strength.

Once Dad and B Company had taken control of the beachhead, they received orders to get everyone together from the various landings, do a headcount to find out how many men had been lost or injured, and then press on to the centre of Bernières. Dad remembers seeing a beachmaster, some sort of naval figure who'd clearly been in Normandy for several days with a commando force who had secretly recced the whole set up. 'He obviously knew exactly what was what,' said Dad. 'It was chaotic with fighting men, stretcher parties and captured Germans all over the place, and it certainly needed organising, but his main job seemed to be to do a lot of shouting ... and very loud shouting it was too!'

'He was extraordinary,' agreed Doug. 'He just kept shouting, "Over there! Get bloody well over there!"' The men were told to look for a large black and white building which they could see clearly from the English Channel and, amazingly, considering the pounding that the whole area had taken from the combined forces of the Royal Navy, the RAF and Luftwaffe, it was still standing when the Royal Berkshires arrived. Even more astonishingly it still stands to this day.

Throughout the day there was sporadic German machine-gun fire and some bombing by the Luftwaffe, but mainly the enemy activity in that area was surprisingly low key. For other troops, particularly the Americans who landed on Omaha Beach, the fighting had been savage with a huge loss of life. The US forces who landed on Omaha lost more than a third of their fighting men in the main attack.

Despite the relatively muted resistance from the Germans in the Juno area, the men of B Company of the 5th Royal Berkshires still faced a constant threat of danger. As they made their way up from the beach to secure the wider territory, the biggest problem for Basil and his men was coming from the enemy snipers. Once the Royal Berkshires had got dug in and mounted their guns, the snipers went understandably quiet, but later they reappeared with a vengeance. Sickeningly, their main target seemed to be the wounded as they were lying on stretchers waiting to be loaded on to landing craft and taken back to hospital in England. As Dad noted in his diary, the Germans were fighting a dirty bloody war.

Several men, including many already wounded, were hit by one particular nest of snipers who were reckoned to be working from the roof of a château that overlooked the ambulance and loading station. What followed in amongst all the horrors of the day was pure farce. Lieutenant Tarrant and his men crawled or zig-zagged to the massive door that formed the entrance to the château, making their way nervously through some 200 yards of open country to get to the door. Now they were close under the walls of the magnificent old building, no sniper could get a shot from the roof. Once assembled, Dad and a small handful of Hackney's finest tried charging the door with their shoulders. No use: it was solid reinforced oak. They tried hammering it with the butts of their rifles. Still no use. A couple of rounds of live ammunition fired at the ancient lock also achieved nothing. Then a wonderful cockney voice came from twenty yards away in the trees, where the rest of the platoon were taking cover: 'Why don't you try the fuckin' 'andle?' This they did, only to witness the door immediately swing open.

Once inside, Dad charged through, leading three others, with them all covering each other in textbook style. As they got to the main hall, Basil could clearly see somebody in full battle dress coming down the stairs directly opposite him. With instincts honed from the long months of training, Dad swung round his Sten gun and fired immediately. The shattered glass from a huge antique mirror came down all over the stairs in front of him. What Basil had seen as he came charging through the door was his own image in the mirror.

It was the stuff of black humour but there was no real time to savour the moment until much later, which of course he did again and again in years to come. But for now there was still a potentially dangerous building to be cleared. In the end it turned out there was no one on the roof and the ancient château was completely empty. So where was the gunfire coming from?

The source of the sniper fire was eventually located in the old church tower of Bernières, from where a female sniper was believed to be operating, either working alone or with others. Private Desmond Illsley remembers vividly his first awareness of her: 'It was said she was a French bird who had married a German and borrowed a rifle and a uniform from one of his mates. Man or woman she was a pretty good shot.' Illsley went on: 'I remember lying at the top of the beach, a good 400 yards from the church, and I found myself next to a Canadian captain who was looking through his binoculars. I asked him if he could see anything and the next thing I knew he rolled over on to the sand with a hole in the middle of his forehead.'

The bell tower was the perfect spot for a sniper: it was impossible to get up to the very top without being shot at and it was thought very probable that she or they would be able to get away under cover of darkness. The last bit of access was just a narrow set of stairs, which of course the snipers had covered, and there were believed to be several exits. The concern was that the sniper could disappear when night fell, only to reappear somewhere else the next day. Something clearly had to be done.

On the beach they now had ack-ack anti-aircraft protection and facing the church was a massive Bofors gun. Angered by the continuing damage that this particular sniper, or group of snipers, was doing to his troops, Basil called to the sergeant who had been standing patiently by his gun waiting for German planes since early on D-Day morning.

'Have you hit anything?' Dad asked him.

'No sir,' he replied. 'I haven't actually fired it yet.'

'Do you think you could hit that steeple from here?'

'I should think so,' said the sergeant. 'But it is a church.'

'Well, cross yourself, man, and then hit it,' said Dad.

The sergeant made the sign of the cross, looked to the heavens for forgiveness, then seconds later there was a massive boom as the shell hit the top of the old church.

The sniping fire was silenced with that one blast but there was an extraordinary twist to this already sorry tale. Men were detailed to go up carefully and bring any bodies down from the tower. The lads came back down and threw out several dead bodies in bloodstained German greatcoats. On closer examination one was found to be the body of a woman, but there was another door to the rear of the tower and another detail came down and flung out another body, again in a greatcoat, and that too was the body of a woman, still holding a mangled gun. There had been two of them. The legend of the woman sniper had clearly been true, and in fact they were a double threat, but now that particular danger was over. As Private Illsley said, 'Whoever they were, whatever their story was, now they were just brown bread.' Dad added, 'Male or female, anyone who shoots at wounded men on stretchers can expect no mercy from any of us ...'

Even in the midst of all this, there were some comic moments. One old Frenchman they met as they were clearing the area said, 'Have you seen any Boche?'

'Yes, loads of them,' said the Gurkhas, 'all over the place.'

'Well, why don't you shoot them?' said the old Frenchman.

One of the lads replied, 'We're trying to, but they just won't stand still long enough.'

Communications on the ground after the landings were frequently chaotic. Captain Mike Pardoe got an SOS from head-quarters saying that they were being heavily mortared and that an enemy patrol seemed to have infiltrated into their area. It was requested that an immediate fighting patrol come and check the German advance. This puzzled Mike as resistance up till now had been surprisingly light, hundreds of prisoners had been taken and the whole area now seemed to be made secure, so he suggested that they were suffering from hallucinations. This was vehemently denied and he was told in no uncertain manner that it was almost certainly the first part of a massive counter-attack with the aim of pushing the Allies back into the sea – 'They have to be stopped at all costs ... message over.'

Mike was still unconvinced but dutifully called Basil Tarrant and his platoon to search the area and kill or take prisoner all

Germans they met. Dad and his men searched the whole area thoroughly but found nothing but dead bodies and abandoned rifles. Not a single live German was to be seen.

Mike says: 'As I had expected, the reports of heavy German mortar fire had been nothing more serious than the crack of HMS *Rodney's* 16-inch shells as they passed overhead on their way to a target several miles inland – but this story may cause a blush on many manly cheeks, so perhaps it had better be forgotten.' And so it probably remained ... until now.

In the midst of all this day's activity, some magnificent homemade cider was found in what appeared to be an abandoned French farmhouse. The lucky lads who discovered it were allowed just the one glass at the time and then, later that evening, they came back for more ... although it was shared out carefully because there was a real fear of a heavy German counter-attack overnight. Counter-attack or not, the whole lot disappeared very quickly; it would certainly have gone down well after the events of that epic June day. In the morning, though, it transpired that the farm wasn't actually abandoned at all. The farmer with his wife and children emerged tentatively from a cleverly concealed hiding place in a haystack. Luckily they couldn't have cared less about the cider, which had all gone; they were just glad to be free at last from German occupation.

It had been less than twenty-four hours since the Allied invasion and some Frenchmen still feared that the Germans would bring in reinforcements and occupy Normandy all over again. However, most of the French families sensed that, for Hitler, it was at last the beginning of the end. Not everyone was happy with this turn of events – some French men and women who had collaborated with the Nazis during occupation were to realise they had backed the wrong side and were now in danger of their lives. In the coming weeks, many such traitors were hunted down and humiliated. Women who were suspected of having sexual liaisons with the enemy had their hair cropped and were paraded through the towns of Normandy, or tied to trees and left in the market square. Many other collaborators across northern France were summarily executed.

But in Bernières-sur-Mer and St Aubin there was mainly rejoicing and the townsfolk appeared delighted to see the Allied troops. To commemorate their liberation the people of Bernières later named one of the roads from the beach Rue du Royal Berkshire Regiment. But this was not the only lasting legacy of the Royal Berkshires' part in the liberation; there was also another unusual object that was acquired by Basil and the Hackney Gurkhas at the end of D-Day. The men were so pleased, indeed positively amazed, by the comparative ease with which they had all landed on French soil that when they got to the old railway station at Bernières they decided to take the station sign as a memento. The men all signed it and somehow got it back to England – an extraordinary journey in itself – and it now nestles proudly over the reception area of The Rifles Berkshire and Wiltshire Military Museum in Salisbury.

Years later I went there with my father and Toby, my son. We had a fascinating day and, egged on for the first time by his grandson, my father revealed just a little about the war. He was incredibly amused by the railway sign and the three of us were pictured underneath it. Toby and I got up on to the desk and spent a long time trying to spot my father's signature on the sign, among all the others scrawled there. One or two were still legible, but most of them were very faint and dusty and we couldn't spot Dad's name amongst them. There were a few names that we were just able to decipher, though, and as I called one or two of them out I noticed Dad's eyes just briefly mist over before he looked away. Only months later did I realise how insensitive I had been and how painful it must have been for Dad ... some of those names would have been ones he hadn't heard for more than sixty years, and some of them would almost certainly have been young men, less than twenty years old, who'd died fighting alongside him in France.

In amongst nicking French railway signs, Basil and his men spent much of the rest of the day clearing mines and taking prisoners. In all there were well over 1,000 German prisoners taken on the day and of course they all had to be transported back to England in our own landing craft.

As the war dragged on towards its conclusion, the problem of surrendering Germans got worse as the sheer weight of numbers became more and more difficult to accommodate. In the main it does seem from the military records that we were far gentler with the Germans that we took prisoner than they often were to us. But it was massively draining on our resources, transport and manpower.

Not all prisoners of war were taken back to England. Many were taken to Holland and Belgium to be kept prisoner there after those countries were liberated later in 1944. Often they were imprisoned locally, in châteaux or large buildings that had been taken by the Allies. Hitler's propaganda machine insisted that these men had not been imprisoned at all but were ready to proudly march out again to fight for the Fatherland. Dad poured scorn on this in his diary: 'This would have been tricky as they were all in chains and, in any case, our guards were all under orders to regularly parade the bedraggled prisoners manacled through the streets so that it could clearly be seen that they had been beaten in battle and were very much in our hands as prisoners ... Mainly we did look after them but they were a bloody nuisance and tied up more and more manpower.' I always wonder what he meant by the 'mainly' in that sentence.

As 1944 drew on, an increasing number of Germans were just glad to give themselves up. But there still remained some fanatical, hard-core Nazis who didn't care if they died as long as they took a British soldier with them. In the bitter winter of 1944–45, many of the SS wore two tunics with camouflaged battle dress on the outside. At first the Allies didn't cotton on to this tactic. They would search the outer tunic of a prisoner of war and strip him of any obvious weapons. But the Germans would keep a pistol knife or even a grenade under the second tunic. When the guard's back was turned they would take out the weapons and kill a guard or two before they were invariably shot themselves.

But these horrors were still to come: for now the immediate priority was to clear the beach for the easy passage of further waves of incoming Allied troops and to escort the prisoners on to the waiting boats. As this necessitated getting back into the sea, Captain Peter Prior, a man my father had great respect for and who was later to become the chairman of Bulmers Cider in Somerset, commandeered a floating rubber life ring. He says, 'We were constantly worried about the lads drowning in the deep water, especially when the tide was full, so I just "borrowed" the life ring. It said Royal Navy on it, which was a bit of a clue that it wasn't ours, so I got my batman to cross the word Navy out and replace it with the word Berks!'

Harmless enough – and there was a war on … but here's the twist. When many survivors went to Juno Beach in 1994 to mark the fiftieth anniversary of the D-Day landing, with my father and Peter Prior among them, they found themselves among a large group of French locals. As they stood, listening to the speeches and watching the laying of a wreath, a determined woman pushed her way through the crowd. She was called Madame Micheline Trannoy and she made her way to Peter and said, 'Excusez-moi, monsieur, but you left this behind!' Beaming, she then handed Peter the life ring still with the words 'Royal Berks' painted proudly on it. She had stored it in her cellar until 'the day the Royal Berkshires came back'.

Prior himself had an eventful war. For six months before the Normandy landings he'd been one of just four men in the regiment who had been secretly briefed about the plans for D-Day and, after that day, he went on to be captured twice by the Germans – only to escape both times.

For Dad, it was the only other time he was to visit the shoreline of Juno Beach. The second time was obviously altogether quieter, but must have been full of memories. Perhaps it exorcised some of the demons – I'll never know. I do remember that on his return, when I asked him how it went, he said, 'I just didn't realise how close the Germans were,' but then typically said nothing more and went quietly out into the garden. I didn't follow … the subject was closed.

On D-Day itself, one other downright strange event happened to Dad. It was an extraordinarily busy day and by late afternoon it had seemed a very long time since early-morning tea and hard tack biscuits. He and his sergeant, with a small patrol of men, were checking through German trenches and making them fit for their own possible use, when they came across one trench occupied by a dead German corporal. Chivalry clearly did still exist, at least on this first day of the invasion of Europe, so Basil decided they should move the body for proper burial. Finding a wheelbarrow conveniently parked nearby in a field, Basil and the sergeant trundled the corpse away to a quiet corner, with its arms and legs hanging over the side of the barrow. Then they had a bizarre experience. When they did the routine check of the dead man's pockets and papers they found a picture of this young NCO smiling happily, in what was presumably his garden at home – but lying in a wheelbarrow with his arms and legs dangling over the side ... the same pose, the same picture, almost exactly how they had just left him. It was a macabre end to what had been an emotionally and physically exhausting day.

CHAPTER SIX

Over the Seine

D-Day saw the turning point for the Allies' campaign in Europe. Although Hitler continued to insist that there must be no surrender, forcing many of his generals to be shot or to commit suicide rather than accept defeat, many of the German Army began to realise for the first time there was a chance that the war might be lost. Now, it was their turn to start worrying about how they might get home alive.

For Montgomery it was a huge triumph. It was he who had convinced both Roosevelt and Churchill that his invasion plan would succeed. It had gone almost too well. In the eastern sector of the front, British and Canadian troops had successfully pinned down the main force of Field Marshal Rommel's defences, making it impossible for them to follow Hitler's frenzied instructions to drive the invading battalions back into the sea, while the Americans were pushing forward up the Cherbourg peninsula. At this point Eisenhower and Montgomery were talking in all seriousness about finishing the war before Christmas.

However, for all the euphoria of the Allied commanders at the success of the invasion, they failed at first to get the foothold in

Caen that they badly needed. And in the months ahead, the battle-hardened panzer troops were to continue to check their advances time and again, frustrating any thoughts of ending the war as soon as had been optimistically hoped.

Nevertheless, despite heavy Allied losses, D-Day had been a tremendous morale-boosting success. A liberating Allied force was now in northern Europe. Of course there was still a major task ahead to liberate first France, then Belgium and Holland, before entering 'the Fatherland' to give Hitler a good hiding on German soil. This would be a colossal operation which would take many more men than had landed on 6 June. But all agreed it had been a glorious start.

The amount of planning and organisation that went into the cause of European liberation was mind-blowing. A massive infra-structure of communications, supplies, transport, food and ammunition had to be established immediately to enable the Allied push into Europe. Once the beach area had been secured and cleared of all German occupying forces, my dad and the Royal Berks lads of 'No. 8 Beach Group' had a new, mammoth and back-breaking job ahead of them. They were to be responsible for the unloading and movement of the many thousands of tons of equipment, ammunition and supplies that were to cross the Channel and land after dark every night over the next six weeks. One of their tasks was to lay tracks across the beach to prevent the supply trucks sinking in the sand and to minimise the distance they had to carry the heavy boxes and containers from the beached landing craft.

The daunting task was not just physically demanding, it was dangerous as well, in no small part because the sand and shingle still hid a vast number of German landmines. Many of these mines were covered with wood, which sounds primitive but was actually lethal because they couldn't be picked up by metal detectors. In addition, although Lieutenant Tarrant and B Company had managed to secure the area from ground attack, the RAF couldn't completely clear the air space. The Luftwaffe would fly overhead nightly, desperately trying to impede the beach group's progress by showering them with anti-personnel bombs and dropping further mines into the Channel. The anti-personnel bombs were dropped from canisters that contained thirty of these small but deadly devices, peppering the beach as they dispersed.

Dad and his Royal Berkshire beach group set up anti-aircraft guns all along the shoreline but, tragically, having survived the landing on Juno Beach, many men were lost during these nightly operations over the next few weeks. Some were killed by direct hits from bombs, some stumbled on to the mines hidden along the beaches, some really unlucky ones were hit by shells from long-distance German artillery. In addition to these casualties, several men were killed by accidents unloading ammunition.

The demand on Dad's beach group was exhausting. Thousands more Allied troops were pouring into northern Europe, and vast numbers of larger landing craft were beginning to bring in serious bits of kit, including ammunition trucks, Jeeps, Red Cross vehicles, personnel-carrying lorries and tanks. This had necessitated the building of a 'Mulberry harbour' – a temporary but substantial landing dock – by the Royal Engineers, as the larger, much heavier landing craft couldn't get right up to the beach. The massive causeway was floated over the Channel and then secured to huge concrete and steel pontoons sunk into the seabed.

Interestingly, two battalions of the Wiltshire Regiment – the 4th and 5th – were among the new arrivals, landing on 19 June. They'd missed the carnage of D-Day but, by early August, as they moved to the French interior around Mont Pinçon, twenty miles south-west of Caen, they were thrown almost immediately into savage fighting with highly trained German regiments and lost hundreds of men within just a few days of arriving in France. My father didn't yet know it, but the decimated Wiltshires were to become a major part of his war.

But not just yet. First, No. 8 Beach Group had twelve full weeks of bringing in men and supplies to back up the invading Allied armies as they pushed deeper into France and on up towards Germany.

At times even the elements seemed to conspire against them. Two weeks after the D-Day landings, a hurricane hit the northern coasts of France and caused massive damage. The storm raged for seventy-two hours, bringing gale-force winds and driving rain. The sea was wild and very dangerous, craft of all kinds were washed ashore and wrecked and the Mulberry harbours were severely damaged. Most of the temporary port American sector was out of action altogether for a while but amazingly at no point did the Royal Berkshires' unloading stop – when the DUKWs, the six-wheeled amphibious vehicles, were unable to reach the ships, unloading continued from the coasters which were beached on the turn of the tide. Losses due to this freak storm amounted to nearly 2,000 vehicles and over 140,000 tons of stores, but the Royal Berkshires refused to give up.

Eventually the storm abated and the work of the beach group continued with renewed vigour. To give an idea of the scope of the work, here are two typical days from the regimental diary at the time:

30 June 1944 Bernières-sur-Mer FRANCE

Tonnage for the day: 4,452.

D company moved away from the ammunition dumps to carry out emergency repairs. Called back urgently twice for ammunition loading as more supplies arrived.

Training programmes carried out at night.

Fatal accident 199 GT Company. One man killed in DUKW accident.

73,586 tons of supplies discharged on company beaches since June 6th. These figures would have been even higher but for the fact that weather considerably hampered the work at times.

3 July 1944 Bernières-sur-Mer FRANCE

Slight enemy air activity directed at shipping off shore.

04:30 hours unloading commences.

08:00 hours off-loading commenced.

08:35 hours mine exploded forward of gun site on beach near advanced HQ.

Three wounded – two Royal Naval personnel and one gunner.

Type of mine: S type. This type and a British Mark Three had previously been cleared around the gun position but not detected as of wooden type.

The diaries are full of snippets and incidents that give a flavour of these weeks. 'Enemy air activity, beaches machine-gunned but no casualties' … 'Rocket landed in minefield 200 yards west of B Company HQ' … 'Bombs seen dropped in the sea to hamper shipping. Royal Navy informed' … 'One Allied plane crashed into sea north east of beach area. Crew bailed out before crash launch proceeded to rescue' … 'One plane believed to be Junkers 88 with fighter on its back believed shot down' … 'Torpedo painted grey three prongs on nose may be floating in anchorage or washed ashore. First sighted eastern end of Sword Beach. Anyone sighting it please report at once' … '22:00 hours: A company report landing craft approaching in direction of cookhouse. Five rounds fired at cookhouse. No injuries, officers' mess damaged' … 'Explosion in ammunition area some casualties but none fatal.'

Despite these incidents, the Hackney boys were soon settled into the exhausting routine of unloading supplies. With boats coming in twenty-four hours a day, the sheer range of supplies that arrived was extraordinary. As well as trucks, tanks, massive guns and ammunition, every conceivable little item was brought in that might be needed for the months ahead: beer, biscuits, bandages, torches, socks and condoms. One morning Basil and co were surprised to hear barking in the distance, coming from the sea. It turned out to be the Royal Engineers' No. 2 dog platoon who were specially trained for bomb disposal and sniffing out mines. Sapper Donald May remembers coming in to Juno Beach: 'We were several weeks after D-Day so the first great battle was already over but it was still a horrible place to come ashore and the sea was absolutely pounding. There were twelve of us in our unit with twenty-nine dogs, all specially trained to sniff out mines. The lads were all delighted to see us, as even though a lot of the area had been cleared there were still large areas where the Germans had hidden mines and booby traps as they retreated.'

Doug Botting says it was the unpredictability of the mines that spooked them: 'You were aware of heavy artillery fire coming towards you and you knew all about trying to duck below the line of machine-gun fire, but the thought of standing on a mine was always terrifying.' The dogs were a key element in the detection of these terrible weapons. Donald May says, 'I was actually in the Highland Light Infantry but they wanted volunteers to work with dogs. So because my dad was a gamekeeper I enjoyed working with animals and I put my hand up. I liked the idea of training dogs but they didn't tell me they were doing mine detection until it was too late. But they were amazing. They were trained to sniff out explosives and then lie down just in front of the mine as a marker. Then the engineers would come in and defuse the mine. Wonderful animals. We took twenty-nine out and twenty-seven came home.' Over the next few months those dogs were to save literally thousands of lives.

Considering the sheer amount being unloaded by very tired men, it is remarkable that there weren't more fatalities among the regiment during this unloading period. But some of the regimental diary entries reveal a tragic waste of young life. On 10 July it was reported, 'AM. Private Bailey received fatal injury by accident. Gunshot wounds.' Similarly on 19 August: '17:30 hours Private Plank fatally injured by mine explosion at clifftop near mortar range.' It wasn't all one way, though. On 14 July, the diary reported: '19:29 hours Messerschmitt shot down. One man seen parachuting down, others presumed dead.'

There was little to raise the spirits of Lieutenant Tarrant and his men through this rather frustrating time. They wanted to get on with the fighting but knew they had this long, back-breaking period ahead of them. In addition they were still taking casualties and losing men, despite hardly ever seeing a German.

However, a couple of notable visits during this period had helped to provide a little cheer for the troops. Just ten days after D-Day, with no warning, King George VI flew out to Normandy to thank these brave young men for what they were doing. Doug remembers him clearly: 'It was great for morale, of course, and the lads all loved him, but I got up really close and he unmistakeably had heavy make-up on. Max Factor it must have been. Really thick. At the time I just thought it was weird, but years later I realised he didn't want any of us to know how ill he was. Apparently his real colour was ghostly pale.' The king was already suffering from lung cancer, exacerbated by the stress of war, and he was to die less than seven years later, aged just fifty-six.

A few weeks later, on 22 July, Winston Churchill and Field Marshal Montgomery came over to see the Normandy battalions at Caen – now in Allied hands – which was another great boost for the troops. Delighted with the success of the landings, Churchill praised the soldiers' achievements and reassured them how well the war was going. Churchill and Monty were much admired by the British troops. They had both seen active service in the First World War (Churchill in the Boer War too), and the men respected their integrity and grit. Basil was thrilled to see them both in the flesh. Later Churchill wrote of the trip in his diary: 'Went to France. It was a very nice day. Things going well.' Echoes of my father's brevity in his diary entries.

The other thing that encouraged the troops was the daily news bulletins that were set up for their benefit. So often soldiers feel they have no real idea what part they are playing in the overall context of a war, so this was to make a huge difference. At night, Jeeps with loudspeakers would give them the latest news from the front, and all companies were regularly given situation maps to show clearly how the Allied troops were doing in their push into France. How much of this information was doctored we can't tell but my father and his platoon found this gave them a real sense of involvement as they unloaded one landing craft after another. They were also given a daily breakdown of how much equipment they had shifted – an enormous amount each day.

At first, Basil proudly kept a tally in his diary of the tonnage they had unloaded and transferred to trucks each night, but the novelty soon wore off and the diary entries stopped. The regiment's war diary, though, shows that an average night saw them unload 7,000 tons of assorted 'stuff' from the many landing craft that shuttled backwards and forwards, under the cover of darkness, across the Channel. The nightly tonnage varied, depending on the weather and the frequency of enemy air attacks, but by the end of August Basil and the lads had landed and shifted a staggering one third of a million tons of vital supplies and equipment. An extraordinary achievement by Dad and the Hackney Gurkhas and it gave the Allied forces a huge backup to support the march towards the Rhine.

Towards the end of August it was considered that everything needed for the liberation of Europe was now safely on French soil, or at least every last thing that was available at the time, so the job of No 8 Beach Group was done and they were disbanded. Of course, it was hardly redundancy – they were already tough, battle-hardened infantrymen and they would be sorely needed elsewhere.

So it was that, after twelve long weeks of unloading supplies, the 5th Battalion of the Royal Berkshire Regiment finally got the news that they were to be sent off to join other regiments. Half of them, including Basil, were to be transferred to join the Wiltshires.

This announcement didn't make the Hackney Gurkhas very happy but of course a lot of it was just resistance to change. Dad commented that he'd never witnessed such a degree of undying parochial loyalty and regimental pride, and it meant that some men became rather bolshy when they heard the news. He said later: 'I don't know what they were making a fuss about. I don't remember them being very excited about being in the Royal Berkshires in the build up to D-Day, especially as half of them had never even seen Berkshire before – they were cockneys from the East End. But, in the end, they were a good bunch and they knew we had no choice. We were soldiers, there was a war on and we just got on with it.'

Dad, who actually was born and bred in Berkshire, didn't seem to mind the change of regiment himself. In any case, he was pleased that a major concession to comradeship had been made, as they had not been totally split up: they were reassigned to other regiments as whole platoons.

About half the force stayed on as the Royal Berkshires and fought their way deep into Germany. Meanwhile Basil and a large number of the original Hackney Gurkhas set off in lorries and tanks to join their new regiment. They travelled well into France like this and then there followed a long march in blistering heat until they joined up with the Wiltshire Regiment boys at Vernon, on the banks of the River Seine about halfway to Paris.

The march was tough. Wearing heavy battle gear and carrying full packs of arms and ammunition, the Hackney Gurkhas were surrounded by the smell of death. Doug Botting says it was just horrific: 'The weather was baking hot. We were all super-fit with rippling muscles after the weeks of unloading but it got really tough. Men were passing out from the gagging heat and the air was filled with the cloying, sickly stench of death.'

'It wasn't just dead soldiers either,' said Robbie Purver. 'There were dead horses everywhere and bloated cows, pigs, goats, cats and dogs that had been hit by the heavy artillery fire. As we marched, the smell was overwhelming.' Doug added: 'A lot of men were throwing up as we marched but there was no time to stop. As well as the smell of death there was the cloying stink of diesel from hundreds and hundreds of blown-up trucks and armoured vehicles. It was like a scene from hell. And even to this day, seventy years later, if I get a whiff of that smell, whether I'm out walking or just sitting quietly at home, all sorts of bad memories come back.'

Robbie Purver also remembers a particularly disturbing episode that has remained etched in his mind for nearly seventy years: 'A lot of animals had been killed or horribly wounded by shellfire from the artillery on both sides. As we were marching through France in the heat and stink, a farmer came up to me, calling "Monsieur!" and making sign language for me to follow him. A couple of us went with him, carrying our guns, to a field below his farm. There we saw a horse, alive but dreadfully wounded, with its guts hanging out. It was a terrible sight. Clearly he wanted me to put it out of its misery. Even though we'd already killed a lot of the enemy since we landed on D-Day, I hadn't killed any animal and I really hated the thought of it. But I realised the poor thing was in agony so I finished it off with a few bursts from my Sten gun. It was the only humane thing to do but I hated doing it.'

These were the horrific scenes that Basil and his men had to face. 'We knew we just had to keep marching,' said Dad. 'At night when it cooled, the stench went away for a while, but in the morning as the fierce August sun got up, the smell came back. It was a tough time on everybody.'

In addition, there was real danger from mines laid by the retreating enemy. As the marching men got hot and their feet ached, they preferred to travel over grass whenever possible. It was easier on the boots but of course it was under grass verges that the Germans hid their mines. Dad recalled an occasion when a towed trailer that just touched a Teller mine was blown up into a tree, killing the men immediately beside it and flattening men several yards around with its blast. Dad said, 'We could never relax. Even when things seemed OK they never really were or at least never for long. I never really relaxed from the day we landed in France.'

Meanwhile, the battalion they were heading towards, the 5th Wiltshires, had been having an even worse time. As Dad had seen, the Wiltshires hadn't actually arrived in France on D-Day; they'd landed thirteen days later as part of Montgomery's ongoing invasion force. But if they'd missed the D-Day landings, they'd certainly been in the thick of it since. In attempting to clear Mont Pinçon, about twenty miles inland from Juno and Sword, they had taken heavy casualties from the Germans dug in at the top. In fact the regiment was decimated: they had lost more than 200 men in a series of bitter fire fights.

Then it got tougher. The brief for the Wiltshires was to cross the River Seine as part of their push north towards Belgium. But the Seine at the place where they arrived, near Vernon, was heavily defended by German troops who set themselves up on high ground looking down on the river. They were in a perfect position to fire down upon anyone trying to cross it. The Germans had already blown the bridges so the Wiltshires' orders were to get across the river by boat and take the hill. The Seine at that point was perhaps 200 yards wide.

A plan was quickly hatched. The RAF was to drop a string of smoke bombs on to the river so that the Allied troops could get across quickly in boats with outboard motors, safely camouflaged by the temporary smoke screen and thus not presenting any visible targets to the Germans. It was a good tactic. However, what happened next, on 25 August, was a disaster.

Unbeknownst to the Allies, there was a series of sand banks just under the surface of the river, halfway across, and several of the boats became grounded on them. Then, tragically, the wind changed as the lads were crossing, blowing the smoke away and leaving them completely exposed in mid-river to the German machine guns. They were sitting ducks.

It was a bloodbath. The men were mown down where they sat, hopelessly trying to hide in their boats. Young boys who'd been photographed grinning and giving the thumbs-up just minutes before, as they quietly loaded their heavy wooden boats into the river, were now floating dead downstream. There were very few survivors.

Jackie Dryden, the assistant curator of The Wardrobe – The Rifles Berkshire and Wiltshire Military Museum in Salisbury, showed me a poignant black and white picture of a whole group of these young lads, smiling for somebody's camera, sitting in one of the boats. There were thirty or more of them preparing to push off. Grimly she told me, 'Within less than a minute all of them were dead.'

Lieutenant Tarrant and his men arrived soon after the disastrous attempted crossing. As they arrived, the Wiltshires were still coming to terms with their huge losses from that one terrible, failed attack and were very glad of the reinforcements. The former Royal Berks beach group had originally been assigned to the Wilts because of their losses at Mount Pinçon, but now they were needed more than ever.

The Seine still had to be crossed, though, and later the new regiment regrouped, crossing in flat-bottomed landing craft under the cover of night. They hastily assembled a floating pontoon bridge, replacing the one that the Germans had blown, and over the next few days there was a bloody series of battles as the newly strengthened Wiltshires secured the whole area.

Although British troops were now safely across the Seine, other troops following their footsteps were still fired upon by the enemy, from German positions on high ridges overlooking the north-eastern side of the river. The new 5th Wilts B Company dealt with one of these machine-gun positions on high ground then climbed further to take another, even larger German position on top of the cliff.

Tragically this was to cause more men to be killed in action, in the most horrific way. Dad had been instructed to lead his men up the hilltop at night. They made their move to take the summit just on daybreak. Robbie Purver remembers, 'Basil was leading and in the early morning light we all felt very vulnerable. It was a flat-topped hill with an open field right at the peak. The Germans were dug in at the far side of the flat ground.

'The plan was our usual one – to pound them with artillery first and only then would we, the infantry, go in. It was the usual tactic. To be honest it didn't always work because often the enemy would dig themselves in, lying low until the artillery pounding stopped and then come up again and start firing at us. However, on this occasion they didn't need to: the artillery had got the range wrong and instead of landing perhaps 100 yards in front of the advancing British troops, the shells landed right amongst our boys.'

Robbie thinks that they must have advanced further and faster than the artillery anticipated and were therefore right in the line of fire for the shells meant for the enemy. His memories of that dreadful day are permanently etched into his brain. 'I lost several of my closest mates. There were many casualties – several men lost their legs, one lad sat there dying with his lungs hanging out and one poor blighter had his head blown off completely. It was horrific, just his blood-soaked body was lying there. We could only find out who he was much later by going through his pockets and finding his pay book. It was awful, sickening.'

This was the real horror of war. Young men lying dead some-where on a hill in northern France blown to pieces, in a tragic accident, by their own artillery. And of course for Lieutenant Tarrant and his shattered men there was no going back; they still had to carry on and take the hill. With heavy fighting but not too many more losses, they eventually achieved their aim.

I asked Robbie Purver how you pick yourself up from a tragedy like that, with your friends dead and wounded around you, and carry on into battle. Of course he said, 'You have no choice, you just do it.' Maybe that's true, but it's courage and grit that I and most of my generation can't even begin to contemplate.

This action saw a lot of bayonet fighting which I have always found a sickening thought, and I still find it hard to imagine my own dear, kind father killing someone in this way. Doug Botting explained, 'We'd only done it with straw dummies in training. The real thing was very different. It's horrible to think that we could ever do it, but we did ... of course we did. It was me or him. You had to.'

Another of the Wiltshires, talking about bayonet fighting, said, 'At first I dreaded it but we soon realised that the Germans were totally inferior at it. They would always charge at you with arms raised and their bayonet in the air, all you had to do was duck under their charge, parry and then stick them as they came on to the blade.' Of the remaining Germans they encountered, some ran away, some were killed in action, but many of them just came out with their hands up, surrendering to the Wiltshires. They took many prisoners that morning.

Days earlier they'd found the bodies of more than fifty British soldiers dead at the side of a wood, shot in the head by the SS, and after everything that had happened that morning it must have been tough to show mercy when they captured German soldiers. But whatever his inner feelings, Dad seems to have always kept to the Geneva Convention and the prisoners were taken unharmed and sent back down the line. For some it was clearly a relief that their war was over. One young blond German was found looking positively calm in a trench at the top of the hill. 'Good morning, gentlemen,' he said, happily raising his hands. 'I've been waiting for this day for four years.'

The Germans who had been guarding the Seine were eventually defeated and by the end of this battle more than 100 German prisoners of war had been taken back down the line. The Royal Engineers could now safely get on and construct a Bailey bridge over the river, allowing the safe passage of many more Allied troops and vehicles.

The area around the new bridge was still a bottleneck, though, and a huge backlog of Allied vehicles was building up as they prepared for the big push into Belgium. Clearly the bridgehead had to be extended with more river crossing points. This meant other German-held villages nearby had to be cleared so my father and B Company moved up to the village of La Chapelle, which was still held by the enemy. At 10:30 a.m. on the morning of 28 August, with B Company on the right and D Company on the left, they started to make their way slowly forward along the two edges of a cornfield with thick woods on either side.

It was very uncertain where the Germans were, or indeed how many of them there were. It was essential to stay quiet, so they crept silently through the cornfields and orchards that fringed the road all the way to La Chapelle. It was almost too quiet. Then they heard a car driving towards them so they all froze and took cover. It was a German staff car and an officer got out to have a good look around … and have a wee!

The Wiltshires had a big anti-tank gun camouflaged on the edge of the field which would have blown both the car and passengers to smithereens in an instant, but it had its nose cap on

116

and to remove it someone would have had to break cover to get to it. So they stayed silent and the car eventually moved away. That German officer can have had no idea how lucky he was.

It was still too quiet but little opposition was met until Dad's B Company platoon got almost to the village. Then, all of a sudden, they came under concentrated short-range machine-gun fire from some very innocent-looking corn stacks. Three section commanders were killed at once and the remaining men threw themselves flat to the ground. One sergeant quickly brought his two-inch mortar into action and the company commander, a man named Major Norris, displaying extraordinary cool courage, calmly walked across the road where the tanks were moving up and directed their fire on to the enemy positions. At this point Basil and the rest of B Company jumped up and charged the now-terrified Germans who came running out with their hands up. In all, 160 German prisoners were taken. There were no further casualties among the Wiltshires that afternoon but three more officers had been lost.

It was still only August but Dad must have already been wondering about the odds of his own survival. So many officers had been killed since they landed in Normandy. An infantryman's average survival rate in the Second World War was just seven weeks and for an infantry officer just four. Already Dad and the remainder of the original Hackney Gurkhas were on borrowed time.

Doug Botting says that by now he was becoming very impressed with Basil, but thought he was perhaps slightly mad: 'He was obviously a very brave man but I thought he was a bit of a nut. We were being picked off by sniper fire at one point so, as we lay huddled down below a wall, Tarrant said, "I'll move forward, keeping low, and then put my head up. As they fire, you all look where it's coming from." So this is what we did. He very quickly showed his head, the sniper fired and we saw Lieutenant Tarrant fall. We were pretty sure he was dead but we saw where the shot came from and took them out straightaway. Then Tarrant got up and said, "Did you get them?" His plan worked, but it was a crazy thing to do. Brave but barmy!'

Doug had his own theories about Dad. 'It was like he always had something to prove. He was full-on all the time, in the thick of everything, always active, always. He never asked any of us to do something that he wouldn't, but it was as if he was always thinking, "I'll show 'em, I'll show 'em!" '

Looking back now, years later, I wonder whether he wanted to prove that he was worthy of officer rank, that he wanted to live up to his position. Nobody seems to have ever suggested that he couldn't do it, but perhaps he just wanted to prove it for himself. When Doug mentioned this it struck a real chord with me because, knowing Dad as I did in later life, he displayed the same characteristics in the company that he worked for, always wanting to be the best ... 'I'll show 'em, I'll show 'em!' It was a characteristic he displayed throughout his whole life.

There were of course still many battles to come, but for now Basil and his men could enjoy the sense of a job well done: the German stronghold overlooking the Seine had been taken so other troops were now able to safely cross the river in great numbers, and the surrounding villages had been cleared. Together the Wilts had successfully infiltrated the area and liberated it from German occupation.

My dad and the rest of the lads took a well-earned break in the nearby village of Gasny in upper Normandy, as August turned to September. The French were naturally pleased to see the Allies, knowing they were being liberated, although one French woman berated the Wilts and chased some of my Dad's lot down the road, cursing and yelling in French, 'Who's stolen my chicken?' Well, even liberators have to eat.

My dad remembered a story from when they first came into Gasny. As they came to a remote farmhouse on the outskirts, Basil and his men found all was quiet. As they entered, the only sign of life was an old French farmer, silently pointing to a hatch in his kitchen floor. The men very carefully opened the chute, pointing their machine-gun barrels down into the void, and two very frightened-looking Germans came out of the cellar with their hands up. They were taken prisoner and quick-marched back to HQ with the grinning old French farmer giving them a mock bow and bidding a sarcastic 'au revoir' to his hitherto oppressors.

The French, perhaps typically, were in general a little cool and much less effusive with their gratitude than the Belgians and the Dutch were about to be, but the Wilts did get one taste of knowing what they were fighting for that warm summer's evening. They were moved to hear a large number of patriotic French voices floating on the breeze, singing their national anthem, 'La Marseillaise'. They were celebrating being a free nation once again after four years of German occupation.

Due to the massive losses sustained while crossing the Seine a few days earlier, the original 5th Battalion of the Wiltshire Regiment was barely recognisable and Dad and all the new wave of Hackney Gurkhas were now an integral part of the revitalised unit. They'd taken off their Royal Berkshire flashes and replaced them with those of the Wilts and any reluctance to be part of the new regiment had quickly disappeared under fire. There were still glimpses of the usual humour, though; when the Royal Berkshire men first settled in with the Wiltshires there was a certain amount of banter from the Reading boys along the lines of, 'Well, we were there at D-Day ... where were you?' However, the newly reinforced regiment had already seen so much heavy action that there was no time for squabbling, and the two groups of men quickly settled in together, realising they had to rely on each other just to stay alive. After what they had been through together, they had been bonded for life.

The cockney humour of Basil's boys always made them stand out, though. As many of them had worked on barrows selling fruit and veg before the war, they drew on their old street traders' cries to become a bizarre rallying call whenever they went into battle. Whenever there was an attack on a German position, Dad's Hackney boys would go in, guns blazing and grinning, to a chorus of: 'Lovely tomatoes, lady, ten for a pound', 'Lovely Cox's Pippins, lovely Cox's Pippins' and 'Get the baby off the barrow!' – all yelled at the top of their voices in rich cockney accents. The Germans must have been bewildered. Incidentally, if you are as puzzled as I was by the latter cry, the full market trader version was actually 'Get the baby off the barrow, it's pissed on all the strawberries!' Dad always thought this whole barrow-boy pre-battle ritual was very funny but as always it was tinged with tragedy, because so many of them were so young and were cut down by machine-gun fire still grinning and shouting.

The two-week stay at Gasny, though, felt like a hard-earned honeymoon period in the French late summer sunshine. The Germans had moved off to try and regroup although their morale was now believed to be very low. Reconnaissance showed that they were at least fifty miles away.

This was the first time the Hackney Gurkhas had a real chance to rest and relax since they'd arrived on Juno Beach, although several of them reported they still found it very difficult to wind down. One corporal says he remembers going to the cinema and, although it was a good film, playing in English, he found it impossible to concentrate. After all that they'd seen and gone through since 6 June, it was hardly surprising.

The war seemed a long way away at this moment but the opportunity was not lost to rebuild the magnificent fighting machine that had been tested so harshly in the last few weeks. Training was carried out every morning. Lieutenant Tarrant and the Wiltshires had been reinforced by the North and South Staffordshire Regiments and, along with a hard core of original Wilts survivors, by now they were all feeling very much one regiment.

The fortnight spent at Gasny will always be remembered by the men who were lucky enough to enjoy this strange respite from the horrors of war. They hadn't been welcomed everywhere by the French but the hospitality of the charming villagers in Gasny was overwhelming. Dances were held nearly every night, football matches were played by the lads against the locals and a battalion concert was organised starring a lady who apparently was very famous on French radio – she stole the show, although perhaps this was an easily pleased audience. There was good food and lashings of French wine, and the brave young infantrymen were showered with flowers and kisses everywhere they went. And of course there were plenty of women who wanted to thank their brave young liberators more personally! After all, they were fit young men, heroes in the truest sense. For the men's part, their needs were the same as any other young nineteen- or twenty-year-olds, except that they were heightened by a very real sense of not knowing what awaited them round the next corner. In many cases, wives and girlfriends back home were forgotten for a while as the men took a little brief comfort where they could. Whether my father ever succumbed to the temptations or not, I'll never know. He was deeply in love with Joan but there was every chance that he'd never see her again.

The highlight of this brief rest stop was the arrival of the splendid Flanagan and Allen, a wonderful old-time singing duo who sang all the songs the lads remembered from back home. The Wiltshires knew every single word and sang along with them at the top of their voices. Dad led the singing – well he would, wouldn't he? The squeaky boy soprano from the choir back home in Reading had come rather a long way.

So the warm summer days drifted on for a whole blissful fortnight. It was the first time Basil had rested at all since the beginning of the year. As he and his men swam every day in the Seine it must have seemed a very long time since he was diving in and out of the icy waters off the coast of Scotland. Deep in northern France it was high summer; the corn was stacked, the vines were full of grapes, there were apples everywhere. They picked the first blackberries. It was beautifully warm and the whole region was bathed in sunshine. Dad and the men seemed to quickly forget or perhaps just ignore the fact that only days earlier that same river where they swam had been swollen with dead British bodies. For those who survived, life had to go on and the river just kept rolling on through the valley. The lads dived from high rocks and held races across the river, which is very wide at that point. And the favourite activity for everyone was riding up and down the river in a captured German motorboat – rumoured to have once belonged to Rommel.

Sadly for Lieutenant Tarrant and his company, all good things had to come to an end and on 13 September the orders came for them to catch up with the rest of the war. However, there was still a feeling amongst the men that the worst was over, that the

Germans were in disarray and full retreat, and that the war could well be finished by Christmas. The next few weeks were to prove any such ideas to be horribly wrong ...

CHAPTER SEVEN

The Battle for the Railway

For Lieutenant Tarrant and the rest of the Wiltshires, with batteries now fully recharged, it was back to the harsh realities of war. The next few days saw a lot of travelling. British troops were already in Belgium and the speed of their advance had caused chaos among the Germans and thrown them into confusion, exactly as they themselves had done in 1939 and 1940 right across Europe.

Montgomery and the Allied High Command were so pleased with the speed at which they were moving that it was decided to keep up the momentum and push into Germany itself, crossing the Rhine. The British, American and Canadian troops now had complete command of the area north of a line from the Normandy beaches right across to the Swiss border. But they still had no secure sea port as a base to bring in supplies. They desperately needed to take Antwerp or Rotterdam to speed up their communication lines, otherwise the massive thrust into Germany would not be possible, especially with winter approaching. The liberation of France was already well underway and could now be completed by less battle-hardened troops.

For Dad and the hardy Hackney Gurkhas, however, the resumption of their war meant heading for the push across the Rhine, which involved covering some long distances as quickly as possible. On 13 September, they travelled 190 miles in a single day by truck into Belgium to a point just north-east of Mons called Laugrenee. It was remarkable progress, especially given they were repeatedly stopped the whole way. Dad recalled this as 'one of the most unforgettable, extraordinary days of my life'.

Dad and his men must have thought that peace was imminent because the streets were lined with liberated Belgian people cheering them and thanking them all the way with gifts of flowers and fresh fruit – a rare and very welcome luxury to men who had spent much of the past few months living frugally on basic rations out of tins. Apples, pears, plums, tomatoes, greengages and huge bunches of delicious black grapes would come flying through the air to be deftly caught by the delighted soldiers. In one town, where the column halted for a few minutes and every vehicle was besieged by the happy Belgians, an elderly man pushed his way through the crowd and, addressing some of the troops in dignified and excellent English, said: 'Thank you for coming, Tommy. Good luck and God bless you.' Then he turned and walked away. It was a touching tribute and a timely reminder of what they were fighting for, as it expressed what was clearly in the hearts of all the Belgian people.

The next day they moved another ninety miles to the village of Lummen, just to the west of the Albert Canal. In the main, casualties on this leg of the advance were light. There was very little enemy fire, few signs of German aircraft or artillery and most nights they were able to billet down in farm cottages, cellars or barns, rather than digging themselves into holes in the ground. The days were still warm but the nights were starting to get cooler.

Washing facilities were virtually nil so most of the men will have smelled pretty grim – in fact they must have stunk to high heaven. However, it was a very British thing that every day the men shaved, usually in cold water, sometimes in a few leftover drops from a cup of tea for just a bit of warmth on the razor blade, while the Germans went bearded for weeks. Boots were frequently left on for at least a month at a time and underpants? Let's just not go there ...

The diet wasn't so great either, although it had to somehow keep the strength up for whole battalions of fighting men. The drinking water always tasted of chlorine, thanks to the tablets that had to be dropped into every precious can, so too of course did the tea. After the war, Dad, a keen swimmer, always swam in the old public swimming baths at Kings Meadow that the River Thames flowed into. He hated the flashy new municipal pool that I learned to swim in because of course it smelt of chlorine. When I got my first house with a swimming pool he wasn't too keen on that either.

The food rations provided were adequate – just – but predictably uninspiring and repetitive. Breakfast always arrived before daylight, as everything had to be done before the Germans could spot where the Allies were dug in. Often they had arrived in the small hours so it was vital to eat the supplies quietly and with minimum movement. It was always bacon, apparently very good bacon, with a rare treat of a sausage and always some powdered egg creation. Then there was the 'all-day sandwich', because that was literally how long it had to last – until dark. It invariably involved tinned sausages and baked beans. Dinner seemed to almost always be very fatty corned beef, or 'bully beef' as Dad always called it. This was served with rice and more baked beans. Potatoes in any form were a real treat. For many years after the end of the war Dad couldn't even look at the outside of a tin of corned beef, let alone open one. And he wouldn't ever, ever eat a baked bean.

It was frequently rumoured that some delicious treats, like tinned peaches and pears, arrived in the supplies – but they never got through to the lads on the front. Their only dessert, and that was rare in itself, was tinned rice pudding.

Dad's company did once capture some German rations from a position that they overran, and were amazed to see that the panzer divisions' fighting rations were even worse – horsemeat that was coated in a thick yellow fat. No wonder they lost!

That autumn had seen the official start of what High Command rather dreamily called Operation Market Garden. It turned out to be anything but a picnic. British and American airborne troops were dropped to the north of the Rhine, near Arnhem in the Netherlands, preparing the way for the big push into Germany. However, the great plan would only work if the bridge could be kept clear for the invading column. Notoriously it was the bridge too far.

On 19 September, Basil, still somehow without a scratch on him, and the rest of the 5th Wiltshires, took their place in the column of soldiers making their way to the action. Starting at nightfall, they drove along a dangerous narrow corridor, dubbed 'Hell's Highway', up through Eindhoven in the Netherlands. Disaster nearly overtook them all there when Dad's entire column got on the wrong road in the darkness and they found themselves driving straight towards heavy German armour. Luckily, an American patrol guided them back on to the right route, and they went on through the night to the great bridge at Grave, where they rested up till daybreak.

They were aiming for Nijmegen, a city in the east of the Netherlands near the German border, on the southern side of the

Rhine, but had to stop five miles short as word was coming back of fierce German resistance in that area. A recce party was sent to investigate while the others tried to get some much-needed sleep. American troops had been dropped on most of the bridges leading up to Arnhem, but from Nijmegen German resistance was too heavy and the airborne troops coming in by parachute and glider were cut off until access could be got to them. The roads were narrow and very muddy and the tanks and lorries were getting bogged down, causing bottlenecks. Most of the infantrymen were having to get out and march but they were without protection from their heavy armour.

In addition to this, a completely unthinking or irresponsible US officer had taken the full operational plan for Market Garden with him into an attack and the Germans took the crucial top-secret document from his dead body, hardly believing their luck. The full plans were quickly trucked back to the German High Command who were able to always be a step ahead of the Allies over the next few days of battle.

And, as if all that wasn't bad enough, the Allies also had to contend with the complete breakdown of radio links through to Arnhem, which made communication with the massed but isolated airborne troops hopeless.

Dad always referred to anyone who'd been at Arnhem as 'those poor sods'. There was a really lovely man who lived along the road from us in Reading as I grew up. He'd been a paratrooper and as a kid I really liked him. Terribly nice but with a lot of his face and jaw missing. He'd been one of 'those poor sods'. Apparently he'd been machine-gunned in mid-air as he was coming down under his parachute.

How much detail the officers and men of B Company knew at the time about the beleaguered troops at Arnhem is not now clear, but it seems they did know there was a large Allied force cut off across the Rhine and there was a real sense of frustration that they couldn't get through to relieve them.

By 22 September, the Guards and the Americans had successfully captured Nijmegen Bridge, after some fierce fighting, so Basil and his full battalion would now be able to cross the river and continue northwards towards Arnhem. While they waited, one of their own Bren gun carriers exploded, apparently due to overheated ammunition, setting fire to other Allied vehicles around it. The accident killed four men and wounded sixteen others. Nothing could be done to save the dying. Fires raged and the sound of exploding shells filled the air for many hours. As if the young men didn't have enough to deal with, these occasional events were such a tragic waste of life.

At the end of the day they could at last cross the river on the north side of Nijmegen, establishing a regimental headquarters in Lent, before moving on to the village of Elst. Dad said, 'Our orders were to extend the bridgehead by advancing on foot along the Arnhem railway line, then capture and hold the crucial railway crossing, which was the only gap in the embankment for several miles where large numbers of troops and armour would be able to get through. It was a vital strategic spot and our orders were to hold it at all costs ... but Command seemed to have forgotten that we actually had to take it in the first place.'

The danger was all around. As they were approaching the railway line, Robbie Purver remembers they heard some trucks coming towards them. Dad motioned for everyone to get down and stay quiet. As they lay there, thankfully made invisible by a field of tall sweetcorn, a whole cavalcade of German troops went past them in countless lorries and staff cars. Attack would have been futile so their only option was to let them pass – but it gave them an idea of the strength of German forces in the area.

That night, Basil's B Company was told they had to lead the attack ahead of A and C Companies. They advanced for more than two miles in darkness but were stopped in their tracks when they heard the sound of German voices ahead of them, apparently coming from a nearby signal box next to a railway embankment. Once more, Dad gave the sign for everyone to get down and stay very quiet and still. They were too far beyond the rest of the battalion to attack, and they didn't know how many enemy they were facing on the other side of the embankment, so the men dug in silently where they were to wait till morning. The Germans had no idea they were there – one German officer even strolled over the railway line right into their company, where he was quickly captured and taken prisoner.

Basil and the lads caught a couple of hours' sleep by the signal box, only to wake at 6 a.m. to the sound of yet more German voices. As the dawn light illuminated their surroundings, they discovered they were only fifty yards from a huge German encampment on the other side of the railway tracks, hidden by the embankment. You'd think their first instinct might well have been to get the hell out of there, but no, they prepared to somehow take the signal box, despite now knowing they were hugely outnumbered. Meanwhile, A and C Companies stayed back, defending Elst and their HQ in Lent from German attacks. It seems this was a pocket of Nazi resistance that was going to be hard to overcome.

B Company had advanced the farthest forward and were now the most exposed by far. Any movement in daylight would be seen. They were dangerously isolated, with both flanks open to enemy fire and lines of communication covered by sniper fire. No food could be brought up to them and they had no cigarettes. But of course the English Tommy, especially the cockney Tommy, will always improvise. For food they killed and cooked some chickens they found in the garden of the signal box and for cigarettes they used dried leaves rolled up in paper.

Once again you have to take your hat off to the bravery of these boys. Totally cut off from Allied reinforcements, and even the rest of their own regiment, they were completely outnumbered by the enemy, and yet they tenaciously hung in there, without a thought of surrender or defeat. The Germans knew they were there, but fortunately were unsure how big a force they were, so it became a very wary stand-off on both sides. Dad recorded, 'Thank God the enemy didn't realise just how few British soldiers we had in place or things might have worked out very differently.' In fact, there were only 180 men in Basil's unit.

Despite the immense danger they were facing during this siege, the Hackney Gurkhas found ways to keep their spirits up. The things that young British soldiers will do under pressure are truly wonderful. In this predicament, they did what anyone would surely do in these circumstances: they found a goat, tied a red signal flag from the signal box round its middle and a green one round its hindquarters, stuck an apple on to the end of each horn and painted its tail with tar. They then quietly crept up with it on to the railway line, gave the bewildered goat's bottom a good spank and sent it trotting off to say hello to the astonished Germans. Don't ask – it's a cockney thing.

Although they clearly managed to maintain their sense of humour, these three days trapped by the railway line must have been horrendous. Robbie Purver told me about the appalling conditions they had to endure in their small damp 'slit' trenches: 'No food, no cigs, no sleep … body aching with tiredness … eyes burning ... closing one then the other in turn ... afraid to fall asleep. It was a dreadful time.'

Men were killed on both sides during the three days of this siege, and as the area had also seen fighting prior to B Company's arrival, the surrounding land was still scattered with corpses. Robbie remembers: 'Men and cattle were lying dead everywhere, bodies grotesquely distended as they started to decompose and rot. There were abandoned, mangled tanks and guns strewn all over the place. The air was full yet again with the stench of death and diesel. The smell alone was sickening.'

It must have seemed a lifetime since Dad and the Hackney boys were swimming in the Seine and singing along to Flanagan and Allen, but in reality it was less than a month. Only two weeks ago they were being showered with gifts as they marched as conquerors into Belgium.

Their situation was very serious but fortunately the Germans didn't seem to be able to pin down their exact position, and they still weren't sure of the British strength. At one point the worrying call came on the radio, 'Fall back! Fall back! We are being overrun! Fall back!' ... and sure enough a large German force appeared, marching fast towards them. Dad and B Company withdrew, taking up a defensive position, expecting the worst, but then on looking again realised these were not hardened SS troops in the sights of their guns, but a most extraordinary mixture of old men and teenagers in a rag-bag assortment of uniforms. Dad later described this shambolic unit as a bit like a German Dad's Army. There were even several very young boys and old men in ill-fitting German air force and navy uniforms.

Once B Company understood that they were no real threat they couldn't bring themselves to open fire. 'I had one old boy right in my sights, but I couldn't shoot the poor bugger,' Robbie Purver told me. Instead they were rounded up at gunpoint and taken prisoner. It was actually a good thing that Dad's lot did show such compassion because in fact the whole charade had been a typically heartless and cynical ploy staged by the SS. The idea was to round up this disparate bunch of old and young from the local villages, dress them in any German uniforms that came to hand, and sacrifice these expendable men simply to draw British fire, in order to find out where the British were and in what numbers. They never did get back to report and funnily enough they didn't seem too bothered.

A lot of strange things happened in the battle for that signal box. Doug Botting remembers, 'One evening I was told to creep up and take over the guard on the side of the railway line. When I got there I couldn't see any guard but eventually I did spot one bloke who appeared to be kneeling. I called out to him a few times in a whisper, but he didn't reply. I crept closer and just tapped him on the shoulder so as not to make him jump, but he just fell slowly forward on to the line and I realised he was dead. I now had no information about what I was actually supposed to be doing or looking out for in that eerie place, not a clue what I was supposed to be guarding, so I crawled low into a trench and trained my rifle on where I thought the enemy might come from. But that trench absolutely stank. I didn't dare show myself or get up again and get out but it was just vile. God knows what was lying at the bottom of that trench but it stank unmistakeably of death and decomposition and human excrement. I couldn't wait to be relieved at midnight but in the event nobody arrived until after 4 a.m. That was the longest, most physically gut-wrenching night of my life.'

After three days with several losses, very little food and virtually no sleep, B Company must have been elated to see other Allied troops being dropped close by their trenches to relieve them and allow them to rejoin the rest of the Wiltshires in a nearby farmhouse on 24 September for a much-needed break. B Company had shown great determination, though, and had somehow held in check a vastly more powerful German unit.

By this time it had become apparently clear that Arnhem was lost and Operation Market Garden had tragically failed. It had been impossible to get to the trapped Allied troops and on the night of 25 September, Montgomery reluctantly admitted defeat. The order was for the Allies to cut their losses and get as many men out as possible, but for too many it was already too late.

The strength of the German resistance and the problems of getting access up the gridlocked roads and over the bridges had made it a hopeless cause. Nearly 1,500 British paratroopers were killed at the Battle of Arnhem, which had been raging just ahead of where Basil's company was positioned, and almost 6,500 were taken prisoner. The US 82nd Airborne Division lost over 1,400 men and the 101st over 2,000. Some 4,000 lucky men were ferried away or escaped downstream but the failure of the operation overall was a cruel blow and all thoughts of nice Christmas dinners back in England were forgotten. The war continued to drag on relentlessly. A rampant Führer raged at his generals: 'Now is the time to wipe out our fleeing attackers and push them back into the sea.'

One of the men between the sea and the SS was, of course, Basil. Dad recalled: 'For many of the men this was a real low point. As the news trickled through of the disaster at Arnhem it became clear that there would be more loss of life. And no sign of things changing any time soon.'

German morale was arguably even lower: they had themselves suffered massive losses since June and had been forced back to their own border. But now the remaining troops were really battle-hardened. In addition, Hitler's propagandists talked noisily about secret weapons in the manufacture that were going to turn the course of the war. In reality of course they had no such thing, but it gave the exhausted Germans some hope. They were clearly not a nation that liked to give up.

The brief respite for B Company in Elst, therefore, after their ordeal near the signal box, was all too short. Their orders now were to take and hold the land enclosed by the River Waal and the lower Rhine between Nijmegen and Arnhem, which was known as 'the Island'. It was flat and exposed but was part of a crucial route up into Germany.

This period saw some of the toughest fighting yet. The Germans, determined to push the British back, moved south and started shelling the Wilts B and D Companies. Corporal Robbie Purver remembers: 'I was exhausted and we were all getting thoroughly cheesed off by this point. We were constantly going out on night patrol. We had no night sights or anything like that; we didn't dare shine a torch. The privates had bayonets; as a full corporal I had a Sten gun and officers like Basil usually carried a Sten or a Bren gun. The Germans were as afraid of bumping into us as we were of meeting them.' B Company lost huge numbers of their men in this period. More officers were killed almost every day and the odds against Basil making Christmas, or ever seeing Joan or his parents again, were reducing all the time. It was still only the beginning of October.

Sapper Donald May and the dog platoon remembers the whole area around Nijmegen as terrifying. 'So many died in all that chaos,' he said. 'The dogs were particularly busy here because there were mines hidden everywhere and in two particular areas the dogs' skills were unbeatable. The Germans hid a lot of Schu mines and Teller mines in wooden and plastic containers which of course couldn't be picked up by the engineers' normal metal detectors, but the dogs could sniff them out straight away. Also the whole area was criss-crossed by railway lines which the Germans loved to booby trap and again the detectors were hopeless amongst the metal of the lines. But the dogs were perfect and must have saved hundreds of lives.'

Despite the dogs' best efforts, Don still describes this period as 'carnage'. He recalls: 'The Germans did so many terrible things. On the way to trying to relieve the bridge at Arnhem we came across a poor dead young British paratrooper. His revolver was showing and one of the lads thought he might as well take it, when some sixth sense told me to scream, "Don't touch it!" – don't know why. But on closer examination we found the poor dead boy's body had been completely booby-trapped. There was a Schu mine hidden under the parachute with a further Teller mine underneath that. We would have been blown sky high.'

New young soldiers were being brought in all the time to replace the losses but the Cockney Gurkhas described them as worse than useless. Dad wrote, 'It wasn't their fault but we'd become real veterans in just a few months and these poor young kids had no chance. It was tragic. Some were killed or badly wounded within days or, in at least one case, within less than an hour or two of arrival.' In the same entry he wrote: 'I saw many men dreadfully wounded, crying out for their mums, but I never heard one calling for his father.' It's a reminder of how young these boys were.

Despite everything they had gone through and all the horrors they had witnessed, or maybe because of all that, compassion and mercy could sometimes still win the day. Robbie remembers one time when he had an SS soldier clearly in his gun sights. He had every intention of shooting him but then at the last minute thought, 'Oh sod it, let him go,' and took him alive instead. Robbie took his pistol off him and gave it to his mate Huey Kennedy, who Basil was later to have reason to describe as the very best kind of British soldier. Dad always called him Jock, even though in fact he came from Newcastle upon Tyne. It seems Dad had no great ear for accents.

As the Hackney Gurkhas carried on into the beginning of October there seemed to be a noticeable increase in German activity. There was a good deal of shelling overnight and reports were coming in to the battalion HQ by telephone and wireless of a mass of German infantry and tanks arriving at specific points. B Company hurriedly got dug in along the side of the railway line again, near a crucial level crossing, where they were hidden by the high ground of the embankment. They had one 25-pound gun, which they moved up so that it could concentrate its fire all along the German line, on the other side of the railway. This caused tremendous slaughter, but still fresh enemy companies kept arriving.

The crossing was evidently seen as having huge tactical importance and the Wilts night patrols continued to bring back more news of increasing enemy activity. Transport, tanks and infantrymen seemed to be piling up in the enemy lines. Clearly something was about to happen – but what?

At 10 a.m. on 2 October, a tremendous concentration of artillery fire came crashing down on to B and D companies. It was easily the heaviest fire they had ever come under. There had been nothing like this since the Normandy landing. Over 100 German guns were pumping shells at them from everywhere they looked. The Allied phone lines were shot to pieces but radio links worked, confirming that a large German infantry attack force was on the move. This was the standard tactic used by both sides – first the enemy would be pounded by artillery and then the backup soldiers would advance with machine guns, grenades and bayonets.

Luckily, B Company, and the others alongside them from D Company, had been well dug in when the shelling started and casualties were surprisingly light. The Germans, on the other hand, were for once very exposed as they advanced and consequently their casualties were high.

Initially the Germans were repelled but two hours later they came back again. One British captain, whose voice Dad recognised, came crackling through the radio, shouting: 'There are more Germans than I have ever seen in my life about fifty yards away!' However, he then directed the artillery fire with superb accuracy and the Germans retreated in disorder, leaving many dead behind them.

And so it ebbed back and forth all through that long day. By nightfall there had been individual acts of heroism everywhere among the men of the Wilts. More than twenty of the crack 156th Panzer Regiment had been taken prisoner and by late afternoon the shelling had died down. The Germans were clearly running out of men and ammunition.

By 9 a.m. the next day the Wilts were once again established at the level crossing. There had been so many losses and casualties, including all the officers of D Company, that it was decided to combine B and D Companies under Captain Rudd MC, a man who after the war Dad would mention with some respect. Rudd now called upon the exhausted men to attempt one last full-scale attack on the enemy later that afternoon.

The battered survivors managed to rally themselves, winning one more brutal victory. They then recaptured the forward positions by the railway line. The 5th Wilts, including my father, were relieved by the 4th Battalion later that day. The whole area was at last back in Allied hands. Nevertheless, sporadic fighting continued for another twenty-four hours. The company

HQ suffered a direct hit later that evening and the reserve ammunition exploded.

It had been a horrific few days. The survivors were exultant but exhausted and emotionally drained. They had lost so many friends so quickly. But at last, by five o'clock in the afternoon of 5 October, the responsibility for the whole area was handed over to the 101st US Airborne Division. Basil and his exhausted company made their way to the village of Weert for two whole days of rest and recuperation, re-equipping and refitting, before the whole cycle began all over again.

Among the casualties that terrible week was a young engineer called Private Lewis Curtis. He'd been with the regiment since Normandy. He'd come from Liskeard in Cornwall, had worked in the Co-op until the outbreak of war and was just nineteen years old. He was killed in the main artillery barrage on 2 October and was buried in a shallow grave where he fell. Although Basil and the other officers liked to give the men they lost some sort of dignified grave, it was just not always possible. In Lewis Curtis's case his grave markers were washed away when German military engineers blew up a dyke on the Rhine to flood the whole area, halting the Allied advance. Among many others, Private Curtis's burial site was lost to his family and the only information they received was that he was believed to have died somewhere in Belgium. In the chaos of war so many young men were lost without trace and the graveyards throughout northern Europe are littered with crosses over unnamed graves marked 'Known unto God'.

However, in 2003, nearly sixty years after Private Curtis's death, his remains were found by builders excavating the old Dutch battlefield to make way for a new housing estate. A Dutch forensic team, using scientific tests including DNA analysis, took another five years to discover his identity. Only after old dental records were uncovered did they finally discover the true identity of the young Cornish soldier.

According to Geert Jonker, the head of the Royal Netherlands Army's Recovery and Identification Unit, the lengthy process required to confirm the identity of the remains is not uncommon. 'It can take anything from three days to seven years to be able to identify remains because it's important to get it right for the next of kin. So when we can make a positive identification it makes all those years of research worthwhile. It's the ultimate reward, but sometimes it's about luck. In this case it was only because we went for a second opinion on the age of the soldier that told us he was a lot younger than we originally thought. Initially his remains seemed much older than his nineteen years but once we had that information we had seven new names we were considering, three of whom had dental records. One of which was Lewis, who was a perfect match.'

Private Lewis Curtis was eventually laid to rest in Arnhem-Oosterbeek Cemetery on 3 October 2012, close to where he was killed in action almost seventy years before. He was buried with full military honours. Representatives of Dad's old regiment were in attendance at the ceremony, including Robbie Purver. Robbie said he was honoured to be there, and it helped lay a few of his own personal demons to rest in the process.

Private Curtis's family, including his twenty-year-old great-nephew, Rifleman Richard Edwards, who had just returned from Afghanistan with the 5th Battalion The Rifles, the Wiltshire Regiment's successor, were also in attendance. Sadly the discovery was too late for his sister Alice but her children Susan and Robert, who still live in Liskeard and grew up with tales of their Uncle Lewis, flew to the Netherlands for the burial. Susan said, 'Mum was always talking about Lewis so it's unbelievable to be here now to finally lay him to rest. After so long of not knowing it's been quite an emotional rollercoaster since we found out.'

Private Curtis's tragic story is just one of way too many, but the highly personal nature of it is a useful reminder to my generation that this was about real young men who were robbed of long, fulfilling lives ahead of them, something my own generation and my kids have been fortunate enough to take for granted. It's a sobering and somehow surreal thought to realise that had a German sniper aimed a little this way instead of that way, my father could have ended up in that shallow grave, and I would not have been born to write his story. Too often we rattle off statistics about war casualties, without really thinking about the awful ripples each death caused through grieving families. Every single one of those countless thousands has a personal story every bit as important as, and no less touching than, that of Private Lewis Curtis.

CHAPTER EIGHT

A Pre-Christmas Decoration

So many men from Basil's unit had died now, or been sent home wounded, that there were only a handful left who'd crossed with Dad on D-Day. He was one of the most experienced of all by now, having come through Dunkirk as well. He was never particularly religious but the gods did seem to be looking after him. In addition, he was an astute man who'd clearly learned very fast how to stay alive in battle. Despite this, surely even he, by now, must have been wondering how much longer he could avoid the one single bullet, the exploding shell or, God forbid, the blade of a bayonet that would spell the end of his run of luck. By now he'd seen so many close to him die exactly like that. How much longer did he have?

Luckily the Wilts were not to fight any major battles from mid-October through to January but life was anything but easy for Basil and the remaining Hackney Gurkhas. The Wilts' regimental war diary makes constant reference to refitting, re-equipping and training. There was a constant influx of new young conscripts being shipped over to replace the dead and wounded. For all new arrivals the training had to be fast and fierce. At first the new rookies were more of a liability than a help, so the art of survival was passed down from veterans like Dad, Robbie, Jock and Doug, who had evolved into battle-hardened warhorses in a short matter of months.

There was also further training for the seasoned troops, as new weapons were constantly being developed and invented. For example, a new, improved version of the anti-tank weapon, the PIAT, had been created which was extremely powerful and could be used to annihilate large buildings, not just vehicles and tanks. This was to prove highly useful in the coming weeks, with so many German-held dwellings to overpower and take out. The Wiltshires were now based in the small Dutch town of Mook, south of Nijmegen, where they would stay for the next three weeks.

The Wiltshires' orders were to routinely defend their current position, but of necessity much of that defence was aggressive and inherently dangerous, as they had to clear the area again and again of enemy patrols. Dad didn't like night fighting – who would? – but he was evidently very good at it. For a big man he could move without a sound, not even the snapping of a twig. His dad had taught him how to do it when watching badgers or deer back home on the Berkshire Downs. Most nights the order was to find the enemy, get the details and grid references of their precise location back to HQ and then the artillery would pound that position at daybreak. Basil led a lot of these patrols. They would go out till the small hours, often in thick darkness, deep forest and fresh minefields. It was extremely dangerous work.

As if things weren't hard enough for the troops, the winter of 1944–45 turned out to be particularly harsh weather-wise as well. At the start of October it was raining heavily most of the time and by the end of the month that had turned to snow. In the evening, the temperatures dipped way below freezing, yet many nights the men had to sleep rough in shallow 'foxholes', with the bitter cold getting through to their bones. Food was limited, much-needed cigarettes were in short supply, and even when it was your turn to sleep you always kept half an exhausted eye open for enemy patrols, artillery shells or aircraft. Dad said this period made him marvel at just how much the human body can actually stand. It must have been utterly dispiriting and they'd been doing it most nights since June.

Sleeping in a trench was exhausting – and first, they had to make it. The men all carried either a small pick or an entrenching tool in their kit and, when they couldn't find alternative billets, two-man trenches were dug straight into the earth – a tough job even in high summer but murderous when faced with the rock-hard, frosty earth of winter.

Trenches were perhaps two foot wide and four foot six deep. There was angled earth at the base of the trench to take water away but of course it never did this properly and Dad's and most of the lads' feet were always wet. Trench foot was a common problem and made marching agonising, and pneumonia was commonplace. They had no blankets, just gas capes – a sort of poncho made from thin rubberised material – and they slept with their steel helmets on. Often they'd been out all night on reconnaissance, so sleep had to be grabbed in the daytime. Sometimes, if the enemy were believed to be close, they would literally force one eye at a time to stay open while their head screamed for sleep. The men's eyes were often in real agony doing this and it could cause hallucinations. All day and night they were dreading the urgent call to 'Heads up' – which meant they needed to move out fast.

Many years later when I was going off on an all-night fishing trip, I remember Dad hinting that I was 'a bit of a jessie' for taking a small tent with me. 'Why don't you just dig yourself a foxhole?' he enquired with a knowing grin and the usual twinkle in his eye. I had a vague idea what he was referring to, but didn't fully understand. Of course he was only joking, but it's a little humbling now to discover just what grim conditions those brave young men endured every night.

As the nights lengthened and the weather worsened, all sides must have been exhausted. Doug Botting remembers it with a shiver: 'Of course, sleeping out in a slit trench in the ground was rough but you got used to it and you felt just a bit safer below the skyline. You were never really dry; there was always water running over your feet. Trench foot was a big problem, or catching a chill that could turn into pneumonia, but you did become hardened. You were always tired. We all knew the experience of marching for miles, while actually asleep, and often you were glad to just collapse into your trench. At one point, in some battle or other, I lost my shovel and for night after night I had to dig my foxhole with my bare hands. I didn't dare tell anyone I'd lost it or I'd have been on a charge.'

The idea of Doug having to dig a trench with his bare hands 'or I'd have been on a charge' seems shocking, but it does show that even amongst these hard-core infantrymen, who'd been together through so much, British Army discipline was never relaxed for a second. I think both Basil and Doug would have been philosophical about this and some of the harsh decisions that officers like Dad had to make. Dad definitely had the attitude that 'there could be no exceptions in the thick of things: there's a war on and that's how people get killed'.

Doug told me that on one occasion during this period he became briefly stranded from the others and the only way he could get back to the unit was through what turned out to be a minefield.

He always had a real fear of mines more than anything else, and he was sweating and terrified as he made his way agonisingly slowly back through the field, always dreading hearing that awful *click*. Dad had trained all his blokes what to do if they ever heard it. Doug said, 'It was the one noise that all infantrymen knew meant you'd got one or both feet on a live mine. You knew if you lifted your foot you would be blown sky high, taking anyone nearby with you. It may blow you up at once, of course, but if you just heard the click, you kept your feet flat down, not lifting them whatever you did. Then the drill was always to scream out 'Mine!' and stand very, very still. It gave everybody else at least some chance of getting down below the blast, but you were almost certainly going to lose both legs or die.'

Mercifully on this occasion Doug did not hear that awful *click* and made it back to his unit alive … only to be told off by my father for being late!

It was now midway through October and they had been in the Netherlands for about three weeks. The Dutch were delighted to see the Allies. They had really suffered through the German occupation and they were starving. In many areas they'd been reduced to eating tulip bulbs for food and thousands of Dutch children were suffering from rickets, typhoid and diphtheria, mainly caused by malnutrition. Wherever the Allies went, they were welcomed with open arms by the Dutch people.

The lads were thrilled one day to be offered the simple forgotten pleasure of something resembling a shower, when a Dutch farmer rigged up a hose for them – the first real all-over wash they'd been able to have since D-Day. There was even soap and – oh joy! – toothpaste.

But such pleasures were short-lived. On 16 October the regimental diary reports that 'strong fighting patrols led by Lt

Tarrant and Lt Stapylton-Smith wrought considerable havoc among fighting positions'. At 3 a.m. that day, Basil Tarrant and twenty other soldiers out on patrol had found a number of Germans in houses outside the town. Puzzlingly, the report says Tarrant and his men were challenged by the German sentries but they took no action. The Wilts patrol then stormed the house with machine guns and grenades, killing two Germans and taking a number of others prisoner. It had turned out to be an enemy headquarters.

Quite why the sentries didn't call the alarm as Dad's platoon approached seems to make no sense. However, there are reports in the company diary of many German deserters being taken prisoner by the Wiltshires in that area at that time. So it seems probable that, with the heavy losses that they were taking and the worsening weather, many of the Germans were becoming utterly demoralised and the sentries either gave themselves up or just ran away at the approach of the British patrol. There were, of course, still many die-hard, fanatical Nazis who were more than willing to fight to the very end for Hitler, but for obvious reasons they had all been diverted to the frontline, not left on mundane sentry duty. Dad and his men would soon face many of them in bloody battle.

Some of the stories from this period were hair-raising. One B Company night patrol was searching a cellar in what seemed to be an empty house when they heard German voices coming from above. Cautious investigation revealed that a superior number of heavily armed Germans had come into the house while the patrol were downstairs in the cellar, and they were now making themselves at home upstairs. Further surreptitious reconnaissance revealed there was now an armoured car and a tank in the yard outside. The Hackney boys couldn't get out without disastrous consequences, so their only hope was to bed down and pray that the Nazis didn't need anything from the cellar that night.

For the next several hours the boys slept very uneasily on the floor, with guns trained on the cellar door ready for the moment when they were discovered. Using the radio to call for reinforcements was out of the question as they would have been heard, so they braced themselves for what would no doubt be a fatal firefight when the Germans found them. However, when they peeped through the cracks at first light on a freezing late October morning, they discovered all was wonderfully quiet and the Germans had moved on – leaving hot water in the kettle so the boys could all make a nice cup of tea before reporting back to base.

One strange and shocking affair happened at this time. Dad had to take over command at one time as the officer in charge and his batman had gone out on a patrol and had failed to return. Although HQ feared the worst, there were some unconvinced mutterings from the ranks, as this just happened to be the same officer who, extraordinarily, had missed out on D-Day as he had a bit of a high temperature. Both officer and batman strolled back unconcerned the following morning, miraculously safe and sound, having achieved surprisingly little. Quite what the lieutenant's story was isn't clear but it wasn't believed. Dad had been forced to cover for him on more than one occasion. This particular officer was renowned by the men for having a string of excuses for going missing at the first hint of danger, and never being in the frontline, so was quite naturally despised by them for not pulling his weight. According to Robbie Purver, he was eventually court martialled for desertion/cowardice and sentenced to eight years in a military prison.

As October turned to November, the Wilts continued to advance steadily towards Germany, mopping up the pockets of resistance they encountered on the way. A weary routine had established itself: nocturnal patrols would silently go ahead to establish the enemy's whereabouts. Then the information would be radioed to the artillery so that the RAF could bomb the location in the daylight.

On occasion, however, it was decided that the ground troops could take out certain targets themselves, so some nights they would return to clear German-held buildings and billets with mortars, grenades, machine guns and bayonets. By now they were based in Groesbeek, just north of Mook, getting ever closer to the German border. In early November, A, B and D Companies of the Wilts were given instructions to take out various enemy targets, which they had previously mapped, over three consecutive nights.

A Company were first to go, successfully blasting and 'beating up' several German-occupied buildings. Unfortunately though, their activities attracted enemy shellfire and their young patrol leader, Lieutenant Jack Kleinman, was killed. D Company went out the next night and wasn't terribly successful, though they suffered no casualties, despite being fired upon. All this, especially knowing his opposite number in A Company had been killed in a similar sortie, puts my father's bravery on the third night into real perspective.

On the night of 7 November, it was Basil's turn. Lieutenant Tarrant's instructions were to take out his patrol of sixteen men from B Company under cover of darkness to pinpoint and hopefully silence two key enemy positions at the far end of a minefield. There were two farmhouses at either side of the field – one was known to be in the hands of the Germans, the other was not confirmed. My father's orders were to take the one out and, if necessary, destroy the other. Intelligence thought that there might be as many as seventy of the enemy in position.

Some time just before 1 a.m. my father and his patrol moved slowly towards the top of the field. They all had their faces blackened and crept ahead quietly and cautiously. There was no moon and it was very dark and horribly quiet. Dad made sure that all the men had a Bren light machine gun each and carried a lot of ammunition, as he wasn't quite sure what they were walking into. Basil was carrying his usual Sten sub-machine gun and they were all equipped with grenades.

The men had to approach the target zone across a built-up road, which they thought might be a problem if they had to face sudden oncoming traffic and headlights, but when they got to the crossing there was just the same eerie silence. Dad made signs to the men to come across and they silently obeyed. There was strictly no talking, not even a whisper. Dad had a sick feeling that they might be walking into an ambush.

My father took one volunteer and together they crawled across the road, discovering a whole network of slit trenches had been dug at the far side. Luckily they were empty, so the Wiltshires used them for cover while they regrouped and prepared to advance across the minefield towards the first farmhouse.

First, the engineers went in with metal detectors, hoping to trace a line through the deadly field that the platoon could follow in darkness. When they had safely achieved this, the rest of the boys made their way agonisingly slowly through the minefield, all trying to step on exactly the same footsteps as my father who was slowly leading the way, all of them dreading hearing the unmistakeable *click* that meant that, in the pitch darkness, one of them had put one or both feet on a mine.

Progress was at a snail's pace, but the engineers had done their job with painstaking perfection and, after what seemed an age, they got within striking distance of the first farmhouse. They could hear voices speaking in German and could see sentries posted, but they showed no reaction as Basil and his platoon silently moved into place. Then, on his signal, all hell broke loose. Round after round of machine-gun fire was pumped into the farmhouse, grenades were hurled in through the windows and the sentries died at once.

My father's diary takes up the story: 'Some men came running round from the back of the building, but they were all shot up as they ran towards us. It was dark so how many we killed, wounded or whatever, we don't know, but the place went very quiet again in perhaps less than a minute. There were only the groans of the wounded and the dying ...'

After all this, any hopes of secrecy for the second half of their mission were of course lost and, from the noise coming from the other farmhouse about half a mile away, it was now abundantly clear that it was also occupied by Germans, who were screaming at each other and shouting into the darkness. Dad, using all his quick wits, swung his platoon round and they made their way towards the second set of buildings from a completely different direction, so they came from behind.

This time the sentries knew something was coming, but not how many or from where. Before any of the sentries could make out what was happening, Basil screamed the signal to attack and went racing in, firing his Sten from the hip while the rest followed up with a stream of Bren gunfire and grenades. Later Dad recalled: 'We were challenged this time and straight away we fired on the sentry, who screamed out before he died. I should think he was certainly killed. The building erupted and soldiers came running out, shouting. They had no idea where we were coming at them from and we were able to pick them off at will. Then one of my chaps threw a smoke grenade. I don't think we were supposed to have a smoke grenade, I think it had been issued wrongly or something, but it didn't matter – it was an absolute gift because it landed in the middle of the building, caught some curtains alight and set the whole of this very large farmhouse alight, so we could shoot at it and all around it without any return fire. We were just picking off our targets lit up by the firelight … I think there was some German fire at the beginning but it soon went very quiet.'

Many Germans were certainly killed in this action, possibly as many as fifty or sixty, a lot more were badly injured, and a few ran off into the night in a panic. It was an enormously successful sortie but, even more extraordinarily, Lieutenant Tarrant brought all his men back without a single scratch: 'We came back home, no casualties. The buildings then got the usual final crescendo of artillery fire that accompanies operations of that sort. At that stage the British Army had artillery ammunition that they were just dying to use and as we came away I should think they had a complete divisional artillery shoot on these two buildings which must have absolutely flattened them – end of story.'

Sixteen men had been led out and sixteen returned. This is exactly why the boys said they liked to follow Dad into battle. Obviously there were no guarantees in a war as brutal as this, but clearly Basil's instinct for the survival, not just of himself but for his men, made him the sort of officer you'd want to be with in a fight. As military historian Paul Reed explains, 'This is the best possible type of infantry officer – he did his job but at no time unnecessarily sacrificed the lives of his men.'

Others also noticed Basil's cool command and impressive leadership that night. Shortly after the incident, Lieutenant Tarrant was recommended for a Military Cross by his commanding officer. This was an enormous honour. The MC was then the second-level military decoration – coming after the Victoria

Cross – awarded to officers in the British armed forces, granted in recognition of 'an act or acts of exemplary gallantry during active operations against the enemy on land'. Since the start of the First World War when it was first instituted, this has been one of the highest awards for gallantry that could be bestowed on a serving member of the armed forces.

The recommendation for Basil's 'Immediate Military Cross' was signed all the way up the chain of command, not only by Lieutenant General Horrocks, who Dad always spoke very highly of, but also – and this will have made a huge impression on Dad – by Field Marshal Montgomery. It was well known that whenever possible 'Monty' liked to hear of all acts of exceptional courage by his men. As a soldier's soldier, he took a great interest in them and Dad would have been as proud of his signature at the bottom of his recommendation as the medal itself.

Reflecting many years later on the moment he received the actual MC, Dad was typically, infuriatingly low-key about it. 'So some weeks later, somewhere in a cinema in Holland, the Divisional Commander handed me the Military Cross,' he said. 'When I was able to show it to her after the war, my wife was very impressed and, many years later, so was my grandson.'

Incidentally, equally impressed was Christopher, his son – who still has it to this day, locked carefully away, and who one day will pass it on to Toby. It is an inspirational and elegant object – an ornamental silver cross with a Royal Cypher in the middle, attached to a white ribbon with a central stripe of deep purple. It is a tangible symbol of my father's bravery and, as such, I will treasure it forever.

What I still find almost surreal is that, although we all knew that he'd won the MC, and the letters 'MC' were often still used after his name on correspondence addressed to him, until I went filming with Channel 5 I had never been told the slightest detail of how he won one of the highest military honours.

Quite naturally I was immensely proud of Lieutenant Tarrant MC when I heard the full story of what he'd achieved, and under such terrifying circumstances, but I still find it hard to equate his heroic and expedient – but nonetheless bloody – actions with the very laid-back, naturally funny man I was proud to call 'Dad'.

CHAPTER NINE

Into Germany

On 9 November 1944, Montgomery decided that the Canadians were to take over responsibility for the Groesbeek area, so the Wiltshire Regiment made yet another long journey south, this time to the Maastricht region. They marched through that night and eventually settled themselves into the small Dutch mining town of Brunssum, to the south of the country, with an HQ in nearby Malden.

This was the closest they'd been to the German border, but it was a strangely pleasant and peaceful rest stop. The Dutch were delighted to see them and Dad and the Hackney Gurkhas had forty-eight hours to regroup, service their weapons and, above all, get some decent food, a few strong Dutch beers and a couple of nights' sleep in the dry. It had been a long, relentless struggle since June, they had marched several thousand miles, they had slept rough, they had seen many horrors along the way and lost many of their friends, but the sense that they were almost in Germany coupled with the wonderful hospitality of the Dutch gave them new strength yet again.

And bizarrely, for a while at least, things got even easier after they crossed the border. On 11 November, Dad made a note in his diary: 'Entered Germany for the first time.' This must have been an emotional day for him and for all of them. I don't suppose there was a sign up saying 'Welcome to Germany' and there probably wasn't a check on passports, but it will have been of enormous psychological significance to the men. At last they were in Hitler's back yard. They had driven the Germans back over their own borders and, with the Russians doing the same on the Eastern front, there must have been a real sense that they were finally entering the end game.

The Germans, of course, still were refusing to lie down, and although for many of Hitler's soldiers the writing was on the wall, others had no intention of giving up and, if anything, the arrival of the Allies on their home soil made them even more determined. Surrounded by dead German bodies after a vicious battle on the Dutch border, one young American GI said, 'It just doesn't make sense. Why do they keep fighting?'

However, for ten days, the Wilts were doing very little fighting as they established themselves in Birgden. Billets for Lieutenant Tarrant and his platoon were found in nearby villages and, although they were almost on top of the enemy who were believed to be no more than five miles away, life was almost comfortable. Dad set guards in frontline trenches, but the rest of the lads took over the cellars of abandoned local houses.

These cellars were a real godsend. Almost every house and cottage in that part of Germany had a cellar, usually with beds and bedding. In most cases the lads created some sort of Heath Robinson stove, although mainly they could only be lit at night for fear that the smoke would give away their whereabouts to the enemy. Not only were these cellars warm and comfy to a degree virtually unknown since before D-Day, they also provided maximum protection against enemy artillery. Only a direct hit would really impact men down in a cellar. They could even read their maps with impunity, rather than trying to make sense of them by torchlight hidden under a blanket in a trench. It may not sound much but breaks like this were a real luxury to the weary infantryman and undoubtedly gave them the strength to carry on when they were called again to the front.

Doug Botting remembers these nights taking over the local houses: 'We were very puzzled as we kept coming into houses with no one in them, just groups of young boys, maybe eight or nine years old, smoking fags. I suppose everyone else had run off and hidden when they saw us coming but I don't know what those young lads were doing there. Gradually the rest of the families would creep back after a day or so and we'd live alongside them, but both sides would still be wary of each other. They were civilians, so they were probably just innocent victims of war, but there was always the possibility that they were spies.'

Outside, the weather was getting worse. It was the wettest winter in that part of the world since 1864 and by now in many places the rain had turned to snow. The drifts were thick and troops and armoured vehicles would soon become increasingly bogged down in a sea of slush. But in their nice cosy German cellars, life for Dad and co – for a little while at least – was almost good. They were virtually safe from shells and mortar fire and they were warm and dry. The cellars were well stocked with beer and bottled fruit and the gardens had plenty of fresh vegetables, chickens and pigs.

Basil, the keen fisherman, was deputed to get trout from the streams that crisscrossed that area. In spite of the fact that most of the streams were frozen, he developed a technique that many years later he threatened to use when he was losing to me badly in a two-man fishing match on the River Thames. It wasn't a particularly sporting or a remotely skilful method, but it was apparently very effective. It consisted of finding a nice deep pool where there would invariably be several trout collected together and lobbing in a grenade. As I say, not particularly sporting but highly successful if you didn't mind your trout tasting of just a hint of cordite. Naturally, with this trick, Basil became the great trout provider for B Company.

In another instance, Corporal Purver remembers they even caught a goose, a wonderful delicacy that was quickly dispatched, plucked and divvied up amongst the hungry men. They were inside an old barn, keeping lights and talking to a minimum as usual, but they each managed to cook up a portion of the goose on their little stoves and eat from their army-order tin plates. The goose was delicious and there were murmurs of approval all round, but one young infantryman complained that he hadn't managed to cook his piece of goose properly because his little stove seemed to have run out of fuel. Foolishly he poured more petrol directly on to his little cooker, with inevitable results. There was a great whoosh and the whole roof of the barn caught light. Chaos reigned, with everybody desperately beating the fire out with their greatcoats and blankets.

At this unfortunate moment, an enraged officer appeared and held a pistol to Robbie's head, screaming at him that he was to be court-martialled for giving away their position to the enemy. Mercifully the young lad came forward to admit his guilt and things calmed down. The fire was put out, there was no enemy shelling, there was no court martial and peace returned – but it was a tense moment. 'Shame really,' says Robbie, ''cos I hadn't finished my bit of goose.'

But the war was always around them. It was in the middle of

Right: The official arrival of Basil Avery into the world, 22 July 1919.

Below: Baby Basil with his mum, my granny Edith.

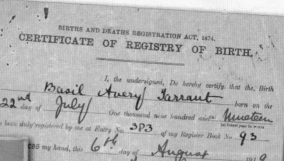

Above: Dad down by the River Thames with his father, Stanley, and younger brother John.

Left: Basil in the garden aged eight – he was very mischievous, even back then.

Left top: Basil looking very smart in his uniform in the 5th Royal Berkshire Regiment, circa 1944. He would have been twenty-five.

Left bottom: Joan 'The Iceberg'.

Above: D-Day, 6 June 1944. The Hackney Gurkhas landing under heavy fire on Juno Beach.

Below: The regiment before D-Day, 1944. Dad's in the back row, second from right. He was one of the few to survive from this group.

Top: Happy times for the 5th Wiltshires, singing round a piano in Vernon on the bank of the River Seine. These brief moments of happiness would not last long.

Middle: After the beachhead at Juno was secured, captured Germans carried their wounded to the beach for transportation to POW camps in the UK.

Right: The local Reading paper carrying details of Dad's part in the savage fighting at Kleve.

Goch.

Capt. Tarrant took over a company when his company commander became a casualty, and led them on to their objective against very heavy opposition, particularly from German self-propelled guns and artillery. It was a daylight attack, and Capt. Tarrant describing it said: "We got into trouble near our start line and lost some 20 chaps in 200 yards of road. Our road was on a ridge and Jerry, in position on the opposite ridge, definitely had us under observation. Our stretcher-bearers had been knocked out and all sorts of people were doing wonderful work collecting the casualties. We finally had to take shelter in a small farm building. The orders came that we were to start the attack again at night."

The company had the task of securing some buildings on a main road for a start line. This time they got in successfully, only to find when daylight came that the enemy were right on top of them.

"We had run into a mare's nest," said Capt. Tarrant. "The enemy were occupying a building only 150 yards away on our left. They were also in trenches 200-300 yards ahead and in the wood on our right. We got a heavy early morning stonking from the Germans."

But the company, held on to its precarious positions throughout the day until the arrival of supporting tanks and an attack by another battalion eased the situation.

Above: Photos from Dad's locket of the wedding day, first day of spring 1945, and a message from Mum to stay safe and come home soon. Dad kept these memories of home close to him during the fighting. Amazingly both he and the locket survived.

Below: Just before the ill-fated Seine crossing. Within minutes nearly every man in this picture was killed by German machine-gun fire.

Above and bottom right: My father's Military Cross and the clear reference in the regimental paperwork to 'Bar to MC', his second Military Cross, but he never received it.

Top left: A British tank that supported the battalion, lumbering through Arnhem trying to clear the town of German resistance.

Bottom left: The exhausted men from 5th Battalion, Wiltshire Regiment waiting in the streets of Nijmegen before another push towards Arnhem.

Bar to MC.
...mmander was wounded ...pt Tarrant immediate... ...forward, under heavy... ...icer cooly and skill... ...That night the Com... ...Gropps of houses. ...werful opposition,... ...this position under... ...ers, until the next... ...orders, and still u... ...unded.' His courage,...

Above: Me aged five. Butter wouldn't melt …

Right: Facing Dad's savagely fast bowling in our back garden.

Above: The MOTHS. A brave and wonderful group of men who'd seen it all and come home. Basil is in the front row, second from right.

Right: A programme for the annual MOTHS Armistice Dinner, which always included cartoons of their mascot.

2" LOOS SKROOS"

BERNIERES

EXIT

Above left: Basil in the Loos Skroos. The moustaches were much funnier than the act.

Above right: 'Grandad, we love you.' Basil about to get on a hammock with Toby and Sammy, my two youngest.

Left middle: This whole family's mad! My father (left), my grandfather and a bewildered-looking Helen, my eldest.

Bottom: Dad, Toby and me at the Regimental Museum, beneath the nicked railway sign.

BASIL AVERY TARRANT
1919 – 2005

Always that smile … I miss it so much.

the night soon after this that Corporal Robbie was out on patrol with just a couple of the other men when they all but stumbled right on to a whole group of Germans, setting up a machine-gun position in the darkness. Before they even realised what was happening, the Hackney boys shot up the whole lot of them. There were no survivors and, on a macabre note, when they were going through the dead bodies in the morning, there was a perfect hole in one of the Germans' hats, with Robbie's Sten-gun bullet still inside it. Seemingly it had killed him outright and bounced straight back off his shattered skull. Robbie was still only nineteen at this time.

As well as the usual patrols, an urgent priority for the Wilts was the laying of telephone cables. Communications were obviously essential as they were very much in enemy territory, although things were mainly strangely quiet and casualties were light at this time. The biggest danger came from landmines. As the Germans moved back, they still wanted to cause as much injury to the following Allied forces as they could. The Germans had a real genius with booby-traps, mines linked to trip wires, particularly the notorious Schu mine which would blow off a foot as soon as the pressure pad was released. In addition, as they moved back along many of their own roads, particularly into the forests, they would leave felled trees as barricades and would booby-trap the area around the tree so that anyone getting out of a truck to clear the road could easily step on a mine.

On 23 November, the Wiltshires set up their HQ in the village of Bauchem, near Geilenkirchen, but there was heavy shelling soon afterwards, mainly seeming to come from the nearby district of Tripsrath. On 25 November, the battalion CO, Lieutenant Colonel Kenrick, decided that it was time to clear any remaining German resistance from the area. This proved far tougher than they envisaged – and for one soldier in particular it was to prove a decisive moment of the war.

Lieutenant Tarrant and his men formed part of a large fighting patrol who were sent to clear all houses in the area, but they badly underestimated the strength of the Germans. One house was easily taken but then just as easily lost again to a large German force as the enemy called in reinforcements. Meanwhile, Corporal Robbie Purver was with a patrol trying to take a German-held château. He had managed to get right up to the imposing building unscathed, but, in order to position himself to fire in through a window, he made himself a sitting duck for a Nazi sniper inside. It was in this battle that Robbie, one of Dad's longest-lasting Hackney boys, was hit in the chest by Spandau fire. He'd already been injured twice by shrapnel but this time his war was over.

Later it turned out that there were more than forty heavily armed panzer troops inside the castle, and he'd been asked to take it with just five men. Robbie recalls thinking that they were under-manned and grossly ill-equipped for the task that they had been given, but of course they had to do as they were told. He felt they should have had artillery back-up pounding these large, heavily armed buildings, but instead they were sent in with hand-held weapons. Eventually the British tanks had to be called up to reduce the château and the Germans inside it to rubble, but for Robbie it was too late.

Basil was sorry to see him go; Robbie was one of the few remaining faces from before D-Day. But at least he was alive. He was passed back through the line, heavily bandaged but with blood still pouring from his wounds, dosed with the usual heady mix of penicillin and morphine. He survived from what could have been a fatal wound, though it took him many months to recover in a hospital in Belgium. Although obviously in a lot of discomfort, it was the first time he'd slept in comfortable and peaceful surroundings since before the landing on Juno Beach.

His wounds healed, although he was left with permanent disfiguring scars on his arm. Worse, though, were the mental scars. Robbie had a tough time with his memories of everything they'd gone through and had a long battle with post-traumatic stress disorder, although of course it wasn't officially recognised as a medical disorder at the time. He later discovered he'd become very deaf. As he says, 'Firing a Sten gun almost every day, sometimes almost all day, is bound to damage your hearing. And it did. Of course it did.' Robbie survived, though; came through it all; married three times – the third time to a German girl – and, as I write, is eighty-eight years old and still very much alive and well in Derby, a very proud father and grandfather.

In this same action Private Doug Botting also got badly injured – he was hit by machine-gun fire with four bullets in the stomach.

'I'd always wondered what it was like to be hit,' said Doug. 'God knows I'd seen enough of my mates go down since D-Day. Well, I can tell you it burns, it really burns. There was blood pouring out everywhere. It was very painful but above all I had a feeling of anger, of rage. I kept saying, "You bastards, you bastards," over and again. I hated the Germans at that moment so much. I wanted revenge on them but of course that wasn't going to happen. I knew my war was over but at least I was alive.'

Recalling the moment when he was hit almost seventy years later, Doug was strangely philosophical. 'I did become very bitter towards them for what they'd done to me but then I remember thinking maybe it gives you a learning experience that will reshape your thinking for the rest of your life. I think it did for me.' Strange conclusions for a man with a stomach riddled by German bullets, perhaps, but Doug is a fascinating, thoughtful and intelligent man.

After he was shot, they got him to the basement of a converted monastery that was serving as a hospital and a brilliant Scottish surgeon joined two sections of his bowels together, which apparently had rarely been done before.

'Everybody got very excited about the operation,' says Doug. 'I was just glad not to be dead. The surgeon even produced a bottle of champagne and said I must drink a glass every day to celebrate!' It was all very bizarre but then they were in a war zone.

Eventually Doug was flown back to Swindon and was in hospital for weeks. 'I flew home with a wounded American Air Force pilot. I was rather excited about being flown home but he hated it. After his experience he never wanted to be up in a plane again.'

Doug fully recovered back in England but he had nightmares for years, 'and for a long time I could never talk about the war to anyone – only other soldiers. I could talk to them because they understood but I couldn't find any way to talk about any of it to my two daughters … just couldn't.' When Doug said this to me, I heard such an echo of Dad.

Basil had now seen two more of his best long-term infantrymen shot and sent home and the way this battle was going it could be his turn any minute. Once they realised they'd walked into a hornets' nest at Tripsrath, the Wiltshires got out fast to regroup around HQ. Getting the wounded back off the streets, where several of them lay, was done under fire with great courage, while the call went back for heavy artillery back-up. The next morning a much stronger attack was mounted. C Company led the way in, with Dad and the depleted B Company following up. Heavy shelling of the enemy preceded their move back into the town and the Germans suffered heavy casualties. When Basil and the boys went back into the houses, they discovered that many of the Germans had dived into the cellars to avoid the bombardment, but of course this meant they were trapped. They were either bayonetted or taken prisoner when they emerged.

The Germans retaliated with relentless shelling and mortar attacks over the next few days. The maintenance of telephone cables, food and ammunition supplies became extremely hazardous and in some cases fatal. Eventually on 29 November the 5th Wiltshires were relieved by the 4th Battalion, and were not sorry to say goodbye to Tripsrath.

The plan now was to push further north into Rhineland. However, this strategy was switched after a few hopeless days because heavy snow and ice were making travel impossible, especially with trucks. Then news came that the Germans had started a massive offensive to recapture the vital seaport of Antwerp in Belgium. Hitler had called for thirty divisions to make one great thrust deep into the American lines in the Ardennes to smash their way back through to the Channel and cut off the Allied supply chain. In the event they mustered a total of twenty-eight divisions but they were the toughest soldiers that Hitler still had under his command – the 5th, 6th and 7th Panzer Armies – and at 5.30 a.m. on 16 December, almost 2,000 German guns started simultaneously firing at the US lines. It was as terrifying as it was unexpected.

For the armies in the Ardennes protecting Antwerp it was the beginning of several terrifying days and nights, with heavy casualties. However, for Basil and his confused battalion, it meant a swift move away from Germany, back over the border, to defend Liège in Belgium instead and to hold the bridges across the River Meuse. In the event, the Germans never got that far and the Wiltshires spent a surprisingly good Christmas in the Belgian town of Tongeren (Tongres in French). The Belgian hospitality was probably the best they had encountered, and they celebrated the birth of our Lord bringing peace on earth in traditional style, with both Belgian and English beer, wine, chickens, ducks and geese, roast potatoes with all the trimmings, oranges (a rare treat) and even Christmas pudding. The newly liberated locals just couldn't do enough for the English Tommy. Even the weather was kinder: still cold but bright. As US General George Patton put it: 'A clear, cold Christmas, lovely weather for killing Germans.'

All too soon, the New Year came in, bringing another wave of freezing weather right across Europe. There was still a feeling amongst the men that they must be close to the end but it was a belief tinged with desperation. With the 5th Wiltshires now back just over the border in Birgden, Germany, Dad wrote: 'We are almost over the Rhine but maybe it's more hope than reality amongst the men that this may soon be over for once and for all. They are getting very low. In this bitter weather, digging trenches into the rock-hard frozen ground each night is getting tougher. It's almost impossible to ever get properly warm. Their breath is always thick and steaming in the air when they wake from what little sleep they do manage and quite often their stubbled faces are actually frozen to the white earth. It's gone on for so long and it's just getting harder.'

The unexpected massing of hard-fighting German troops in the Ardennes just before Christmas had made both Eisenhower and Montgomery more cautious. Although the commander of the Third United States Army, General Patton, had pushed back the savage German offensive, and frustrated Hitler's attempts to get a foothold in Antwerp, it had been very costly in American lives, as almost 20,000 US soldiers were killed and tens of thousands more wounded or captured. German figures are harder to work out but nevertheless it had been a major defeat for the Germans who lost more than 16,000 men killed, with some 35,000 wounded and anything up to 30,000 missing, most of whom had been taken prisoner. They lost most of their tanks and guns.

Hitler's traditional New Year broadcast to the German people did nothing to lift the mood of his country. It was usually a rousing affair but his last speech in January 1945 didn't refer at all to the Ardennes, a sure sign that the great push had failed, and it was delivered in such an untypically flat manner that many thought it had been pre-recorded or was even a fake. Rumours continued to circulate that Hitler was already dead.

Eventually, Lieutenant Tarrant and the Wiltshires moved on further into Germany as part of a massive mobile strike force backed up by Churchill tanks from the 4th Battalion, the Grenadier Guards. As they lumbered forwards into Uetterath in the Breberen area, one tank was blown up when it went over a mine, but the great force of over 100 armoured vehicles moved irresistibly on across the snow-covered fields, looking like a mighty fleet of warships. The German forces seemed to be completely overawed by this terrifying spectacle and came streaming out with their hands in the air. More than eighty prisoners were taken and as always sent back down the line. This had been so successful, with very little actual need to fire their big guns, that many Germans nearby didn't seem to realise that the town of Uetterath had fallen into Allied hands. This became clear the next morning when, to my father's surprise, a small party of Germans marched straight into the arms of B Company, completely unaware of what had happened overnight. They were simply marching in to relieve the guard. They showed no resistance, just bewilderment, and quickly joined the rest of the prisoners.

The word seemed to be that enemy resistance was collapsing throughout that area. There was very little enemy shelling; the only casualties came from the minefields that the Germans had left all around that area. The only other threat from the Germans was propaganda, which they dropped at night on to the Allies. This went mainly along the lines of, 'While you are out here invading our country, the Americans are all over England screwing your wives and girlfriends.' Far from demoralising the men, it was a source of real amusement. The East London boys responded by making plenty of jokes about the relative merits of German and British women, along the lines that at least our women were worth screwing! This was of course followed by derisive hoots from the rest of the lads, so the great German propaganda campaign didn't seem to be having the desired effect.

With the Breberen area secured, B Company were moved yet again to Nijmegen to join a vast number of Allied troops being gathered together for the push to the Rhine. For Lieutenant Tarrant and his men, this was a time of high excitement. They were on one hour's notice and had to be ready to move in full battle gear at any time. It was at last feeling like an end game.

However, what they weren't to know was that the next month would see some of the heaviest fighting yet. If they thought the Germans had been softened up by their recent losses, they were very much mistaken.

CHAPTER TEN

A Scene from Hell

On 8 February 1945, the order came to drive the armoured advance into the battered remains of Kleve, just south of the Rhine and over the German border from the Netherlands. From the hills around the old town Basil and his men could see the devastation. The town had recently suffered intense RAF bombing raids: 287 aircraft had dropped 1,384 bombs, according to the Allied report. The town itself was almost obliterated; whole streets had been flattened and there was rubble and debris blocking virtually all the roads. Dad says, 'When I came into the town I thought just for a fleeting moment, "My God, what have we all done?" The city was absolutely flattened. It was like the surface of the moon, a sea of mud, blood, broken-down tanks and armoured cars. It stank of death; there were bodies everywhere and hardly a building still standing.'

Sapper Don May remembers Kleve with horror. 'I've never seen anything like it – complete devastation. It was absolutely flattened. Just shells of buildings wherever we looked. But there were still Germans all over the place and even in those areas where they'd been forced out they left booby traps everywhere. I don't know how they found the time to set them but it was our job to move from ruined house to ruined house with the dogs hoping to sniff out the mines before the infantry came in. It was very frightening, like a scene from hell.'

The combination of bomb craters and a big snow thaw followed by heavy rain had left the access roads into Kleve in an appalling state. In addition, the Germans had blown up the dykes farther upstream, so the Rhine and the floodwaters were dumping thick mud everywhere. A lot of the Allied trucks became hopelessly bogged down, so the Wiltshires had to move into the town in tanks and other tracked vehicles. Dad never liked travelling on the tanks; he said they were 'too exposed, too vulnerable'.

The Wiltshires were part of a massive army and, after the pounding the RAF had given the town, there was a feeling of invincibility among the men. Yet again that was not to last long ...

What happened in Kleve over the next couple of days was horrendous, brutal and chaotic. Both sides were caught unawares. The Allies thought that taking Kleve would be a push-over as it had been so comprehensively bombed and 'softened up'. The orders were to mop up any remaining German resistance, creating a clear corridor through the town for the 43rd Division to pass through and take Goch, to the south. It sounded simple enough, but it certainly wasn't. For their part, the Nazi troops stationed there seemed to be caught completely off guard, so they weren't concentrated in one defensive mass to hold off the Allies, but were scattered in smaller groups all over the town. Whether they didn't realise the Allied infantry was so close, or whether they thought they would be left alone after the carpet bombing raid, history doesn't record, but they seemed to be completely taken by surprise when the Wilts rolled into town. The upshot of all this was chaos in the worst possible sense of the word.

The approach to Kleve was bloody. German resistance was much heavier than expected. In fact, as they were on the back foot now on their own soil, those that had not been killed or taken prisoner seemed to be more fanatical than ever. And their numbers in Kleve were far higher than expected. Several British officers were killed or injured early in the fighting, including B Company's own Captain Masterman, who had been badly wounded, so Basil had to take full command.

It's interesting to note here that the regimental war diary records Basil as Captain Tarrant, not Lieutenant Tarrant, during this battle. Officers' ranks often floated up and down according to the needs of the regiment at any one time. It seems that because senior officers had been killed on the approach to Kleve my father was unceremoniously promoted on the spot to act as captain, putting him in charge of B Company. He was clearly highly regarded by this time and was first choice to replace dead or wounded higher-ranking officers. Whatever personal pride he might have had in this promotion, though, he would have quickly realised that taking command in Kleve was a poisoned chalice. Very few of us have ever heard of the battle of Kleve but it was one of the most savage of the whole war.

The fighting was as fierce as it was shambolic. Both sides kept facing the wrong way or getting completely cut off behind enemy lines. Because of the appalling state of the roads, the Wilts took different routes and got split up. Dad and the lads of B Company, seeing a possible way through, swung right into the western part of the town, isolating them from the rest of the regiment. Driving into the ruined old town, they were impeded further by bomb craters and had to change direction and get out on foot under heavy German fire. With round after round of machine-gun bullets whizzing all around them, Dad and his sergeant made a dash for the cover of some houses, which they quickly commandeered. This turned out to a brilliant move because they discovered that from the rear windows they had a clear view of the fields bordering the town.

Just in time they spotted German reinforcements moving swiftly on foot across the open ground towards the town. With quick thinking and intense fire from Basil and his sergeant, all the reinforcements were wiped out or sent fleeing for their lives. The whole thing probably only lasted a matter of minutes but it was as violent as it was short.

According to the regimental diary: 'Infantry led by Captain Tarrant and Sergeant Latton made a dash for the excellent firing position afforded by the rear windows of the houses on the right of the road. No German reached closer than 50 yards.'

Two German tanks then appeared on the hill. Machine-gun fire alone wasn't going to halt them quite so readily. The tanks got within 100 yards and were firing shells straight at the houses which my father and the men were using as their firing position, threatening to obliterate all of them.

What happened next is best told in the words of my father from his interview. Talking about Kleve, he said:

As the tanks came into sight, they started firing on us in these houses in which we had taken refuge. We were lying so flat to the floor it was unbelievable. They were firing low in the room but it was going over our heads. It was a very frightening situation. I was now caught with the leading platoon and I didn't know where the PIAT was so I was really thinking, 'What the hell do I do now?'

A SCENE FROM HELL

At this point a chap with a broad Scots accent [Private Huey 'Jock' Kennedy] comes tearing through with a PIAT in his hand and races up the bedroom stairs. Apparently Jock had seen the situation and was laying flat in the garden outside the house we had taken shelter in. He weighed up the situation, grabbed the PIAT with a number of Scottish oaths, and raced up the stairs with his number two carrying ammunition. There he got to a back window, put the PIAT on the outside sill of the window and fired at the first of the tanks, which had now got to within fifty yards. He didn't destroy the tank – you don't destroy a tank, a Tiger, with a PIAT, even at that range – but the big bang and the yellow flame frightened the tank driver, who reversed. The Germans had spent a week digging an anti-tank ditch all round Kleve, and he reversed right into it. His backside went down the hole and the whole of his belly was on show, so Kennedy fired a second shot, hit the underside of the tank and set it alight. The crew bailed out and B Company fired at the Germans who were running away. The second tank took similar action and we fired at them as well.

Now that was the action of a private soldier – no orders, just using his own initiative and great bravery, he tore up the stairs, didn't even know where his officer was. In actual fact I followed him up but he didn't know where I was and he did this all of his own accord. I've always thought that was the bravest single action I saw by any soldier.

Jock Kennedy was awarded the Military Medal for this action, on Basil's recommendation, and Dad always used this action as his perfect example of how good his soldiers were. Later, in the same interview, he said: 'The British soldier is as good as any in the world. Not many have got the initiative that Jock Kennedy showed, but if he is properly led, the British soldier is as good as any anywhere.'

The British soldiers were certainly finding their mettle tested in the hornets' nest of Kleve. Because the Allied troops had become fractured into smaller units as they entered Kleve, and because the Germans were caught napping, suddenly finding the Allies right in the middle of what they thought was a German stronghold, fighting was splintered and localised. The Allies had accidentally put themselves behind enemy lines, which was a very dangerous place to be. Each platoon had to deal with its own mini-battle. Normally in battle, the two sides face one another, with a no man's land in between, and you know who the enemy are and where to fire. In the sudden, terrifying pandemonium of Kleve, a lethal hail of bullets, mortars and tank shells were flying in all directions. There must have been nearly as much chance of being killed by a bullet from your own side as from an enemy bullet.

The fighting was so chaotic in Kleve that the usually detailed and coldly accurate regimental war diary produced daily back at HQ has scant entries during this period, because it was impossible for them to keep tabs on what was actually going on.

There were no clear winners or losers in such sporadic fighting, so it must have become a war of nerves and bravado at times. At one point a handful of Nazi soldiers descended on part of B Company and asked them to surrender. Dad's oppo', Captain Maggs, didn't waste words. He simply said 'No' and shot the Germans. C'est la guerre.

House after house had to be cleared by the Allies, much of it by bayonet and grenade, as a lot of the armoured reinforcements just couldn't get through. Captain Tarrant and B Company were caught in a series of terrifying running battles for the next thirty-six hours. They had no sleep – it was simply too dangerous – and the whole situation was very confused. Whole companies and platoons were getting split up and at various points Basil and his men got cut off inside German lines. On one occasion they had broken cover from the houses they'd been in and had advanced deeper into Kleve to a major crossroads by the town cemetery, where they were hoping to clear the route through to Goch, but they suddenly found themselves completely surrounded by hordes of German troops. It must have felt a pretty hopeless situation, and there was a lot of very bloody fighting, with many dead and wounded on both sides, but somehow the tenacious Wilts triumphed again.

The more things like this that I discover, the more I am astonished that Dad kept surviving all these traumatic events, and, against all odds, lived to tell the tale ... except of course he didn't ever actually tell the tale, not to me at any rate, but he did survive, at least. I think it must have been a combination of good soldiering on Dad's part and a huge measure of good fortune. I never really thought of my Dad as a particularly lucky man, but I now realise that he was extremely so. Then again, he always told me you had to recognise good breaks in life, to work them and ride your luck when it comes. It's something I've always done and it's kept me in work all my life, but the way he did it was infinitely more important – it kept him alive.

It was not just Basil who got cut off and had to rely on his wits to survive. When B Company withdrew at the end of the second night, they had two vital anti-tank guns, but only one remaining carrier. Another of the men that Dad rated highly was a Corporal Buckle, and now the young corporal volunteered to remain with his crew to look after the gun until another carrier could be sent. Unfortunately, as the main company withdrew, the enemy overran Buckle's position and he and his small group of men were forced to hide in the cellar of one of the houses. The Germans had no idea that they were there.

Buckle, creeping up the stairs, smelled cooking coming from the kitchen and saw a sentry at the door with a Tiger tank parked outside the house. The marooned B Company boys took turns to cover the cellar door through the night with their machine guns. If they were detected, the British men were determined that they would take quite a few Germans with them before probably being killed themselves. As the hours went by, though, nothing happened, and most of the lads fell asleep. Creeping upstairs at about seven o'clock in the morning, Buckle was amazed to find that the Germans had all gone and even more surprised to see that his own anti-tank gun was still there. Looking quietly out of the window, he could see that the Germans had regrouped back on the hill where they'd been twenty-four hours before. Although they were not sure where B Company actually were, the boys decided to make a run for it and, although they were fired at twice, they got back to their lines safely and were able to tell the commanding officer where the enemy was.

Later in the morning, though, after a bit of brekkie, they decided to try one more time to get their gun back. So Buckle and his men took a carrier and, running and ducking through machine-gun fire, managed to hook the gun on and get it safely back. It was yet another story of extreme courage by individuals taking the initiative.

There were a lot of casualties but slowly the British forces took control of the town, killing many of the enemy and taking nearly 200 prisoners of war. By the end of the second day Kleve was safely in the hands of the Allies.

Kleve saw some of the worst fighting of World War II. The Germans were clearly determined to hold off the Allies at all costs before they could cross the Rhine. From the safety of his headquarters in Berlin, Adolf Hitler continued to harangue his generals about their lack of stomach for the fight and ordered them never to surrender – they would be hanged if they gave in to the Allies. But if many of the German senior military personnel had had enough of a war that they were evidently losing, there were still a good number of battle-hardened troops that had no thoughts of giving up. As they emerged from the flattened town of Kleve itself, these were the ruthless Nazi troops that Lieutenant Tarrant and the battered remains of B Company encountered on 13 February 1945, as the 5th Wiltshires began their assault on the German-held position on the ridge alongside the Forest of Kleve.

The Wilts were quick to gain foothold on a neighbouring ridge, but this made them all the more vulnerable. They were isolated and exposed, continually shelled by German artillery and frequently raked by heavy machine-gun fire. For Basil and his men, who had just survived Kleve, this must have been almost too much. They had been fighting now with heavy casualties on both sides night and day for over a week. The Germans had been ordered to recapture the ridge at all costs and Basil and his men had to fight off repeated counter-attacks from the 15th Panzer Grenadier and 116th Panzer Divisions. Both sides must have been completely exhausted but the 5th Wilts stood their ground for two days.

Around 300 men on both sides were wounded or killed in this battle. At times it seemed almost suicidal, but there was no way back and Dad and the hugely depleted Hackney Gurkhas somehow held on. The odds against my father surviving this must have been overwhelming. How he hadn't been hit or even scratched by one bullet, one shell, even one fluke ricochet was extraordinary. A lot of skill learned the hard way. But somehow he just kept on going. As if this wasn't hard enough, his platoon commander, Captain Maggs, a bloke Dad had tremendous respect for, had been badly wounded and yet again my father found himself the senior officer in charge. But in charge of a hell on earth …

B Company, commanded now by Captain Tarrant, were ordered to secure and capture a group of houses on the extreme right of the ridge. In this they were successful but at a heavy cost. My father recalled afterwards: 'It was a daylight attack and we came against a very heavy opposition, particularly from German self-propelled guns and artillery. We got into trouble near our start line and lost some twenty chaps in the first 200 yards of road. Our road was on a ridge and Jerry, in position on the opposite ridge, definitely had us under observation. Our stretcher-bearers had been knocked out and all sorts of people were doing wonderful work collecting the casualties. We finally had to take shelter in a small farm building. The orders came that we were to start the attack again at night.'

Captain Tarrant and B Company postponed the attack until well into darkness and then, with extraordinary courage and strength, went in guns blazing. This time they successfully took all the houses they'd been detailed to take, and dug in for the night, thinking their job was done – mission accomplished. However, when daylight came, they discovered once again that the enemy were right on top of them. They were just 150 yards away from other German-held houses and a whole line of densely populated and very active German trenches. The Germans opened fire on them as soon as they were visible targets but somehow Basil and his men managed to hold off the much greater number of Nazi troops until Allied reinforcements arrived later in the day, allowing the vital ridge to be snatched from the enemy. In all, an unbelievable 1,000 German prisoners-of-war were captured.

Dad's bravery made the local newspaper back home, when news of his attack reached Britain. 'We'd run into a mare's nest,' Captain

Tarrant is quoted as saying in a short piece entitled 'A Tough Fight: Reading Officer Led an Attack'. He continued: 'The enemy were occupying a building 150 yards away on our left. They were also in trenches 200 to 300 yards ahead and in the wood on our right. We got a heavy early morning stonking from the German artillery … One platoon kept the Germans in the building low all day. Then later the tanks came up. Jerry's tanks formed up, too, but we got the medium guns on to them.'

It was an amazing escape, an extraordinary, heroic action against huge odds, and yet again Basil Tarrant lived to tell the tale. Several officers were mentioned in dispatches for distinguishing themselves in this brutal battle, including Lieutenant Money, Sergeant King, Corporal Lancey … and Captain Tarrant. So now he was to get another reward for his heroism – or was he?

For his bravery and initiative leading his men in this action, Captain Tarrant was recommended for a second Military Cross. They call it a Bar to the MC, and quite clearly in the 5th Wiltshire's logged orders at the time it says:

CAPT TARRANT B. A. MC 'B' Coy. Bar to MC

On the morning of 14 Feb, 'B' Coy Commander was wounded on the way to the start line for an attack. Capt Tarrant immediately assumed command and took the Company forward, under heavy fire. The attack was postponed, and this Officer coolly and skilfully organised the digging in of his men. That night the Company attacked a strong enemy position in two groups of houses. Capt Tarrant led the attack against powerful opposition, and it was completely successful. He held this position under very heavy fire, and with much depleted numbers, until the next evening. He then withdrew his men, on orders, and still under shell and mortar fire, evacuated the wounded. His courage, leadership and skill were outstanding.

After the war Dad was always referred to as Major Tarrant MC and Bar. In all military correspondence from Brock Barracks he was always referred to in this way. The blokes back from the front always talked about Basil as a man who had been awarded not one but two military crosses. But, for whatever reason, it was never officially stamped. The order for his second military cross was either never received by High Command or overruled.

Dad never seemed that fussed about it, but the more I've learned about what he did on that extraordinary day, the more it rankles with me. As far as I have been able to discover, there are two explanations. One is that in the chaos at the front, the recommendation simply never got through – and that does seem very possible. The other is that it did get to High Command but someone made the decision that one Military Cross was enough. So many men were doing so many amazingly courageous things that perhaps they felt it would have been diluting the honour to bestow the award too often. Apparently the British generals did the same during the First World War, when it was felt they were giving away too many Victoria Crosses.

Obviously I disagree. Not just because he was my dad but because, if anything, the second action was even more extraordinary than the earlier one for which he was awarded the first Military Cross. Sadly, though, Basil was never to see his second MC for his extraordinary efforts in combat.

But for how much longer would he and the Hackney Gurkhas have to keep fighting? After days and nights of virtually non-stop combat, with many losses, the 5th Wilts did get some well-deserved rest and recuperation time in Bedburg, but towards the end of

February they were on the move again. Continuing south-east, they met with little resistance apart from the occasional mortar attack – until, outside Kalkar, on the last day of February, four more of the boys were killed and another seven wounded. Even with the Germans in retreat, progress was difficult and the casualty rate continued to mount steadily as they flushed out the last stubborn enemy resistance. In addition, bridges had been blown up, roads were cratered and many tanks were still bogged down and abandoned in thick mud from the snowmelt. As they rested and awaited orders, a small recce patrol of one officer and two snipers went out after darkness but didn't return. It was later discovered that they had been ambushed, wounded and taken prisoner by the SS.

The main job of the 5th Wiltshires was now to take the German-held town of Lüttingen to the south-east of Kalkar, allowing the gathering Allied troops safe passage across the Rhine. The land was flat and Dad and his men felt very vulnerable but, as always, running and moving from one side to another they showed enough massed strength to frighten the Germans. After hours of fighting on 8 March 1945, the Germans surrendered, but there had once again been heavy losses to both sides.

It was time to join the rest of the now massed regiments poised to take the Rhine and move into the very heart of Germany. Operation Veritable was complete but at a high price. In this one battle for Lüttingen, seventy-nine more men from the Wiltshires were killed or wounded.

At last, as the Allies prepared for the mass invasion, there was some well-deserved R&R just back over the German border from Goch. There were football matches, ENSA concerts and even an inter-battalion athletics competition. As the men massed on the banks of the River Rhine there was at last a real sense of 'one final push'. It was the best time they'd had since Christmas, which to those who'd survived Kleve seemed a very long time ago.

But Captain Tarrant missed out on some of this – because he had another very important appointment elsewhere ...

CHAPTER ELEVEN

One False Move

An extraordinary thing arrived on the mat of number 52 Blenheim Road in February 1945.

It was a letter addressed to Joan Cox from her beloved Basil, saying words to the effect of: 'I'm hoping to get a few days home in March. Could we get married? Please have everything on standby.'

It wasn't the most romantic proposal, perhaps, but there was a war on. They had talked about it a lot before Dad left for D-Day, but he had been away for more than ten months now and it was only his letters that let her know he was still alive – and each one of those was out of date by the time it arrived.

The couple had been corresponding regularly since Basil had been at the front. The forces' postal service was a lifeline for the troops. Mail planes from home seemed to be able to get to them almost anywhere. The troops could send as many letters home as they liked and, more importantly, they could receive letters and packages from family, friends and loved ones back home. It was a free service and its importance can't be overstated. They received food parcels, little treats, cigarettes, photographs and heartfelt letters with family news and touching sentiments that must have helped remind them what they were putting themselves through this for.

Similarly, for the mothers, wives and girlfriends left at home, the letters brought much-needed comfort and reassurance that their loved ones were still alive – though of course for thousands of couples in this pitiless war, the letters arrived but the sender was already dead.

Basil, though, was still very much alive and wanted to get married. He and Joan had talked about it when he was last on leave, of course, and, even though they never actually got officially engaged, they had decided they just wanted to be together forever, no matter how short forever might turn out to be.

This was what Joan had been waiting for. She excitedly told May, her younger sister, that Basil was coming home to marry her and that May was going to be a witness and bridesmaid. She also told her parents, who were rather less keen. They were very fond of Basil but their daughter had already had her world shattered once by this war and they must have wondered whether it was worth her risking going through it all again. Although it seemed as if the war was coming towards its end, there was still every chance that the young Basil would be killed by a stray bullet or forced to spend the rest of his life in a wheelchair or, God forbid, blinded. 'Had she really thought this through?' Of course she hadn't, but she was twenty-six years old, he was twenty-five, and they were hopelessly in love. Three weeks later, Basil turned up back in Reading and got a message to Joan to tell her where to meet.

Home at last, after such a long and traumatic time away, Basil went back to see his parents, had a rare bath, made himself presentable and then told them he was popping out as he 'had something to do'. A few minutes later he had a joyful reunion with the woman he had left behind some ten months ago. Joan had brought her birth certificate, Dad had his regimental identification papers, and Joan's sister May and another girl from the aerodrome were rounded up as the two witnesses. Together they just strolled round to the registrars' in Thorn Street and, after a few hours' wait, got married.

It sounds extraordinary but in wartime it could be done – and it was done by many young couples just like Basil and Joan. With no one knowing what tomorrow would bring, why should they wait? It was better to grab a chance of happiness now, as it may be the last chance they would have.

Basil and Joan were now Captain and Mrs Tarrant. No matter how many problems lay ahead, and these were of course potentially enormous, they were ridiculously happy. They loved and laughed and made plans for when this damn war was over. They wouldn't even discuss the possibility that Joan might be widowed for a second time, although they were both grimly aware of it: for now it was just great to be young and alive.

They found somewhere to stay together, not at either of their homes, and for Basil it must have been wonderful to spend three nights in the arms of his new wife as opposed to sleeping in a hole in the frozen ground. It must have been pure chance, in the middle of a bitter war, but the date of the wedding couldn't have been more romantic – 21 March 1945, the first day of spring. They ate well – at least as well as rationing would allow, they drank, they made plans for the future ... although in the back of both their minds was the sickening awareness that in just a couple of days he would have to go back to the front again. But for these few days it was enough just to be young and hopelessly in love in England in springtime. The daffodils were out, the first buds were on the trees and it seemed a thousand miles from the Rhineland.

They told both sets of parents. Harry and Elsie, Joan's parents, were happy but worried for both of them, telling them that they should have waited until the war was over. It was all very sensible but Joan and Basil didn't want to be sensible, that was the whole point. In any case, there was that wonderful feeling that only the young really understand – that it's too late now, what's done is done and there's nothing anyone can do about it!

Basil's parents went through the motions of congratulations but were clearly not at all thrilled about it. They never quite got over the fact that Joan had been married before. More than anything, though, they just wanted their son back home, married or not. But it was all too soon before Basil had to go back and rejoin the fighting.

Basil and Joan must have had one of the shortest marriage celebrations on record. Dad, in his diary, talks about his 'three-day honeymoon', for that's as long as they got. What it must have been like for both of them to be together, knowing that they were so soon to part, and not knowing if they would ever see each other again, cannot be imagined. But they'd made a decision to marry and, like thousands in wartime, it was just how it was. It was a statement to Basil's disapproving parents, it was a confirmation of what they felt for each other, and it was a reminder that they would be together till death did them part. As Dad went back to the German front there was every chance that it might do just that.

The parting at the station was harrowing. Joan's make-up was ruined with tears but she waved him goodbye as the train full of soldiers pulled out of Reading General Station. Alone again, she went back to her room in her parents' house at Blenheim Road and her work at the aerodrome. For Dad it was also an immensely painful journey all the way through France and Holland back to the front. He was missing his new wife, reflecting in his quieter moments whether they had actually done the right thing and wondering what had been happening while he was away. Who was still alive and who had died? He was soon to find out.

After a couple of days' travelling, Basil was back at the Rhine.

'Hello, Basil,' his adjutant said when Dad got back to the front. 'Good leave?'

'Yes, thank you, sir,' said Dad, 'I got married.'

'Good for you,' he was told. 'By the way, you're now a major.'

And not only that, Dad discovered he was now in a position of 'command'. This, as always, was because other officers had been killed or injured, meaning he was now in fact the officer commanding the whole of B Company of the 5th Battalion the Wiltshire Regiment. This is one of the very rare occasions, in any records, that Dad admits to a moment of fear. This is the third time he'd been made the officer in command of the company and he found himself thinking that it must be his turn next. 'But then again,' he jotted in his diary, 'I am very experienced by now, I've got this far and I've learned a lot about staying alive.'

Major Basil Avery Tarrant, MC & Bar, had certainly come a very long way from the fresh-faced seventeen-year-old who had volunteered to become a peace-time private in the Territorial Army in Reading, offering his services as a humble clerk. He'd seen things and done things you pray your own children will never have to experience, and he was still only twenty-five years old. It's a humbling thought when I think how naïve and unworldly I was at twenty-five, and how my dad never seemed to resent that fact that perhaps his own best years had been stolen from him. Now, at this young age, he had a huge weight of responsibility on his shoulders.

Rested and revitalised after their rest stop, the 5th Wilts were preparing for the final push over the Rhine. It was a strange period. Although only pockets of German resistance remained, these consisted of hard-core SS and panzer divisions who would fight to the last drop of blood. In addition, the Allied armies were not at all sure what the reaction to them would be from German civilians. The bombing of Germany by the RAF had reduced thousands of homes to rubble and killed a very large number of German people, particularly old men, women and children. The controversial indiscriminate bombing raid and obliteration of Dresden, massacring vast numbers of its civilian population, had only happened a matter of weeks earlier and now we were doing it again right in the heart of a virtually defenceless enemy ... but until their leaders would surrender it had to continue.

The actual crossing of the Rhine was a complex operation on a scale almost as colossal as D-Day. In the early hours of 25 March, the 5th Wiltshires were concentrated by the Rhine at Lüttingen again. Large numbers of Allied troops and their leaders had assembled along the banks of the Rhine in waiting for the historic crossing.

There is a wonderful story about how, in the small hours of the morning, a figure quietly made his way through the sleeping ranks and sentries on to the banks of the Rhine, where he proceeded to urinate into the river. It was unmistakably Winston Churchill. As he buttoned himself up, he turned with a huge smile and said, 'I've been waiting to do that for some time!' General Brooke, chief of the Imperial General Staff, who was with Churchill that day, later wrote: 'I shall never forget the childish grin of intense satisfaction that spread all over his face as he looked down at the critical moment.'

Just after daybreak, dense clouds of smoke were laid down to cover all equipment and crossing points and everything was set for the final push into Germany, and on to Berlin. Airborne assault divisions and commandos were dropped into the enemy gun areas and, although there was some resistance, it was not as intense as the Allies expected. Major Tarrant and the remainder of the Wilts crossed with the rest of the battalion by a pontoon bridge, stopping just north-west of a village called Rees on the eastern side of the Rhine. Everything seemed unnaturally quiet; there was no sign of aircraft or enemy artillery and the battalion were able to settle themselves about a mile from the river. During the next few days they were occasionally shelled by mortars, but many Germans were surrendering, including over seventy from the 6th German Paratroop Division. Clearly many of these prisoners of war were now broken in spirit and just wanted to survive.

Major Tarrant and his fellow officers were busy most days organising the transportation of hundreds of these surrendering Germans, moving them off to Holland and Belgium. Dad said it became increasingly clear that most German soldiers and civilians were desperate to give themselves up to the Allies rather than be taken by the Russians. As the two great armies moved towards Berlin, the savagery of Stalin's troops was almost unprecedented. Many of them had of course suffered from the brutality of the SS, but their treatment of captured German soldiers was vicious and the raping and gang-raping of German women, of almost all ages, was grotesque. The numbers of women who came forward after the war to tell of their horrific ordeals at the hands of Russian soldiers ran into many thousands.

But if the Germans knew that losing the war was inevitable, many of them were still as dangerous as any wounded animal and the remaining pockets of resistance proved tough to finally subdue.

One young medical officer wrote about the scene that he witnessed at daybreak, just after they'd crossed the Rhine. 'In the half light an enemy paratrooper appeared and began to direct bursts of machine-gun fire into our vehicles on the bank, pinning everyone to the ground. An officer dashed along the mound firing a rifle from the hip, hitting the German who fell. He was rising and attempting to return the fire when the officer sprang at him ... and killed him with the bayonet.' Later, in that small area alone, more than forty prisoners were taken and thirty-four enemy dead were counted. They were back in the homeland but they would never see home.

The retreating German armies were also leaving landmines everywhere. It was at this time that Sapper Donald May of the Royal Engineers' No. 2 Dog Division realised his worst fears, the thing that all bomb-disposal men dread. He and his dog were carefully sweeping a wide area looking for German mines when he heard that awful *click* that the men feared more than any sound on earth: the unmistakeable noise that betrayed that he had just stood on a mine. He knew he had just five seconds before he was blown to bits. In terror, he screamed: 'Mine! Everybody down!' He stood rooted, thoughts blurring, heart racing, as they dived down all around him and waited and waited for five seconds.

Ten seconds passed. Then thirty. It was perhaps a minute before anybody spoke. Convinced at any second there was still going to be a huge explosion, Donald lifted his foot and slowly moved away. Everybody in turn gradually got to their feet. The engineers came in gingerly, examining the mine. It was very much live and had definitely detonated after five seconds ... but incredibly there was no explosive in it! Which was of course why his dog, having already swept the area, hadn't picked up any scent from it. At some point, weeks or maybe months earlier in an armaments factory in Munich or Dusseldorf, somebody had omitted to pack any explosives inside the mine – and the only reason Don and I could even laugh about it now, nearly seventy years later at his house in Kent, was because someone in super-efficient Germany hadn't done their job properly. And I was able to tell my kids I'd met a man who stood on a landmine and lived to tell the tale.

Not everyone was so lucky, of course: sometimes the deeply hidden landmines brought casualties among invading Allied units, but every day also saw fresh incidents of individual heroics. Typical great courage was shown by one young corporal of the battalion's stretcher-bearers. He was making his way along the edge of a mined area when a man was heard calling for help from about twenty yards inside the minefield. In full knowledge of the danger all around him, the corporal went without hesitation to the young infantryman's assistance. When he got to the wounded man, he found that his foot had been severed by the mine. He was in great pain and bleeding profusely. The corporal called in another stretcher-bearer to assist him and together they rendered first aid and extricated him from the minefield. Undoubtedly their prompt action saved the life of the injured man.

My father always spoke with great warmth about what unsung heroes the medics were. Their name was always the first called when any company had a man down. The cry of 'Medic!' was screamed over the machine-gun fire and exploding mortar shells and it was they who had to race in first, frequently unarmed and under heavy fire, to where injured men were lying. He said in many ways the medics were the bravest of them all.

Interestingly, although the number of wounded casualties among Allied troops throughout the war was on a par with the First World War, the percentage of actual fatalities was much lower in 1939–45. This was because of the general availability of medicine, particularly penicillin, which saved the lives of hundreds of thousands of men and women who otherwise would have died of wounds – particularly from gangrene. Morphine, too, was readily available. It reduced pain and combatted the shock of a life-threatening injury.

Despite these occasional casualties caused by the retreating Germans, there was still an exhilarating feeling of optimism in the air. The lads could surely sense that victory was really now just around the corner. Disillusioned and fatalistic German soldiers were surrendering in droves, especially Polish conscripts who had no real loyalty to the Nazis anyway. Major Tarrant must have been proud to lead his men into what seemed certain to be the end of the war. He would soon be home to Joan and this time they could have a proper honeymoon.

Having ventured successfully across the Rhine and set up bridges for the armour to get through, they moved briefly back through the Netherlands into the Dutch town of Hengelo, where the Dutch people were delirious with joy at their liberation, before continuing virtually unopposed back into Germany. Dad said at the time: 'Back into Germany, hopefully for one final time, here I am a major commanding my own company for the handsome sum of twenty-eight shillings a day, plus field allowance. I'm rich.' He must have felt that life was pretty good at that moment: married; promoted to major; with the war about to end and not a scratch on him. Little did he know what was waiting around the corner ...

With Major Basil Tarrant at the front, the company joined an armoured thrust towards Holte, on the way to the important German city of Bremen. They spent a night in the woods near the town of Brogbern, digging into their foxholes yet again and sleeping through a still cool early April night. Although the freezing weather had passed, it was still chilly and wet, and the rivers and the ditches were all in flood, not helped by the Germans blowing many dams.

The next morning, on 10 April, they made their way through the German village of Flechum, with a lot of the lads in lorries and the rest travelling about ten at a time on the top of tanks. Then, without any warning, they came into heavy fire as they came round a bend. The Germans had cut down trees, dropping them right across the road to slow down the Allied advance and give them a firing position from behind the thick brush cover. Basil and his men all dived down behind the tanks to duck the spraying machine-gun fire and he frantically radioed company headquarters to let them know that there were Germans still in some numbers holding the area.

Dad and a few of his troops then ran at full tilt in a flanking movement along the edge of a fir wood, while the tanks came up in strength and the enemy hastily backed off, realising they were outnumbered. Major Tarrant then tried to contact HQ again to let the battalion headquarters know it was all clear for the advance to reassemble and continue, but the wirelesses often wouldn't work in thick woodlands and he couldn't get through.

For reasons that he said for the rest of his life he will never know, instead of just sending a runner he decided he'd go to HQ himself to report that they had cleared the road. In the interests of speed he decided to take one of the Red Cross Jeeps that trundle along behind each company when advancing to pick up the wounded, rather than something better fortified. He said to the driver, 'Race me down to the HQ, can you? I want to tell them it's all clear and then I'll hitch a lift back on one of the tanks.' It was a left-hand drive so Dad jumped into the passenger seat and held out a Red Cross flag in his right arm, in the hope this would prevent them from being fired upon.

As they came round a bend, he saw a line of sandbags that the Germans had been firing from only a quarter of an hour earlier.

There was no sign of the enemy – they'd clearly retreated fast – but Basil could see there was a small opening between the sandbags and some trees that they'd left in the middle of the road.

'Just go for the gap,' Dad told the driver and they raced on through, with Basil still holding the flag just outside of the vehicle. The wheel of the Jeep just touched the grass verge on the off side … and suddenly there was the most tremendous explosion and the Jeep was thrown high into the air.

Both Basil and the driver landed unconscious in separate bloody heaps. They'd gone over a Teller mine, which is a massively powerful weapon normally used for blowing up tanks. It was one of twelve that the engineers later discovered the Germans had buried in that spot. Sadly the Royal Engineers' sniffer dogs hadn't gone through this area so Basil was one casualty they didn't manage to avert, though the rest were detonated before they could do any harm and the tanks were able to pass on through towards Bremen. The Jeep was of course blown to bits but extraordinarily both men were still alive.

The driver, miraculously, seemed to have nothing worse than a few cuts and concussion but because Dad had been holding the flag outside the protection of the Jeep, his right arm was blown to pieces. Somehow the two men came to and started to stagger ahead on foot, bleeding, dazed and in pain, especially my poor dad. What happened next is described by Dad in his interview:

I walked something like half a mile and around the corner were three tanks with a friend of mine from the Grenadier Guards. They were all lying out in the sun; it was a lovely morning. 'Hello Basil,' he said, and then – and I can hear him now – 'Bloody hell!' He came down and he was the first to give me a shot of morphine, marking my forehead with the mystic letter

M. The battalion advanced and I can see myself now with the provost sergeant from the 5th Battalion, a sergeant I had never really liked during our days together. I was never very friendly towards him and yet he made such a fuss of me on the grass verge waiting for the ambulance. If he is still alive now, I am sorry I misjudged him. Such a kind man, he came along on his motorbike and really looked after me, holding me up, wiping away pint after pint of blood and trying to bandage my arm. If I ever tried to see what was going on he would whip my arm away. 'Don't look,' he kept saying, 'don't look, Basil, it looks worse than it is, you'll be fine, you'll be fine.' He was terrific, such a comfort, a really lovely man. He looked after me until the ambulance arrived.

With blood pouring from his shattered arm, in agony when the morphine wore off, and drifting in and out of consciousness, Basil was moved back in a series of ambulances and stretcher rides towards the Channel. Clearly his war was over. Although badly wounded he had actually been terribly lucky – he was still alive and his eyesight hadn't been injured (always his particular fear), although it looked like he would lose an arm.

The first part of the journey home was all right, apart from the burning pain and the cries all around him from other wounded men. They were flown back to RAF Lyneham near Swindon and then transferred to an ambulance train that went through the night very slowly towards Coventry. The resources were very limited – there was very little water for the thirsty, wounded men and many of them were bleeding heavily through their bandages. There just weren't enough nursing staff to look after them. It was the journey from hell and Basil emerged in a very dark mood, in pain and terrified about what sort of a future he had. He was transferred at last to a bed in the military hospital at Lichfield and Joan quickly joined him there to try and bring him some comfort and help him recover. Above all, she just wanted him to realise that by the grace of God he was alive and she would support him through whatever the years ahead would bring.

Basil remained in hospital for many weeks. He was grimly amused to discover that part of the hospital was previously a home for the mentally handicapped. With no hint of political correctness, he wrote, 'It was actually a loony bin and sometimes it seemed to us battered souls it was a fitting place for us all to end up in, after all we'd seen the past year ...'

Bizarrely, whenever a senior officer came into a ward, however badly they were injured, the men had to try to salute and bring their broken bodies to attention, with their heels together, while lying on their backs beneath the sheets – 'thumbs in line with the seam of your pyjamas, lad'. This always struck Dad and his mates as comical if not absurd. For some of the men with one or both legs in traction it must have been farcical, and God knows what punishment they could possibly be handed if they failed to comply. These lads in hospital wards all over Britain had surely given enough but it was one remaining example of the sort of army bull that Dad always hated.

Major Tarrant was blown up on 10 April – ironically the same date that Mum was to die at the age of ninety-two, nearly seventy years later. Hitler committed suicide on 30 April and German troops in Berlin began surrendering on 2 May followed by the rest throughout Europe on 4 May, so Dad nearly made it to the end unscathed. Having fought his way from Normandy right up through the Netherlands into Germany, he managed extra-ordinarily to not get so much as a cut, until just three weeks before the end of the war.

Mum and Dad saw the fireworks of VE Day on 8 May through the window of the military hospital. Dad had black periods of deep depression about the prospect of losing his arm but mainly he stayed very positive and realised that, compared to many of the others in the wards, he'd got away comparatively lightly. He was heavily bandaged and frequently injected with penicillin to avert gangrene. His left arm was fine but the right one just hung loose with seemingly no feeling at all. For a man who'd always been so fit and strong, facing life as an amputee was awful. In more recent years, paralympians have proved that almost anything is possible but in 1945, Basil, alone in his hospital bed at night, would have thought the worst. How could he support his new young bride with only one arm? What employer would take him? He wouldn't be able to play any sports ... wouldn't be able to drive a car ... never again play his beloved drums ...

Mum said he went into really black despair at times, repeating the same hopeless phrases over and over again: 'I so nearly made it ... just three weeks before the end, after all I'd been through ... *why* did I get into that stupid Jeep?'

Then one morning, a young surgeon doing his routine rounds of the wards said, 'Basil, did you just move your fingers?'

'I've no idea,' said Dad, 'I don't think so. I might have just twitched them a bit maybe. I honestly don't know.'

'Well, whatever you just did,' he said, 'do it again.'

So Basil did it again and, as they both stared at his hand, they could see there was the tiniest movement at the end of his bandages.

'Well,' said Dad, fed up and unimpressed, 'so what does that mean?'

'It means,' said the surgeon, 'it's still connected. It's barely working but it *is* working. Basil, I can save that arm but it's not going to be pleasant.'

And it wasn't. Over the next few weeks, Dad had a series of

skin grafts, with skin taken from his leg and his stomach to rebuild the wrecked right arm. I grew up completely at ease with the sight of my father stripped down to his pants or swimming trunks with a great raw expanse of his stomach muscles actually showing. It gave Dad no pain and his right arm actually worked. It wasn't brilliant – he had to teach himself to write with his left hand – but he could drive a car, hold a pint and even bowl quite a fast cricket ball at my head in the garden. He could even still play the drums, all with his rebuilt right arm.

As I pieced together what actually happened the day my father was blown up on a landmine and the weeks in hospital that followed, two things have been rattling around in my head.

One is that, in spite of never telling me or even Mum anything but the broadest detail of the day he came closest to death, I found out purely by chance in conversation with Toby, my son, that not only did my father tell him in great detail exactly what happened that day but he even drew out a detailed map of the whole incident for Toby on a table napkin when the two of them were having lunch many years ago. 'This is where the cut-down ambush trees in the road were … This is the route we took as we tried to steer round it over the kerb … This is where the mine was hidden that blew us and the Jeep sky-high …'

Now why would Dad find it so much easier to pass every detail of what must have been a terrifying experience on to a young boy of maybe nine or ten rather than his own wife or son? Did the age gap somehow make it easier to unload those years of buried pain? Was Toby supposed to tell Mum and me because it was too painful for Dad to explain it to us direct? He certainly never did, nor would I have expected him to. I think the young Toby saw it as a lovely big secret shared with his grandpa. He only even mentioned it to me more than ten years later when he was an adult. Like so many things I've uncovered these past two years while compiling and writing this book, every time I unearth something I only find more puzzles that baffle me further.

The other intriguing thought is about Dad's shattered but rebuilt arm. When Toby and I visited the regimental museum at Salisbury with my father and we saw the French railway sign that he and his men had taken, signed and somehow got back to England, Toby and I spent a long time hunting through the dusty, barely legible names for Dad's signature. We never did find it, which was terribly disappointing for us all. However, now I have realised that perhaps I know why we couldn't see it. After Dad's right arm was so badly damaged, he taught himself to write all over again with his left hand. For all my life, his handwriting, although a poor scrawl, was unmistakeable. It's only now, so long later, that I realise I would never have known my own father's original signature with his right hand.

I can see now that I must make another pilgrimage back to the museum to go through all the signatures once again. Maybe this time I'll find the name that means so much to me.

CHAPTER TWELVE

The Beginning of the End

Only a week or so after his operation, once his muzziness had gone and he was feeling stable enough, Dad was actually typing letters from his hospital bed with two fingers of his one working arm, to ask if he could continue his military career. Even though he'd been invalided away from the front and brought home, he wanted to remain in the Royal Berks or Wiltshire regiments.

While waiting for a response from the War Office, every day more recently wounded men and women were still coming into the hospital. They all brought news from the front and through them he got to hear what his old regiment had been doing.

After Basil had been flown home on 10 April, the old original gang he'd known who'd stayed on with the 5th Battalion of the Royal Berkshires, including Bill Pyke, had gone on to Xanten in Germany. Their main brief was to keep established bridges open and wipe out any last pockets of resistance. They were taking hundreds of prisoners and dealing with many more hundreds of displaced people. Many had no form of ID and no home to return to, and others were using the chaos and lack of papers to try and get away.

These are just a few extracts from the 5th Royal Berks diary at the time:

1 April: Guarding Rhine bridges . . . normal.

2 April: Battlefield clearance begins.

6 April: Deserter from German Army apprehended . . . Disposed of at POW cage after interrogation.

15 April: Wanted war criminal apprehended. Obersturmführer August Schruff . . . engaged in labour camp as guard. Disposed of for trial.

20 April: Deserter from German navy posing as Dutchman apprehended. Disposed of at POW camp.

26 April: Private Collins killed by exploding torpedo. Covered by dirt and unrecognisable. Explosion is thought to have been caused by heat from nearby fire.

8 May: Announcement of unconditional surrender by Germany.

And, tragically . . .

14 May: Lieutenant [John] Craddock killed while engaged on duties of battle clearance.

During the same period, after Dad's accident, the 4th and 5th Wiltshires were part of a massive mopping-up force making their way up to Bremen. They encountered some pockets of resistance, although even the most hard-core panzer grenadiers didn't really want to lose their lives when the war was so clearly over.

On 26 April, the Wiltshires went into the city, and Dad learned that by the end of the second day, Bremen had fallen. Among those taken prisoner was a fine mixed bag of two German generals with all their staff officers, a vice admiral and the Nazi Bishop of Bremen.

The Wiltshires continued to police the area right up to the North Sea coast for a few more days until news of the German surrender came through. In that time, though, one unit from the Wiltshire Regiment had discovered a concentration camp at Bergen-Belsen and they were ordered in to administer it. But what they saw as they opened the gates was something even the most battle-hardened warrior could never have been prepared for.

One of the first in was Private Geoff Young, who later wrote a memoir of his experiences: 'When we arrived at the gates, we were greeted with the most gruesome sight imaginable. It was unbeliev-able. Through the wire we witnessed young German soldiers already at work hurling the dead bodies of the poor unfortunate victims into huge pits. Bulldozers were moving back and forth, digging even more pits, soon to be filled to capacity. The stench was so overpowering that even hundreds of gallons of disinfectant could not hide it. The vision of that first view of Belsen would live with us forever. We returned and explained to everyone in company headquarters what we had witnessed and warned them of the shock awaiting them.'

When the news got back to some of the Wiltshires, they were sickened and furious. Doug Botting said, 'If we'd known we never would have taken prisoners.' Similarly, when the details began to filter through to Lichfield, Dad was appalled. 'Sick, stomach-wrenching ... what they'd been doing was almost beyond belief. How could any human beings treat others in such a disgusting way? We just had no idea, just no idea ...'

It does appear that Eisenhower, Churchill and the Allied High Command knew at least some of what was being done as part of Hitler's final solution for the Jews. The statistics from the

Holocaust are mind-blowing and clearly information about this mass programme of murder would have reached those at the top. More than 6 million Jews out of a pre-war total of 7.3 million Jews living in countries ruled by Hitler were murdered, along with 3 million Soviet prisoners of war, 5 million Soviet citizens, 1.8 million Poles, 150,000 mentally handicapped and 10,000 homosexual men. All died in the camps before the end of hostilities. An average of 27,000 people a day died between September 1939 and August 1945.

But how little the average soldier knew of what had been happening in the camps is clear from Private Young's recorded thoughts on first witnessing the horrors of Belsen. In other camps, Allied troops raged against the perpetrators when they discovered what had been going on, shooting guards out of hand, and whether Dad or any of his comrades would have been so observant of the Geneva Convention in their handling of prisoners had they known about Belsen, Auschwitz, Treblinka and all seems very unlikely. If nothing else, it gave Dad a new conviction that Britain had been morally right to take on Hitler. He'd seen so many young men die horribly at the hands of the enemy, some quite brutally, but he'd accepted it as the realities of war. But once he learned many of the unspeakable things that were done in the name of the Third Reich in those camps, his attitude hardened against all things German for the rest of his days. He never forgave them.

This whole business of hating the enemy is very difficult for the generations that succeed men who've experienced the savagery of war. Sometimes I found it difficult with my own father, and I'm sure my own children would find it even harder to comprehend. However, I understood it, even if I couldn't totally endorse it.

Under Emperor Hirohito's regime in Japan, almost 13,000 British soldiers and another 2,000 British civilians died in their prisoner-of-war camps in the Second World War. Tens of thousands more barely survived torture, disease and starvation. My dad's brother John, a lovely, kind man who had fought against them in Burma, hated them forever, and although Dad had no first-hand experience of them, he'd been told by many of his soldier mates of their brutality. Some of the stories were almost too shocking to believe, although of course by now Dad and the rest of those who had survived the war in Europe knew only too well of the horrors of the concentration camps on our doorstep in Germany and Poland.

So when it was announced in the autumn of 1971 that the Emperor Hirohito was coming for a state visit to Britain, my father and John, and millions of others who'd fought and risked their lives for all our freedom, were disgusted. They felt it would be exactly like giving a state reception to Hitler. To them, a man like Hirohito was a mass murderer and should never be forgiven – he should be tried for war crimes. But he never was and instead he was paraded through London as any other visiting head of state would be. The crowds refused to acknowledge him, showing their disdain with a stony silence as he passed by, and hundreds of surviving prisoners of war very pointedly turned their backs on him.

It was all over the evening news and, in the bar at the TV studios that evening, we had a heated debate. Many of us younger ones were of the opinion that it was twenty-six years ago and surely it was time to forgive, forget and move on. But there was a lovely old guy in the corner, a very well-spoken set designer, who looked at us with unusual antagonism. He was about sixty years old by then, tall with a mop of silver hair and a big beard. He was normally a kind, gentle giant of a man. 'I'll never forgive the bastards,' he piped up. 'Never! Never!' We were all stunned into silence – he'd never spoken like that before – and then he produced a creased black and white photo from his pocket, of a skeletally thin figure with huge bulging eyes, ribs like a xylophone and a stomach distended from starvation. 'That was me,' he said. 'Changi Prison, 1944, building Death Railway. I was one of only eleven of my group out of 300 that came out alive. I'll never forgive the bastards, never …' and he went moodily back to his pint. We slowly left the bar one by one, feeling ashamed.

I rang Dad the next morning and told him what had happened and he said, 'Well, what do you expect? Of course he can't forgive them, and bringing Hirohito here is insulting to the memory of all who died in their camps.'

It's easy for my generation to say we have to move on, and of course we must, but we cannot dismiss the opinions of those like Dad, who went through what they did in the war, saw so many horrors and lost so many friends and comrades around them. Many have gone to their graves never, ever forgiving. Dad never forgave either, but he was realistic and even funny about it. He could do business in Germany without having to like them. He told me once about a football match between his company and their German equivalent in 1948. His arm was much stronger by now but it was only three years after the war and the memories of everything they'd all been through were still horribly recent.

It was, unsurprisingly, a bad-tempered game with a lot of physical shenanigans going on that the referee did well to control. But nobody was actually sent off and eventually the Germans won 2–1. Dad managed a sort of sporting handshake with his opposite number, who smiled and said in broken English, 'Vell, ve have beaten you at your national sport.' 'That's all right,' said Dad, 'we've just beaten you at yours.'

When I first started to make a few quid I thought I'd treat myself to a new Mercedes. Foolishly, it never really occurred to me that they were German cars – to my mind they were just very good motors. Dad didn't actually hit the roof when I turned up in it, but I could tell he wasn't impressed and I heard him muttering something about, 'Why couldn't I have bought a Jaguar?' Then, about a year later, I decided I needed a second car for fishing, kids and wet dogs, so I bought a 4x4 Toyota Landcruiser. This time he did hit the roof. 'Well,' he said, 'all you've got to do now is buy an Alfa Romeo and I'll have all three Axis powers out on my driveway.' He was joking, I think, but only half-joking. With Dad it was sometimes hard to tell. He could always do a very good straight face – maybe that's where I got it from on *Millionaire* ...

And then there was the World Cup final in 1966, England versus Germany. I dived into my parents' house just before kick-off only to find Basil waiting for the referee's whistle wearing all his medals and standing to attention. 'Dad,' I said pathetically, 'it's only a game of football.'

'This is not a game of football,' said my father. 'This is war.'

See what I mean? He was joking but only half-joking ...

Why Dad wanted to stay in the army after everything he'd been through is a great mystery to me, but clearly he did and when the news came through from the War Office that he was no longer fit for active service he was extremely depressed. When he emerged from hospital his arm was slowly mending, the war was over and he felt he could continue to serve at some level – he certainly had a lot of experience to pass on to other young soldiers, although hopefully nothing like it would ever happen again in his lifetime. Maybe it was all he felt he knew now. Maybe he was secretly frightened of the real world in peacetime. In the end he adjusted extraordinarily well to civilian life in peacetime with no sign of mental scarring, unlike many others who had been through what he had.

I did ask Mum once if Dad ever suffered from nightmares after his experience in the war. It would have been perfectly natural, after all – he'd seen so many men die all around him, many of them screaming – but Mum just said, 'Of course not, don't be so daft.' Doug Botting, who served with Dad for many months and witnessed the same horrors, had nightmares for many years and Robert Purver had years of stress trauma and medication, but for many of the others like Dad their way of coping was just to keep everything inside them and bottle it up. Clamming up was simply a way of getting it out of their minds, even though it is hard to imagine how effective it was, given the horrific things they'd seen. Like millions of others, Basil just closed the book and moved on, keeping his memories to himself and counting his blessings that he'd been one of the lucky ones, he'd come back alive.

Some 60 million didn't survive the war, of course: 27 million Russians, nearly 7 million Germans, 5 million Poles, 6 million Jews and 3 million Japanese. British losses were almost light by comparison: 449,000, slightly more than the 418,000 Americans who died. They were comparatively 'low' numbers but nearly all of them were very young and every death was unnecessary.

The disruption this war caused to the world can surely never happen again. By the end of the conflict, there were millions of displaced men and women of every nationality, many of them with absolutely nothing left – their possessions and homes gone, family dead or missing, some hundreds or in many cases thousands of miles from home, trying to get back to make what they could of the rest of their ruined lives. For more than five years, in nearly every corner of the globe, the horrific had become the norm. Young dreams were dashed, families were ripped apart, towns were blown to bits, whole villages were executed, husbands were murdered in front of their wives, mothers and daughters were raped in front of their fathers and sons: the grotesque had become commonplace.

Now, at long last, it was over. For Basil, still only twenty-five years old, with a shattered arm and an uncertain future, it was time to move on. But he would never forget.

Fatherhood
Part Three

CHAPTER THIRTEEN

Just the Three of Us

One year and seven months after their wedding on the first day of spring 1945, Basil and Joan were preparing for the arrival of their firstborn, namely me: Christopher John Tarrant, born on 10 October 1946. The nineteen months since the wedding and the three-day honeymoon had been fairly busy – in fact, if you include my dad being blown up on a landmine and nearly losing an arm, Hitler committing suicide and Japan being hit by two atomic bombs, it had been very, very busy.

It had also been very cold. It was down to minus twelve the winter I was born – they were driving buses across the frozen Thames that year – and the following spring Reading was hit by floods from the melting snow and ice. The *Reading Chronicle* reported in March 1947: 'Thousands of Reading inhabitants have been forced to move to the top rooms of their houses because the ground floor has been flooded to a depth of several feet in many cases.' Power cuts occurred as the gasworks and power stations ran out of fuel, and coal frequently couldn't be delivered in the freezing streets. As a result, factories had to run their machines by hand, shop displays were lit by paraffin and candles, dentists used foot-powered drills and greyhound meetings were cancelled because there was no power for the hare. Dad and the other returning soldiers must have wondered what they were coming home to.

Nevertheless, once my dad had recovered from his injuries, Basil and Joan had moved into a small terraced house in Reading, which was where I grew up. No pets – just me, Mum and Dad. Mum's parents, Harry and Elsie, were lovely and came to visit us a lot, although I learned years later that Dad's parents didn't come to see me at all until I was over three years old as they were still harbouring ill-feeling about my parents' marriage.

Despite this rift, Basil Avery, Joan Ellen and little Christopher John were a happy, close-knit family. I was to have no brothers or sisters. Whether or not being an only child made any real difference to how I turned out is difficult to judge. I was certainly never spoilt. Dad was very strict and, even as a little boy, I knew that what he said went. It was clear he was officer material, I suppose.

Around the house there were lots of pictures of Dad in uniform. This was pretty normal, I think, right across Britain after the war. In most homes, a picture of the man of the house took pride of place on the mantelpiece, with messages like 'Home soon, darling' on the bottom of the photo. Of course in thousands of homes he hadn't come home. This so nearly happened to my own father, but here he was, safe and sound, and he and Mum were a strong unit.

Many men, including my own dad, wore a rather shiny, ill-fitting demob suit – the mass-produced suit issued to all servicemen on their return from the war – although one of the first luxuries he and Mum felt they could afford was to buy him a suit of his own that actually fitted. Certainly men in uniform were still a regular sight on the streets as I grew up, and from my earliest days I remember the house being full of men wearing either uniform or demob suits. The talk of course was all about the war. For the survivors of that generation, all around the world, nothing in their lives ahead could possibly ever be so traumatic. The talk was of friends they'd lost and friends who'd come back but been terribly wounded. Other families had lost their houses and everything they possessed in bombing raids and some others, men and women, had just simply disappeared.

Over the years, some of these men who'd been missing in action did return. One of my dad's brother's mates reappeared one day, long after the war had finished, after being imprisoned by the Japanese. He'd been rescued barely alive by an American platoon and been in hospital in Singapore for over a year. I once saw him stripped to the waist washing and, even to a little boy, his chest and rib cage looked hideously thin. That was probably three or four years after his release.

Our house had all sorts of wartime memorabilia around the place, but puzzlingly it nearly all seemed to be German. There was a German Iron Cross medal, there was a huge German bazooka shell that we used as an umbrella stand in the hall – there was even a swastika flag. Obviously these were all taken in action from the German enemy, but it was always a bit of a family joke in later years when we would say to my father, 'Dad, exactly which side were you on?'

My early memories of Mum are that she was always working. Not in a paid job, though, because like a lot of women after the Second World War she didn't believe in mothers working at all. She was of the generation that thought that mums should always be there for their children at home, even though there was only me in the house. Not that she was in any way downtrodden; she was no feminist but she totally ruled the roost in the house. She was brought up like millions of other women to believe that the man goes out to earn the money but the wife runs the home, buys and cooks the food and sorts all his clothes for him every day. It seems extraordinarily outdated now, but she was born in 1918, Basil was born the year after, and for them and most of their generation it worked. They rarely quarrelled, Dad didn't abuse his position and they were together for over sixty years. Dad would comb and shape his thick black hair with Brylcreem, but everything else was done by Mum. She kept his shoes shiny, shirts crisp and white, and his suits beautifully ironed for all of his working life. Meals were waiting for him every evening and breakfast was cooked every morning, for both of us.

The house was spotless – she was obsessed with cleanliness and was forever polishing, sweeping and hoovering. Dad and I were viewed as a thorough nuisance whenever we had the audacity to come into the house. If we came in from the garden, shoes were grabbed before we dared come over the doormat, and if we came back from fishing when I was older, woe betide either of us to even breathe inside the back door with muddy coats and boots. We reckoned it was a lovely house, but it would work better if we lived in the garage.

Mum couldn't have been more opposite from her war-hero husband. Like him, she was very chatty and funny, but she never drove a car, was wobbly on a bicycle, could swim a bit but not very well – and she would never, ever fly in an aeroplane. She would have been absolutely petrified. She lived in a perpetual state of worry about everything – she was terrified in cars, on buses and trains, and was never totally sure about the pavement either. She was constantly worried about Dad, me, all her relatives and, in later years, her grandchildren. She was convinced that we were all about to have some dreadful accident at any minute – perhaps a legacy from the war years when she was forced to wait helplessly for Basil to come home safely. Yet, funnily enough, on the odd occasion when there actually was a crisis, she became icy calm, totally organised and showed complete control.

She was also incredibly kind. She came from an extraordinarily caring Berkshire family who would do anything for absolutely anyone. Her mum was like it, her sister May was like it: they were all enormously generous with their time and whatever little money they had, they would give you in an instant.

Dad loved these qualities in her and was secretly hugely proud of our house. He used to love showing friends around, remarking how spotless it was, even though everybody was tiptoeing around in their socks with their shoes in their hands. Our house always smelled of Lifebuoy soap, and we had Gibbs pink toothpaste in a little tin. We always had a bath on Saturday night and Mum put Dettol in the water, which really stung if you had cuts, which I always did. She gave me cod-liver oil every day which was disgusting – still is! – and syrup of figs to keep us regular ('opening medicine' Dad called it, rather graphically). Mum also frequently gave me a horrible brown syrup called Virol, which was used as a revolting kind of general multivitamin.

We had carpet in as many rooms as Dad could afford and linoleum in those that he couldn't. Nobody had central heating. We had gas for lighting, heating and cooking for years, as electricity was still quite a luxury. There was no phone in the house, of course; we had to go to a corner call box – all intact and unvandalised in those days – with a pocket full of coins. You had to press button A when the person you were calling picked the phone up at their end, or button B to get your money back if there was no reply. We had a brand new Hoover, costing twenty-five quid in 1950, six weeks of Dad's wages, and – Mum's pride and joy – a washing machine. We were also the proud possessors of an indoor bathroom and one loo indoors, although we still had another in the garden.

In 1950 less than half of the population had an indoor lavatory.

Mum was a great cook. We always had a cooked meal at breakfast and in the evening. To Dad and me her cooking was truly wondrous and she could do clever things like trifles, cream cakes, scones and even lemon meringue pie. In addition to all this cooking, washing and ironing, she also painted and wallpapered the house for many years because Dad, with his shattered arm, couldn't do it. The knock-on damage from driving over that landmine still affected our lives so many years later. But at least Dad was home and, unlike so many, he had survived.

If our house was spotless, the streets outside were pretty grim, mainly because they were caked with horseshit. Dad was always out with a bucket, collecting dung for the roses in our back garden. Horses were still a regular sight in the streets well into the sixties, pulling carts and delivering milk, bread and coal to most houses. The coalmen were wonderful characters, all absolutely blackened by the coal that they delivered to each house in huge sacks. Most houses had a coal fire and chimneys all along our road belched out black smoke all through the winter months. Sometimes the fire brigade would come racing to a house where they couldn't afford to pay for a regular chimney sweep and their chimney had caught fire. Luckily Reading had escaped most of the bomb damage that many other towns of its size had suffered, so I didn't have the experience of playing in bombed-out ruins that many other boys of my generation had.

We lived in London Road, near Cemetery Junction (now immortalised on celluloid by Ricky Gervais), opposite Palmer Park, named after one of the Palmers of Huntley & Palmers Biscuits fame. We had a small back garden that seemed to mainly consist of dirt, a small amount of grass, and dog poo – even though we didn't have a dog. The house was located right next to the main road that went into the centre of town and Mum and Dad went to elaborate lengths to make sure I never went out of the front door of the house without one of them to keep an eye on me. Even though there was nothing like the motorcar traffic there is now, there was still enough rumbling past every day to spell danger, especially for someone of my mother's nervous disposition. It was a terraced house and we lived in the downstairs part only.

It's very strange how the brain forever retains minute detail from a long time ago and how certain things are etched forever into a child's memory. The couple upstairs were called Esme and Ted Lickfield – they were very nice and they always babysat me when Mum and Dad went out. I remember vividly waking up one evening and being horrified as I went toddling around the house to discover that my parents weren't in. I became terribly upset and started calling out in floods of tears. Happily the Lickfields heard me, and Esme came down to give me a cuddle and reassure me that Mummy and Daddy were coming home very soon. It was probably only ten o'clock in the evening but of course it was the middle of the night to me. Just then, while Esme was cheering me up, my parents came in through the front door. Mum was wearing a very nice white coat, Dad had his suit on with a red tie, and I was wearing blue stripy pyjamas. My slippers had rabbits on and Esme Lickfield was wearing a red cardigan. I repeat these details now because I can still see everything as clearly as I could then, more than sixty years ago. Many years later, with Dad's help, I worked out exactly when this must have occurred – I cannot have been quite three years old.

The other event that every child remembers clearly, of course, is Christmas. The festive season was always great in our house – we always had a big tree that Dad used to go and quietly rustle from the common, and even though there were just three of us on Christmas Day in my early years, we would wade through a huge turkey and mountains of roast potatoes and parsnips before listening to the King broadcast on the radio. Mum and Dad would then almost invariably nod off and I would play with my new toys, then later we'd eat the cold remains until we were groaning and Mum would start making a turkey broth that would last us for several days.

Every Christmas I seemed to be wearing a new cowboy suit – I think Dad got me a new one several years running and a six-gun with caps. I spent a lot of time playing on my own in the back garden, hiding behind a little bush jumping out and shooting imaginary Apaches. Then one year when I was about was four, I got my pride and joy: my first bicycle – well, tricycle actually – a light blue Gresham Flyer. I was only allowed to cycle on my own in the back garden round and round the dog poo but it had one of those long extending poles on the back so Dad could push me for miles when we went out together.

I loved everything about Christmas – I still do. I have so many memories and they all seem to centre around my father. Dad and I getting scratched to bits collecting the holly … Dad insisting on going out and joining in with the carol singers (well, he had been head chorister although it was a bit much when he started shaking the tin for Mum and me to put money in) … and of course then there was Father Christmas, whoever he was. I was a real believer in Santa – I used to look out of my bedroom window into the sky after I'd been put to bed extra early on Christmas Eve and one year I was sure I could hear the sleigh bells. I was so sure that I actually pulled the sheets over my head because Dad always told me that if you had even the tiniest glimpse of the sleigh then Father Christmas and his reindeer would go straight past.

I guess I would have been maybe five when I first began to wonder about Father Christmas. I was not yet a definite non-believer but clearly someone at school had sown the first seeds of doubt. So I hatched a clever little plan. In fact for a five-year-old it was as cunning as the most cunning fox.

When I pinned my usual list on the pillow by the chimney at the foot of the bed I ended my note with: 'Thank you very much, Santa … please can I have your autograph?' Simple and yet brilliant! Bearing in mind that my dad with his war-damaged arm had an unmistakeable scrawl for his signature, this would surely be the clincher that Father Christmas had actually been Father Basil all the time. Exhausted – probably from my own cleverness – I slept well and heard nothing, but the next morning when I tiptoed to the end of my bed, there was my stocking, there were the presents bulging inside … and there was my note with no autograph, just a big sooty thumbprint on the bottom!

These were happy, innocent days at London Road. The area has changed a lot in character now – there is a large immigrant community, curry houses have sprung up all over the place and it's hardly recognisable, but our house is still there with a brightly coloured front door.

About fifty years after we'd left the house, as Dad and I were driving through that part of town, in a moment of madness he suddenly said to me, 'Let's go and look at the old house.'

'Dad,' I said, 'don't be so daft. It'll be unrecognisable, everything will have changed and we won't be welcome.'

'Of course we will,' said Basil the bold and he drove to our old street and marched up to the front door, knocking on it loudly. I erred on the side of cowardice and stayed in the car. For a few seconds nobody came and I thought we were going to get away with it but then the door opened and an enormous bearded Sikh gentleman appeared, looked my father up and down, saw me squirming in the car and said, quite abruptly, 'Who are you and what do you want?'

'Hello there,' said my father, 'I'm Basil Tarrant, that's my son out there in the car, and we used to live here.'

'Well, you don't live here now, I do. So piss off!' he said curtly, and slammed the door.

Inside the car, I was in hysterics. Dad came back looking flustered. 'He was going to show us round, but he's a bit busy,' said Dad, covering his embarrassment. I just stared innocently into the middle of the windscreen but couldn't wait to tell Mum when we got home.

After the war, Dad returned to work at Huntley, Boorne and Stevens. No night sweats, no trauma. His attitude seemed to be 'Been there, done that – back to work'. In spite of everything that he had witnessed he just came home and took up where he left off. I know that he was resentful of some of the other young men in the company who seemed to have been promoted in his absence while he was away fighting. But he knew he was lucky: several from HB&S who had gone with him had been killed. Those who had remained must have had their reasons for not going to war. Perhaps they were good reasons, possibly they weren't.

He still retained a strong connection with his army life, though. He joined a wonderful group of old soldiers called the Memorable Order of Tin Hats, the MOTHS, who met every month in the Ship Hotel in the middle of Reading. This was to form the basis of one of the most important friendship groups of his civilian life.

Formed originally in 1927 in Durban, South Africa, the idea of the MOTHS caught hold almost immediately in the UK, cementing great friendships that had occurred during and after the First World War. Each area created a local headquarters or 'shell hole' where men who'd served could get together every few weeks, bare their souls to each other and raise funds for others who had not come back from fighting for their country in one piece.

For Basil it was just what he wanted and probably just what he needed. By pure chance the first UK shell hole was established on 21 September 1928 in Reading. It was called Windy Corner and became well respected locally for its terrific charity work. By the time the Second World War had finished there was a whole new population of exhausted and shell-shocked ex-soldiers who needed a focal point for their memories. The MOTHS' aims were to maintain the camaraderie of all men who'd had service in an active theatre of war, to assist the wounded in military hospitals with gifts and occupational equipment and to honour the war dead. Their proud motto all through the years was: 'To today's fighting men we offer friendship; to veterans we extend comradeship.'

As a surviving, decorated major, Basil was one of the leading lights of Windy Corner, and in the coming years he became the host and key speaker at their annual general dinner. It was a real gentleman's club – wives were occasionally welcomed, but mainly it was all boys together. Above all, it must have been the one place where they could all relax and maybe relive experiences with the only people who could really relate to them – men who'd been there and somehow survived.

I got to know quite a few of the MOTHS as a little boy and Mum and I loved to have them around the house. Some of them had been in even more horrific situations than my own father, including Japanese prisoner-of-war camps. I didn't realise it at the time but over the first year or two of the organisation, Dad quietly weeded out the lightweights, the bullshitters and the bluffers, making it gently clear they weren't welcome. The men who became his real close friends for years to come had all been there at the sharp end.

They had killed and come close to being killed themselves. They had lost many friends. There was no glorification of war from them, only a horror of what they'd seen. But like Dad they kept it locked away. They were the real deal, they were hard core.

I always loved it when Dad let me sit up with them. Even at the time it seemed that my father was letting me into something very special and it made me feel very privileged and grown up. The MOTHS had a real unspoken power about them but, like Dad, they were mainly very kind, gentle blokes. They were all extrovert and full of funny stories about the absurdities of the army, but about the actual detail of war they hardly ever said a word.

CHAPTER FOURTEEN

A Post-war Childhood

When you're a little boy of only five you just assume that all other families are pretty much like yours. So when you discover that your father is called Basil you just naturally assume that there will be thousands of Basils in charge of thousands of houses just like yours all over England. You also presume there will be just as many men called Avery, his middle name. Well, I never did meet another Avery, not a single one, and the first Basil I ever met was Basil Brush. I was about thirty years old and he and I starred in my one and only panto – *Babes in the Wood* at the Beck Theatre, Hayes in Middlesex. Years later I came to love Basil Fawlty, and I once watched Basil D'Oliveira batting in a test match, but apart from those three (and one of those was a fox) I never came across any other Basils. I also assumed that the country would be heaving with Pomeroys, because Basil's best friend was called Pomeroy! A lovely man – Uncle Pom we called him – but I have to say Pomeroys were even thinner on the ground than Basils. I never even heard of another Pomeroy in my life.

It all sounds rather grand, but we certainly weren't. We were a pretty normal middle-class family. Dad worked, Mum washed and cleaned and, in the early days at least, I'm pretty sure we struggled to pay the bills. However, it was a middle-class dream in those days to send your son to private school. Dad really believed in education, probably wanting to give his son the schooling that he never had. He'd worked hard but the school he went to wasn't great. So with a few quid that he'd managed to save, he got me a place in one of those rather twee little fee-paying schools that are based in grand, old but rather crumbly Victorian houses. It was at number 9 Christchurch Gardens, so they'd catchily named it the No. IX Preparatory School.

Years later, on a trip down memory lane with Toby and Sammy, my two youngest kids, I decided to proudly show them their father's first seat of academia. They were rather excited, but when we got to Christchurch Gardens number seven was there, and number eleven was there, but number nine was just a big pile of bricks and a bonfire! Toby and Sammy were somewhat unimpressed ...

Dad thought it was very important that it was an all-boys' school. I think he thought that, apart from Mum, girls were a bit ... well, girlie. And of course there had to be plenty of sport. Dad loved all sports. Luckily, so did I, and it was a great bond between us all of our lives, as it is now between myself and Toby, my own son. We watched football and cricket anywhere we could and often went to the White City stadium to watch athletics. I seem to remember a bloke called Derek Ibbotson being Dad's sporting idol, along with Billy Wright, the captain of the England football team, who, years later, I was to work with at Central Television. Dad and I even went to Billy's *This Is Your Life* – for Dad, it was a great thrill to sit amongst his all-time heroes. Basil just loved anything to do with sport and, like Grandad Stanley, he walked everywhere he could. After nearly a whole year of those long route marches in full battle dress carrying forty-pound packs and weapons, walking across Reading or through the Berkshire countryside would have been but a gentle stroll.

So the No. IX School (motto 'Parendo Artem Regnandi Discimus'; how weird am I to still remember that?) was an all-boys' school – no soppy girls wanting to play kiss-chase. We were very much encouraged to play sport: cricket, football and lots of PE. It was a noble idea but all these activities took place out in the playground, which had a surface as hard as rock. The play area had goalposts at either end and the pitch was a mixture of ground-in builders' rubble and concrete. If you fell over you cut your knees, it was simple as that. The masters' attitude was equally simple: 'Well, don't fall over, boy!'

Then there was the school swimming pool, which, presumably for economic reasons, we built ourselves. We clearly had not been taught how to use a spirit level for when the pool was empty, it looked like there had been a nuclear attack. Unfortunately, it was often empty because it had a terrible leak, which we never did find or mend. The depths were like a fairground ride designed by a madman – it went from six inches to six feet in a matter of a yard or so, and then lurched violently back up to plateau at about four and a half feet, which occupied a lot of the middle of the pool, except for an eight-foot gully which, terrifyingly, ran along one whole length hard against the side. If you slipped in, you disappeared. All together now: 'Well, don't slip in, boy!'

The application of chlorine was very hit and miss, depending on how shaky the swimming master's hands were in the mornings, and could vary from a teaspoonful to about three pints. Oh, and it was right next to the school poultry shed which meant that the surface was constantly full of floating chicken shit.

We wore grey Viyella shirts with matching grey shorts and socks. Classrooms were low-lit with ancient, dark-brown desks and old-style blackboards. The masters wrote in chalk and wiped them with blackboard rubbers – which could be turned, in an instant, into a deadly missile to hurl at any little oik talking or firing ink pellets. Some of them were deadly accurate and they could hit you squarely between the eyes with a board rubber from thirty feet away.

I was easily distracted in class, as was my father before me, and I distracted those around me. My reports regularly said that I seemed bored in class and 'bored boys have to be disciplined'. I think the masters were as bored as we were, but I was only six so I couldn't cane them back. When Dad used to ask me what I thought of the school, I always said, 'Really nice, thank you, Daddy.' I just felt that it was what he wanted to hear. I didn't want to whinge about the caning and the cut knees and the chicken shit. I think I just wanted to please him, because he wanted me to be pleased.

All the time I was at school, whenever I was caned or punished, I wouldn't dare tell Dad – he would have been more angry about whatever I had done that caused me to get a clip round the ear than the punishment itself. Labels like 'teacher brutality' simply didn't exist in those days. It's what happened to Dad at his school when he misbehaved and his father before him. And I think, after the real brutality that my father had witnessed in France and Germany, a bit of corporal punishment in the classroom would have seemed pretty insignificant. He clearly expected me to be tough.

Then one day in 1952, in the middle of a particularly dull Latin lesson, the headmaster came in and whispered something in the Latin master's ear. It wasn't a very good whisper because we all clearly heard the words: 'The King's died.' The school was closed for the next couple of weeks, as the whole country mourned

King George VI. Dad was clearly moved by the death of the monarch. It didn't mean much to me at the time but I can imagine now that he was very sad about the loss of the man who had ruled the country and stayed loyally in Buckingham Palace, with his Queen, throughout the darkest days of the Second World War. And of course he had visited the regiment in France. Dad came home with a copy of the *Reading Chronicle* the day after the King's death on 7 February 1952. The paper carried its own very sombre editorial tribute, all edged in black.

On Wednesday morning, with a suddenness that stunned the intelligence, the nation learned of the death of the King, whose passing was peaceful. Unhappily it synchronised with the absence from England of his elder daughter, the heir to the throne, to whom, but a few short days ago and with a long lingering look, he had waved farewell on her journey to distant lands as his emissary of goodwill. It is a tribute to the native character of the British race that while monarchs have fallen like autumn leaves in Europe, the British throne has stood like a rock ... Elizabeth II comes to her task not wholly unprepared. Now she takes up the sceptre in an era with difficulties as many and problems as searching as any that faced her puissant namesake nearly four centuries ago. We all will wish that, under divine guidance, her reign may be long and peaceful and that both she and her consort may be blessed in their endeavours.

Not the sort of editorial you will ever find in a Murdoch red-top, but Dad thought it was wonderful and kept it for years. It was one of the things I found in his desk after Mum died. He was always very pro-royalty and had been saddened by the King's death.

Despite their grief, my parents and the whole nation were united in their excitement about the coronation of the new, young Queen. None of my little schoolfriends really understood what a coronation was, but we all agreed that the new young Queen Elizabeth looked lovely. We had no television set – in 1953 most people didn't – but we all jammed into the front room of a house down the road and watched it in black and white on their set.

A few days later, Dad got into his best suit and Mum put on her nicest dress, plus of course her fur coat and hat, and the three of us watched it all over again in colour on Pathé News at the Gaumont cinema. Afterwards Dad led us out on to the packed streets where there was some sort of coronation celebration going on and we all waved our Union Jacks at nothing in particular.

Once I'd started school, Mum used to take me shopping every Saturday morning. Dad did everything he could to avoid it. He used to go off and dig his allotment, where he grew cabbages and potatoes, but he used to hand over what seemed an enormous amount of money to Mum before he went.

My main memory of those early years was a drabness everywhere. Nobody seemed to wear bright colours, just grey and brown. And Reading itself was dark. The buildings were grey and old. The shops all had low ceilings and were very gloomy inside. There were none of the bright neon lights or glaring decoration of modern supermarkets. The only really bright buildings in Great Britain in the early fifties were newly built ones in those areas where there had been heavy bombing. Otherwise there was a lack of colour everywhere. There was also a lack of money and food was still rationed until 1954.

The shops were all proper old-style establishments with personal, helpful service. There were no supermarkets in Britain after the war until eventually someone called Mr Sainsbury opened the first 'self-service store' in Croydon. Mum and I would go to the grocer, the baker and, my favourite, the butcher. I was fascinated by the massive bacon-slicing machine swishing up and down and I loved all the smells of the various meats, the sausages (even though they were about 70 per cent bread) and the chickens – a luxury that most families, including ours, could rarely afford. I can still picture the array of strange delights like tripe, black pudding, sweetbreads, pig's trotters and kidneys dripping with blood. The bill would be something like a pound for the whole week's shopping.

Dad, in those days, earned about five pounds a week. Mum would buy things like Rinso washing powder, which was one shilling and sixpence (about seven pence), Kolynos toothpaste, one shilling and three pence, Camp coffee which was one shilling and two pence, and Robertson's Golliberry jam, one shilling five pence and a halfpenny. Kolynos toothpaste may still exist, I think, and I even spotted some Rinso not too long ago somewhere in Spain, but you will definitely no longer find Golliberry jam anywhere.

I seem to remember quite liking shopping, although it may be a trick of memory because Dad always hated it and, for all my adult life, so have I. But at four years old I just remember people in the shops being nice to the little boy with the pretty mum. They'd give me sherbet fountains and Spangles, and Mum found me my comics to keep me quiet while she sorted out what she needed to buy. I loved my comics – The Beano and Dandy were firm favourites. Korky the Kat, Dennis the Menace, The Bash Street Kids; I loved all of them.

Dad avoided shopping but always took me for my haircut. I loved going out with him. Growing up I felt I could go out with Mum any old time but going out into the town felt much more special with my father. We always got our hair cut together – there was no styling, just short back and sides. And when they finished with the clippers they did a very strange thing that I never understood and still don't. After the actual cut, they went all over my father's and my head with a lighted candle, just singeing the ends! It cost an extra penny but was supposed to be very good for our hair. I've no idea why – but they did it to the two of us for years, luckily never catching light to our heads. Then the barber would smear Dad's hair down with Brylcreem and out we'd go.

If Dad ever did get coerced into doing the shopping, we were in and out in about ten minutes flat. He'd race round, grabbing whatever Mum had put on the list and his own cigarettes. He'd always smoked quite heavily – it seemed to me all ex-soldiers seemed to smoke. In fact, cigarettes were army issue to the infantrymen. They were a rare comfort and I don't suppose long-term health risks were a major concern at D-Day, Kleve or Arnhem.

Dad would usually buy ten untipped Senior Service. Occasionally he'd smoke some vicious things called Capstan Full Strength – you could buy them in fives or, if Dad was really short one week, you could even buy them in singles. Woodbines, Black Cats and Weights were some of the other brands I remember Dad and his ex-soldier mates smoking in our kitchen. It was very normal but I can tell you that on the top of a bus, where everybody was allowed to smoke, sitting next to your Dad smoking a Capstan Full Strength was pretty grim. In the early morning everybody was coughing and some of them were almost certainly very ill, but there was little health awareness. Most of these men and women had come through six years of a bitter war, so it was just how it was, but I'm sure all us little boys arrived at school smelling strongly of tobacco.

And then – and this would make the modern-day anti-cigarette brigade apoplectic – if the masters were smokers, which most of them were, they used to smoke in class as well. Sometimes a great long ash would grow and grow as they leaned over us, tut-tutting at our work, and then ash would fall all over our blazers or even in our hair. Our maths master, a really aggressive man who would hit me hard around the head with bony knuckles again and again for not being able to do division or fractions, used to smoke all the time ... and frequently nod off in front of us all with a lit cigarette in his mouth. Because he was so bad-tempered, we never dared take it out of his mouth just in case he woke. Miraculously he never set the school on fire. Funnily enough, even though he knew that the man was particularly fond of cracking me round the head, my father rather liked him – for two reasons. One was that he taught me my first real basics of bowling at cricket and the other was that the poor soul had been gassed badly in the First World War. Clearly the fact that he was both an ex-serviceman and a sports lover raised him in my father's eyes and counterweighed any criticism of his classroom management skills. My dad would always take the side of someone who had suffered in a war – and a cricket fan to boot!

Eventually when I was about eight, my irascible cricket and maths master became so friendly with my parents that he would give me and a boy who lived up the road a lift home and an hour's extra maths tuition each. This was in exchange for a couple of extra shillings, a nice cup of tea and a cake. The journey was something else – if he hadn't managed to set the school alight with his cigarettes he surely would with his old banger of a car. It was an ancient Vauxhall and it was a moving death trap. It was OK in the summer but in the colder months the two of us sat terrified in the back while our teacher would ignite a precariously wobbling, evil-smelling, upright paraffin stove that he had plonked on the back seat between us!

I tried to explain to Dad that we were travelling in a mobile bomb but he seemed rather amused by the whole thing. I suppose he'd seen rather a lot of bombs and they didn't faze him – but they certainly fazed me and my little friend. Our maths master's car was just waiting to explode. Mercifully it broke down once and for all before he blew up most of Berkshire, and his new one, a Ford Popular, actually had that rare new-fangled luxury … a built-in heater.

By comparison, my grandad's first car, which he bought in 1954, was positively luxurious – a brand-new Morris Oxford. I think it cost nearly eighty pounds and Dad and I were very proud when he parked it outside our house. Back home he kept it in a lock-up about a quarter of a mile from his house, as hardly any houses in the early fifties had a built-in garage simply because most families didn't have a car. So sitting comfortably in the Morris Oxford with Grandad puffing away on his evil-smelling old pipe became a regular feature of our family days out on Sundays. Mum was more or less accepted now, as was I – but it had taken a long time to reach this point.

The relationship between my father Basil and his father Stanley became warm as time went by, but the marriage to Joan had caused a big rift for the first few years. My grandparents didn't understand him hurrying to marry in the middle of a war and they hated the fact that Mum had been married before. Certainly Joan and Dad's mother never really saw eye to eye. My grandfather was a lovely warm man, incredibly kind to me, so I have found the discovery of this period of bitterness between him and my parents very painful.

Like so many things I have unearthed recently, it was news to me: I had no idea how deep the feud was between them. Both Stanley and Basil were very strong, stubborn men. Stanley and Edith didn't of course come to the wedding and simply refused to come to see me until I was nearly four years old. In the end, I think, as an ex-naval man himself, my grandfather could not but be proud of what his soldier son had gone through and achieved in the line of duty, and they begrudgingly welcomed Joan and me into the family. Too many families had lost their sons in the war; it was ridiculous not to fully enjoy their own son's safe return.

So once they were reconciled, every weekend the five of us had what became lovely, happy outings in Grandad's shiny new Morris Oxford – perhaps a picnic or a nature walk (during which Grandad was a mine of information) or sometimes they'd be longer, all-day affairs to places like Hastings, Wittering and Hayling Island. I absolutely loved our days at the seaside. Grandad was very calm on these days. Born towards the end of the nineteenth century, he used to amaze me with descriptions of 'watching the troops come marching home from the Boer War'. He'd fought in World War One as a sailor at Jutland, both his sons had come back safe from World War II and he had enjoyed a successful career as a businessman. He was always preparing to retire, which he finally did in 1959, when he bought his own house for the princely sum of £800 cash. Nevertheless he did not enjoy much calm at home: he and Granny seemed to fight for their entire married life. She literally used to chase him round the house with a frying pan or once, to my horror, with one of my cricket bats. It has to be conceded that he was a bit of an old rogue, but I absolutely loved him.

Grandad became an enormous part of my life. I loved every aspect of the countryside, more keenly even than Dad, so in some ways, Grandpa was closer to me than he was to his own son. He loved and understood all aspects of the country way of life and taught me about fishing, birds, eggs and badgers. At the seaside he, Dad and I would spend all day paddling about in rock pools catching tiny fish and crabs. The weather was almost always dreadful, but we didn't seem to mind. We had our plastic macs and Mum and Granny would sit under a brolly next to a big canvas windbreak. We made tea on a methylated spirit stove that Dad had bought, which we took everywhere. In my memory they were lovely, blissful days with the people I loved most in the world.

One late Sunday evening, crawling home from West Wittering, the idyll was rather spoiled by me sneaking a bucketful of live crabs on to the floor in the back of the car and, halfway home, there was a loud scream as one pinched Granny's leg. Grandad narrowly avoided an accident from an oncoming car. I got a thick ear from Dad on a par with one from my maths master and was called 'stupid, stupid, stupid' – a fair summary, I think, on reflection. All the poor crabs were hurled, bucket, seawater and all, on to Petersfield Common.

I was forgiven by about midweek and we continued our Sunday adventures. One regular visit was to a common outside a village called Hurstbourne Tarrant in Hampshire. Well, as a family we just had to, didn't we? Actually it was a great place with perfect grass for cricket. We had a good bat and new stumps from Woolworth's. I would bat while Grandpa and Dad would fire at my head with a succession of bouncers. Dad could still bowl pretty quickly with his bad arm, although it tired easily at which point he would switch over to slower spinners. Granny and Mum would chat, make tea and we would eat a pile of what I think on reflection were pretty horrible sandwiches, with fillings like salmon paste, Marmite and a dreadful lumpy creation in jars called sandwich spread that looked and smelled like vomit. These days out were great – always just the five of us, as there was no more room in the car. 'Not enough room to swing a bucket of crabs,' I joked once, but it went down pretty badly.

We also started to go on holiday with my grandparents. Our best-ever holiday was two weeks on a farm in Polperro, Cornwall, with Grandpa puffing his pipe all the way there. It rained non-stop every day. Fair enough, we were in England and it was August. Nevertheless, we all loved it. The three of us fished in a little stream that ran next to the farmhouse and I helped with the sheep and was taught to milk the cows. We went to the seaside some days, but I was just as happy wandering about on the farm with Dad. We did have one nasty scare one evening when Grandpa got charged by an enraged bull, but we managed to scramble my grandfather over a tall bramble hedge in the nick of time ... Dad and Grandad had both faced much scarier situations in wartime but that was one very angry bull!

I remember the rock pools in Cornwall being very good, but after the earlier incident of the crabs in the car I was very careful to put all of them safely back into their natural home. Dad and I swam a lot on this holiday because the waves were great and I loved diving into the surf. Mum was terrified, of course, but Dad kept a careful eye on me and I was a very strong swimmer. He taught me to swim when I was very young and emphasised over and again that if I ever got into trouble in the water I must never panic. I always preferred the warmer water of public swimming baths, but my father loved swimming in the chlorine-free sea and he always seemed to actually enjoy the shock of the first cold wash of English seawater. Hardened by his pre-D-Day training in the icy waters of Scotland, perhaps. He would always do the same routine ... run manically down the beach then straight into the waves, without any pause for temperature adjustment. Then he would just thrash about doing front and back crawl until he'd warmed up.

People sometimes used to look sideways at the scars on Dad's stomach as he lay in just his trunks on the beach, maybe even smirk a bit, but then look away in embarrassment if they were caught staring at them. It was almost a private joke in the family. Dad never seemed to mind and, to Mum and I, they were badges of courage. He'd lost a lot of the tissue off his stomach to save the arm that he'd so nearly lost in Germany. No one should ever laugh at the scars of those who came back and I was always rather proud of them, even if none of the smirking imbeciles had the foggiest idea how he'd got those injuries.

Dad continued to have a close relationship with his parents for the rest of their lives, though we couldn't help but notice that their own relationship was still fairly atrocious. After years of my grandparents squabbling non-stop, in 1979 their sons and their families were all invited to celebrate 'Stanley and Edith's Diamond Wedding Anniversary – sixty happy, loving years together'. We all turned up to pay homage to the loving couple with just a hint of cynicism in the air.

A year or so later, I was round Dad's house when the phone rang in the hall and I heard my father, usually a very polite man, saying, 'Don't be so daft … No … No! Absolutely not! Don't be so ridiculous … No, no, no!'

'Who on earth was that?' I asked him.

'Your grandfather,' said Dad. 'Silly old sod! He's packed a case and wants to come and live with us! Says him and Mum are incompatible! I told him not to be so daft, after more than sixty-two years, and just unpack his case and get on with it!'

But when Edith died, about a year later, Grandpa was absolutely distraught. It was harrowing to see him. At one point, sobbing, he tried to get in the grave. We all came home terribly upset and Dad gently told me to prepare myself because often when one half of a long-married couple goes, after so many years together, the other one goes very soon after. They seem lost and just give up. The thought of this really depressed me. Grandpa was now living alone and we all rallied round as best we could and took turns to keep him company, but he didn't seem the same – he was eighty-six by now and clearly very lonely. Then one evening the phone rang and Dad passed me the phone, saying, 'It's your Grandad.'

'Chris, there's something I need you to give your blessing for,' said Grandad. 'I've spoken to your father, but it's you I want to give me the go ahead.' Why he'd suddenly chosen me as the family moral arbiter I don't know. I had vague worries that he was contemplating euthanasia but then he went on: 'I'm thinking of getting married again.'

I was absolutely delighted. 'That's wonderful news,' I told him, 'I'm really thrilled for you.'

'But it's not as simple as that,' he continued, 'she's a much younger woman.'

Fearing the worst now, I had visions of some young bimbo cleaning out the last few quid he had in the world. 'Oh, Grandad,' I said with trepidation, 'how old?'

'Seventy-four,' he said.

It sounds pretty daft ... well it was, but of course to him the twelve-year age gap was a yawning chasm. She was terrific, though. Her name was Peggy. Dad and all of us loved her straight away and she put another ten years on Stanley's life. He lived till he was ninety-six.

In these latter years, Grandpa and Dad became much closer. They were both very funny men, yet also very proper. There was love, but there was also mutual respect. Some men fall out with their fathers and only get that bond back towards the end of life. Some of my best friends have never achieved it at all, usually to their great sadness when it's too late to try to mend bridges. My grandfather and father mended things when Dad was still quite a young man with a new son and they were strong forever afterwards. I was also lucky in that I was always very close to my own father, even though there must have been times when he totally despaired of me. I always felt loved, though perhaps not always understood, and of course, as we now know, he had whole areas of himself that were completely off limits.

The bond between father and son is a very precious thing and I cherish it with my own son Toby. The bad news for him is that he's horribly like me and, even worse, he's horribly like his grandfather.

CHAPTER FIFTEEN

A Close Call

Dad was very anti-television for a long time, especially commercial television. I think, like a lot of people in the fifties, he was wary of it, thought it would never really catch on and was quite possibly the instrument of the Devil. Strange really, given that his son ended up making his living out of it. The first advert on television came in 1955 for Gibbs SR toothpaste but Dad was having none of it. In fact I think we were one of the last houses in our street to let the ghastly ITV into our house. It didn't matter much to me as a growing boy except you couldn't join in some of the popular playground games because you didn't know the stories. Some people were so determined to look as if they were on the bandwagon that they just pretended, putting an aerial on their roof without actually owning a set.

Dad would have none of this nonsense. What he loved, and the whole country loved after the war, was the radio. My earliest memories were listening with Dad on a Saturday and Sunday morning, while he read the paper. We'd listen to a man called Uncle Mac, who only seemed to have about four records. One was about an old lady who swallowed a fly, one was about a runaway train, one about a troll that lived under a bridge and one was a dreadful thing by Max Bygraves about a pink toothbrush. Good grief! Years later, when I was on Capital Radio in London, Dad, with his best serious face on, said: 'Why don't you play some of those tunes you used to love as a little boy?' I explained that I didn't feel the sophisticated London audience would thank me for starting their day by saying: 'Coming up later this morning, the Stones, Bon Jovi and Guns N' Roses, but first … Max Bygraves with "You're a Pink Toothbrush"!' Dad appeared puzzled by me turning his big idea down and then burst into manic laughter.

What was great about those days was the way most families would sit down to listen to the radio together. Sunday lunchtime was the big Sunday roast and then Mum, Dad and I, along with almost the whole country, used to listen to *The Billy Cotton Band Show* and *Two-Way Family Favourites*, and Dad and I both loved *Hancock's Half Hour*. There was also a ridiculous programme called *Educating Archie*, starring Peter Brough and Archie Andrews. This was a ventriloquist act – on the radio. The whole idea of radio ventriloquism was daft enough, but Dad's standard joke was that 'even on radio you can hear his lips move'.

On Sunday evenings, Mum, Dad and I would always listen to *Sing Something Simple*, then I would play outside for a while until Dad called me in to read me my bedtime story. As I got a little older, I would go out and kick a ball with my friends under the street lamps until it was time for bed. And then no arguments, in you came. Dad was always very even-tempered but he took no messing. I think he probably only actually spanked me three or four times in my life, but I always knew that he would if I crossed the line. Mum, on the other hand, spanked me endlessly but, bless her, it didn't hurt and she would just make empty threats that she would tell my father, which she invariably never did. She did once smack me when I was eighteen and over six foot tall, which just ended with both of us bursting out laughing.

Although it was now a decade after the end of the war, troops on the streets were still a regular sight. Two years' National Service was still obligatory for all young men over seventeen and that didn't stop until 1960. Luckily I missed it, though there are those who think it would have done me rather a lot of good. And although we were at peace there were always fears of another war. Dad hated it when people even mentioned the possibility – surely that was what they'd all been fighting to avoid? – but since the dropping of the atomic bombs on Hiroshima and Nagasaki in 1945 we all grew up convinced that the world was about to end in a nuclear war between America and Russia. On a couple of occasions it very nearly did.

In the event, thank God, it never happened but there were a number of other conventional emergencies in Aden, Borneo, Suez, Korea and Cyprus, amongst others, in which British troops were involved. The woman next door to us lost a son who was killed by the Mau Mau in Kenya. And in 1956 hundreds of refugees from the Russian invasion of Hungary came to England. Dad always took a keen interest in world events and he and I went with some of the MOTHS to take food, clothes and blankets to the refugees at a church hall outside Reading. They'd been some of the lucky ones who'd escaped from the Russian tanks that had poured into the streets of Budapest. But they looked desperate; they were just sitting against the walls, staring into distant space through fearful, empty eyes. Dad and the MOTHS were wonderful with them and even as a ten-year-old boy I realised that these will have been exactly the same sort of shattered, displaced souls with the same drawn, frightened faces that Dad and the others would have seen thousands of times in the battle for Europe. For the first time I could appreciate that the horror of their war was not just about bombs and bullets and people dying; they would also have been scarred by witnessing the wretched daily misery that the war brought to so many millions of innocent lives.

Dad was very quiet on the way home but he did remark that he'd seen thousands of eyes like that in Holland and Germany towards the end of the war ... the look of men and women who had somehow survived but seen much that was horrific.

On a happier note that year we moved to a new house, the first my parents actually bought. It was just outside Reading at number 58 Delamere Road – a semi-detached with a nice big garden. It cost the grand sum of £2,000 and featured Mum's new pride and joy – a GEC electric cooker. We had electric lighting (a real luxury item), no fewer than two inside loos and even French windows into the garden. Mum predictably spent hours polishing these and woe betide me if I put my mucky little fingers on them.

I became friends with two bigger boys who lived next door and the three of us were constantly being told to be careful when playing anywhere near the French windows. How delicious then for me when Mum and I came home from shopping one day and Dad and the two lads next door were standing in the back garden, shuffling and looking at their feet. Dad carefully took Mum's shopping bags, put them down and said, 'Darling, there's been an accident ...' There certainly had. It turned out that Chris, the youngest boy, had been in goal, being German goalkeeper Bert Trautmann, and Philip, the other boy, had been Real Madrid's legendary Alfredo Di Stéfano. Dad, being Bobby Charlton, had dribbled skilfully past him and blasted an unstoppable swerving shot past the hapless keeper into the back of the net. Except unfortunately there was no net – instead it had gone smashing straight through the shiny new French windows. There was glass everywhere, all over the brand-new lounge carpet, and a couple of ornaments and an ashtray were also shattered in bits. Mum went upstairs. Doors were slammed. Trautmann and Di Stéfano tiptoed away and Dad spent the afternoon getting bits of glass out of the carpet. The next morning a glazier came and put in new windows and Mum didn't speak to Dad for a week.

Always, though, just the mention of Bobby Charlton brings back a much sadder memory. As a little boy, as well as supporting Reading, aka 'The Biscuitmen', my other main football team were Manchester United. They had flair, they were exciting, they had a terrific manager, Matt Busby, and a whole string of great players. I had them all on my cigarette cards and I cut all their pictures out of my comics – Dennis Violet, Roger Byrne, Billy Whelan, Tommy Taylor, Harry Gregg, Duncan Edwards and Bobby Charlton. But on one very foggy night in February 1958, Dad came in late from work looking ashen.

'Something terrible's happened,' he told me, with a real catch in his throat. 'The Manchester United team have had a plane crash. Many of them are dead.' Billy Whelan, Tommy Taylor and Roger Byrne had been among the twenty-three who perished. Matt Busby and Bobby Charlton were injured and, some days later, the name of the young, sublimely gifted Duncan Edwards was added to the death toll. Dad and I had always bonded over sport (as I later did with my own son, too) and this tragedy brought us very close together. It shocked the world and later that night Dad held me as I cried myself to sleep.

Our own football team was Reading FC and Dad and I used to go regularly on a Saturday afternoon. A lot of walking was involved – of course it was! – as we used to walk about a mile to the trolley bus, then walk another mile with all the fans from the centre of town to Elm Park. It was all right on the way there, but on the way home in the winter, especially if we'd lost, which happened a lot, it wasn't a whole barrel of laughs. But I loved these occasions with Dad and the virtually all-male crowd. Dad used to worry about some of the fans' language but when I was younger it all washed over me, and when I got older I knew all the words anyway! It was a great atmosphere. There was never any fighting or trouble – we just had one policeman on each side of the pitch for crowd control and they loved it because they got to see the football for free.

In those days, of course, we were in Division Three South. There were no luxury coaches, not a single Ferrari in the players' car park – in fact, most of the players made their way to the ground by public transport, and the farthest they played away was Oxford or Bournemouth. They all had other jobs during the week and couldn't afford the time off work or the travel fares. The teams from the north played in Division Three North, so the farthest Dad and I ever went to an away game was Swindon.

When we weren't walking we used public transport, which mainly meant the trolley buses that ran through Reading. One day Dad came home for lunch on a huge rusty bicycle that had apparently once been owned by a policeman, which he'd bought from a bloke in the office for a pound. I have to say he looked pretty silly on it as he could barely touch the pedals. Mum was appalled – it looked ridiculous and it was clearly unsafe. Rather crestfallen, Dad cycled back to work and it was never seen again. It's interesting that although Dad was unquestionably head of the household, if Mum ever did really put her foot down he did as he was told.

But then sometime around 1955 or '56, we entered a whole new world. Still flush with having bought our first home, Dad now bought his first car. The job at Huntley, Boorne and Stevens was going well; he was on £80 a week by now and the firm gave him a big Wolseley 1500. It cost the company nearly £600. To give this context, a gallon of petrol was four shillings and sixpence (about 22 pence).

The Wolseley had a wooden dashboard and smelled strongly of real leather. Mum was very proud and spent hours shining it up, inside and out. I loved it but hardly dared sit inside it in case I made a mark. It was great for all of us at weekends, though – now we could take Grandad out for a change, and Mum and I felt happier because Basil was a better driver than Stanley and didn't smoke an evil-smelling old pipe. Dad joined the AA motoring organisation, which meant you were covered for breakdown and you could sport a very smart chrome and yellow badge on the front of your car. If any AA patrolman saw you go past he would salute you.

There was tremendous excitement when the M1 opened in 1959. I remember Dad and I watching a Pathé newsreel at the Gaumont cinema about the motorway's opening night, with just one lonely Ford Consul using the middle lane and the Minister of Transport appealing to more people across the country to use it. Often when I am sitting in a solid tailback somewhere near Newport Pagnell, I wish the right honourable minister had kept his mouth shut.

As if a new house and car weren't enough excitement, it was around now, on my birthday, that I got my own new technological wonder – a Dansette Major. This was the first record player that could play more than one record at a time. Until then you had to race back to the gramophone after each record ended otherwise it would just keep making a horrible click-clicking noise until the needle broke or you lost the will to live. Dad was a big Glenn Miller, Bing Crosby and Sinatra fan, so he insisted on playing a lot of those artists' songs on what I thought was my record player. But I had a couple of Tommy Steele records, and within months, I had a Cliff Richard and even an Elvis Presley.

Our house had always been musical. Dad had a great voice and sang loudly from the bathroom every morning as he washed, always thoroughly and always naked. I think after the long months in 1944–45, when he and his men barely washed at all and shaved in ice-cold water, being able to thoroughly wash and shave every day in the warmth must have been a real pleasure. It was always a joyously loud affair as he sang 'Love Is a Many-Splendored Thing' or 'The Man from Laramie'. Bizarrely, he hardly ever sang anything by his heroes Frank Sinatra or Bing Crosby; he always said they were too good for him to copy. A strange notion. I sing all my favourites all the time – really badly – but they can't hear me, can they?

They were fast-moving times. Mum and two of my aunties went to see a singer who'd come over from America called Johnnie Ray – he sang about a little white cloud that cried and all the girls in the audience, presumably including my own mum, started squealing and sobbing. This squealing and sobbing lark was something very new and Dad, and just about every other man in the country, thought the women of the world were going mad. 'Silly nonsense,' Dad called it, but he seemed to forget that there had actually been a bit of this nonsense from the female fans of the young Sinatra. And compared to what was to come in the sixties, it was just a ripple.

In spite of our house with its new wonders – and new French winders, come to think of it – life continued pretty much along the same lines as it always had. Mum kept the house, and us, spotless. Dad had a slightly new routine in that he marched me to the trolley bus that would take me to school each morning, then went back and got the car to drive himself to work. He seemed to like our morning chats, although most of my conversation still came out in puffs and gasps. We were still very close and he enjoyed giving me the occasional treat. Every Friday he brought home a giant bag of broken biscuits – one of the perks of being part of the Huntley and Palmers group. I always thought that it would have been great if he worked in a bank and came home every Friday with a bag of ever-so-slightly damaged five-pound notes – but we just got ginger nuts and custard creams.

We still only ever holidayed in this country. By 1960, 3.5 million Brits a year went abroad for their holidays but Mum, with her fear of flying, would never be among them. For the princely sum of twenty-eight pounds and seventeen shillings (£28.85), you could have a week in Majorca, flying with someone like Horizon. I always thought Mum's fear of flying was very frustrating for Dad, particularly after he retired, but he never complained and as he rose higher in the company, he got to travel more, firstly in Europe – France, Belgium, Holland and even to Germany again – and eventually to places like Chicago and Toronto. His trips to Germany were always edgy. He openly said he could do business with them and smile and shake hands on a deal, but could never trust them. He said to me once, 'I saw too much.'

Perhaps it was as well that we didn't take any holidays in Europe. We happily continued to take our holidays in places like Paignton, Polperro and Bridport, which I loved. I do remember an epic holiday at Falmouth in Devon, when we were in a bar, a rare treat for me. Dad was enjoying a beer, Mum a gin and tonic and I was munching my Smiths crisps, with its little blue bag of salt inside, when Mum – who never normally gambled in her life – idly put a shilling in one of those new-fangled slot machines and pulled the handle ... and she won the jackpot! The machine kept pouring money out for what seemed like hours. Everyone crowded round Mum, congratulating her, Dad bought the most enormous round of drinks for everyone in the bar and, with cheers following us all the way out, we went home with Mum's handbag still bursting with cash. It's not every night you win fourteen quid!

And then there was the fishing incident that Dad and I used to tell and retell over the years. He and I were fishing in the harbour, catching mullet on bits of bread and taking it in turns to share the one rod we'd brought. Mum was sitting behind us and a few of the Devonshire locals were starting to watch us approvingly as we'd caught a few, but then we started to run out of bread. 'No problem,' said Dad, 'there's a bakers the other side of the harbour. Jo, can you keep an eye on our tackle please, make sure nobody nicks it? I'll take Chris.'

We'd only been away maybe ten minutes, but as we got back there was a huge crowd gathered around Mum. A man was holding her round the waist and she was screaming at the top of her voice. Dad and I started to run, trying to work out what the hell was going on. Then, as we got closer, it became clear ... Mum had, as requested, wound our rod in and kept an eye on it. However, she hadn't realised that she hadn't wound it in fully and a bit of bread was still hanging halfway down the side of the harbour wall. Mother was screaming because she'd hooked a large, and now clearly very angry, swan that was roaring round and round the harbour beating its wings, still attached to the hook, our rod and my mum, who was all but being pulled in. Eventually a man from the RSPB arrived in a launch, somehow managed to placate the swan, get the hook out and release the bird, who flew off indignantly. The crowd dispersed, we decided that fishing was probably over for the day and Dad and I remained in hysterics as we drove a very red-faced Mum back to our hotel.

Then in around 1959 an extraordinary thing happened – I came home from school and there was a strange brown object in the corner of our lounge. Yes, Dad had finally cracked and bought a television set. Mum and Dad had strongly resisted hire purchase for years, and always believed in saving up for everything, but slowly Dad realised this was virtually impossible. You started out saving for a particular item, but by the time you'd eventually got the money together, with raging inflation across Europe, its price had doubled. So HP became the norm.

Having a TV changed our lives. It was only black and white, of course – typically Dad didn't go to colour till long after everyone else. The family next door had one straightaway but Dad always hated the idea of 'keeping up with the Joneses'. Next door, they had everything. Most of the early TV sets were pretty small, but next door they had a giant magnifying screen to go in front of the set, which was great if you were sitting directly in front of the box, but meant you could see virtually nothing anywhere else in the lounge. Then they acquired a coloured gauze that gave the black and white picture a sort of non-specific tint. They were very excited by it, but Dad said their screen just looked as if it needed a bit of a clean. The greatest gizmo of all was a colour screen that adjusted so that you could set it to have, say, blue sky at the top, brown cows in the middle and green grass at the bottom – which was great until the picture changed to a big close-up of a man with blue hair and bright green teeth.

Dad fell for none of it, but even he had to admit the range of programmes available did open up a whole new world. Most of it, just like today, was utter rubbish – game shows like *Take Your Pick* with Michael Miles and *Double Your Money* presented by an absolute slug of a man called Hughie Green. As a boy, Dad used to say to me, 'This man is an odious creep,' but when I met him years later in real life, he was much, much worse!

One programme that made a big impression was called *Quatermass and the Pit*. It was the first science fiction I had ever seen and I found it absolutely terrifying. I suppose at that time the world coming to end in a nuclear war, or being invaded by aliens from another galaxy, were the two things foremost in all our minds – certainly mine – and the Quatermass invasion seemed horribly real. I loved it in a hiding-behind-the-sofa kind of way, but I started to get nightmares and after a few episodes, in spite of my pleas, Dad stopped me from watching it altogether.

Much more child-friendly was the BBC teatime show *Crackerjack* – a strange but very popular programme. Eamonn Andrews, Michael Aspel and Leslie Crowther were just some of the presenters over its very long run. You would win prizes like pens and pencils if you got it right, and a cabbage if you got it wrong, and the key gimmick was that every time the presenter said the word 'Crackerjack!', everyone in the country shouted it back. Dad used to come in if I was watching it, snort derisively and disappear into the kitchen. Years later, when I introduced him to Michael Aspel on my *This Is Your Life*, he told him how much he used to love *Crackerjack*. I don't think Michael believed a single word.

Dad loved some of the dramas, all the news and sport, police programmes like *Dixon of Dock Green* and eventually the much grittier *Softly, Softly*. In the early sixties he was one of the first to understand the brilliance of David Frost and *That Was the Week that Was*, a live satirical show that rocked the establishment and pricked the pomposity of many of our peers. I remember being quietly thrilled that Dad was one of his generation who got it. For all his military officer background, he was often surprisingly progressive. Years later he loved *Spitting Image* and *Have I Got News for You*. He voted Tory but had very little time for most politicians, loved Hugh Gaitskell and Jo Grimond and he had never understood how Winston Churchill got thrown out of 10 Downing Street, directly after the defeat of Germany. He, like most soldiers, absolutely worshipped Churchill. 'He'd just won the war, for God's sake, what else did he have to do?'

But Dad's absolute favourite programme was *Morecambe and Wise*. Dad would literally cry with laughter while watching it. Almost as soon as Eric appeared he would have tears pouring down his cheeks, often actually falling off his chair and rolling around on the carpet. We all loved them, they were wonderful, but I can think of nothing before or since that had such an effect on my father. He was like a man out of all control. It was joyous, and his infectious laughter had the whole room howling.

So television, even in our house, was clearly here to stay. By 1960 there were ten million television licences bought in Great Britain, probably one for every other household, but although it was very exciting I certainly didn't sit in most nights watching it. In any case, once I was sent off to bed I could listen to Radio Luxembourg for a while under the bedclothes on my transistor radio. We used to call them trannies although that means something altogether different now (and would be a very different thing to have under your bedclothes).

I was starting to get into plays at school, which I really enjoyed. I got very nervous until I was actually on stage then I was fine. I confided this to Dad one evening and he said, 'Don't worry, I still feel the same. I'm very nervous before I make a speech but as soon as I'm up and get the first laugh I'm fine.' He didn't tell me what was supposed to happen if you didn't get that first laugh. Several times in later years I was to find out.

It was about this time that Dad said to me one evening, with a hint of nervous pride, 'I've started up the Loos Skroos, just for fun...' I was none the wiser. Eventually it emerged that the Loos Skroos were a trio of what might just about qualify as entertainers who, according to their flyer, 'have packed out local pubs, dance halls and one theatre' (I never got Dad to quite pin down which one). Apparently Basil and two of his closest ex-army mates had thrown together 'a mixture of music, merriment and mirth' which they felt the world – well, small corners of Berkshire – needed to experience. Basil seemed to be compere, lead stand-up gag merchant and drummer, which obviously involved a lot of running about in the manner of a headless chicken. Accompanying him were John (backing vocals and lead banjo) and Eric (the other backing vocal, harmonica and occasional assistant drummer). They all wore silly hats and false moustaches that fell off a lot. Bearing in mind that Dad was a senior sales executive by now and the other two were equally successful corporate high-flyers, it's probably as well that in the 'stampede' – Dad's word – for bookings, none of their employers ever witnessed their act.

Round about the same time as the Loos Skroos were playing packed houses all over Reading, I'd really got into my local Scout group. Dad had been a keen Scout and it took over my life for several years. I made a real gang of mates there – some of whom I still see to this day – and learned all sorts of things about knots, first aid, nature, cycle maintenance, even how to cook a hedgehog – a skill I've never really followed up. They were wonderful days and the annual camp was the highlight of the year. For the considerable sum of one pound and one shilling, we were all packed off to live under canvas and fend for ourselves for a fortnight. We all loved it. We fished, caught rabbits, played games, swam, ran, wrestled and made fires without matches, just as my own father had done fifty years earlier. For young growing boys, who'd mainly never been away from home before, it was a magical time.

That is until one year when, for no sensible reason, our Scoutmaster took us swimming near Seaton in Devon. Unfortunately, the place he chose as our swimming spot turned out to be just along from the mouth of the River Axe, which came swirling into the English Channel at that point and was a known danger spot. Known, it seems, to everyone except our Scoutmaster. We were learning to float on our backs, so lying there, star-shaped, with my ears under water, it was a while before I became aware of a lot of shouting going on around me and maroons going up in the sky. We were in a strong undertow, off the back of a turning tide.

The next few minutes were a blur. All around me, boys were screaming with fear. I knew from Dad's swimming lessons it was essential not to panic, and I tried to remember that, but although I was a strong swimmer I could make no headway against the strong current – I just seemed to be going sideways or backwards. People were trying to swim out from the shore but couldn't get to us fast enough.

Eventually I came to some jutting rocks and somehow dragged myself up on to them. Several of the other Scouts were hanging on to them too, dazed, vomiting and exhausted. We were all pouring blood from the sharp barnacles on the rocks, but just kept hanging on. Eventually, after what seemed ages but was probably only five or six minutes, a small fishing boat appeared and an old guy carefully got us aboard one at a time while his mate kept on the oars to keep his ancient boat clear of the rock. We flopped, one by one, shocked and crying, into the bottom of the boat. We got to shore and were wrapped in blankets, bleeding and shivering. Our Scoutmaster was manic, running everywhere, checking everyone and getting us into ambulances. He was a really good guy but we all absolutely knew he'd dropped one massive bollock. One by one we were all checked out by the doctors, our cuts were bandaged and around teatime we were told we could leave hospital.

We all knew it had been a close call, very close. We went home at the weekend and the next evening our Scoutmaster went round to every single one of our houses to explain to our parents that things had gone 'a bit wrong' and that he'd 'made a bit of a mistake'. Mum and Dad absolutely loved him, but I heard Dad's voice raised and he was white when he came back from nearly half an hour at the door. He was very, very angry. In fact it was probably the angriest I ever saw him. He was angry with me for not even mentioning what had happened and absolutely furious with the Scoutmaster, but I think above all he was sick with shock to hear how close his eleven-year-old son had come to death. I'm sure the irony was not lost on him that he had survived five years of being bombed and shot at during the war, only to nearly lose his son on a Scouts' camping holiday.

CHAPTER SIXTEEN

Another Scare

B y 1959 I'd already passed my Eleven Plus, but Dad wanted me to stay on and take a thing called the Common Entrance exam to see if I could get into public school. If I didn't pass my Common Entrance, it meant I would still be able to get to grammar school, but Dad was hoping for higher things. It meant of course that I would board and be away from home for months for the first time in my life. Mum dreaded the idea but I was rather excited and, in any case, just accepted it.

So it was that I was packed off to King's School, Worcester, after passing the exam. It seems a strange thing to do to your only son, but to Dad it was just a progression, a desire to give me a better education than he ever had. I think it was also a social thing: you put your child in one end and a perfectly formed little Hooray Henry came out the other end. Unfortunately this was the sixties and that didn't quite turn out the way he expected!

I went away to school in 1960 and by the time I finished in 1964 the Beatles and the Stones had happened and the world was changed forever. But that time at King's School was where I spent the formative years of my life. The fees were made slightly more affordable by a grant from the cathedral, but I know my parents made a lot of sacrifices just to keep me there. Dad was working harder than ever, and they didn't have a holiday for four years.

On the first day, Dad drove me to school and came in to meet the new housemaster. Mum sat sniffling into her hanky in the car. The housemaster was a Mr Bailey, known to all the kids as 'Basher' because he was very keen on the use of the cane, and he and Dad seemed to circle each other, with me as the nervous little piggy in the middle. 'Oh dear,' said my father, 'I didn't realise I had to take him back at the end of each term. I presumed you'd just keep him till he was eighteen!' I was horrified and Basher looked bewildered, then we both realised it was just one of Dad's jokes. Well, thanks for that one, Dad. Thank God Mum didn't hear – the car interior would be awash with tears.

Having established that I was only there for one term at a time, home for half term and allowed out one in four Sunday afternoons, there was a more important matter to be discussed. I'd done quite well in my exams, so well in fact that I was a year ahead – which sounds good but actually meant I had to choose there and then between arts or sciences before term started the next day.

'Science,' I said at once, 'it's the way ahead for the future.'

'Arts,' returned Dad instantly. 'You're OK at maths but only OK, and you're much better at English, history and drama.'

I wheedled and pleaded but Dad was convinced he was right. Basher wouldn't take sides – after all, he had only known me three minutes – and eventually I weakened and arts it was. No science, no physics, biology or chemistry, ever. And of all the things I am grateful to my dad for, that was the best decision my father ever made on my behalf in my whole life. I would have hated going down the science route. My maths got worse and worse and I only just scraped an O Level in it – by cheating (another day, another book). Whereas my love of the arts just grew and grew, all the way to university and beyond. Thanks, Dad. Perhaps it was the result of his leadership instincts having been honed during the war but he didn't hesitate for a second and he was absolutely right.

That first night in the new dormitory a lot of the boys cried after lights out. After all, we were all only thirteen and most of us had never been away from home before for any length of time. I'd only ever been away staying at Grandpa's or camping, but I was determined not to cry. I remember thinking if I cried it would mean that Dad and Mum had made a big mistake, so I mustn't. I was pretty homesick, though, and I wrote a letter home first thing in the morning about nothing in particular, mainly just gossip about some of the boys and the masters that I'd met so far. Dad sent me stamps in with my tuck parcels and that first term I wrote home almost every single day. The second term I wrote home six times and the third term just the once. Sounds cruel and unthinking, and it probably was, but I was pretty typical.

School was OK. The masters were very old-fashioned; they all wore gowns and I was caned a lot, but then I was used to that. The only thing that was odd was that the prefects were allowed to cane us as well. Strange as it may sound, being caned by an old gentleman was, at the time, completely normal ... but a thirteen-year-old being bent over and caned by a seventeen-year-old, now that was weird! I'm fairly sure it happened in every public school in the country at the time, but it's still weird.

Mum and Dad came up the first Sunday we were allowed out – or, to use the Latin language I loathed from the age of five, an 'exeat' – and we went out to tea and back in time for curfew. It was great to see them but already I felt I was growing just a little bit apart from them and I think they felt it too. It had always been the three of us, at home together, and now the routine was changed, the circle had been broken. I didn't realise it then but, apart from school holidays and the odd week here and there, I was never to live at home again.

This affected my relationships with my old friends as well as my family. When I did go back for the Christmas holidays, it was good to see some of my old mates from Scouts again, but I was a bit out of touch and I found over the next few years that I drifted apart from a lot of my old gang because I was away so much. Also, if you're at a boarding school, your holidays are always longer so everybody else would be back at school and I'd be Johnny No Mates for another week or two, just me, Mum and Dad, and my Dansette Major.

Music was becoming an increasingly important part of my life by now. I bought a mass of Elvis records, along with Cliff Richard and the Shadows. As most of the bands of the time were guitar-based, Dad bought me a little ukulele. I never really mastered the instrument, although I could twang out a mean 'My Bonnie Lies Over the Ocean', not exactly a rock classic but the first tune in the accompanying instruction book. However, although I wasn't very good at playing the ukulele I was great at posing with it. I used to secretly sing into the hall mirror, curling my lip, gyrating my hips and twanging away. Dad caught me once. I went bright red and he just went away, shaking his head.

The next big social craze that absolutely bewildered my father was the idea of DJs playing records in the dance halls. Until now, if you'd gone out to hear music you would go to a 'hop' in the local hall and there would be a band singing the pop tunes of the day (usually really badly). But the DJ was a brand-new phenomenon. Now a man at the front of the stage would play records on his giant Dansette Major, tell us what the records were called, and we'd all dance. Well, the girls would dance; us boys would all just line the wall. Mum and Dad had always gone every week to dance to a live band but the idea of paying good money to go and see someone play records that we probably had at home anyway made no sense to my father at all. He wasn't against it, just thought it was utterly ridiculous. He thought that a lot over the next few years. Parents all over the country did.

Then when the Beatles came along he was convinced I'd finally gone mad. My hair was long and he was forever telling me to get it cut. He and I were really growing poles apart. He didn't like the way I was turning out, or my music. I was not at all the Hooray Henry they'd been hoping for. Instead, as they saw it, I was a bit of a yob.

But I had become swept up in an unstoppable force. John, George, Paul and Ringo were huge. They conquered America and Beatlemania took over the world. In April 1964, I was proudly able to tell my father that they were in the US Billboard chart at numbers 1, 2, 3, 4, 5, 31, 41, 46, 58, 65, 68 and 79. They were also number one and two in the album charts. Quite simply at that moment they were the most popular four people on the planet and even Dad had to begrudgingly admit 'they're actually not too bad'.

Of course the worst thing any parent could have said was that they quite liked the Beatles. I immediately switched over to the Rolling Stones. The whole point was that you didn't want your parents to like what you liked: I think it took Dad's generation a long time to understand that. Anyway the Stones were perfect. They were ugly, didn't look like they washed much, behaved appallingly and got arrested a lot. Dad absolutely hated Mick Jagger, who wore girly smocks and had shoulder-length hair. 'Big pouting cissy,' Dad called him. To Dad he was the anti-Christ.

He believed men should look and behave like men. Never look at yourself in a mirror or a shop window and don't ever, ever use a comb in public. This must have been a hangover from his days in the army, when it was all about short back and sides haircuts, washing and shaving every morning and above all carrying yourself at all times like a man. For someone who had been through a war, the Stones represented the worst sort of louche hedonism.

Back at King's School, Worcester, I continued to disappoint. I joined the school cadet force but to Major Tarrant's understandable shame, I was absolutely hopeless. I hated all the marching up and down, being shouted at by the sergeant major. I was always losing my cap or one of my boots. I even managed to lose my gun once when we were out on field day. Dad came to see me once just as I was coming out of Saturday morning cadet force – my least favourite two hours of every week – and he was absolutely horrified. Far from being the smart, upright soldier that he'd been so proud to be, I looked like I'd crawled out of a hole in a hedge. I'd lost my cap – yet again – and my belt, my boots weren't shiny and, worst of all, I'd cut my own hair. Well, actually, my mate Neil McLauchlan had, with a pair of nail scissors. I thought it looked pretty cool, but Dad thought I looked like a mad monk.

We chatted for a while and then he drove home. He must have been in despair. What with my overall shabby appearance, my crazy haircut and my Rolling Stones albums, he must have wondered why he'd bothered to send me away to an expensive school. I think most of the parents in the country were going through the same sort of problems with their children but, nevertheless, Dad was disappointed. The one time he actually got angry was after my mock O Levels. I did really badly and in my end-of-term report the teachers all said I wouldn't pass the exam.

One or two would have been bad enough, but they were unanimous. Dad hit the roof, told me I was lazy and that I was wasting my time and his money. 'Don't worry, Dad,' I told him. 'These practice ones are pointless, I'll pass them in the summer.' And I did. All nine of them. After that, I think Dad let go of the reins a bit. Maybe he thought the four years at King's School for young gentlemen might have been worthwhile after all ... but he still hated Mick Jagger.

By the time I was eighteen, Dad had more or less stopped bothering me about my need for a haircut. I'd come through King's, Worcester without being expelled and had three good A Levels, so I was off to university in the autumn. Dad was really busy in those years; he'd been promoted to sales manager and was driving all over the country working long hours and grabbing a sandwich when he could. He was drinking quite a bit, too, which suited me because it meant he and I could go for a few beers once in a while. Although I still looked pretty bad, the mad monk's fringe had grown out and I think he realised that all across the country kids were behaving pretty badly and, by comparison, I wasn't as wild as some. I didn't steal and never did drugs, so that was a compensation. I was chronically untidy, which I still am – I think it's a direct reaction to Mum's obsessive tidiness – but I did a string of casual jobs to help pay for university and he and I got on more like a couple of mates, rather than man and boy. Maybe he could see I was growing up at last, starting to take some responsibility. Certainly we began to become closer again after the distance that had grown between us while I was away at boarding school.

This new work ethic meant I took on some truly dreadful jobs. I dug holes; I laid bricks; I picked apples; I was a barman; I was a security guard; I worked from 6 a.m. every day for a while on a conveyor belt. I have never been so bored in all my life. I was even a lorry driver, which I loved. For years afterwards, I thought if I don't get a job I like, I'll be a lorry driver.

But I couldn't take a big artic out at weekends and I badly needed to get a car of my own. I was working hard but putting a lot aside for university and there wasn't much left. I didn't like to, but I asked Dad for help and he had what I thought was a good idea. 'I'll go halves,' he said. 'You save up half and I'll give you the other half of whatever you need.'

'Great!' I said. 'Can I have an E-type Jaguar?'

''Course you can,' he said, 'but you've got to find the other half.'

'Hmmm, OK then,' I said, 'I'll find something a bit cheaper.'

And so it was that about four weeks later, after a lot of extra shifts, I became the proud owner of a green Standard van. Dad stumped up half, good as gold, and it's something I've done with my own kids ever since – I'll pay for half of their first car but they have had to find the rest. Dad never wanted me to get something for nothing; he was a firm believer that you had to pay your way in life.

I was at the University of Birmingham reading English Literature for three wonderful years. I loved the place, loved the freedom, drank excessively and had a string of disastrous love affairs. We were always going to parties, not because we were part of any social elite, but because in those days everybody just gatecrashed. Somehow the word would get out that there was a party tonight at such an address and you just turned up with a seven-pint pipkin of Watneys Red Barrel, said, 'Hi, I'm a mate of Dave's,' and you generally got in. The parties themselves were usually dreadful. The idea was you would get drunk and pull girls … mainly I just got drunk. Dad thought I was clearly a very popular student always being invited to parties; I hadn't the heart to tell him I just gatecrashed.

I also didn't tell him that I topped up my grant by betting on the horses, which I became very good at. Unbeknown to my father, each term I put half my grant aside for living on and invested the other half in the Selly Oak bookies. I really made a study of it. If I'd done a degree in horse racing, rather than English Literature, I'd have got a first. Out of the nine terms I was at university I was well ahead in seven of them.

Years later I was trying to explain my years following horse racing to my dad and he said, 'You never told me about any of that.'

'Well, what would you have said?' I asked him.

'I'd have been bloody furious!' said Dad.

'Well, that's why I didn't tell you,' I replied and he laughed. What else can a dad do at these times? In any case I was too big for a damn good hiding, I had been for years. By the time I went to university I was six foot two and Dad was still five foot eleven and a half, and carrying a bit of weight from expense-account living.

And then, halfway through my second year, I got a call from one of Mum's neighbours. 'Chris, can you come home? Your dad's very ill.' They wouldn't tell me any more details and I raced down from Birmingham to Reading, fearing the worst. When I got home there were cars in the drive and there seemed to be a lot of people I didn't know indoors. Mum's face was red with tears but, as always at these times, she was icy calm.

'He's had a heart attack,' she told me. 'You can go in and see him but he won't recognise you.' I hugged her and went into the bedroom. There were nurses by the bed who let me through and I saw Dad lying unconscious on his pillow. He looked horribly white but he was still breathing. It was the first time I'd ever seen my strong father not in control. He looked helpless. I held his hand and mumbled something to a doctor. 'The next few hours are vital,' he told me. 'They often have a second attack, quite soon after the first.' I couldn't bear it. I had to get out of that room, I felt sick and panicky. I ran into the garden, streaming tears. 'Please God, he can't die,' I said over and again, 'please don't die, Dad, I love you so much,' and I beat my fists into a tree till they bled.

We hardly slept at all that night. Mum and I were both very frightened and feeling terribly alone, although the house was full of people. We felt lost without the man we both loved. I hadn't even had a significant final conversation with him. But we must have dozed off sometime around dawn, because the next thing I knew there was daylight coming through the curtains and a nurse was gently shaking us. 'He's awake,' she said, 'and asking for you.' I started crying all over again and remember rushing to the bathroom to wash my face. He wouldn't approve of my tears. When I went into his room he sounded very hoarse, but had some colour back in his cheeks. He was holding Mum's hand and gave us a weak smile. 'Sorry about that,' he said.

Dad was in bed for six weeks. I stayed at home with him most of the time. He was getting stronger gradually and started muttering about 'all this fuss' and needing to get back to work. He made light of how close to death he'd been. After all, he'd been there before in Germany in 1945. We hadn't had any idea that he'd had a heart condition – it had come completely out of the blue – but from that point onwards Mum always insisted that it must have come from being blown up in the war, and I think she was very probably right. Either way, he'd had another lucky escape. It was a warning and something must have sunk in because he completely changed his lifestyle from then on – he never smoked a cigarette again, he gave up beer and spirits altogether and only drank white wine for the rest of his life. He ate more healthily, lost a couple of stone and, within months, looked fitter and sharper than he had for years. It had been a warning.

CHAPTER SEVENTEEN

'I Am the Face of the Seventies!'

Back in Birmingham I had a degree to finish and my finals to get through. We then went through a nonsensical graduation ceremony, with all of us long-haired oiks somehow squeezed into mortarboards and gowns, then all 2,000 of us queuing up the stairs to meet the wonderful, but very ancient, W. H. Auden, shaking every single one of our hands with his bony fingers and saying the three magical words, 'I admit you.' It was pure slapstick and we all headed straight for the bar afterwards in our mortarboards. I found out later from Mum that Dad was deeply hurt that I hadn't invited either of them to the graduation ceremony. I feel ashamed now but I honestly hadn't realised that it mattered to them. I was twenty years old, selfish and thoughtless.

After I'd got my degree, I was in no great hurry to get a job – mainly because I didn't have the foggiest idea of what I wanted to do. In some ways I still don't; I just drifted into something forty years ago and I'm still doing it.

I have to say there was no immediate stampede by employers to get first use of my great knowledge of Shakespeare's sonnets, and the *Duchess of Malfi* – in fact there was a distinct lack of interest. I kept working at various jobs, though, because I needed some money to run my van and pay off my large overdraft. The betting on the horses had had to take a back seat while I was frantically revising for my finals and I owed the bank rather a lot. I never told Dad about my overdraft, but then I never told him about a lot of things that happened while I was at university, like getting into fights, becoming involved in disastrous relationships, being thrown out of my hall of residence, living in my van or spending two nights in a Spanish prison! I didn't want to anger him or worry Mum, as she was always worrying anyway. Over the years that followed I told him everything but, by then, it was old news and he'd just smile with a look of feigned despair. I think not telling him at the time was the kindest way, though it was also the coward's way.

During this period Dad and I spent a lot of time fishing together. I've fished all my life, thanks to my grandad and, to a lesser extent in the early days, my dad, although I have to rather ungratefully say their tuition was pretty basic and by the age of nine or ten, in terms of knowledge and skill, I'd outgrown the pair of them. Dad was keen but he was never that keen. However, it was a great way for us just to be together, often with no one else around for miles. When I was very young he used to push me to the river on my Gresham Flyer and, once in a while, if we caught some pike, we'd bring them back tied to my crossbar – poor things. Mum would try to cook them and make them appetising but they usually ended up feeding next-door's cat.

As I got older, after I'd left university, we used to fish together a lot. I used to love just being out with him one to one; he'd talk about my work and his work, whatever Grandpa was up to, whatever Mum was worried about, anything he was concerned about. He'd quiz me about the state of my finances and I had to be really honest with him, not try to fob him off. He'd always end up offering to bale me out and I'd always refuse. I think we were as proud and stubborn as each other. He'd be nosy about my love life and as we both got older the language would get more adult. I would never have dared swear in front of my father at sixteen, but by about twenty 'bloody' and 'sod' were acceptable, and by about twenty-five the 'f-word' was in common parlance between us – but interestingly never, ever in front of Mum. I'm not even sure she knew the word.

These fishing trips with Dad were some of my favourite times with him. He used to get up at the crack of dawn with the aim of catching some really big fish. But he had no idea of stealth at all – he would stand up on the bank in a bright white shirt and wonder why all the fish had disappeared, or clump about noisily in a boat and loudly bash his old pipe out on the side of it, frightening everything beneath the surface for miles. For an intelligent man it was strange that he just refused to accept that fish respond to noise. No, Dad wouldn't have any of it – so crash, crash, crash he'd go, before he chucked out his bait and lit his pipe. He only ever smoked his pipe when he was fishing. He once told me that Stanley had bought him his first pipe when he was about fourteen and Dad, feeling very grown up, lit up very publicly in his local snooker hall, had a couple of puffs, as if he had been smoking it for years, and was then violently sick.

But if he had eventually mastered the complexities of pipe smoking, he hadn't really acquired a lot of technique with his fishing. Once we were fishing on the little River Loddon in Berkshire on a cold winter's day – gloves, woolly hats, heavy coats, the lot – he cast out and then became convulsed with laughter, literally rolling about on the muddy bank and howling uncontrollably. It must have been cold because I didn't feel a thing but, somehow, he'd accidentally managed to hook the pompom on my woolly hat and cast it all the way across the river. Of course, when he wound it back, it was absolutely soaked and useless to my freezing head for the rest of the day.

On another occasion a few years later, unbeknown to me at the end of a long day's fishing, he sneaked a herring into my fishing bag. The weather was hot and I was busy in London, so I drove around with my car getting increasingly smelly for about a fortnight until eventually I opened the boot and my fishing bag almost crawled out on its own. The herring was rancid and the smell gut-wrenching. Yes, thank you, Dad, very funny! When I rang him to tell him what I thought of him there was no hint of apology, just great gasps of laughter coming from the other end.

I can recall many other such stories about my dad's warped sense of humour. I once called his name in the boat and, without meaning to, he just turned and accidentally threw a whole bucket of soaked bread and maggots all over me that he was just about to throw into the river by his float. Again, howls of laughter. When I was about fifteen I hooked what was clearly at that time the biggest pike I'd ever seen. It fought hard for ages but when it finally started to tire and its great body came across the surface of the lake towards me, he somehow managed to reach out with my landing net ... and poke it off! At least this time he didn't howl with laughter, he just said, 'Sorry, Chris, I think that was quite big.'

As well as fishing, we used to attempt other father-and-son bonding activities, though we were never very good at them. During the fallow period after university I used to help Dad with jobs around the house and in the garden – God knows why we even tried because we were both absolutely hopeless. We were the

Chuckle Brothers of DIY, bungling and bodging our way through what to anyone else would be the simplest task, interspersed with numerous tea breaks.

Unhappily, the sheer frustration at our incompetence would send my normally very easy-going father into the most dreadful rages. It was the one thing that really wound him up. I think some of it would have been the frustration and helplessness caused by the damage to his right arm; I of course had no such excuse, I was just bloody useless. We once spent hours making a wall outside the house but I think we put in too much sand and not enough cement so when we were nearly finished the whole thing just fell apart. At this point Mum appeared with two cups of hot chocolate and my father, apoplectic about the collapse of our whole morning's work, shouted, 'Hot chocolate? I hate bloody hot chocolate!' and hurled the cups at the side of the house, smashing them both to pieces. Mum got the drift that tea might have been a better bet and quietly scuttled off. A few calming minutes later, Dad picked up all the broken china and crept into the house to apologise. He never stayed in a bad temper for long but any sort of DIY brought out the beast in him.

Eventually, in a moment of madness, I briefly decided that perhaps I should follow my father into sales and marketing. I got myself a suit – no rubbish, eighteen quid – got my hair tidied up a bit and went for a series of interviews with people like Olivetti, Unilever and Marks and Spencer. Dad used to ask me how each interview went. 'Pretty good,' I would tell him, 'they seemed fascinated!' I think they were, but in a kind of 'what on earth is it?' way. I began to accumulate several very polite letters saying, 'We have no immediate vacancy but we will of course keep you on file.' Trust me, the file is the waste bin. I never heard from any of them again.

After rather a lot of these, my father sat me down one evening and said that he knew a lot of people in marketing and could make a few calls and get me a job. It was a genuine offer, but I thanked him and turned him down. I think he was quite affronted but I didn't want to get a job like that, I had to make it on my own. I really wanted to somehow stand on my own two feet, and I secretly dreaded the thought that if I was working for one of Dad's closest mates, I just might let myself and therefore my dad down. So I carried on for a while, working as a petrol-pump attendant, labouring and even working in the bedding department at Bentalls.

Then, over a chance conversation in the pub, a mate of mine told me that, as a graduate, there was decent money to be made as a supply teacher. The basic wage was high because they sent you round the toughest schools in London, and then you got more on top of that for having a degree. Dad thought it was great – at last my great knowledge of English literature was to be put to full use. Within only a few years I could be a housemaster, then headmaster, then who knows? Minister of Education?

It didn't quite work out like that. My first posting was at an all-boys' school in New Cross in south London, and I was to get the fourteen-year-old bottom stream. They were a very mixed bunch, some of them very large, and there were a huge range of nationalities – West Indians, Turks, Greeks, Indians and a smattering of Irish and English. There were forty-two in my class, and at least two towered over me. I probably wouldn't be doing much *Duchess of Malfi* then.

I just about controlled my class most days, but I taught them very little and only very basic stuff. I hated it. Many of them truanted and even though the masters knew exactly where they were, it would be madness to try to get them back. The system had failed these kids totally. It was a shambles. But Mum and Dad seemed proud of me and kept talking about me having a proper job at last. Bearing in mind that Dad had been off in France fighting a war when he was this age, I think he was just relieved that I wasn't drifting around aimlessly any more.

I lasted one whole year. Never mind being moved round from one rough school to the next, things were so bad in my school I wasn't moved for twelve whole months. Then, yet another chance conversation in yet another pub – this time the Pineapple in Vauxhall – revealed that there were vacancies at the Central Office of Information, in their television department, writing scripts for government films. I got the job and we made films to show everybody all around the world how jolly clever and nice we British were.

I had three blissful years. Dad was a bit unimpressed, I think partly because he couldn't see any of my work on the telly. Well, not unless he moved to British Honduras or Sierra Leone. Mainly, though, I think he didn't really see the point of the whole department, particularly as it was funded by the taxpayer, and with hindsight nor can I. However, we had a very nice time and I learned how to research items, do interviews, write scripts, edit, even direct. I travelled all over the place. I was sent out to Trinidad for two months, filming their carnival. I even got to sign the Official Secrets Act although I didn't actually know anything.

Then, one day, we were filming at a big agricultural show somewhere in Hampshire and I began idly watching a bloke who was the reporter for the local TV news station. He did a couple of pieces to camera, basically saying where he was and why there were cows all around him and finished with an interview with a farmer who specialised in pedigree Aberdeen Anguses. I watched him say goodnight to the studio and then drive off in a very nice car, and I thought, 'Well, that's not much of a job!' And, don't tell anyone, but of course it isn't, and I would soon be doing 'not much of a job' myself and have been ever since.

That night I sat down at Dad's old typewriter and wrote a letter to every television station in Britain. I still cringe when I think about some of the wording but it included the immortal phrase: 'I am the face of the seventies, this is your last chance to snap me up!'

Understandably I had doubts about my strategy and I showed Dad before I sent it off. He read it without emotion and then turned and said, 'I'd give you an interview if I got that letter, just to see what sort of lunatic wrote it.' He was wrong, but he was also a little bit right. The vast majority of the TV stations I wrote to sent me the 'no particular vacancy at the moment' reply, but two of them, ATV and Yorkshire, asked me to come for an interview, just to see what sort of lunatic wrote it.

On went the suit again and I was off to Leeds and Birmingham. Even more amazingly, ATV offered me a job. I could join them for a week's trial on their nightly news programme, as soon as I was free. Free? I was doing nothing, just living in Dorset and fishing every day on the wonderful River Stour. They kept ringing and I kept procrastinating about 'finishing a script', but eventually I gave in and went off to seek my fortune in Birmingham. If you check my records, the fishing season finishes on 14 March ... and I started with ATV on 15 March. Well, there's a coincidence.

Dad thought my new job as a news reporter might just be a good move, and this was reinforced when other family members started ringing Mum and Dad and excitedly telling them they'd 'seen Chris on the telly'. I was on every night, six till six-thirty. I'd started off doing the heavyweight news stories with MPs and shop stewards, at which I was absolutely hopeless, so they'd given me the lighter '... and finally' sort of items, which I absolutely loved but didn't have much gravitas. I may have omitted to tell my parents that. One night, unbeknown to me, my parents booked themselves into a hotel in Woodstock so that they could watch their young, thrusting, investigative reporter son in action. Unfortunately that night I was interviewing a man walking sixteen miles from Worcester to Evesham with four live ferrets down his underpants. 'Oh well,' said Dad, 'you can always go back to teaching.'

And then ATV asked me to present a new Saturday morning children's show – three hours live each week for an extra twenty-five quid. Yes please! It was called *TISWAS* and it changed my life – took it over, in fact – for the next eight years. It was a huge success. Of all the things I've done, it's still the thing I get asked about more than anything else since. It was supposedly for children but the antics of myself, Sally James, Lenny Henry, Spit the Dog & co also achieved cult status with every student in Britain. Dad didn't see it for a long time because it was originally only screened in the Midlands, but he came to watch it being filmed one weekend and said to me and Sally after the show, 'Well, it's certainly different, in fact I've never seen anything like it. One bit was quite funny.'

One bit? *One* bit? We'd just done three hours. How dare he? I suppose Dad, by now in his late fifties, probably wasn't really our target audience, but he and Mum did eventually become fans of a sort, and were regulars in the studio.

Then something else happened. I had a baby. Well, not me personally, but by now I was married and my wife produced the most beautiful, healthy daughter, Helen, followed a couple of years later by Jennifer. Basil was now a grandad and, after a lot of protestations early on about 'not being very fussed about babies', he became absolutely besotted with them. He and Mum were the most amazing grandparents, planning weekends with the girls, taking them to all sorts of wonderful places and spoiling them rotten. As my family got larger and larger, over the next few years, the tough ex-soldier Basil became an absolute softie, brilliant with all the kids and showing boundless energy for playing with them.

One thing he would always do was put on silly hats for them – the hats weren't silly in themselves, they just were when he wore them. Although Dad was a fairly well-built man, he must have had a tiny head because he just couldn't wear a hat. Any hat he ever put on just slipped down over his ears and looked ridiculous. Naturally, he would do it on purpose for the grandkids. I would often hear him and the kids howling with laughter, a joyous sound. Mum was always saying that he did too much, that he'd get exhausted. She was always worried about his heart, but he was as fit as a butcher's dog. I remember several years later looking out the window into the garden and he was playing on the climbing frame with Toby and Sammy, my two youngest. To my horror, he was dangling from the top of the frame, upside down, by his ankles, like a demented bat.

I knocked on the window and shouted out to him, like you would to a naughty child: 'Father, get down off that climbing frame!'

'Why should I?' he said, still upside down.

'Because you're seventy-nine years old!'

Helen, my oldest, always says that the first word she thinks of when she thinks about her grandfather is 'mischievous'. Basil was always the chief instigator and my children were willing followers. Mum told them that knickers was a very rude word, so Dad would suddenly shout out 'the other word of pants!' to shock, and they would gleefully spank the living daylights out of him. He was always up for a bit of silly play-acting. My daughters used to play 'restaurants' and Basil would pretend to be a troublesome customer, knocking over plates and tables with his 'broken leg', so that they were delighted to kick him out of their café. There was much singing, too, with Basil doing the harmony, but his choice of songs weren't your standard nursery rhymes. My daughter is currently teaching 'Horsey lift your tail up and let's see you poo' to Daisy, who would be his great-granddaughter. It's clearly a song that needs to be passed down through the generations like a family heirloom.

Even though he was from the 'stiff upper lip' generation, there was always deep affection and kindness. It may not have been communicated in words or touch, but my children knew he was desperately devoted to them. There was nothing he wouldn't do for them. Maybe because he was actually a big kid himself. My daughter says she has many memories of him laughing until the tears came streaming down his face.

His energy was extraordinary, too. He and Mum lived in a sort of ranch-style house with the kitchen and lounge upstairs, so whenever he came into the house, we'd hear his key in the lock and then he'd run up the stairs. Always. Mum was constantly telling him to slow down but of course he wouldn't. He was inexhaustible, still bounding up the stairs until well into his eighties.

Once the grandchildren arrived, he'd often make a weekend of it with us. He'd come to see us after *TISWAS* and then stay with us in our house in Warwickshire and play with the grandkids. They were wonderful days: my career was going well, and I was now producing *TISWAS* as well as presenting it. The show had brought national fame to all of us and meanwhile Dad had been appointed to the board of Huntley, Boorne and Stevens so he was also enjoying his own success.

TISWAS was great fun, but Dad was still worried that the bubble might burst and then what would I do? It is the constant fear of our industry, everyone's 'fully booked till tomorrow', but in myself

I wasn't particularly concerned. I was young and had two kids, but I was confident the money would keep coming in. I was more worried about being typecast – I didn't really want to spend the rest of my life rolling about in custard and I didn't want to be seen only as a children's entertainer. Nor did Lenny and the others, so we decided it was time to move on.

In 1982, we were commissioned to do thirteen adult versions of *TISWAS*, to go out late and live on a Saturday night. It was called *OTT* for 'Over The Top' and the controller said to me, 'I want you to really shake people up, but just don't get me arrested.' We were briefed to shock, and we certainly did. It got huge ratings but, for the first time, we were roasted in the national press. There were repeated cries for the show to be axed. I had become the anti-Christ and for my parents it was obviously a really tough time. They hated reading the vicious headlines slagging me off each week; they'd never had to experience anything like it before. Neighbours who'd been only too pleased, until now, to come up to my parents and revel in how well I was doing, suddenly started to look away, embarrassed. But Mum and Dad were amazing. Dad almost thrived on the criticism. 'Stuff 'em!' was his attitude: 'You'll come through all this.' Both he and Mum remained very strong. Underneath though, they must have been very worried – their son's career could be going down the pan.

It didn't help that in the middle of all this I got divorced. It was my own fault – I'd been busier and busier since the heyday of *TISWAS* and was never home. It hurt like hell but Dad was like a rock. He chatted to me for hours when I was low, tried everything he could to help salvage the marriage and, when it was clearly irreconcilable, made absolutely certain that the kids saw all of us as much as ever before. He and Mum helped me look after the girls every weekend. Thankfully, work kept coming in. I was offered a series at the BBC with Mike Harding and did a spell at *TV-am* with Greg Dyke, probably the best producer I ever worked for.

Then, out of the blue, I got a call from a radio station in London called Capital Radio. I wasn't very keen at first – I didn't know anything about radio and Dad thought it would be a step backwards career-wise. 'You're a TV man,' he reckoned. I agreed but thought that people like Wogan, Everett and Aspel managed to do both and maybe it would be handy to fall back on, if things on the TV front went a bit thin.

So I went along to do a pilot for Capital – I just turned up really with a bag of Rolling Stones and Pink Floyd albums, and wittered into a microphone for three hours. I absolutely loved it. It was empowering. I adored the immediacy of it, the freedom and the fact I could play the music I loved ... and I've been wittering into a microphone ever since.

I did the Capital Radio breakfast show for the next seventeen years, and Dad seemed to listen every morning. OK, I'm pretty sure he didn't listen right from the 6 a.m. start, but I think he listened for an hour or so every day before he went to work. Mum said the sound of the Capital breakfast show turned up loud even replaced his warbling 'Love Is a Many Splendored Thing' in the bathroom.

Occasionally I'd get a phone call while I was on air, referring to something I'd said, and my producer would say, 'Bloke on line three, says he's your dad, but I think he's a nutter ...'

'No,' I'd say. 'That'll be Dad!'

CHAPTER EIGHTEEN

Dad Makes a Memorable Entrance

A t the age of sixty, Dad had the option to retire or to continue working for another five years. He was earning a good amount of money by then, with directors' bonuses, and the company really wanted him to stay on. So, after long discussions with Mum, he carried on till he was sixty-five. When he was approaching that milestone, in the weeks leading up to his final days at work, several of his mates quietly confided in me that I should keep an eye on him. A lot of people, they told me, go downhill fast after retirement. When they've been as manically active for as long as Dad had, suddenly having no work to do can have a big effect on their mental and physical health.

I was quietly worried, but I needn't have been. He absolutely loved it. Now he had so much more time on his hands to be a husband and grandfather. He and Mum had lunches and dinners with friends they hadn't seen for ages, and they spent a lot of time in Devon with no great urgency to come back. 'I don't know why I ever did those extra five years,' he told me, 'I'm loving this.' And he clearly was. The one great shame I always thought was that Mum still just wouldn't fly, so they couldn't travel and see the world. He did get Mum on a ferry a few times to Belgium, Holland and France, revisiting his war days, but that was as far as they ever got.

He was as fit as a fiddle though, and really enjoying life – still walking miles and always running up the stairs. He spent a lot of time on the Thames in his best friend Pomeroy's motorboat. Mum even took to driving it and amazingly was really good. This elderly lady, who'd never even sat in the driving seat of a car, took to chugging up and down the Thames and expertly mooring up in the locks as if to the manner born.

Dad and I continued to go fishing year after year, because I loved his company and there were always ridiculous tales to tell when we got back. Once, when he was in his eighties, I got permission to fish a very exclusive bit of the River Test in Hampshire. On arrival I asked the gamekeeper, who ran the estate, where would be easy for Dad to get to and give him a chance of a few fish. 'Well,' he said, 'the bit in front of the old mill is good at this time of the year and it's not much of a walk for him. But first he can have a go in the One-Cast Pool. Only one cast, mind!' It was called the One-Cast Pool because it was a breeding pen stuffed full of trout laying their eggs before they were put into the main river.

So, thanking him profusely, I showed Dad where to start and told him just to have the one cast and then to join me on the lawn in front of the old mill. I went off downstream, caught a few fish but, after perhaps three-quarters of an hour, there was still no sign of Dad. I got a bit edgy – perhaps I shouldn't have left him, maybe he'd had a heart attack, maybe he'd fallen into the powerful current in the Test or got trapped in the weeds. I walked back quickly, getting more and more concerned.

I needn't have worried. He was sitting by the One-Cast Pool with a huge grin on his face.

'This is great,' he told me. 'Absolutely brilliant.'

'How many have you caught?' I asked him.

'Forty-one,' he said.

It was about now that I was awarded the OBE, much to my parents' pride. My dad was thrilled for me even though with typical humour he always referred to the OBE as standing for 'Other Buggers' Efforts'. Of course I had to take my parents along to the presentation of the award at the Palace – going some way towards making up for not inviting them to my graduation ceremony, perhaps. Dad was very excited, teasing my daughters about how this would give him a chance to wear a really big hat.

Unfortunately Mum was ill on the day and unable to attend, but Dad and I got ourselves done up in our tailcoats and with two of the girls we had a splendid morning at Buckingham Palace. I met the Queen and the whole family thought it was wonderful. It was only on our way to the reception afterwards that Dad and I thought we ought to put our hats on to arrive looking elegant – we'd just carried them up to now – but I'd rather forgotten how ridiculous Dad looked with any form of hat. I don't know what size we'd ordered but it was huge: it literally went over his ears and as we pulled up to meet the guests everyone burst into hysterical laughter. The kids of course thought Grandpa had done it on purpose but I genuinely don't think he had. He just couldn't do hats.

All in all it was a terrific day, and I felt enormously happy to have been able to share it with my father. But as I carefully put away the OBE into my desk that night, I knew in my heart of hearts that it would never match up to my dad's MC.

Mum and Dad by now were spending more and more time with their growing army of grandchildren. By now I had four children of my own, three girls – Samantha, Helen and Jennifer – and a son, Toby. Plus two great stepkids, Fia and Dexter. My parents adored it. They loved having a couple of them to stay at a time, taking them to places like Windsor Safari Park and Legoland, with a detour to Toys R Us on the way home. They even used to take Sammy ice-skating. Mum used to just sit and watch with Toby, who was never keen, but Grandpa used to go with Sammy out on to the ice at the age of nearly eighty years old.

Then Stanley, my grandfather, died. Even though he was ninety-six it hit us all very hard. He had gone quietly into a coma from which we were told he would not emerge. I sat with him for hours, listening to his breathing and hoping for a miracle. We were so close and I was desperate to have the chance to have just one more conversation with him. Dad came to say his own farewell but, even though Stanley hung on for another week, Dad wouldn't return to see him one more time. He said, 'I'm not going back. I've said my goodbyes.' At the time I thought he was rather callous but I think now that Dad was hurting like mad but didn't want to show it. It had been his way since he came home from Germany.

A few weeks after Grandpa's funeral, Dad took Mum on the ferry across to Normandy and went to a huge war grave 'for the fallen'. He hadn't been there since June 1944 and this was nearly half a century later. Mum said Dad was for once very quiet, alone with his memories of friends who'd fallen during the first attack, fighting to capture that beachhead. There was row upon row of crosses to mark the graves of British and Canadian soldiers. Dad stood beside Mum for several minutes giving a long silent salute, then he broke away looking emotionally drained by his own thoughts. At last he just said, 'All so young, so young,' and walked slowly away. This is one of the things that struck me years later, reading the names and ages on hundreds of crosses in a war cemetery in Holland. It was full of row upon row of graves of those from the Wiltshire Regiment who'd died in the battle for Kleve. So many of them were just seventeen, eighteen or nineteen – finding a grave of anyone much over twenty was rare. Such a terrible waste.

By the time Toby was eight he'd been studying history at school and had learned for the first time about the Second World War. He started to ask questions like 'Were you in the war, Grandad?' I used to just quietly listen to these conversations, sometimes interjecting with, 'You never told me any of that!' 'No,' he said, 'you wouldn't have been interested.' Of course I would, but it was Dad's quiet way of saying that the matter was closed. He'd briefly opened the box, but it was now firmly shut again. It went on like that for several more years but then, five decades after D-Day, he started to open up more than ever before. He told me he'd been asked to do an interview about his war memories for the local paper ... and, amazingly, was actually considering it.

'Be very careful if you do,' I told him. 'Don't trust any of them.' I rang the newspaper office myself and gave the guy there a really hard time, telling him that they were not to make any reference to me apart from the fact that I was his son. I was determined that the article would be about Dad, not me, and that they had better be absolutely faithful to Dad's words. Poor bloke! I think he was terrified, but he was actually a decent chap. He kept absolutely to his word, sent a good journalist, and a couple of weeks later a really sensitive interview with Dad made the front page of the

Reading Evening Post, making Mum very proud. It has to be said, Dad gave them some pretty sketchy information. He glossed over things like receiving the Military Cross, but at least it was something. This, along with a more in-depth interview he gave for the regimental museum at Salisbury, also in May 2004, was the first detail he'd given to anyone in fifty years.

And then I did something that I have regretted and will regret for the rest of my life. I had set up my own production company and made a beautiful programme about polar bears, which I financed myself, and which eventually went out on ITV on Christmas Day. I also made some fishing films and a lot of radio shows. But then, around the time of his newspaper interview, Dad unexpectedly said to me, 'I've got an idea for your new company. You and I could go to Juno Beach and talk about D-Day and then the film could go out on 6 June, the fiftieth anniversary!'

'Great idea,' I said, 'but there's no way we can make it in time.' It was already May and even if we could make the film and edit it in four weeks the likelihood of ITV or anyone else commissioning it and scheduling it for a month's time was absolutely nil. Television schedules move at the speed of a racing slug and the chance of getting anything commissioned, even for two or three years ahead, is almost hopeless. Gently I explained to him it was just not possible.

Dad didn't really understand what I was trying to tell him nor did he seem particularly upset, but I'm sure now he will have been. It seemed that after keeping so much locked away for so long he had at last decided it would be therapeutic for him to open up. Also, after his own father had died, perhaps he was beginning to feel more vulnerable himself. Maybe he realised there were lots of things that happened in his war that should be recorded somewhere before it was too late.

It was such a big turn-around from how he'd steadfastly been for fifty years I think it caught me by surprise. But what a mindless idiot I was to turn him down. How stupid was I? Even if the film had never seen the light of day in public, I should have just seized the offer with both hands. My father was proposing, for the first and only time, to talk to me about D-Day, and I rejected it. Sometimes still in the small hours of the morning, my own thoughtlessness comes back to haunt me. How could I have turned my own heroic father down because I couldn't see beyond stupid TV scheduling? I will regret it bitterly forever.

Then we had another family shock. Early one morning the phone rang in the studio at Capital. It was Dad sounding close to tears. Apparently Mum had had a bad fall and he was holding her at the foot of the stairs, waiting for an ambulance. 'Chris, please get here,' he said, 'she's in so much pain.' Fearing the worst, I finished my radio show as fast as I could and raced to the Royal Berkshire Hospital in Reading. Mum was sitting up with Dad holding her hand. Her head was badly bruised and she'd broken her hip, but she was conscious and managed a weak smile. 'Your Dad's been very worried,' she said, 'it's a lot of fuss about nothing.' But she was clearly in a great deal of pain from her hip. Dad was sitting beside her bed, looking almost white, just stroking her hand. I stayed with them most of the day. Dad never moved from her side and eventually, when I had to leave, he stayed the night beside her. They were both in their early eighties by now, and they were clearly frightened but still devoted to each other. The next day I came back again, straight after my show. They'd been reassured by the doctors that there was no other damage done to Mum, apart from the broken hip, and Dad was a lot calmer.

The following day, at the Hilton Hotel in London, there was a tribute lunch being held for me. Mum and Dad were scheduled to be special guests and Dad was to be one of the speakers. Obviously I didn't think that would happen now, as Dad had to stay with Mum. 'Don't be silly, Baz,' said Mum, 'you should go.' Dad was torn and felt he should stay, and I thoroughly understood, but Mum insisted, 'No, you should go, you must go.' So I made arrangements for a car to pick Dad up from the hospital the next morning, take him back to their house to get a wash and a suit (he hadn't been home for two days) and then run him up to the Hilton. We moved him up the running order, so he could be first speaker, and then arranged to race him straight back to be with Mum at the hospital afterwards.

So the next day we all had a splendid lunch at the hotel. There were a lot of old mates and some real surprises for this so-called 'tribute' lunch – it was more of a 'roast' – and Dad arrived just in time to speak first. He set the tone brilliantly.

'Good afternoon,' he said. 'I am, for my sins, Christopher's father although, I'll be honest, I haven't been much of a father to him. I wasn't there at his birth' – and then, after a long pause, he added, with a twinkle – 'and do you know I'm still not sure I was there at his conception!' There was a great cheering roar from the audience and shouts of mock outrage from me, the supposed guest of 'honour'. In thirty seconds he had set the tone for the afternoon brilliantly. He was amazing and he went on to absolutely crucify me for the next ten minutes, portraying me as a complete waster and a total nightmare of a son. It was obviously done tongue-in-cheek – well, I *think* so – but he was magnificent. He finished to standing applause, gave me a huge hug, and was raced away in the waiting car back to Mother.

Greg Dyke, chairman of ITV then director general of the BBC and no mean speaker himself, was the next to stand up. 'When I saw that I was due to follow an eighty-year-old, I thought, "Well, that'll be easy,"' he said, 'but I got that wrong, didn't I? This is a poisoned chalice!'

It was a splendid afternoon, but it was Dad who had laid the whole foundation.

I suppose that *Who Wants to be a Millionaire?* was the first TV show that Dad could see me presenting that he might qualify as 'a proper job'. It nearly didn't happen at all. The BBC didn't want it and the then controller of ITV turned it down flat. I told Dad the idea, but he was pretty sure it would never happen and, to be honest, I was equally sceptical. Dad's honest opinion was that there was just too much money involved. Surely no company would risk giving away a million pounds, even if it was all supposedly going to be covered by the income from the phone lines? 'It's a nice idea but just too much,' he said.

Then out of the blue I had a call from David Briggs, my long-term producer at Capital Radio, telling me that there was a new controller at ITV called David Liddiment ... and he loved the idea! We did a couple of pilots and we were on every night from the beginning of September 1998. I had no clue as to just what a monster show it would become in all our lives, but I liked the idea of it and I liked the people I was working with – mostly guys like Briggsy and Paul Smith, boss of Celador who owned the show and a man I'd worked with several times before. I told Dad that it might run for two or even three years if we were lucky and I signed a good deal for a year. Dad agreed that with the back-up of the guaranteed money coming in from my Capital Radio contract, it was worth taking the gamble – there was nothing really to lose. Perhaps I wouldn't have to go back to teaching after all.

Dad was absolutely hooked on *Millionaire*, he just loved it.

This was real people playing for real money that could change their lives forever. Briggsy always used the phrase 'shout-ability' about good radio competitions that he dreamed up for me to do at Capital Radio, meaning people would sit in their cars or in their kitchens shouting at the radio. Well, his first venture into TV had the ultimate ingredients for shout-ability. People all over the country screamed at their screens and the catchphrases got immediately etched into British life: 'Go fifty-fifty' or 'ask the audience' were used everywhere – courts of law, in parliament, even in the American senate, and I've had 'Hey Chris, wanna phone a friend?' shouted at me out of car windows virtually every single day for fifteen years. The audience figures were enormous. Alan Yentob, the controller of the BBC, famously said, 'Who Wants to be a Millionaire? went through the BBC's audience figures like an Exocet missile.'

Dad was wonderfully proud of its success. He and Mum came to a few of the shows at Elstree Film Studios and were treated like royalty. They loved it although Dad was very scathing about some of the contestants. 'That bloke last night,' he'd say to me, 'how could he not know that? What a thicko.' But he couldn't have been more complimentary about the show. He was really thrilled with my involvement on it. 'Best thing you've ever done,' he'd say. 'I love it.'

The only time I think he and Mum weren't that keen was when I was offered the chance to go and do the show in America and Australia. It was very flattering but, from the start, I just wasn't interested in working in America. I'd always found American media types to be manic, panicky and hugely insincere. I'd been very lucky in the UK, as I've always worked with people I respected and who became close mates. I was pretty sure I'd never have found that in America. Also my three youngest kids were still so little; Toby was only six, Sammy and Fia nine and ten, and I really didn't want them growing up in New York. ABC were persistent for a while but it was never going to happen and I've never regretted it for a second.

The one I really fancied, and the one that disturbed Dad, was the Australian version. I love the country and its people and doing TV down there in between series here in the UK really appealed, especially when the weather here got bad in the winter months. ITV had no problem with it, as long as I was available in the UK when required, but the real stumbling block was my contract with Capital Radio. The management and sponsors were very good about most things, but eight weeks off the show, which was what the Australians wanted, was just too long. I understood but was really fed up about it for days. Dad, on the other hand, was delighted – he was always wonderfully supportive but he worried about me being that far away if anything happened to Mum. Interesting it was always about Mum: he never mentioned himself, even though he had just turned eighty. He just assumed and I think we took for granted that he would go on forever. Also, if I did go to Oz, I think he had fears of me liking it so much there that I might eventually disappear to the other side of the world for good, taking their grandkids with me. And of course they would never be able to visit because Mum wouldn't fly.

Anyway it never happened. I carried on pretty happily juggling *Who Wants to be a Millionaire?* most nights and the Capital Radio breakfast show early every morning in London. I was to live like that for years. We received every accolade going. Every year at the National Television Awards at the Royal Albert Hall we won Best Light Entertainment Show or Best Game Show. We won it year after year. I loved it. I always bounded on to the stage like a demented puppy, made a suitably grateful speech, raced through the obligatory press interviews and then grabbed my shiny silver award and made for the bar and the after-show party.

It was always a challenge presenting the radio breakfast show the morning after the awards – the usual routine was to leave the Royal Albert Hall about 2 a.m. and be back on the radio at 6 a.m. Every year I was a little delicate to say the least. 'You sounded pissed,' Dad would say on the phone mid-morning. 'I was!' I'd tell him. One year my 5 a.m. alarm rang and beside my bed was, yet again, another big shiny television award. It was only when my eyes were focusing a little later in the car going in to Capital Radio that I read the inscription – 'Best Dramatic Actor: John Thaw'. Somewhere across London, a little later in the morning, John Thaw woke up to find that he was 'Best Game Show Host'.

Then, one year, I went through the usual routine – got on the dickie bow, won the award, made the speech, met the press as briefly as possible – but instead of hitting the bar it was impressed upon me that I had to go back and sit in my seat again till the end. 'We're doing a montage at the close of the show of all tonight's winners to be run just before the end credits,' I was told. Fair enough, I thought, so I went back to applaud the winners in the other categories. Then Sir Trevor McDonald announced, 'There is one final award tonight ...' and he started to read out a citation about some chap who'd started his career in the Midlands, then went into children's television ... This sounds ridiculous but I really do remember sitting there, thinking, 'Blimey, this bloke's career started off the same way as mine!' It was only when Sir Trevor started talking about *TISWAS* that the penny dropped. The special Lifetime Achievement Award was being presented to me.

The rest is just a blur. *TISWAS*, *TV-am*, Capital Radio, *Tarrant* on *TV* and of course *Who Wants to be a Millionaire?* – he went through the lot, although I was barely taking any of it in. I just remember thinking, 'It just doesn't get better than this.' ... But it did.

To the applause of the whole of the Royal Albert Hall, the public, my mates on *Millionaire* and a lot of my peers, great broadcasters and performers I'd respected all of my life, I went up on to the stage and mumbled some very emotional words of gratitude. But then Sir Trev said, 'And there's one final surprise for you tonight, one more person who'd like to thank you in his very special way,' and to my amazement on came the Phantom Flan Flinger – the masked man from *TISWAS*, the blackest fiend in the cosmos. He menaced me with the custard pie in his hand, but it seemed pretty obvious that he didn't mean to use it. But who was he? It was obviously someone I knew, but who? I could see it wasn't the original phantom, unless he'd lost a lot of weight and grown several inches. He was tall, but not tall enough to be Lenny Henry. It wasn't Sally James, for obvious reasons. I stared through the mask at his eyes. I knew them, but who on earth ...? Then, in front of the audience in the hall, and right across the country in people's living rooms, he removed the mask ... and it was Dad!

Unbelievable. I'd even spoken to him that morning at home with Mum and he'd wished me luck for that night. 'We'll be watching,' he'd said. What I didn't know was that, even then, there was an LWT car outside their house in Woodley waiting to whisk him to rehearsals and a fitting for his black outfit. 'Dad!' was all I could say, 'Dad, it's you!' 'Hallo, son,' he said, milking every second of it. Then I grabbed him in a huge bear hug and we both turned, tears streaming, to take the applause. The whole place, even right up at the top beyond the chandeliers, came to their feet and cheered wildly. I've never felt so emotionally drained as that moment. I had no idea, not a clue that any of it had been planned, but what a moment for us – me and my dear Dad – as we looked right up to the private boxes right up in the gods, acknowledging their applause. I thought, 'Now it really doesn't get better than this!'

And I don't think it ever did.

CHAPTER NINETEEN

I Love You

I think that night at the Royal Albert Hall I felt more love for my father than I've ever felt for anyone else in my life. I told him afterwards, 'I love you, Dad,' and gave him a big hug. 'I love you too, mate,' he replied. It was a natural reaction after such a night but I realised afterwards that, although there was an understanding between us, this was the first time either of us had ever used those words out loud to each other. I said it a few more times over the years to him and to Mum, and they started to say it too. It seems really weird now – after all, my kids and I say it to each other every time we speak – but my parents' generation were just not brought up to say it. I don't think I ever heard Dad say 'I love you' to his own father, or Stanley to him, it just wouldn't have happened. It was the same with crying – I think I only saw my father cry once in his life. It's all another aspect of the British stiff upper lip that stopped people like Dad from talking about his experiences in the war.

I was at home when I got the call. It was 2002, a couple of years after the Lifetime Achievement Award. On the phone was an old friend of the family. She said, 'Your Dad's fallen down at a wedding reception.'

'Oh God!' I said, laughing uneasily because something in her voice suggested it wasn't a laughing matter.

'No,' she said, 'it wasn't that, he only had a couple of glasses of wine. He just fell down but then, within seconds, was up again. He's a bit embarrassed really, and he seems fine, but I think you should get the doctor.'

'Thanks,' I said, knowing that short of taking him along at gunpoint there was no way the stubborn sod would go. I rang him at home that evening, chatting about how the kids were and nothing in particular, and asked him casually how the wedding went.

'It was all right,' he said, 'but I fell over.'

We went through the obvious 'pissed again?' banter and then he said, to my amazement, 'I'm going to see the doctor, get it checked out.'

I was delighted. Clearly even Dad realised it was a bit unusual. Also, although he was well into his eighties, he was still driving – but blackouts at the wheel are never ideal, are they? So off he went next morning to the doctor, who diagnosed that his heartbeat was too slow and occasionally it was stopping briefly for just a second or two – which is pretty scary, although Dad was ridiculously matter-of-fact about the whole thing.

'Anyway I'm going in next week to have a pacemaker,' he told me breezily, 'whatever one of those is. Didn't he sing "You'll Never Walk Alone"?'

'No, Father, that was "pacemakers" as in "Gerry and the …".
This is one that will regulate your heartbeat so if it slows down too much it'll just speed it up a bit.'

'Dead clever,' said Dad.

'Absolutely brilliant,' I agreed.

'Will it affect my singing?' he asked.

'I hope so,' I said, 'it's bloody awful!'

It was all very lighthearted but secretly I knew Mum was worried. His heart, she'd always said, had been weakened by being blown up by the landmine in Germany, but he still seemed very fit and was still running up the stairs every single day. However, he had been looking very pale recently.

So the pacemaker was fitted – an amazing invention, just under the skin, high on the left of his chest, about the size of a matchbox. It seemed to work for at least a year. No more falling down, but Dad was now finding it hard to breathe. The running up the stairs stopped for the first time ever and he suffered a series of chest infections. He was seeing his local GP regularly, but didn't seem to be getting any better.

Eventually, I got a bit exasperated with him. 'Dad, it's your heart, it's pretty important, why are you piddling about with your local GP? I'm booking you into the best heart specialist we can find on Harley Street – and you are coming!' For once he didn't argue. The struggling to breathe was really starting to spook him.

Two days later, we took him up to London to see an eminent heart consultant and, even in those two days, he looked paler and the breathing had become more difficult. He also seemed a bit confused. When we got to the consultancy he was struggling to walk and I had to help him in. The specialist was brilliant, really thorough and very gentle. 'He has a chest infection,' he told us. 'The heart is just not pumping properly and the infection is causing a lot of confusion. I want to take him and put him on an antibiotic drip.'

I rang Mum, reassured her there was nothing to worry about but told her they were taking him into St Thomas's Hospital there and then. He had a big, private room overlooking the Thames, and the staff were fantastic. We got Mum up to see him and various family members popped in and out. I slept on a mattress on the floor and he seemed to be mending fast.

Then, two mornings later, he complained of not being able to see. He was frightened. So was I. He actually couldn't see Big Ben, which was clearly visible through the window. I always knew he had had such a fear of going blind in the war so this panicked both of us.

I called the consultant. 'It's the infection,' he told me. 'There's nothing actually wrong with his sight, but he's having a lot of bad side effects. It will clear.' I relayed this to Dad and it seemed to cheer him, and within two days his sight returned.

He had a hearty appetite and seemed better, so by the weekend we took him home. But he wasn't right. One thing that did catch his attention was Armistice Sunday. It was November 2003. Although he hadn't been at all well for a couple of weeks before, Mum had talked about it to him a lot and he was really looking forward to it. On the Sunday morning he washed and shaved properly, put on his best suit and at eleven o'clock stood to attention in front of the television through the two minutes silence and saluted. When the silence was over he said to me very lucidly, 'Promise me you'll never mock, boy.' I solemnly promised, and of course I never would. Later that day, though, he seemed exhausted and over the next few weeks he looked increasingly white, almost like a ghost, and kept drifting in and out of confusion.

A couple of times he was luckily with me when he nearly fell, and I just managed to catch him. Once I had to bath him. We giggled a lot, probably to cover both our embarrassment, but I never expected to bath my own dad. It seemed his heart was just not strong enough to shift the chest infection and he seemed to be slowly going downhill.

Having said that, it was only a chest infection, we had the best possible private doctors, so he couldn't die … could he? He got through Christmas and into the New Year and we all believed he was mending.

Then, one afternoon in early March, I was on my way to Reading when I got a call from the hospital. 'Your father's been rushed in. Please get here as fast as you can, he's very ill.' There's a song by Mike and the Mechanics called 'The Living Years', which Mike Rutherford wrote about the passing of his own father, and, by a macabre coincidence, I will always remember that was the song that was playing on the car radio when the phone rang.

When I got there the ambulance had only just brought him in. He was conscious but in a lot of pain. He seemed to know he was fading this time. 'Please look after Mum,' he said to me urgently, 'she's the love of my life.' I protested that he shouldn't worry about things like that, as he'd soon be out and about again, but I think this time we both knew that maybe he wasn't coming home.

He was weak but he and Mum celebrated their sixtieth wedding anniversary with Mum sitting alongside him in the hospital, just as they had done all those years before when celebrating VE night in 1945.

By lunchtime he went into a coma and, as the family all began to arrive, he no longer seemed to be responding. The grandkids were crying; I was crying; Mum, as always at these times, remained very strong. Then Toby, the youngest, suddenly said, 'Grandpa, can you wiggle your toes please if you can hear us?' We all stared at the foot of the bed and amazingly his toes clearly moved. It was a wonderful moment, and we all started chatting to him nonstop for the rest of that long day, sure he was hearing us. However, by early evening he seemed to have stopped responding.

I decided to stay beside him through the night and gently told the kids and Mum they should go and get something to eat. If there was any change I'd let them know. And then Toby said something else. 'Can I just have a few words with Grandpa alone, please?' So we all quietly left the room while he had a few private moments talking to his grandfather. I've never asked him what he said that day, but even though he's now a grown man I still love the memory of that twelve-year-old boy and his dying grandad.

Dad actually lingered in a coma for a few more days. We all took turns to be with him, but there were no more signs of life and on 28 March 2005 this amazing man, who was born nearly eighty-six years earlier in July 1919, died. I was empty, drained of any emotion. The grandkids were lost, devastated, and Mum had to be helped through all of it, and prepare for whatever was next for her. She was dreading the loneliness. Their house had a terrible void in it where, for more than forty years, there had always been so much noise and singing and fun and laughter.

The regiment asked us if we wanted full military honours at the funeral, with the coffin draped in the Union Jack and the slow military drumbeat as the body is brought in behind the flag of the Wiltshire Regiment. In some ways it would have been a wonderful tribute to a great soldier, but Mum said the war was over a long time ago and now it should be more about him as a husband, father, grandfather and a great friend to so many people, not just as a soldier. And she was of course right. The church was so full it was impossible to close the doors.

I had spent days writing an oration to him which broke me up every time I tried to read through it, just to myself. I so wanted to say everything I felt but I thought I would never get through it in front of a packed church. In the end I focused on a brick at the very back of the beautiful old church and spoke to that for nine or ten minutes, without ever taking my eyes off it. I never once dared to look down. I could hear a lot of sobbing and I knew if I caught the tear-filled eyes of any of my children I would be in pieces. My daughter did a beautiful reading as well. I had whispered to her to try the brick-focusing trick and it worked a treat. We all got through it, as he would have expected us to, and everybody gave him a terrific send-off.

People came from all over the country to say goodbye to him. A lovely old friend of Dad's, who I hadn't seen since I was a little boy, came over and showed real kindness and concern to Mum, and then turned and said to me, 'He was one of the very best, your father.' And he was. A light went out that day that I've never been able to switch on again. I talk to him at the grave whenever I can and I still miss him every day.

I know that there will be many secrets that will have gone to the grave with my dad, but over these last two years I have learned so much that I had just had no idea about. Sometimes I've felt really angry with myself that I didn't know more about what he'd gone through, and I'm sure a lot of people will ask why I didn't just press him harder for information, but however close you are to someone you can't force them to relive memories that they found acutely painful. Perhaps I should have asked his friends while they were still alive but I think they were of the same breed as him and, in any case, I suspect they'd have had too much respect for my father to tell me more than he wished me to know. They are all gone now, all those remarkable men who sat in their demob suits in our kitchen after the war was over, and they too will have died taking many of their secrets with them forever.

But I must also count my blessings. By being such a great survivor, he gave a wonderful life to me, my mum, my beautiful children, and now my own grandchildren. Of course he was my father, but he really was an exceptional human being – brave, of course, and a natural leader, but also kind, generous, warm and loving, although he felt uneasy with any show of emotion. He dominated any room he walked into and didn't suffer fools gladly, but to those he liked and respected, he was a great friend. He was fiercely loyal and would always make time for people. And of course he was very, very funny with a wonderful sense of the ridiculous. He lived life to the full and it was a real privilege for anyone to say they knew him – even though he kept so much hidden away for so many years.

For a lot of the soldiers like my father who didn't want to talk about their wartime experiences to people who hadn't been there, the one place where they could really let their hair down among those who would understand was with their fellow MOTHS. The get-togethers organised by this society gave ex-soldiers a place to meet and in many cases a real purpose to their lives after the hostilities were over.

Dad clearly absolutely loved being a member of MOTHS. The Windy Corner shell hole met every month in a hotel in Caversham and he became one of the main stalwarts of the organisation for nearly sixty years. His annual address to 'the blokes', as they call themselves, at the pre-Armistice dinner became the stuff of legend. He and his committee always managed to somehow acquire a top guest speaker, usually a much-respected military figure, to come to the dinner every year for virtually no fee, just a few drinks and an outside chance of a lift home.

In 1978, celebrating fifty glorious years since Windy Corner started, they had no less a speaker than Viscount 'Monty'

Montgomery, one of Dad's absolute heroes. Somehow they blagged other brigadiers and field marshals to be their guest over the years and Falklands hero Simon Weston came twice.

In Dad's old oak desk, long after he'd died, I discovered to my delight a whole file of Major Tarrant's speeches to the blokes, including the first time he was ever called upon to address a MOTHS armistice dinner in 1948.

Interestingly, in this very first speech to the blokes, there was all the irreverence and innuendo that was to become the cornerstone of his every armistice address in the many years ahead, but there was also a clearly heartfelt statement of why he was so glad to join the organisation:

When first invited to join this splendid organisation I was thrilled to find so many like-minded friends, new and old, who knew what fighting, its sorrows and its grim humour, really meant. Somewhere where the fine comradeship of the services, probably the only blessing that can come from war, is really being kept alive.

I have detected something much deeper and more serious in this order than just having a convivial evening and swapping far-fetched stories, although happily I'm sure we will all do that for many years to come. Phrases used glibly by others, such as 'lest we forget' and 'we will remember them', really mean something to you blokes and I'm proud to be in your company.

As a bald statement in his very first speech to the blokes it clearly touched exactly the right nerve. Like them, he'd been there and had been one of the lucky ones who lived to tell the tale, but could never forget the many others who fought with him but did not return.

On the first page of the programme and menu for The Memorable Order of Tin Hats' annual armistice dinner, there was a drawing of the Cenotaph with wreaths laid all around it for those who died in battle and the sombre words written at the front: 'When you go home, tell them of us and say / For your tomorrow, we gave our today.'

These sentiments underpinned everything that the MOTHS did for more than another half a century at Windy Corner. Not that the proceedings were sombre, though. Far from it, they were clearly riotous – and more than once I heard Dad returning home from the MOTHS well after midnight, singing something by Sinatra ('In the wee small hours of the morning ...') and having strange difficulties negotiating a normally very straightforward Yale front-door lock.

Certainly the after-dinner speeches he gave at MOTHS set the tone of the evening and give an idea of what raucous affairs these events were. His opening gambit in virtually all of the speeches I uncovered seemed to be that nobody appreciated him. Some of his lines give a flavour of the man: 'I was just asked by the commanding officer if I was ready to speak now or if I should just let the men enjoy themselves a little longer' ... 'I'm rather nervous this evening – and believe me, I am nervous, because I know how thin my material is' ... 'My parents christened me Rover – they really wanted a dog.' Or my particular favourite: 'Please don't shout abuse, as I'm not very good at dealing with hecklers. However, I do love coming down there and kicking you in the bollocks.'

Yes, Daddy was clearly a class act, but once he got through his opening subtleties he got into all sorts of other murky areas: 'Gentlemen, it has been said that after-dinner speeches were invented by old men too feeble or too drunk to dance, but I can assure you that I am as eager as you are to get on the dancefloor tonight, especially as I'm told that we will be doing the Quaker dance. This is a very splendid dance indeed – twice round the floor with a lady of your choice and then both outside for your oats ...'

And then, over the years, some of his references became downright surreal: 'On this day, 11 November, in 1656, Isaac Newton discovered that if a common or garden snail crawls up your right trouser leg – and it has to be the right trouser leg – it takes just seven days before you say, "Ooh, that's very nice!"'

One year he made a reference to an old friend and fellow member of the shell hole, a lovable Jewish wideboy called Albie Cohen, following a lot of activity on the local rumour mill. Apparently – according to his speech – he'd said to Albie, 'How sorry I am to hear about the fire at your Randolph Road branch,' to which Albie had replied, 'Shush please ... it's not until tomorrow.' Dad then went on to say: 'Albie has recently been badly beaten up fighting for his secretary's honour ... she desperately wanted to keep it.'

Albie was an old mate of Dad's and seems to have been a regular target: 'On one occasion I visited Albie's factory and found a very harassed, twitchy Albie facing a large dragon of a woman screaming, "My daughter thinks she's pregnant and it's you!" "Don't worry," said Albie, "if she is pregnant I'll give her £10,000, and I'll set up a trust fund for the child of a further £10,000 ... now is that fair?" "More than fair," said the now totally subdued dragon woman, "that's very generous ... and if she isn't pregnant, Mr Cohen, will you please give her another chance?"'

Another great story prefaced the introduction of a senior officer from another Berkshire MOTHS shell hole. Dad told the assembled audience that the gentleman in question was recently seen in a local restaurant ordering a Norfolk chicken. An ancient waiter tottered in with a large dish, at which point the distinguished guest inserted his fingers into the bird's backside and said, 'This is not a Norfolk chicken, it is a Suffolk chicken!' The waiter returned some time later with another offering and was treated to more abuse by the officer: 'This is not a Norfolk chicken, this bird came from Essex!' Exasperated by the poor service, he then turned on the bewildered old boy beside his table and said, 'Call yourself a waiter? Wherever did you come from?' At which point the waiter turned round, lifted up his coat tails and said, 'Well, sir, you're the expert, you tell me!'

Some of this material is pretty whiskery now – and I have a feeling some of it may well have been pretty whiskery back in the 1940s, but these extracts from his annual speeches do clearly demonstrate the style of my father's fifty years of addressing the blokes.

Here, mercifully, are just a few more extracts: 'My brother was arrested last week for feeding the penguins at London Zoo. It was probably because he was feeding them to the lions' … 'I went to the cinema last night, the film was so old Long John Silver had two legs' … 'I went to a dreadful restaurant last night. They didn't have a menu – you just look at the chef's vest and have a guess.'

Some of the nature of the material shows just how long ago it was written: 'There was a washing machine in our new house when we moved in last week. I've never seen one before but it clearly isn't working very well. Yesterday I put five shirts in it, pulled the chain and I haven't seen the shirts since.'

Finally, this little gem has a particular resonance for me: 'We've just had a birthday party for my son Christopher, aged five. We invited about thirty kids of the same age and it was absolute chaos in the house. So I took a major decision – I was going to escape. As I went to the front door, one horrible little brat said, "Do you know any games, mister?" "Yes," I said, "I know a good one: I'm off to the pub and you all have to guess what time I'll be back." '

And so it went on and on and on and on for more than half a century … and the blokes who really should have known better loved it. Well, at least that's what Dad always told me!

One spring, having had a series of great speakers at armistice dinners, they clearly couldn't book anybody good because one evening Dad quietly asked me if I would share the stage with him on the Friday before Remembrance Sunday at Brock Barracks. I accepted at once, of course I did, cleared my diary and then spent the next six months absolutely dreading it. I had done a lot of public speaking by then, but never with my own father – the man I loved and respected more than anyone else in the world. My difficulty was that the blokes all loved and respected him equally and, while it was expected that we would both be jokey about each other, getting the tone right was one of the hardest things I've ever had to do. I wrote, polished and rewrote and re-polished that speech over and over again. Mum said she'd never known me so nervous. 'But it matters more than any other speech, Mum,' I told her. 'It's about Dad and it's in front of his men.'

In the end he absolutely ripped into me during his introduction, describing me as a long-haired waster and delinquent for at least half an hour. He closed this assassination with: 'My appalling son even had the cheek to send me a postcard once from his very expensive school whingeing that he wasn't enjoying it much, saying, "Dear Dad, it's a bastard." So I wrote back: "So are you!" '

I managed to string together an irreverent response, alluding to his brutality, his drunkenness and how I wasn't at all sure that he was my father – none of which of course was true but the men appreciated it. They could also clearly see my pride and love for my dad shining through. At the end we exchanged beer and bear hugs and it was a wonderful bonding night for the two of us.

And then I wanted to stand up and say one more thing in front of the blokes, before we all became too inebriated to say anything. It may sound pompous, but I felt it wasn't just from me. Instead I wanted to speak for my whole generation:

You've made me very welcome tonight and I thank you for that. But, above all, as the long-haired, loud-mouthed waster my father very fairly referred to earlier, and the one that you see on your television screens, can I just say I have so much respect for you all. Please never, ever think that we do not appreciate everything that you did for us. My generation can never thank you enough for what you all went through and we honour you and all your fallen comrades . . .

It was from the heart. There were tears in my eyes and in Dad's, and many of the blokes solemnly shook my hand. They then ended the dinner by standing to attention for a two-minute silence in memory of all the comrades that they had lost and, at the end, we all continued to stand as recorded extracts from Winston Churchill's powerful wartime speeches were played.

It was an extraordinary night and, for me, it made very clear everything that the MOTHS stood for. It is seventy years ago now but we must never forget those who fought and gave their lives to check the advances of the evil that threatened to engulf the world. The evening ended with every man saluting as my father read the words from perhaps the greatest of all war poems, 'For the Fallen' by Robert Laurence Binyon: 'At the going down of the sun and in the morning we will remember them.' We all repeated, 'We will remember them,' and then a bugler played the 'Last Post'.

Dad and I went home elated but in virtual silence, each with our own thoughts and emotions. The bond between us became somehow stronger after that night.

I think for the first time I understood.

Acknowledgements

Thanks go to Kate Moore and Elen Jones at Random House for believing in this book from day one. I was often too close to this very personal material to be objective, and they were wonderfully encouraging throughout. Thanks also to my agent, Paul Vaughan; Lindsay Davies for going through every single word with me again and again; to Jane, my best friend, for letting me write at all sorts of weird and antisocial times of the day and night; to Susan, my tireless PA of more than twenty years, for hours and hours of rewriting and shaping my ramblings; to Tony Nicholson for making sense of mountains of military information; and Jackie at the Royal Wiltshire Military Museum at Salisbury; to Jon Cooksey for his expert eye and double checking the facts; and Tim Mitchell for mapping my father's journey.

Special thanks go to five amazing men who fought with my father and who have been wonderful in helping me bring his story to life: Robbie Purver, Doug Botting, Bill Pyke, Michael Pardoe and Donald May. It was an honour to have met and talked with each of you – we all owe you so much.

Bibliography

Beevor, Antony, *The Second World War*, W&N, 2012

Belchem, Major General David, *Victory in Normandy*, Chatto & Windus, 1981

Delaforce, Patrick, *The Fighting Wessex Wyverns: From Normandy to Bremerhaven with the 43rd Wessex Division*, Fonthill Media, 2012

Hastings, Max, *All Hell Let Loose: The World at War 1939–45*, Harper Press, 2012

Hylton, Stuart, *A History of Reading*, Phillimore & Co Ltd, 2007

Jackson, Robert, *Dunkirk: The British Evacuation, 1940*, Cassell, 2002

Longden, Sean, *To the Victor the Spoils: Soldiers' Lives from D-Day to VE-Day*, Robinson Publishing, 2007

McIntyre, Martin, *The Royal Berkshire Regiment 1914–1959*, The History Press Ltd, 2005

McIntyre, Martin, *The Wiltshire Regiment 1914–1959*, The History Press Ltd, 2006

McMath, Captain J. S., *The Fifth Battalion, The Wiltshire Regiment in North-West Europe June 1944 to May 1945*, Whitefriars Press Ltd, 1945

Shaw, Frank and Shaw, Joan, *We Remember the Blitz*, Ebury Press, 2012

Young, Geoff, *Private Young's War: Service in the 4th Wiltshires Through North-West Europe*, The Royal Gloucestershire, Berkshire & Wiltshire Regiment Wardrobe Museum Trust, 2004

Newspapers:
Berkshire Chronicle
Berkshire Mercury
Daily Telegraph
Mail on Sunday
Reading Evening Post
Reading Standard

Index